W

Te

So

D1575107

STUDIES IN WRITING

VOLUME 15

Series Editor:

Gert Rijlaarsdam, *University of Amsterdam, The Netherlands*

Springer publishes the international book series *Studies in Writing*, founded by Amsterdam University Press and continued by Kluwer Academic Publishers. The intended readers are all those interested in the foundations of writing and learning and teaching processes in written composition. The series aims at multiple perspectives of writing, education and texts. Therefore, authors and readers come from various fields of research, from curriculum development and from teacher training. Fields of research covered are cognitive, socio-cognitive and developmental psychology, psycholinguistics, text linguistics, curriculum development, instructional science. The series aims to cover theoretical issues, supported by empirical research, quantitative as well as qualitative, representing a wide range of nationalities. The series provides a forum for research from established researchers and welcomes contributions from young researchers. All studies published in the series are peer-reviewed.

Triantafillia Kostouli
Editor

Writing in Context(s)

Textual Practices and Learning Processes in
Sociocultural Settings

 Springer

Triantafillia Kostouli
Aristotle University of Thessaloniki, Greece

Library of Congress Cataloging-in-Publication Data

Writing in context(s): textual practices and learning processes in sociocultural
settings /
    Triantafillia Kostouli, editor.
    p.cm. – (Studies in writing; v. 15)
    Includes bibliographical references (p.) and indexes.
ISBN 0-387-24237-6 HB (alk. paper)   ISBN 0-387-24238-4 SB (alk. paper)
e-ISBN 0-387-24250-3
    1.   English language—Rhetoric—Study and teaching—Social aspects. 2.Report
    writing—Study and teaching (Higher)—Social aspects. 3. Academic
writing—Study and
    teaching—Social aspects. 4. English language—Written English. 5. English
    language—Social aspects. I. Kostouli, Triantafillia. II. Series.

PE1404.W725 2005
808'.042'071—dc22
2004065381

Printed in the United States of America.

9 8 7 6 5 4 3 2 1   SPIN 11362760

springeronline.com

TABLE OF CONTENTS

INTRODUCTION: MAKING SOCIAL MEANINGS IN CONTEXTS   1
Triantafillia Kostouli

SOCIOCULTURAL DIFFERENCES IN CHILDREN'S   27
GENRE KNOWLEDGE
Alina G. Spinillo & Chris Pratt

ENCULTURATION TO INSTITUTIONAL WRITING   49
Sigmund Ongstad

WHOLE-CLASS AND PEER INTERACTION IN AN ACTIVITY OF   69
WRITING AND REVISION
Linda Allal, Lucie Mottier Lopez, Katia Lehraus,
& Alexia Forget

CO-CONSTRUCTING WRITING CONTEXTS IN CLASSROOMS   93
Triantafillia Kostouli

PRIOR KNOWLEDGE AND THE (RE)PRODUCTION OF SCHOOL   117
WRITTEN GENRES
Debra Myhill

STUDENT WRITING AS NEGOTIATION   137
Christiane Donahue

WRITING FROM SOURCES IN TWO CULTURAL CONTEXTS   165
Shoshana Folman & Ulla Connor

FIRST AND SECOND LANGUAGE USE DURING   185
PLANNING PROCESSES
Orna Ferenz

COLLABORATIVE WRITING GROUPS IN THE   207
COLLEGE CLASSROOM
Carole H. McAllister

REACHING OUT FROM THE WRITING CLASSROOM   229
Linda Adler-Kassner, & Heidi Estrem

REFERENCES 247

AUTHOR INDEX 271

SUBJECT INDEX 279

LIST OF CONTRIBUTORS 281

INTRODUCTION: MAKING SOCIAL MEANINGS IN CONTEXTS

Writing, Literate Activities and Learning Processes in Sociohistorical Communities

TRIANTAFILLIA KOSTOULI

Aristotle University of Thessaloniki, Greece

Abstract. This introductory chapter delineates the basic premises underlying the inquiry that is currently carried out in a variety of fields on writing as sociocultural practice. Different arguments, terms, and methodologies that address writing as a socioculturally constructed and historically embedded communicative act have been formulated in different fields, including, among others, the genre literacy movement (in its various instantiations), various composition research strands on disciplinary writing, the post-Vygotskian sociocognitive research, the interactional sociolinguistics paradigm. While the chapters of this volume may draw in different ways from these traditions, all are united under the premise that writing should be seen as an inherently dialogic and a socially-situated process of making meanings through texts; written texts are not seen as neutral structures produced by autonomous writers but as units of social action conveying ideological meanings. According to this approach, then, learning to write is not simply a linguistic process but a sociocultural one, which requires that learners appropriate those meanings which are constituted in the communities (and the various contexts) within which learners operate and which they themselves construct. The emphasis of this volume is on school and academic contexts of writing across cultures. Analyses indicate how participants, full and novice members of their discourse learning communities, through their written texts, and composing acts, learn how to produce meanings by drawing upon community-valued resources, how they redefine them or, even, diverge from them. A group of chapters focuses on texts produced by student writers of different age groups, illustrating the ways by which students emerge, through their writing, as social actors, by engaging in dialogic negotiations with teachers, other members of the school community and with other texts (other "voices" in Bakhtin's terms). A different group of chapters indicates how contexts around writing get co-constructed in various settings across communities and traces the processes that facilitate or hinder students' appropriation of school and academic literacies.

Keywords: literacy events, activity types, genres, situated writing, writing as sociocultural practice, dialogism, co-construction, mediation, contextualization, sociolinguistic research, sociocognitive research

1   WRITING AS SOCIAL INTERACTION

This volume, through detailed analysis of written texts and literate activities (which are co-constructed by teachers and students of various age-groups and academic

levels in classroom communities across cultures), aims to contribute to current dialogue on writing as sociocultural practice. The chapters included address writing
from a variety of perspectives, including sociocognitive, sociolinguistic and sociocultural ones. It is interesting to note that, while all chapters are concerned with
tracing the social underpinnings of writing acts, composing processes and text genres, the meaning assigned to basic terms (such as that of "social"), the data selected
(ranging from written texts produced by elementary, secondary school and college-
level students to the interactive contexts co-constructed around written texts), the
methodological frameworks employed (from text analysis of specific linguistic
forms to cross-cultural analysis of school genres and from quantitative to detailed
qualitative descriptions of the factors shaping the construction of school writing contexts) point to a considerable diversity in this inquiry. Are there certain premises
researchers agree upon? What are the points of convergence and divergence? Is it
possible to move beyond the plurality of terminological issues and the diversity of
methodological frameworks towards a more holistic approach? This introduction
attempts to sketch the field, and illustrate how the insights of different and, possibly,
divergent perspectives may actually complement one another and be used to enrich
the inquiry into the contextually-shaped nature of writing. In this sense, rather than
taking the social approach to writing as a given or an agreed-upon point of departure, the discussion illustrates that unveiling its constitutive dimensions and theses is
the issue to begin with: What are the methodological frameworks developed (in L1
and L2) for tracing the way by which written texts are shaped in and through various, mutually interlocking social contexts? In what respects – in terms of the assumptions, claims, and premises put forward – does the inquiry into the *social aspects of writing* differ from research addressing the *sociocultural* and *sociohistorical*
nature of written texts and writing processes?

   The incorporation of sociocultural factors in writing research represents a relatively recent development and certainly one that has appeared with many distinct
strands in work concerned with writing in L1 and L2 (for an overview on L2, see
Kern, 2000). Writing practices, written texts, and disciplinary literacies have been
discussed in various settings, including, among others, mainstream and multilingual
classrooms (Bloom, 1989; Christie, & Martin, 1997; Gutierrez, & Stone, 2000;
Hicks, 1996; Knobel, 1999; Lee, & Smagorinsky, 2000), out-of-school contexts
(Hull, & Schultz, 2002), community (Barton, & Hamilton, 1998; 2000; Dickinson,
1994; Heath, 1983; Taylor, & Dorsey-Gaines, 1988), academic (Bazerman, 1988;
Berkenkotter, & Huckin, 1995; Hyland, 2000; Prior, 1998; Swales, 1990), and
workplace settings (Beaufort, 1999; Dias, & Parré, 2000; Faigley, 1985; Faigley, &
Miller, 1982). Genres (capturing socially-valued ways of conveying knowledge
within primary, secondary school, university and professional contexts [Bazerman,
& Paradis, 1991; Cope, & Kalantzis, 1993; Hyland, 2000, 2002; Myers, 1990]),
instructional contexts in classrooms (i.e., the recitation script [Gutierrez, 1994], the
instructional conversation [Goldenberg, & Patthey-Chavez, 1995], etc.), different
types of classroom lessons (teacher-fronted vs. small group peer interactions) are
additional ways by which researchers have represented the contextual influences on
writing and the social nature of literate activities. Finally, the notions of reader response, and writer identity represent a vocabulary of terms through which pedagogi-

cally-oriented writing research (for a survey with relation to L2, see Kroll, 1990, 2003) has chosen to address the socially constructed nature of writing (see also Belcher, & Hirvela, 2001a). While the chapters of this volume reflect this divergence both in the variety of research foci adopted and the different types of data analyzed, the proposals forwarded are united under the premise that writing should be interpreted as social action and interaction (Bazerman, 1994a, 1994b; Cooper, & Holzman, 1989; Nystrand, 1982) that is shaped in and through contexts.

Specifically: The emphasis of this volume is on written texts, literate acts and composing processes in school-constructed contexts (from the elementary and secondary level up to the university), although attention is also directed to the way by which school writing may project, reinforce and/or negate literacy practices valued in various out-of-school community contexts. Foregrounding the notion of school and academic genres, chapters, through analyses of textual patterns and linguistic forms, delineate a variety of approaches to writing; these range from the so-called monologic (or social) ones, asserting that writing be seen as writer's response to certain, clearly identified contextual variables, to more dialogic (or sociocultural /sociohistorical) perspectives, which suggest that writing should be interpreted more broadly as an inherently dialogic, and a historically-embedded process of creating and reinforcing community meanings via texts.

Proceeding beyond decontextualized writing skills, chapters trace the various contextually-shaped (and historically-determined) ways through which students learn how to make meanings, becoming, through this process, specific kinds of writers, and, thus, literate subjects; writers' interactions with texts are not devoid of meanings; these are, in fact, imbued with ideological significance, for they reflect the way a specific writer positions him/herself toward the textual practices of the community s/he participates in. The strategic resources a writer chooses for the purpose of reaffirming or redefining those meanings are not created anew but constitute the social history of meaning making in a specific community. Indeed, as Gee [1990] has suggested, literacy practices are intricately tied up to a specific group's "world view," signalling certain community-specific Discourses and corroborating specific identity kits (see also Scollon, & Scollon [1981] on how children from different sociocultural groups relate to western "essayist" literacy practices).

To understand the similarities and differences in the ways by which the various chapters of this volume talk about writing as social interaction in school learning communities, it is appropriate that I situate the discussion against the background of a more general epistemology on language use from which all chapters draw to varying degrees; this is the sociocultural/sociohistorical perspective. The origins of this approach to language use may be traced back to Vygotsky's (1978) work, which asserted the inseparability of language, cognition, and context, and to Bakhtin's (1981, 1986) notion of intertextuality, which is seen as a sociohistorical construction. Different premises of this perspective have been variously defined, interpreted and extended in a number of diverse fields. Among these we may include sociocultural psychology (Lave, & Wenger, 1991), social semiotics (Lemke, 1989), linguistic anthropology (Ochs, 1988; Schieffelin, & Ochs, 1986), the New Literacy Studies (Barton, & Hamilton, 1998, 2000; Ivanič, 1998). It is worth noting that, due to its pervasiveness in current theorizing on language use, learning, and development, the sociocultural perspective has not only radically reshaped our theoretical understanding of the interaction between knowledge, cognition, and language (which are seen as situationally emergent and mutually constitutive processes); this has, in fact, reconstituted pedagogical approaches to language and literacy education. Succinctly, the sociocultural perspective suggests that "meanings are embedded in cultural conceptions of context" (Ochs, 1988: 307). Accordingly, in neo-Vygotskian research (Kong, & Pearson, 2003; Rogoff, 1990), linguistic and cognitive development and indeed learning are seen as processes directed towards the appropriation of specific mediational tools, and practices which constitute the sociocultural history of a particular community; novices learn how to produce texts in ways that reflect and redefine the textual universe of their community – a process that encompasses one's dialogic negotiations with the voices (i.e., the texts) of community members (Bakhtin, 1981, 1986; Gutierrez, 1994).

Understanding the way by which the core premises of this perspective are taken up by the contributors of this volume to inform their analysis of written texts and composing acts is contingent upon identifying and clarifying two basic themes, those of meaning and text-context interaction, which are acknowledged and explored, though with different terminology and methodologies, in many different chapters. I situate the relevant issues under two general headings, theoretical and pedagogical ones. *Theoretical issues:* What is context? Is it a physical, a cognitive or a social (i.e., an interactionally shaped) construct? How do texts interact with contexts to index and/or reconstruct the literacy practices of a specific community and indeed of other communities? Do notions such as those of activity types and literacy events signify different construals of contextually situated writing? *Pedagogical issues:* How do students' experiences with texts in out-of-school contexts shape students' school writing? How are out-of-school resources brought in and negotiated in classroom contexts? Which contexts created by teachers and students constitute important sites of apprenticeship into school literacies? What are the methodological frameworks developed for analyzing the way contexts shape literacy learning?

2   ON CONTEXT: FROM STATIC TO DIALOGIC PERSPECTIVES

Meaning – a notion of central importance in linguistics – has been explored in a variety of ways, ranging from formal (and indeed rather narrow) linguistic analyses to much broader social semiotic views. According to the latter, meaning does not reside within any given text, it rather arises out of the mutually constitutive relations established between texts and the layers of contexts (local and global/societal) within which texts are embedded (for a recent presentation of this perspective, see Bazerman, & Prior, 2004). It is worth noting that the inquiry into the social situatedness of meaning has had a long tradition in various fields which analyze talk and talk-in interaction, such as sociolinguistics, discourse analysis, the ethnography of communication, conversation analysis, interactional sociolinguistics, linguistic and cultural anthropology.

Interestingly, the inquiry into writing, at least as it was initially carried out in discourse analysis and sociolinguistics (see Chafe, 1982; Tannen, 1982), tended to build on and reinforce binary distinctions of spoken versus written language; these were seen as two distinct modes of communication, associated, respectively, with contextualized and decontextualized language. Gradually, research attention shifted away from writing as a context-free and apolitical skill to unveil the ways by which spoken and written language, as social discourses, interrelate to construct meanings (Besnier, 1995). Indeed, as it became clear, all discursive forms, spoken and written, are socioculturally embedded; as attested by ethnographic accounts of meaning-making practices across cultures and sociocultural groups (Besnier, 1995; Heath, 1983), orality should not be seen as opposing but as complementary to literacy; orality may, in fact, provide a context for literacy to be understood; research interest is no longer concerned with clarifying the distinction between orality versus literacy but rather with unveiling the sociocultural practices, social languages (Gee, 2001) and genres which constitute the "ways with words" specific groups adopt for communicating and negotiating meanings. Literacy, in this sense, is a semiotic resource that reflects social practices, i.e., it signals the socially, culturally and historically situated practices communities adopt with regard to how spoken and written texts may be used to fulfil various social purposes; as shown, writing is used by community members within specific community contexts for a variety of purposes, including, among others, for the purpose of constructing and communicating knowledge, establishing interpersonal relationships (see Candlin, & Hyland, 1999), negotiating and foregrounding aspects of members' ethnic and gendered identities (Anderson, 2002).

It is worth noting, however that, despite the emphasis given to the notion of context and claims made that all speaking and writing acts and indeed learning processes are shaped in and through contexts, context remains elusive. Different approaches may be discerned in the literature, with some placing more emphasis on certain dimensions at the expense of others. Thus, while some approaches have foregrounded the cognitive aspect of the background knowledge writers bring to a particular situation (usually presented through the notions of frames, scripts and schemata [for an overview, see Brown, & Yule, 1983 and Tannen, 1993]), others have attended to its social dimensions, suggesting that context be seen as a dynamic, interactively shaped set of resources which exists and evolves together with the construction of interactive activities (for a survey of related proposals on these aspects, see Mayes, 2002). Another pertinent distinction is between macro-contexts (homes, schools, cultures and even writing pedagogies) and micro-contexts (reading events, writing conferences) (O'Brien, Moje, & Stewart, 2001); alternatively, contexts have been seen as static containers enveloping texts or as units which are co-constructed by the participants themselves as they negotiate meanings (Duranti, & Goodwin, 1992).

Despite such disciplinary divergence, in general, most accounts of situated meanings seem to have evolved away from the initially prevailing conceptualization of context as a static container that envelops any given unit of social action toward tracing the way by which texts index and/or reconstruct contexts, thus, while initially, context was proposed to be fully developed and accept no changes in its internal structure, in current perspectives, the relationship between texts and contexts is seen as more reflexive and co-producing. Texts are seen as both contextualized (ac-

quiring meaning by virtue of being situated in a context) and contextualizing (pointing to a context giving meaning to any given set of utterances) (see Schiffrin, 1994,
for an analysis of how this applies to conversational data); indeed systematic attempts have been made on the part of the researchers (see Relevance theory and
Gumperz, 1982a, 1982b) to illustrate which from the various overlapping contexts
are made relevant in any given case.

Given the multiplicity of meanings assigned to the notion of context, and the fact
that most of the research conducted tended to focus on speaking acts and interactive
processes, it becomes clear that to define situated writing, it is necessary that I begin
by roughly delimiting the field. To do so, I build upon the distinction introduced by
Duranti, & Goodwin (1992) between a focal event and a surrounding field (that of
context). Seen via a hierarchical model, context is presented as the ground which
makes this focal event understandable.

As Duranti, & Goodwin (1992: 3-4) advice us, for the notion of context to be
clarified, we should attend to the terms against which this notion is juxtaposed and
linked to. While certain of the terms used (such as culture, society) are of general
applicability in accounts of situated language use, other terms index more specific
traditions. Thus, the notions of discourse, activity, conversational processes, processes of discourse production and interpretation are usually invoked by research
dealing with talk-in interaction (see Drew, & Heritage, 1992); terms such as text,
genre, literacy events, activity types, discourse communities prevail in research dealing with context-situated writing and sociocultural literacies.

While, in the way delineated above, the two research strands seem to run along
parallel lines, in actual practice integration has been possible. Indeed, certain of the
notions invoked (such as that of the speech event) in research conducted on spoken
language have been instrumental for clarifying aspects of situated literacy practices.
Before presenting this integration, however, which, as to be shown, has been implemented in a different way in L1 versus L2 writing research, let me begin by addressing the clear-cut cases of contextually shaped meanings in spoken versus written
interaction. Two are the basic issues. Firstly: Through what terms has the notion of
"focal event" been conceptualized in various research strands on writing? Secondly:
What is the context against which the focal event chosen has been analyzed?

2.1 Writing in Contexts: Basic Terms

Assumptions, terms, and methodologies that bring out the contextual nature of writ
ing have been formulated in distinct fields. Four are worth noting. This is the New
Rhetoric tradition on disciplinary genres (Bazerman, 1988; Berkenkotter, & Huckin,
1993, 1995; Prior, 1998) which singles out the way language producers, through
genres or systems of genres construct, negotiate and redefine community-valued
meanings), the New Literacies and Multi-Literacies frameworks (Barton, & Hamilton, 1998, 2000; the New London Group, 1996) outlining an ethnographically-
oriented approach to writing, which is no longer associated with school contexts and
the linguistic system; attention is rather directed to the multi-modal set of resources
people use for expressing meanings through written texts produced in various out-of

school, local community contexts), the post-Vygotskian sociocognitive approach (Englert et al., 1992; Lee, & Smagorinsky, 2000; Moll, 1990; Pappas, & Zecker, 2001; Raphael, 1984), which foregrounds the social aspects of literacy learning as participation in communities of practice and the interactional sociolinguistic perspective (Cairney, & Ashton, 2002; Green, & Meyer, 1991; Knobel, 1999; Santa Barbara Classroom Discourse Group, 1992, 1995), which foregrounds the interactive co-construction of literacy in home and classroom contexts.

Influenced by these traditions to different extents, the chapters in this volume explore the negotiations developing writers undertake with the layers of contexts within which their texts and writing acts are situated and through which they acquire meaning. While individual chapters may single out and focus on one contextual layer at the expense of the others, the discussion is carried out against a background that encompasses a variety of terms, and assumptions on contextually situated writing; as a result, in each chapter some notions are necessarily foregrounded, while others are less attended to or placed in the background. However, for readers to understand if the individual chapters, through the claims they make, adhere to (or diverge from) a basic set of premises on contextually situated writing, it is necessary that a more holistic perspective be outlined; this is presented in Figure 1. It is against this Figure that every chapter may be read and its argument may be appreciated.

Two points are worth noting. First, the terms situated in the various layers constituting Figure 1 have been given various readings, probably due to their divergent origins. While differentiated for the purposes of the analysis here, clearly, each layer cannot be studied in isolation from the rest but should rather be seen as representing a part in a system consisting out of many intertwined components. For the nature of each and every term to be understood and fully appreciated, therefore, attention should be given to the way this term interacts with and is shaped by the context or contexts invoked in each case.

Secondly, the structure of terms presented in Figure 1 is rendered coherent through the notion of social practices (which, as Barton, & Hamilton, [2000] note, are invisible). This notion is used, after Barton (1994: 188) in reference to "common patterns of using reading and writing in any situation." To this end, I suggest (a point signalled in the subtitle of the volume as well) that analyses of writing should indicate that, in fact, linguistic forms and interactive exchanges in writing contexts reflect and instantiate community-valued textual practices (i.e., certain ways of using language that pervade and give meaning to the texts produced and the genres valued in any community setting). How are these practices constructed? Individual chapters through classroom learning processes (traced through the texts produced, the participants involved, the activities constructed, and the artefacts employed) focus on and analyze certain moments that are singled out from the rich intertextual history of meaning making practices that are constructed within a specific sociocultural setting or local classroom community. As a result, chapters may give us glimpses only into a long-term and complicated appropriation process, pointing to a number of issues worth exploring further; even so, the issues addressed illustrate the complexity of the processes involved in the social construction of students as literate subjects: What does it mean to be a primary school student and communicate through written texts in this specific Norwegian, Greek or Swiss classroom? What kinds of written texts are valued in secondary schools in France, England, etc. and how do students of a specific classroom community appropriate the culture of meanings that defines secondary education in this cultural context?

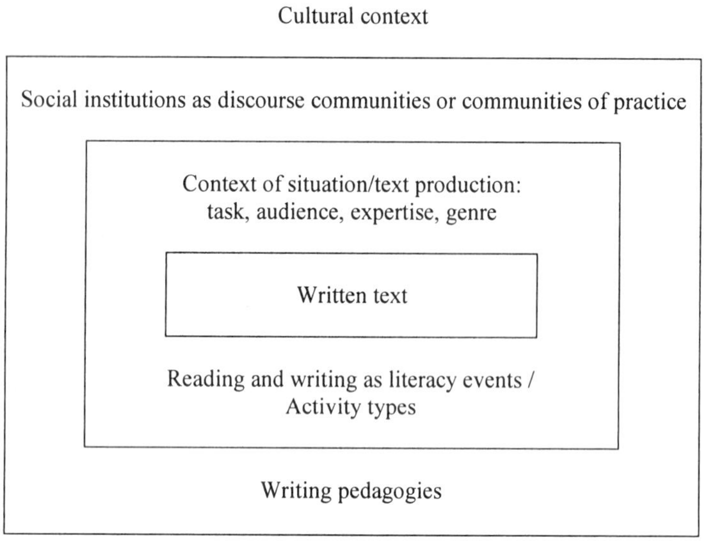

Cultural context

Figure 1. Writing processes and written texts in contextual layers

Given Figure 1, the core premise running through and uniting all chapters in this volume becomes clear. This may be succinctly stated thus:

> Understanding written language, its uses and functions, depends on considering how writing, as a process and a product, is embedded in and co-constructed by participants in a variety of sociocultural contexts. These may range from local ones (capturing genre-shaped schemata) to more global contexts (i.e., schools and other discourse communities). On the other hand, written texts, through their lexicogrammar and patterns of organization, reflect and activate each of these interrelated contexts.

While some chapters, following relevant research traditions, illustrate how schools (seen as macro-contexts) and writing pedagogies (seen as cultures of meaning that instantiate a specific set of premises around writing) shape aspects of language use in any given written text, others suggest that this relationship should not be interpreted as straightforward or linear but as one which is negotiated by people as they use and redefine written texts in micro-contexts (classroom events).

Building upon this Figure 1, we may argue, in line with Cicourel (cited in Gunnarsson, Linell, & Nordberg, 1997: xii; see also Gunnarsson, 1997), that what emerges as important for writing research is to address the kinds of linkages established by participants between these different units within and across sociocultural communities. Analyses need to capture the way by which macro-contexts (especially the values and attitudes certain communities project towards written language and knowledge in general) are constituted in and through the sequential emergence of micro-contexts (literacy events); link the texts produced in a specific school community to the social history of community-valued meanings; gain insight into the textual practices in communities and attend to their interactive emergence. Apparently, independently of the size of the unit selected, analyses of writing can be more informative if built on a more holistic perspective that views writing as a sociohistorical community resource. Borrowing a similar observation made by Prior (1995b) as a result of his analysis on L2 academic writing tasks (see also Ramanathan, & Atkinson, 2000), we could argue that written texts, the tasks used in each classroom, and participants' patterns of response to these tasks make sense only if seen in terms of "a local history of participants' situated actions" (Prior, 1995b: 54; see also Prior, 1991, 1995a).

To clarify the perspectives proposed in this volume and indeed in the literature, it is important that I situate the various proposals presented under two distinct research orientations, instantiating what is referred to as the *monologic* versus the *dialogic* ways of defining contextually-embedded language use (see Linell, 1998). Monologism relies on the notion of the speaker/writer as situated within a clearly delineated context. Dialogic approaches pay more attention to the processes through which texts and contexts evolve together and shape one another.

In what follows, I briefly outline monologic and dialogic developments in research conducted on conversational interaction, and illustrate how these have been (implicitly or explicitly) used in the analyses of contextually-situated written texts and writing contexts. As to be noted, research on the way context shapes spoken and written interaction tends to follow a similar path, from initial accounts building on the clear-cut delimitation of text and context to proposals suggesting the interdependence of texts and contexts as two resources which emerge from one another.

2.2 Context in Conversational Interaction: Monologic and Dialogic Approaches

The best known proposals of context have been put forward by Malinowski and Hymes; context is basically defined as an objective and clearly-delimited set of factors shaping language use. Malinowski (1923, cited in Duranti, & Goodwin 1992: 14-16) talks about the "context of situation", referring to all those extra-linguistic factors which have some bearing on the text itself' (see also Halliday, & Hasan, 1976).

Building upon and refining Jacobson's tri-partite model of linguistic communication (which consisted of the speaker, the listener and the message), Hymes (1974) in his ethnographic research relates social contexts to the processes of language use and interpretation; social context is segmented into a series of culturally important communicative units, namely, the speech situation, the speech event, and the speech act. These units are embedded within each other: speech acts are parts of speech events, which, in turn, cannot be understood unless situated within a speech community; all these units reveal the ways by which communities make meanings. This relationship between various contextual units is captured in Hymes' classificatory grid, known as the SPEAKING grid. The following component elements are included: Situation (setting and scene), Participants (their identities, such as age, gender, etc.), Ends (purposes, goals, outcomes), Act sequences (message form and content), Key (the causal or formal style of speaking), Instrumentalities (channel [verbal, nonverbal, physical]), Norms (capturing both norms of interaction and norms of interpretation), Genre. Though Hymes' work represents a groundbreaking development in the ethnographic analysis of speaking styles across communities, and indeed these notions have been used in writing research as well (see section 3), Hymes' notion of the speech event – which is presented as a clear-cut entity – has been criticized as overly simplistic (see Duranti, 1997).

Subsequent work instantiating the so-called dialogic approach to communication (proposed basically within conversation analysis, ethnomethodology and interactional sociolinguistics) has introduced important revisions to terms and notions, which were assumed to be given or pre-existing. What unites these research strands is the premise that analysis should proceed beyond the "objective" notion of context, as defined through the speech event (where interpretation is presented in a top-down fashion – from global background expectations to linguistic details – and participant roles are static) to trace the way by which speech events (and indeed the goals pursued and participants' roles) are interactionally constructed by all participants involved. In this approach, speech events are "locally produced, incrementally developed," and, as such, they are seen "as transformable at any moment" (Drew, & Heritage, 1992: 21). Thus, speech events, such as an interview, though associated with a pre-established set of expectations, cannot be presented as the static implementation of these expectations; interviews are rather reconstructed in each case anew by the participants involved (see He [1998] on the applicability of this notion to the academic context). This insight has important implications with regard to classroom interactions (and indeed interactions around writing, see section 3.3). The role the teacher and students assume in any classroom interaction cannot be seen as static but as interactively negotiated along with the classroom lesson and the learning activity that is co-constructed. The question is not "what does it mean to be an interviewer or an interviewee / a teacher and a student" but rather: "What does it mean to be a teacher and a student in this particular classroom?" "How do participants emerge as particular kinds of teachers and certain kinds of students?"

In short, in the so-called dialogic perspective, the emphasis is no longer on the way by which certain, pre-established units constrain meanings and interpretations but rather on illustrating how participants themselves through various linguistic and paralinguistic signals – referred to as contextualization cues – construct and index the speech event, and provide, at the same time, each other with guidelines for the sequential interpretation of this activity (Gumperz, 1982a, 1982b; Schiffrin, 1987). Furthermore, in dialogic accounts, the clear-cut distinction between the speaker and the audience is seen as problematic (see subsequent extensions introduced by Goffman [1981] who replaces the notion of speaker by the "production format of the utterance", consisting of three basic roles: author, animator, and principal; the notion of the hearer is replaced by the "participant framework"). Dialogic perspectives are interested in exploring the joint construction of meaning, how speakers and hearers arrive at shared understandings of each other's perspectives (referred to as intersubjectivity, He, 1998; Rommetveit, 1974, 1992). Jacoby, & Ochs have introduced the term "co-construction" to capture the "joint creation of a form, interpretation, stance, action, activity, identity, institution, skill, ideology, emotion, or other culturally meaningful reality" (Jacoby, & Ochs, 1995: 171). Proceeding even further, notions such as those of cognition, culture, identity, and expertise which, traditionally, were assumed to be distinct from language and interaction, are re-interpreted as socially-constructed, i.e., as emerging out of interactive practices (Young, & He, 1998).

2.2.1 *From Context to Contextual Resources to Contextualization*

Seen from a more psychologically-oriented perspective, context has been interpreted as knowledge, i.e., as a set of resources people bring to any given situation for making and interpreting meanings. How do these resources operate when one enters a new community? Are these contextual resources static, i.e., should they be seen as a pre-established set of expectations brought to any communicative situation or as a dynamic and constantly evolving set of expectations people use and draw upon to make meanings? The more static approach to context has been developed by psychological research (Carrell, & Eisterhold [1988]; but see also Labov, & Waletzky [1968] on a different proposal on the notion of schema, related to narrative schemata), which, through the notions of formal schemata, frames, scripts, etc., singles out the cognitive dimension of contextual resources; these are seen as embodying the patterns of prior knowledge people draw upon and use to make sense of and act within the world (for its applicability to reading and writing, see McGee, 1982; Meyer et al., 1980). More dynamic approaches to the social nature of contextual resources (linking constructs developed in the sociology of language, rhetoric and composition research) have been developed within genre studies, which have illustrated how, through genres and through specific textual patterns, one negotiates historically-situated meanings within the community. Rather than assuming the existence of genres as pre-set or given categories, this research advices us that we redefine genres not just as "textual responses to recurring social situations but indeed as ways by which recurring situations are constructed" (Devitt, 1993, cited in Mayes, 2003: 54). A different proposal on the social aspect of the contextual resources used in any act of language use and interpretation has been developed by Gee (1990) through the notions of primary versus secondary Discourses, defined as particular "ways of talking, acting, valuing, and believing" (Gee, 1996: 122-148); these may also encompass the tools, symbols, and objects people use for enacting specific, socially situated identities.

But how do schemata relate to interactive units, such as those of speech events and literacy events (Basso, 1974) that are created within speech communities? The two proposals need not be seen as opposing. Thus, participants' knowledge schemata, and experiences of past similar events and social roles are a valuable resource to be used for the construction of any new interactive event. These resources are instantiated, and thus are made concrete as they unfold in the sequential, moment-by-moment creation of any given speech event.

To incorporate this dynamic process, current research suggested that we shift our attention away from context as such to trace contextualization, i.e., the strategies by which participants establish and negotiate meanings in various social interactions (Bauman, & Biggs, 1990). It is worth noting that, the contextual variables singled out in the past (such as ethnicity, age, etc.) as influencing language use, are no longer regarded a-priori as important. As Gumperz (1982a, 1982b) has illustrated, participants themselves indicate – through lexical, prosodic, phonological, and syntactic choices together with the use of particular codes, languages, and styles (referred to as contextualization cues) – which aspects of the context they regard as relevant for the interpretation of one another's meanings in an interaction.

The implications of this dialogic perspective are very important, since they, in effect, suggest a new way of defining and assessing the notion of communicative competence. Note that in line with monologic approaches, communicative competence has been presented as a discrete set of features to be acquired in contexts (Canale, 1983); dialogic perspectives foreground the situated co-construction of interactional competence (Young, & He, 1998). This new notion integrates the activities of speaking and listening, which, traditionally, were teased apart. The development of interactional competence is presented to be locally shaped, arising out of specific contexts. Indeed, in light of such developments, current pedagogical work in applied linguistics starts from the premise that speaking and listening/understanding should not be seen as existing independently of the interactive practices participants construct.

What does this situated perspective entail with regard to the analysis of texts and the acts of writing which were traditionally defined in cognitive terms? As to be shown, though developed with respect to conversational discourse, this research has been used by writing researchers as a point of departure for conceptualizing the contextual nature of writing and unveiling the processes involved in the construction of writing contexts.

3   TEXT–CONTEXT INTERACTIONS IN WRITING RESEARCH

3.1 Monologic versus Dialogic Perspectives in Writing and Literacy Research

As Figure 1 indicates, the notion of context has been interpreted in many different ways in writing research. In what follows, however, I attempt to cut across this diversity and illustrate that, in fact, relevant research points to two distinct disciplinary paradigms; these may be situated under the categories of "monologic/writing-" versus "dialogic/literacy-oriented" research (for on overview of these approaches through a different terminology, see Lewis, 2001). While both perspectives address the contextual factors that shape the nature of writing, the way by which texts are positioned against contexts and the frameworks through which the text-context interaction is analyzed are quite distinct. It should be noted, however, that adopting one perspective versus the other is not a neutral choice. The use of different terminology to describe "similar" phenomena (writing versus literacies, composing processes versus genre-mediated dialogic negotiations with community resources) entails quite significant implications with regard to the types of units brought into the fore-front of analysis (written texts, literacy events and social practices), the analyses undertaken (from written texts as static units, to texts as dialogic processes), and even the pedagogical interventions designed. Interestingly, even in cases where the same unit, such as that of writing conferences, is selected for analysis by both research orientations, the methodological frameworks employed and the results arrived at tend to be radically distinct (see section 3.3 below).

Writing research basically directs attention to texts and writing processes as situated within specific types of contexts. This perspective builds on a certain way of conceptualizing the text-context interaction; whether focusing on texts or on writing interactions, these units are clearly delimited from their enveloping contexts. Contexts are basically presented as preset scaffolds; certain contextual variables (such as age, social group, etc.) are singled out and their effect to the texture of written texts or writing interactions is traced through specific, quantifiable linguistic forms and interactive patterns.

Stressing the mutually shaping relationship between texts and contexts, the other – more dialogic – perspective suggests that we attend to the social construction of written texts and writing activities, i.e., to the processes through which community members negotiate specific meanings; through repeated interactions, members establish a certain community-valued perspective towards written texts. Attention is not directed to units as situated against contexts but rather to contextualization in Gumperz's sense, i.e., to the processes by which any given unit emerges out of contexts which this unit signals and helps construct. Alternatively, we could argue that in research following along these lines, the *unit of analysis* selected is not the individual writer, the text s/he produces or the path a certain writer follows in appropriating community-valued genres, but the bi-directional interactive processes through which a group of people emerges as a community of learners; this is attained through collective processes, i.e., through learners' repeated patterns of interaction with one another and with community sociohistorical resources. From this more holistic perspective, then, texts and writing contexts play a central role in the construction of the culture of the community (Ramanathan, & Kaplan, 2000). As such, attention is directed toward illustrating how many different units, i.e., writing acts, texts, and practices, interrelate to index and constitute the interactively-built culture of a specific learning community, i.e., its intertextual history.

3.2 From Situated Writing to Socioculturally Shaped Literacies

3.2.1 On Written Texts in Contexts

While initially syntactically-oriented work on writing tended to define writing quality via sentence structure and T-units (Hunt, 1965, 1983; Loban, 1976), through Halliday, & Hasan's (1976) work on cohesion, research attention shifted to the linguistic, micro-structural organization of texts. Writing development is traced by attending to how writers (from different age and social groups) make increasing use of specific cohesive forms (for a survey see Grabe, & Kaplan, 1996); cohesion was proposed to contribute to writing quality (Abadiano, 1995; Cox, Shanahan, & Sulzby, 1990). Though inserted in a very basic social context, written text production is basically seen as an individual activity. The bulk of this linguistically-oriented research attended to specific features (such as connectives, adverbs, noun phrases, pronouns) which were coded, counted, and analyzed as writer's response to a specific, clearly-delimited contextual variable. Thus, a number of studies (note as an example, Crowhurst, 1987; 1991) have traced the ways children learn how to adapt their writing to different audiences or take into account generic features (Knudson, 1992; but also see Kirsch, & Roen, 1990). Though the results may be conflicting, the premise upon which the analysis is founded remains constant: the effect of audience and/or writers' increasing acknowledgement of generic features are identified through the differing use of specific linguistic forms (Collins, 1984; Golder, & Coirier, 1994; Perera, 1984). Writing quality – seen in decontextualized terms – has been correlated with the increasing use of certain linguistic forms (which are a-priori taken as indices of a more complex, maturational style) and later with patterns of topic structure (Witte, 1983). Similar developments may be noted in composition strands, where experimental and non-experimental research focused upon certain variables in predefined assignments (Applebee, 1981; Langer, 1986).

A similarly static way of addressing the text-context interactions is noted in research which focuses on the relationship between macro-contexts (cultures, social groups) and text styles (see Grabe, 1987). An interesting example is work within contrastive rhetoric. Beginning with Kaplan's (1966, 1987) research, initially, most approaches to cross-cultural textual style tended to forward a rather linear correlation between culture (taken as a homogeneous contextual variable) and rhetorical style, with the two levels being linked by specific textual patterns. By asserting such a direct correlation between macro-factors and textual patterns, however, the intricacies of the particular rhetorical situation within which the writer operates have been largely ignored (see Thatcher, 2000). Subsequent work (note for instance Duszak, 1997; Farrell, 1996), attested to the importance of other intermediate factors (such as those of the academic community and of academic genres) and suggested that these be incorporated in relevant accounts of contextually variable notions of academic achievement and writing quality. As a result of the above, the notion of ESL writing, though associated with the acquisition of grammatical and textual competence in a different language, has been since interpreted as a process during which students have to gain access to certain typified ways of making meanings that are socially distributed.

To sum up, we may argue, following Tracy (1998: 6), that, the social tradition in writing suggests a very specific way of addressing the contextual elements that shape written texts; whether attending to the way *macro-contexts* (culture, social group) shape textual style or tracing the textual realization of the *micro-context* (i.e., attending to the way by which the individual writer assesses and responds to features of the immediate context of situation, such as task, text type, addressee, age), in all these cases, context is seen as a variable extraneous to the written text that can be fully controlled; as such, its influence on the text is quantifiable, and discrete, traced directly down to single isolated linguistic forms, rather than to discourse strategies or co-occurrence of forms (see Biber, 1995; Connor, 1995) which instantiate functional concerns.

3.2.2   Writing in Communities

The introduction of new terms such as genres, literacy events and discourse communities (Swales, 1990) with the refinements suggested, through the notions of communities of practice (Lave, & Wenger, 1991), and thick versus thin formulations in the description of communities (Kent, 1999), have led to important new ways of addressing the socially-constructed nature of writing; attention has been directed away from the analysis of specific units (texts or writing interactions) to the collaborative processes involved in the production of texts and writing activities; these processes acquire meaning as part of a locally constructed set of community values and literacy practices.

Formed after Hymes' speech community, the notion of discourse community has been criticized for referring to a "determinate, static, autonomous, and predictable arena of shared and agreed-upon values" (Hyland, & Hamp-Lyons, 2002: 7) around language use. New perspectives brought about by subsequent research (for a review, see Ramanathan, 2002) illuminated the transient and sociohistorical nature of the meaning making processes that characterize a community of practice. Lave, & Wenger define a community of practice as "a set of relations among persons, activity, and world" which exists over time and in relation to other communities (Lave, & Wenger, 1991: 98). Drawing upon the distinction between macro- and micro-contexts, we could argue that the construct of "communities of practice" captures the sequential emergence of the so-called local cultures of meaning; these are not a-priori given but are rather co-constructed by all participants involved, full community members and peripheral ones (see also Casanave [1995] for a similar point).

This notion has specific implications as concerns the analysis of writing processes and literate practices. Apparently, in light of the above definitions, attention cannot be directed to schools as homogeneous social contexts that shape children's writing or to social groups in general but rather to the development of community-specific literacies, i.e., to the culturally-specific and situationally-bound ways by which reading, writing process and speaking acts are co-produced in the moment-by-moment emergence of interactive contexts; these contexts are constructed by the members of a specific school classroom, a specific middle-class or working-class home (see, for instance Gregory et al., 2004; Lacasa et al., 2002). The culture of this local community is reflected in and defined through the *shared history of learning, the relations of mutual engagement and the development of a shared repertoire of negotiable resources accumulated over time* (my underlining) (Wenger, 1998: 76). Thus, in place of static meanings, attention is directed to negotiated meanings, in place of secure understandings to the processes by which participants arrive at partial understandings or even misunderstandings (on this issue, see Bremer et al., 1996) – a process that is shaped in and through interaction; in place of common resources, attention is given to the diversity of perspectives participants bring to any given interactive event and integrate to arrive at intersubjectivity.

If, in light of the above, the literacy culture (i.e., the textual and interactional meaning making system) of a community is not statically imposed but is rather intertextually co-constructed by its members, it becomes clear that questions as to the best practices or pedagogical approaches through which we may teach writing in elementary or secondary schools are rendered insignificant. While the limits that curriculum requirements and general guidelines impose to any local community cannot be dismissed, nevertheless, in each case, teachers and students in their classroom communities construct and redefine a specific version of this curriculum (Bloom, 1989). The interesting issues that arise are these: What does a given writing pedagogy suggest and how can we trace its sequential co-construction over time? What are the kinds of written texts created in the daily routine of classroom life? What kinds of values and positions towards written knowledge do teachers and students in this specific school classroom or university department co-construct?

The answers provided may be simply descriptive (describing what Russell [2002] calls the "depth" and "breadth" of genres within a community) or proceed further to unveil the ideological underpinnings of the resources valued in any given community. What kind of meanings are constituted and which are excluded from this community? What are the processes facilitating students' access to the appropriation of these valued meanings? Drawing upon Luke, & Freebody (1997), we could argue that all school-situated acts of writing are not neutral but deeply political. The kinds of written texts children have access to, the kinds of meaning-making resources they are enculturated to use, and the interactive patterns powerful community members co-construct with students around these texts are not insignificant choices. They rather comprise a system which signals and enforces a certain selection mechanism through which students are enculturated into becoming specific kinds of literate subjects.

Interestingly, while most of the chapters in this volume build heavily on the notion of school genres as ideological resources valued within school communities (Ongstad, Donahue, Myhill, Kostouli), and others draw upon it, although they may not foreground it (Allal et al., Folman, & Connor, McAllister), a slightly different approach is expressed by Adler-Kassner, & Estrem. Adler-Kassner, & Estrem seem to downplay the notion of genre (and indeed the necessity of teaching academic genres), suggesting instead that research into situated writing should be concerned with helping students develop certain strategies that can be used in various, cross-community contexts. This different perspective, in effect, introduces in this volume a long-held debate concerning local versus global knowledge; according to Carter (1990, cited in Beaufort, 1999: 7), this should not be considered as an either-or debate but rather as a continuum "that grows increasingly contextual with greater [writing] expertise." What is the relation, then, between literacy practices, genres and strategies? Since this issue differentiates the nuances of the argument different chapters of this volume advance regarding contextually-embedded writing, some clarifications on genres and strategies need to be made.

3.2.3   On Genres and Strategies in Communities of Practice

Genre – a notion that pervades current accounts of language use, communication and language education – has been variously defined in the literature. Different proposals have been developed in: the New Rhetoric tradition, systemic-functional linguistics, Russian activity theory, rhetorical work on composition, as well as in various social constructivist strands (for a summary, see Hyon, 1996; Johns, 2002; Paltridge, 1997).

Genres have been described as relatively stable textual regularities associated with and constitutive of social practices (Cope, & Kalantzis, 1993), as configurations of semantic resources that members of the culture associate with a particular situation type (Christie, & Martin, 1997), as responses to social situations which are part of a socially constructed reality (Miller, 1984). Genres have been seen as part of the social processes by which knowledge is built up, maintained, transmitted in social oganizations, such as academic disciplines, professions, high school and university programs (Bazerman, 1988; Berkenkotter, & Huckin, 1988, 1993; Yates, & Orlikowski, 1992).

In general, descriptions of genre have progressed away from the exclusive focus on the formal structure of the text itself (described in various ways by the Australian school of thought and by Swales' [1990] and Bhatia's [1993, 2000] ESP analysis of moves) toward more critical approaches which illustrate how genres, as organizing structures of meaning within a community, provide "expectations for the purpose, content, form, participants, time and place of coordinated social interaction" (Yates, & Orlikowski, 2002: 104). Current work aligns with a more generative approach to genres, which are no longer presented as ready-made forms to be statically used by students but rather as "situated forms of cognition" (Trosborg, 2000) that can be creatively reworked by writers, in light of their own purposes. Such a view grows out of the Bkhtinian notion of revoicing, which recognizes, on one hand, the powerful role sociohistorically situated processes play in shaping discourse forms while, it acknowledges, on the other, the agency of the text producer and the significance of the immediate sociohistorical context within which textual interaction takes place. According to this approach, any text is rendered meaningful against historicized patterns of expectations that shape interaction within discourse communities.

While the above work suggests that the construction of genres represents the writer's strategic response to a situation, apparently, such strategic choices are not similar to the types of strategies that have been invoked by previous, process-oriented research (see Collins, 1998 and for an overview of the way post-process approaches address this theme, see Kent, 1999). The strategies most commonly-referred to, i.e., knowledge telling and knowledge transforming (Bereiter, & Scardamalia, 1983; see also Collins, 1998), are seen in cognitive terms. Research attention has been gradually attending to textual strategies, i.e., to the ways through which typical community meanings are made, and certain, community-valued positionings toward knowledge are communicated (Hyland, 2000, 2002). As research in systemic functional linguistics has aptly demonstrated, participation in the school community depends upon children's gaining access to school disciplines; English, history, mathematics, geography and science are literacy sub-cultures, which are constructed and differentiated from one another through linguistic and textual choices (Martin, 1985; Lemke, 1990; Veel, 1997). In light of the above, then, textual strategies, such as the implicit versus explicit way of making cohesion (Michaels, 1991), linearity versus digressiveness (Clyne, 1987), are reinterpreted as ways by which writers index their stance toward historically-situated community resources. If, according to Fairclough (1995), genres are among the main discursive forces in the "naturalization of ideology," any inquiry into genre should bring into the fore-front of analysis the way by which strategies may create certain meanings (over others) as well as establish certain power relationships, and ideological positions (for an overview, see Candlin, & Hyland, 1999). If, in light of the sociocultural perspective, cognition is socially situated and distributed (Forman, Minick, & Stone, 1993), it is worth questioning whether the various types of strategies can be detached from the local history of participants' communities, i.e., from the genres and the communities within which these strategies operate and which they help construct. Composition and discourse analytic research might need to inquire further into the way the cognitive and social dimensions of certain notions, such as that of "strategies", may be integrated.

3.3 Writing Activities and Learning Trajectories in Community Settings: Sociocognitive and Sociolinguistic Perspectives

The shift of emphasis from writing as a neutral, decontextualized skill to genre literacies has led researchers to develop new methodologies for capturing the processes of literacy learning. Given the multiplicity of literacies across communities and the functions writing acquires in and through contexts, it is by now well established that writing development cannot be seen as a process that follows a clearly defined path. Indeed, according to current accounts, the uses and functions of writing cannot be simply transmitted (as in the conduit metaphor, see Reddy, 1979) from one participant to another (from the teacher to the students); students are enculturated into the genres and, thus, into the meaning making system of a transient local culture. In this respect, literacy learning can be traced through students' patterns of participation in reading and writing events. Through their increasingly more dynamic participatory role in such social processes students do not simply contribute to the situated construction of writing acts and written texts (Faigley, & Hansen, 1985); they emerge as community members and may undertake a central role in the construction of the literacy culture of their local community.

The perspectives developed in sociocognitive and sociolinguistic literature offer valuable insights on the way by which literacy is constructed through social activities or literacy events. Sociocognitive research traces literacy learning through the unit of the activity type and the notions of apprenticeship, distributed cognition, mediation, situated learning, and guided participation (e.g., Forman et al., 1993; Lave, & Wenger, 1991; Rogoff, 1990; Wertsch, 1985, 1991, 1998). Following Leont'ev (1981), the "person-acting-in-context" (Cole, 1989, cited in Dias, 2000: 16) is proposed as the unit within which we may locate the situated co-construction of meanings. It is worth noting here that the highest level of analysis invoked, the level of activity, is not just used in reference to the physical context in which participants function; this notion also encompasses participants' own sociocultural interpretations of the context, its various requirements and tasks (see Lantoff, & Appel, 1994: 17). This proposal is a very interesting parallel to arguments developed within the ethnographic and sociolinguistic analysis of classroom-mediated writing processes; in these research strands, attention is no longer directed to preset writing contexts but rather to the contextualization of writing or literacy events, i.e., to how these events are constructed by the teacher and the students as they negotiate writing in classrooms.

Despite this variation and terminological plurality, all proposals in effect suggest this: students' learning about writing should be seen as an interactionally emergent process that can be traced through the paths or the trajectories students follow when participating in recurring interactive activities constructed within a certain local community. Children's understandings and gradually-developing definitions of writing are formulated through the assistance or the scaffolding novice members receive by more expert participants, adults or peers (Hicks, 1997; Lave, & Wenger, 1991; Melzi, 2000; Rogoff, 1990; Tharp, & Gallimore, 1988). In light of this, it becomes clear that what researchers attend to is not learning as such (which is invisible) but how learning processes are displayed in the social contexts created by the participants themselves; students' changing patterns of participation in the writing contexts (i.e., the changes from guided to independent participation) may be an indication of students' learning. As researchers from different fields have pointed out, children learn both what counts as literacy – what meanings and values should be attached to reading and writing in a specific community setting – as well as how they may signal their status within the community and act in community-appropriate ways through the texts they construct, the actions they undertake and by attending to the way their actions are interpreted by other participants.

An important issue that arises concerns the way by which these interactive processes facilitate or hinder students' transitions from home informal literacy experiences to school-constructed literacy contexts (Heath, 1983; Michaels, 1981, 1987) and from school to workplace settings (Dias, & Parré, 2000). School contexts, of course, are not static but subject to considerable variation from one level (elementary school) to the next (secondary school) and even from one subject to the next, since school subjects are redefined as cultural communities themselves (Moje, & O'Brien, 2001). As pertinent literature has indicated, children's acquisition of certain, school-specific ways of making meaning may be, to a certain extent, facilitated or hindered, by matches or mismatches between children's own repertoire of textual schemata and interactive patterns and those school expects for displaying knowledge. What is of importance and should be noted is this: the congruence or divergence in Discourses – i.e., in the ways of speaking and talking about texts participants adopt – are interactively negotiated; various mediational tools, including language, help children move beyond and integrate the divergent cultural resources children may bring to a classroom community; conflicts, and/or the attainment of intersubjectivity (i.e., of shared understandings) are thus co-constructed, and negotiated, in and through the mediation of the teacher or other peers.

A very interesting account of the conflicts children face when attempting to interrelate different social resources has been attested by ethnographically-oriented research on elementary school children's writing. Classroom writing may index a variety of social worlds these classrooms contain, each being associated with its own requirements and definitions on what writing is. In a relevant investigation, Dyson (1993) differentiated between three worlds – the official school world, the unofficial peer world, and the sociocultural community as realized in the classroom – which did not propose similar genres, themes, and ways of using language. As Dyson (1999) has argued, written text production in complex classroom cultures requires that children "differentiate not only phonological niceties and textual features but also social worlds – the very social worlds that provide them with agency and important symbols" (Dyson, 1999: 396). This insight has been restated in Bakhtinian terms by more recent research, which suggests that text production should be seen as the partial re-enactment of prior texts; any current text revoices and redrafts, at least partially, previous discursive forms; indeed, current "practices and activity structures" emerge "from previous (or relevant but different) contexts"; different terms have been used to capture this historically situated process (referred to as "intercontextual practices", "interdiscursive practices", and "intertextual practices", see Kamberelis, & de la Luna, 2004) of making meanings through texts and writing practices; what should be noted is that developing writers draw upon prior resources "for imagining, negotiating and enacting practices and activities in the new contexts" (cited in Kamberelis, & de la Luna, 2004: 245).

If, in line with the above, children's appropriation of school literacies is mediated, supported or constrained by the contextual environments created within classrooms as learning contexts, important issues arise: What are the units created around texts and how do these shape children's acquisition of school literacies? What are the strategies facilitating (or hindering) children's move from the lower ground (i.e., what one can do in cooperation with more capable participants, adults or peers) to the higher ground (i.e., to what one can do on his/her own)?

3.3.1   Writing Contexts in L1 and L2 Literature

In surveying the way L1 versus L2 research responds to these questions, it is appropriate that I re-introduce the distinction between monologic versus dialogic construals of classroom writing contexts (usually writing conferences). The first approach is instantiated in the so called process-oriented research (see Zamel, 1987 for a survey). By situating readers and writers within a given or ready-made context, the writing conference (Connor, & Asanavage, 1994 and for a survey, see Ferris, & Hedgcock, 1998) and defining reader response through a set of comments teachers provide writers on their texts (Ashwell, 2000; Zamel, 1985), this perspective conceives of writing contexts in the same static way Hymes had developed for the notion of speech event (see 2.2. above). As such, the same criticism can be directed against these proposals.

Let me begin by noting some of the issues this research suggests as important for investigation: How do expert versus less expert, native and non-native students participate in writing conferences? How do developing writers process the information on writing they draw from writing conferences? In all these cases, the focal unit selected (i.e., the interaction around writing) is seen as a self-contained entity that can be clearly delineated from its surrounding context. Context is presented as a modifier of the internal activity that occurs in individual language learners. While different types of contexts around writing (such as peer vs. teacher feedback, and teacher-student vs. peer conferences) are compared and contrasted (Conrad, & Goldstein, 1999, Freedman, & Sperling, 1985; Walker, & Elias, 1987; Zamel, 1985), basically, in these process-oriented approaches to L2 writing, writing conferences are taken as given, preset structures rather than as ongoing accomplishments that emerge through the contributions of all participants involved. Indeed, most of the classifications documented (mainly in L2 literature) tend to describe conference talk via a predefined set of categories (for a further discussion on this, see Ferris, & Hedgcock, 1998; Paulus, 1999).

Similar points can be made with regard to readers' feedback. While the significance of the feedback teacher give on their students' text is worth noting, in most cases, feedback is presented as a list of decontextualized comments; in a more dynamic perspective, feedback can be seen as the instantiation of community-valued ways or strategies of reflecting upon texts; feedback is an integral component of the assistance that "expert" community members may give to developing writers so that they appropriate the Discourses of the school community (Anson, 2000; Ashwell, 2000).

It is only recently that L2 writing research questions basic notions – such as that of writer expertise – which were previously accepted as straightforward (see, for instance, Crabbe, 2003). The more dynamic approach to writing contexts – which sees them as constructed by all participants involved (see 2.2. above for pertinent developments on spoken interaction) has been developed by work on the ethnography of classroom processes. Researchers, such as Green, & Meyer (1991), Mercer (1995, 1996), Nystrand et al. (1997), Wells, & Chang-Wells (1992), suggest that the expanding of one's competencies (including writing competencies) is shaped through people's active participation in the construction of a web of dialogic contexts. Through her 3-year ethnographic study, Gutierrez (1994) illustrated how through interactive processes different scripts may be created, which are not neutral patterns of information exchange in schools but rather ideologically-laden mechanisms of information negotiation; these position students differently against school knowledge. Reinterpreting classrooms as local cultures or communities of meaning, ethnographically-based research (see Bloom, & Bailey, [1992]; Green, & Wallat, [1981]; Floriani, [1993]; the Santa Barbara Classroom Discourse Group, [1992, 1995]) suggested that literacy learning should be more profitably seen as a situated process of apprenticeship into secondary discourses (in Gee's [1990] terms). Attention is thus directed away from the design of general writing pedagogies assumed to bring about certain clearly identifiable results toward the investigation of the social nature of each classroom and the way this helps students appropriate specific meanings while it excludes others from this process.

4   THIS VOLUME

This volume presents cross-cultural evidence on writing as a contextually-shaped resource for communicating meanings. The data analyzed consist of texts and writing contexts which illustrate the textual practices of different school communities across cultures. Data is drawn from British, American, Norwegian, French, Israeli, Brazilian, Swiss and Greek contexts.

The research-based contributions to this volume, drawing from sociocognitive, sociolinguistic and composition research on writing, may be situated on various points along the continuum outlined in this introductory chapter, i.e., with some chapters being situated closer to the monologic and others aligning with the dialogic approaches to writing processes, and texts. The chapters draw on different research traditions (illustrative in authors' use of the terms "writing" vs. literacies) and employ a range of methodologies. These extend from semi-structured interviews, used to capture participants' definitions of certain genres, to quantitative and qualitative descriptions of the micro- and macro-structural organization of texts, to the co-construction of writing contexts within which the functions of writing are negotiated.

The chapters interrelate through many different threads and can be read differently, depending upon the type of context they are read against. Taking as a point of departure the domains (the discourse learning communities) that shape writing as a text and as an activity, a first distinction that could be drawn is between articles presenting writing and literacy practices in primary school (Spinillo, & Pratt; Ongstad, Allal et al., Kostouli), secondary school (Myhill, Donahue, Folman, & Connor), and academic contexts (Ferenz, McCallister, Adler-Kassner, & Estrem). When we take as our point of departure the types of data analyzed, we may distinguish between chapters which (i) focus on the linguistic and textual structure of various types of texts produced by children, and college students in either L1 or L2 (Spinillo, & Pratt, Myhill, Donahue, Folman, & Connor), (ii) trace, through quantitative or qualitative analyses, the types of interactions created between "expert" and "less expert" participants around written texts (Ongstad, Allal et al., Kostouli, McAllister, Adler-Kassner, & Estrem) and (iii) attend to the social factors shaping writing processes, such as planning, in these contexts (Ferenz). Interactions may be further differentiated into those created by partners of equal status (peer interactions) and by partners with asymmetrical power (teacher-students) (see Allal et al., Ongstad on school children and by McAllister with regard to college students, which cut through both distinctions), giving us glimpses into the way learners manage interpersonal relationships as well; in negotiating the various meanings of texts, students may seek to establish or redefine their relationships with the other community members who, as vocal or silent participants, may contribute to the construction of writing activities.

The aspects of textual communication analyzed within school communities are as follows:

- *Participants' in- and out-of-school literacy experiences*: How do the textual and multi-modal experiences children have acquired through their participation in out-of-school literacy contexts affect writing in school contexts? This question is addressed and answered by attending to formal school contexts in two ways, a retrospective and a prospective one; some chapters (Spinillo, & Pratt; Myhill) describe how preschool literacy experiences provide children with a set of contextual resources that can be brought to the construction of specific school-valued genres; other chapters (Addler-Kassner, & Estrem) suggest ways by which knowledge acquired in a specific academic setting (first-year writing course) may be used in other communities and other relevant settings.

- *Text production*: How do children use language in a specific text type? What are the ways by which children of different age- and sociocultural groups approach the production of various school genres? How do narrative schemata affect the construction of other genres (namely expository texts) in the school context? Are there cultural differences in the organizational patterns used for shaping meaning? Chapters by Spinillo, & Pratt, Donahue, Folman, & Connor address these issues. Text analyses range from those which are more social (tracing the linguistic forms and textual patterns children employ) to others which are more dialogic; the latter situate text production in the dynamic processes of negotiation students undertake with community-specific resources in the process of appropriating school discourse. Among the text types analyzed are narrative texts (Spinillo, & Pratt), texts constructed from sources and argumentative texts written on the basis of excerpts presented to students (Donahue, Myhill, Folman, & Connor). Different types of text genres are produced by college students (McAllister, Adler-Kassner, & Estrem).
- *Writing Contexts: Negotiation of meaning and divergent schemata on writing*: Chapters by Allal et al., Ongstad, Kostouli, and McAllister address issues on the construction of literacy learning. These chapters focus on writing contexts, i.e., on the various forms of apprenticeship (which may not always involve overt teaching) by which "less expert" writers learn how to reflect upon the texts they or their classmates have produced. Among the issues raised are: How are differences in textual schemata negotiated in the contexts of oral interaction? What role do different types of contexts (teacher-students vs. peer-peer interactions) play in shaping children's developing understandings of writing?

School Communities: On Texts

Spinillo, & Pratt's chapter focuses on Brazilian middle-class and street children's genre knowledge. It documents the different types of textual knowledge these children have acquired as a result of their out-of-school experiences and inquires into the way this knowledge relates to school genres. Analysis traces the criteria middle-class and street children use when asked to identify and produce orally three types of genres, namely, stories, letters, and newspaper articles. As documented, the street constitutes an important – though little researched – literacy context. As illustrated, through their interactions with specific types of print (mainly newspapers), Brazilian street children acquire knowledge of a rather complex text genre, newspaper articles. Interestingly, this genre was not well developed in the middle-class children studied, who, in turn, faced fewer problems in producing and identifying stories and letters. Though psycholinguistic in its design, this study integrates participants' (i.e., children's) perspectives and points to a number of important issues concerning the construction of literacies in Brazilian home and street contexts.

Myhill illustrates how British children's prior knowledge, conceptualized in the form of already-acquired formal narrative schemata and expectations for text layout, facilitates or hinders students in their secondary school writing. Myhill is not concerned with performing a detailed textual analyses of the texts produced by children of different age- and sociocultural groups, but rather with clarifying the notion of prior knowledge; its various constituents inform the different types of choices students make in their written texts (from register choices and thematic patterns to text layout). The analysis, mainly due to the linear relationships established between age/social groups and textual choices, may be seen as an instantiation of the social approach to writing. Myhill, however, hints at the need for a wider perspective, suggesting that the textual data need to be integrated with analyses of classroom negotiations around writing. When it is read from a different viewpoint, Myhill's paper is a clear-cut case of the many contextual layers shaping literacy learning. Note that Myhill outlines the genre pedagogy, which has been introduced in Great Britain with the aim to help children widen their repertoire of choices. Myhill's analysis of the problems students faced with writing school appropriate texts seems to suggest the need that we move away from proposals of writing pedagogies as static bodies of information about writing, which, when applied, would always lead to similar outcomes; writing pedagogies are better seen as a set of claims and assumptions guiding students and teachers when negotiating the meanings of their texts. This negotiation process, as Myhill suggests, is mediated by children's prior knowledge.

Donahue focuses on the problems six French high school students faced when producing argumentative texts in secondary French schools. Her analysis aligns with a more dynamic conception of text construction; the appropriation of argumentative discourse is presented as a rather complicated process which requires that students undertake many steps and employ many different resources, including some which are not very creative, such as copying the ideas and the linguistic and textual structure of the original text presented to them. Donahue accounts for text production within a Bakhtinian-informed dialogic perspective; this perspective suggests that written text production should not be seen as the acquisition of a static set of conventions; text production is rather seen as a dynamic negotiation developing writers undertake as they move with and against given resources, adopt, and divert from available textual patterns and forms to attain their own communicative ends.

Working within contrastive rhetoric, Folman, & Connor attend to the culture-specific ways Israeli and American high school students write from sources – a task that is universally applicable. Important similarities and differences are documented, although for both groups of children this proved to be a difficult task. Such differences are accounted for in terms of the distinct writing contexts schools across the two cultures constructed. Thus, while contrastive rhetoric tended to invoke the notion of culture as an overarching, internally homogenous resource that envelops and shapes patterns of language use in any given text, Folman, & Connor seem to indicate that cross-cultural differences may in fact, be mediated by a variety of variables – including educational guidelines, and classroom processes. While the texts are analyzed in their very final stage (and thus we cannot get insight into the problems students faced during this process and the choices they made to overcome these), the authors outline a very important framework for text analysis; this consists of an interrelated set of dimensions (comparable to Biber's [1995] proposal on register) writers have to integrate in order to produce a text that synthesizes information drawn from many different sources.

School Communities: On Writing Contexts
Ongstad analyzes a very interesting case of a writing activity constructed by two second grade boys in a Norwegian classroom. In this classroom, students could communicate meanings via different semiotic resources, such as drawing, playing and writing about their activities. Apparently, in this rich semiotic culture, the significance of written language had to be established. As Ongstad illustrates, the texts produced by the children cannot be fully understood, unless one deciphers the many different layers of contexts (including genres) which these students recognized and valued as important. The specific text analyzed reflects not just the degree to which the writer, a second grade student, understood school requirements about writing but also signals this student's peer world and the relationships he wishes to establish with his friends. As a result, the text produced – though poor on school grounds – is quite rich in terms of the aspects of the semiotic context it incorporates.

Allal et al. describe three distinct Swiss classrooms in Geneva where teachers and 5th grade students negotiated the meaning of revision. Whole-class interactions are compared to peer interactions. Though the teachers were provided with the same instructional senario, interesting variations were noted across classrooms – a finding that corroborates suggestions noted in both sociocognitive and sociolinguistic literature on the socially constructed nature of literacy learning; the discussion illustrates the role classrooms as contexts play in foregrounding certain kinds of writing competences as more important than others. As Allal et al. note, the activity of text revision should not be interpreted as a given or a statically implemented one; this is rather a dynamic process whose meaning is shaped through the interactions between the specific participants involved, their level of knowledge, and scholastic achievement.

The finding underlying Allal et al. is taken up in Kostouli's paper which analyzes, though with a different methodology, two writing conferences constructed in two 5th grade Greek classrooms, one with a predominantly working-class and the other with a middle-class population. Though a similar philosophy was implemented across classrooms, the analyses illustrate that different writing contexts were, in fact, constructed. Through the data attested, we get information on the discourse processes through which children of different sociocultural groups gain access to literacy learning and on how the learning contexts created through talk within each writing conference may in fact, limit or facilitate children's access to learning opportunities.

Academic settings
The final group of papers focuses on writing processes in academic settings. Focusing on the activity of planning – an activity usually described in cognitive terms –, Ferenz illustrates that even students' choice of a specific language, L1 or L2, during the planning of a research paper, is socially conditioned; this may indicate writer's

consideration for community values, his/her wish to project an academic identity and gain membership into a specific social writing network.

McAllister's study, through the analysis of college writing, sets out to investigate a correlation assumed to be given: does interaction lead to writing improvement? To explore this, McAllister focuses on texts produced over the course of a single semester by students writing papers under three different conditions: independently and in permanent versus changing groups. The semi-experimenal design aligns with the social approach to writing contexts; the three group conditions are seen as three distinct contexts shaping writing improvement. Although analyses do not trace aspects of interaction in detail, participants' perspectives are included and the discussion in this chapter provides us with important glimpses into the negotiations students undertook with each other. The findings indicate that there were benefits to all groups as regards the quality of their final products; however, the students in permanent groups approached and constructed the activity of writing in line with a more socially-oriented pedagogy.

Adler-Kassner, & Estrem's chapter presents the first-year writing program the two authors have designed and implement at Eastern Michigan University. This course builds on the premise that writing in any context, in school or out, should be seen as a situated, public act that makes sense within a constellation of literacy practices. The assignments and their sequencing are presented in detail; as the authors indicate, the whole approach aims to challenge the notion that college-level writing courses should focus exclusively on helping students enter an "academic discourse community"; the authors' (and the course's) focus is on helping students become flexible writers.

Future developments. As a way of conclusion, reference should be made to some research threads developing out of this work. Given the interaction between texts and contexts (captured in Figure 1), it appears that in the future, the inquiry into the contextually shaped nature of writing (a topic addressed in this volume) needs to be revisited in a broader perspective that would explore writing (texts, acts, and processes) as part of an intertextually constructed web of community-valued literacy practices. This introduction suggested a way by which notions and terms from parallel-running fields may be integrated. Further reseach on real data is needed to illustrate how such a reconceptualization would work in practice.

ACKNOWLEDGEMENTS

This chapter came out of many very interesting discussions with the contributors of this volume who helped me develop a number of the issues I address. With regard to the more technical aspects involved in the preparation of this volume, I would like to thank Christos Samantzopoulos for his invaluable help throughout this process. A special thank you is due to Jim Miller and to my graduate students and my colleagues from the Department of Education, Aristotle University for helpful exchanges on literacy. And, of course, I would like to thank Gert Rijlaarsdam for encouraging me to work on this volume and for suggesting in our initial discussions a way to read through the diversity of the perspectives attested here.

SOCIOCULTURAL DIFFERENCES IN CHILDREN'S GENRE KNOWLEDGE

Evidence from Brazilian Middle-class and Street Children

ALINA G. SPINILLO & CHRIS PRATT

Federal University of Pernambuco, Recife, Brazil
& La Trobe University, Melbourne, Australia

Abstract. Texts are an integral part of people's everyday lives in current literate societies. People deal with texts in a variety of social settings: at home, at work, at school and on the streets. Indeed, children may learn a lot about texts by observing adults using them, by looking at print materials, by being read to or by reading books, newspapers, letters and so on themselves. But are these textual experiences the same for all children? How do different social contexts shape children's experiences with texts and written language in general? This chapter addresses these questions and provides answers on the basis of data drawn from a specific cultural context, the Brazilian context. It is expected that some groups of Brazilian children (such as middle-class children) would have frequent encounters with a broad range of text genres and, as a result, their generic textual knowledge would be quite rich. In Brazil, however, we find a special group of children – the street children – who do not live with their families, and do not attend school. What do street children know about texts? Where does their knowledge come from? To explore these issues, we devised a study in which Brazilian middle-class and street children were asked to produce and identify different text genres: a story, a letter and a newspaper article. We also talked informally with the children about their exposure to these genres in contexts created at home, at school and on the streets. The results show that streets can be regarded as an important literacy environment to street children just as home and school is to middle-class children, and that children's generic knowledge is mediated by the social practices around certain types of texts children from different social backgrounds engage with.

Keywords: text genres, stories, newspaper articles, letters, textual knowledge, meta-textual awareness, home literacy, school literacy, street literacy

1   INTRODUCTION

1.1 Home, School, and the Street as Literacy Contexts

Knowledge about written language (e.g., its uses and functions) and about different types of texts is crucial for people's effective participation in society. This knowledge has acquired greater importance in current literate societies, where written texts are the basic means of communication between people in the most diverse circumstances of their everyday lives. However, people's contact with and experiences with written language and texts may vary depending upon many factors. Important research has been conducted in a variety of sociocultural contexts to clarify the nature of these factors and illustrate the extent to which these shape children's literacy development.

Research conducted on many different sociocultural groups has attested interesting findings on children's experiences with texts in informal contexts and has delineated the way this knowledge shapes children's success at reading and writing activities used in formal learning situations (Heath, 1983; Scollon, & Scollon, 1981; Wells, 1985). Children's acquisition of literacy skills is usually described as the result of a long-term process that takes place through children's participation in various interactive contexts created at home, at school, and on the streets (e.g., Carraher, 1984, 1986, 1987; Ferreiro, & Teberosky, 1982; Neuman, & Celano, 2001; Purcell-Gates, 1996; Purcell-Gates, & Dahl, 1991; Scribner, & Cole, 1981). However, as documented by several researchers, within and across sociocultural groups different contexts may be created around written language; these, in turn, shape different routes in children's acquisition of reading and writing skills (e.g., Heath, 1982, 1983; Purcell-Gates, 1996; Rego, 1985, 1995; Sénéchal, LeFreve, Thomas, & Daley, 1998; Scollon, & Scollon, 1981; Teale, 1986; Teale, & Sulzby, 1989). These contexts, which instantiate socioculturally valued practices around written language, influence children's access to various print resources, determine their motivation to read and write, and, ultimately, affect children's level of literacy achievement in school.

In general, research has attested that children from middle- and upper-class backgrounds have broad access to and ample experience with written materials at home. Their home literacy environment provides them with many opportunities to use written language and observe its nature and functions: middle-class children may spontaneously explore print materials on their own; they may observe adults' activities with written language (e.g., reading letters, books, newspapers, magazines; writing letters, writing to-do lists, shopping lists, taking notes) and they may interact with adults in reading and writing activities (storytelling, story reading, writing children's and relatives' names etc.). Children and parents in middle- and upper-class households tend to engage more frequently in interactions which involve direct instruction about literacy (e.g., DeBaryshe, 1995; Fitzgerald, Spiegel, & Cunningham, 1991; Sénéchal, LeFreve, Thomas, & Daley, 1998). These situations do not constitute frequently occurring experiences for working-class children, whose parents are not well-educated or may be illiterate. Indeed, for many working-class children, school may be the only context where they interact with written language as little reading and writing is done at home where written materials may be rare, if not non-existent. In short, the significance of home literacy experiences has been well documented by a number of studies. However, home, as a particular type of literacy environment, may foster different kinds of skills. What are these skills and how do they relate to the literacy skills expected to be used in school?

Directly relevant in this regard is the research by Sénéchal, LeFreve, Thomas, & Daley (1998), which explored the relation between home literacy experiences and the development of oral and written language in middle- to upper-class preschool and first grade American children. Two literacy experiences were analyzed: the storybooks parents read to their children (an activity occurring from the time children were 9 months old), and the instructions they gave their children on reading and writing. No correlation was found between storybook exposure and direct instruction on reading and writing – a finding which reveals that these activities may not be necessarily associated. Interestingly, for the first-graders, book reading and informal literacy experiences at home were found to predict the development of oral language skills only, whereas parents' directive teaching and experiences that included more formal interactions with print predicted the development of skills related to written language only. As stressed by Sénéchal et al. (1998), home literacy experiences should not be considered a unitary construct; rather, storybook reading and parents' teaching may be independent experiences, with different links to early literacy skills and to reading acquisition.

Purcell-Gates (1996) described the ways by which working-class families in the USA use print materials at home, and explored the relationship between these uses and the kinds of literate knowledge children brought to school. In-home observations were focusing on the literacy events in which a focal child participated; his/her knowledge of written language was examined through a set of tasks intended to capture his/her success at learning to read and write in school. The results showed that in some of the families there was a great deal of reading and writing done, while in others these activities were infrequent. The type of print used by the latter group of families was restricted to reading container texts (milk cartons, cereal boxes, can labels), coupons, TV notices, and writing to-do or grocery lists. Complex texts, like stories, letters, and newspaper articles, were not widely used. It was noticed that children who held a more sophisticated knowledge of written language were those who experienced activities that involved the use of language for creating structurally and linguistically complex types of texts; it was this use that proved to be more beneficial toward improving children's knowledge about written language.

Working in a different culture, Carraher (1984) provided interesting evidence on the attitudes working-class Brazilian mothers had toward literacy, which, in turn, shaped their homebound uses of literacy. From the mothers' perspective, literacy had essentially a face-saving function: illiteracy stigmatizes the individual and it should not be exhibited. In relation to the everyday uses of literacy at home, it was found that the majority of the participants reported uses associated with simple activities, like reading and writing letters; interestingly, only a third of them read books, newspapers and magazines. Children's books were practically nonexistent at home, and even mothers who were literate very seldom read books to their children. It was found that children whose mothers read stories or letters to them were more likely to succeed in school.

Spinillo, Albuquerque, & Lins e Silva (1996) outlined the way by which differences in socioeconomic background shape Brazilian children's understanding of the uses and purposes literacy serves in their lives. Using a clinical interview technique, Spinillo et al. (1996) asked middle- and working-class first graders a very simple but key question: "What is reading and writing good for?" Middle-class children reported a large variety of uses and purposes for written language in their everyday lives: reading and writing letters to relatives and friends, reading and writing notes, scanning the newspaper for information on the date and place of a theatre play or of a movie, reading books, comics, magazines etc. Interestingly, this group of children associated the acquisition of literacy with school success and the development of high-level intellectual abilities. On the other hand, for working-class children, becoming literate basically meant being intelligent, being able to achieve school success, ridding themselves of the stigma of being illiterate, and being able to get a good job and salary to support their families financially. These findings are consistent with those reported by Carraher (1984, 1986, 1987) which illustrated that, in contrast to middle-class children who attribute immediate social uses and functions to literacy, working-class children attribute to literacy uses and functions that were related to future activities and gains.

A different line of research has demonstrated that, besides the home and the school, there is a third but equally important type of literacy environment, the street. Streets are a place full of print material of all sorts – signs, logos, words, sentences etc. – which serve a variety of literacy purposes. Despite the fact that much reading is done on material found on the streets, this environment has not, as yet, received much attention. Yet, in some cultures, such as Brazil, there are children who actually live on the streets. Brazilian street children do not live with their families and do not attend regular schools. The street is the only literacy environment available to this group of children, and under these circumstances, streets might be as important to their literacy development as home and school is for middle- and upper-class children. It is, therefore, worth investigating how, through this print-rich environment, these children gain access to written language.

Neuman, & Celano (2001) conducted one of the few studies that analyzed the nature of this literacy environment. This study investigated the kinds of access American working- and middle-class children had to various types of print. Analyses were carried out within the neighbourhoods where the families lived, and were centred on: (a) the types and variety of print materials found on the streets: books, magazines, newspapers, signs, product labels, street signs, logos (Pizza Hut, McDonald's) etc.; (b) the reading done in public places, such as bus stops, coffee shops, restaurants, convenience stores, bookshops, drugstores, grocery stores etc.; and (c) the access to books in child-care centres, schools and public libraries. This ecological analysis showed that there was a considerable disparity between children's access to and exposure to print materials and the kinds of opportunities children were offered to read this material. In contrast to middle-class children who had at their disposal a variety of opportunities for understanding the forms and functions of reading, working-class children lacked exposure and experience with print, and the environmental features in working-class neighbourhoods were not propitious to reading.

Building on and extending this line of research, this chapter explores Brazilian middle-class and street children's knowledge about different text genres. The analyses presented below describe the similarities and differences in children's generic knowledge in terms of certain features that typify these text genres (content, structural organization, function) and suggest hypotheses regarding the social origin or the social contexts shaping the differences that were found.

1.2 Children's Knowledge about Text Genres[1]

Children's genre knowledge can be deciphered by gathering information on children's ability to produce (through spoken or written language) different types of texts, such as narratives (stories, personal narratives), informational texts (news reports, science reports), personal letters etc. (e.g., Cain, & Oakhill, 1996; Hicks, 1990; Kamberelis, & Bovino, 1999; Langer, 1985; Spinillo, & Oliveira, 1999; Zecker, 1996). We can situate the work conducted in this area under two research strands, one following a psycholinguistic experimental design, and the other the sociocultural paradigm. While in the former tradition, it is the researcher who selects specific genres and sets up experiments to assess different aspects of children's genre knowledge, in the latter tradition, attention is focused on school genres, that is on text types actually produced by children within classrooms.

The studies conducted so far in both strands have investigated children's ability to produce texts that exhibit the basic characteristics of the macro- and/or microstructural organization of different genres (see Langer's [1985] work on stories, informational texts, and personal letters; Zecker's [1996] analysis of stories, letters, and grocery lists on three different occasions; Kamberelis, & Bovino's work [1999] on fictional stories and science reports). Other studies traced children's developing ability to employ various linguistic forms (connectives, tense forms) in ways appropriate to the genre under investigation (Hicks, 1990; Spinillo, & Oliveira, 1999). The findings documented so far on text production by pre-schoolers and early elementary schoolchildren may be summarized as follows: (1) children are more familiar with stories than with other types of texts, at least as concerns the construction of well-formed texts; (2) children at the early elementary school level are capable at distinguishing between different types of texts in their productions; (3) there exists a developmental progression in text production, which is most evident between the first and third grades of elementary education; and (4) children's texts improve considerably when produced in situations where children receive interactional scaffolding by adults.

Although important, production tasks alone cannot properly capture all relevant facets of children's knowledge of text genres, such as children's capacity to deliberately reflect on the structure and linguistic conventions that characterize a particular genre. This ability is referred to as meta-textual awareness.

Numerous linguistic levels have been employed in classifying the different types of metalinguistic awareness; these, as proposed by Garton, & Pratt (1998) and Pratt, & Grieve (1984) consist of: phonological awareness, word awareness, syntactic awareness, and pragmatic awareness. Gombert (1992) adopts a similar classification,

---

[1] *"Text type" usually captures differences with respect to patterns of organization in texts; "genre" is used in Australian and North American research in reference to classifications of communicative events or to units of social action. Genres usually refer to a higher-order level capturing a meaning potential, i.e., a set of obligatory and optional elements which are variously realized by language producers in their texts. The term of text genre used in this chapter reflects a combination of these perspectives; it captures both the set of choices available to language producers and the texts produced which instantiate some of these choices.*

but adds a new element to it: meta-textual awareness. This is defined as the capacity to reflect on the structure and organization of texts. This capacity requires that the individual focuses on the text, is familiar with the properties that characterize it and distances him/herself from its use.

Few studies have considered children's textual knowledge from this perspective. Even fewer are the studies (Albuquerque, & Spinillo, 1997, 1998; Rego, 1996), which deal with children's textual and meta-textual knowledge in cultural contexts other than American. Interesting questions arise in this respect. Do children across cultures use the same set of criteria? In what order are macro-structural patterns employed compared to features and elements that refer to the micro-level organization of a text?

Rego (1996) has examined the criteria adopted by 7-year-old Brazilian children to define stories. Conventional stories, stories with unconnected events, and incomplete stories were presented in both long and short versions on four separate occasions throughout the school year. Based on the justifications given, the criteria children used in their judgements were: the size of the text (long texts were considered stories, while short texts were not); and the presence of a typical story beginning ("Once upon a time..."). As documented, it is by about the age of 8 that children come to develop an awareness of the formal characteristics of a narrative text and adopt the story schema as a criterion in their judgements.

A similar study has been carried out by Albuquerque, & Spinillo (1997), who investigated the criteria 5-, 7-, and 9-year-old Brazilian children used to discriminate between different types of texts. A text was read to each child who was asked to identify it as a story, a letter, or a newspaper article. Justifications were asked after each response. It was observed that the criteria adopted by the children incorporated linguistic features, the social function of the text and matters of content. Interestingly, identification criteria varied as a function of the text genre: newspaper articles were generally identified through content alone (real and of public interest); letters were identified through content (personal and emotional) and through function (saying something to someone); and stories were identified through content (fictional), as well as linguistic and structural criteria. In general, structure was not often utilized as a criterion. The authors concluded that children's capacity to identify texts belonging to different genres progresses from the use of undefined criteria to the use of precise criteria that vary in regards to the genre under analysis.

In a later study, Albuquerque, & Spinillo (1998) sought to determine if 5-, 7-, and 9-year-old children were capable of reflecting on the structure of different texts if they were presented with incomplete texts, that is, with texts in which some of their constituent parts were omitted. The children were asked to determine if texts from three different genres (stories, letters and newspaper articles) were complete or incomplete, and to justify their response. A large number of children were found to use structure as a criterion in their judgements and especially in relation to text types (such as stories and letters) whose structure is more clearly and conventionally defined, and is, therefore, more evident, than the structure of a newspaper article.

2   THE PRESENT STUDY

Building upon and extending research conducted along the lines of the psycholinguistic paradigm, this chapter sets out to investigate children's knowledge of different text genres in two different situations: text production and text identification. Two groups of 24 Brazilian children participated in this study. One group consisted of middle-class children aged 7-8 years attending the first grade of elementary school. The other group consisted of working-class street children aged 9-10 years who had lived on the streets for at least one year and had little contact with their parents. Most of them were illiterate, although a few of them had once attended part of the first grade. We investigated groups with rather distinct social and schooling characteristics so that we could capture (what we hypothesized to be) the wide range of different text genres these groups of children would have expectations about and make some suggestions as to the types of social contexts fostering such differences.

Brazilian street children live on the streets of big cities and come from extremely poor families. Many of them leave home to escape domestic violence and poverty. They believe that on the streets they will find freedom, they will be respected, and will have better financial opportunities. Some of these children do not abandon their families completely, and help their parents and younger siblings financially. They form unstable groups, which co-exist, in accordance with the area where they live, and the trading activities they engage with. It is not unusual to find these children begging on the streets, or taking part in informal commercial activities, such as selling fruit and sweets in street corners, washing car windscreens at traffic lights. Some of them have, at some point in their lives, got involved in minor criminal acts, or even committed more serious crimes. They have a history of failure and dropouts in the education system. Together with other children, adolescents or even homeless adults, these children sleep in shelters, or on the streets outside shops, in car parks, and other public places such as squares and parks. Some of these children receive support from government and non-governmental institutions.[2]

2.1 Procedure and Experimental Design

All participants were interviewed individually in two sessions by the same examiner. In the first session, they were asked to produce an original story, a letter, and a newspaper article orally (Task 1 – Production of text genres). In the second session, children were read a text and were asked to judge whether this was a story, a letter or a newspaper article (Task 2 – Identification of text genres), and justify their response. Both sessions were audio-taped and transcribed for analysis.

In Task 1, children in each group were divided equally into three different orders of text presentation. In Task 2, the experimenter read nine texts (see Appendix A for some examples translated in English) one at a time, and the order of presentation

---

[2] *More information about this sector of the population, which lives in a context of social exclusion, can be found in official documents and in several scientific publications in Brazil (e.g., Campos, Del Prette, & Del Prette, 2000; Carlo, & Koller, 1998; Craidy, 1998; Ferreira, 1979; Martins, 2002).*

was randomized with the restriction that texts of the same genre would not be read in succession. The text genres selected were those existing literature suggests are important components of the literacy culture created in children's homes (though to different degrees); it is, therefore, expected that children will have directly or indirectly interacted with them from their preschool years.

2.2 System of Analysis Adopted in Task 1

Studies of children's generic development (Kamberelis, 1999) have demonstrated that in their initial attempts at text production children seem to have greater control over the global or schematic or macro-structural level of the text than over its micro-structural elements. This finding formed the basis in our selecting the classification criteria we use in Task 1. Task 1 explored the extent to which children's texts adhered to the set of conventions for the type of macro-structural organization and for the information (or content) that is expected to be used in each of the three genres under investigation. The texts produced were classified into three general categories, and analyzed by two independent judges. A third independent judge, whose classification was considered final, resolved cases of disagreement. The categories identified are described and exemplified below.[3]

Story Production

On the basis of their macro-structural organization, each story was assigned to one of three categories identified by previous research (see Rego, 1986; Spinillo, 2001; Spinillo, & Pinto, 1994).[4] These were the following:

Category 1 (non-stories): This category contains non-stories, texts that consisted of simple descriptions of actions without any characteristic of story style (i.e., conventionalized story openings or closings). Some of the children produced a report of a personal experience, a song, a rhyme or a passage from the Bible. Examples:

> Deus fez as plantas e todas as árvores. Deus fez o mar e a terra. Deus fez as árvores e os animais de todos os tipos. Deus fez o homem e a mulher. Deus gosta do que criou. *(God made the plants and all the trees. God made the seas and the land. God made the trees and animals of all types. God made man and woman. God liked what he had created.)*

> Eu, meu primo e meu amigo estava nadando na piscina. Meu avô chegou e pediu prá gente sair da piscina. A gente se escondeu debaixo da água. Ai ele pulou na água e ele chou a gente lá. Foi isso que aconteceu naquele dia. *(Me, my cousin and my friend were swimming in the swimming pool. My godfather arrived and asked us to get out of the swimming pool. We hid ourselves under the water. Then he jumped into the water and he found us there. That is what happened the other day.)*

---

[3] *The general argument as to the schematic structures or superstructures characterizing text genres and specifically stories, letters and newspaper articles is taken from Van Dijk (1992, 1995, 1997).*

[4] *These categories are based on story grammars (e.g., Brewer, 1985; Johnson, & Mandler, 1980; Mandler, & Johnson, 1977; Prince, 1973; Stein, 1982, 1988).*

Category II (incomplete stories): Some of the texts included in this category contained the beginning of a story, introducing the setting and characters with conventional story openings (e.g., "Once upon a time" or "One day..."). They also contained an event with information that marked some changes in the character's environment. The stories were regarded to be incomplete if they did not contain a resolution and a closing. Example:

> Era uma vez uma galinha que queria fazer uma casa. Ela construiu uma casa. Mas ela queria uma casa com janelas para poder morar com seus pintinhos. *(Once upon a time there was a hen who wanted to build a house. She built a house. But she wanted a house with windows to live in with her little chicks.)*

Category III (complete stories): This is used in a general way to include texts which contained a central event with a resolution of the plot; conventionalized story openings and closings were also present, though some stories did not contain both. In this study, we are not interested in analyzing all possible sub-categories of stories, as other studies were, such as Berman, & Slobin (1994) on English, German, Hebrew, and Turkish children; Shapiro, & Hudson (1997) with American children and Spinillo, & Pinto (1994) with Italian and English children. Example:

> Era uma vez uma menina que jogava futebol. Ela caiu. A mãe depressa levou ela pro hospital. O médico disse que era um cortezinho, mas ela não acreditou e começou a chorar. Quando elas chegaram em casa a avó olhou para sua netinha e começou a chorar. No outro dia a menina estava melhor e sua mãe e sua vovó fez uma festa para a menina e suas amigas comemorar. *(Once upon a time there was a girl who was playing football. She fell down. The mother quickly took her to the hospital. The doctor said that it was just a small wound, but she did not believe him and started crying. When they got home grandmother looked at her little granddaughter and started crying. The following day the girl was better and her mother and her granny made a party for the girl and her friends to celebrate.)*

Letter Production

Each letter was assigned to one of three categories, previously identified by Albuquerque, & Spinillo (1998), as follows:

Category I (non-letters): These texts consisted of sentences without any characteristic of letter style. Some of these texts were a comment, an expression of a wish or a brief message. Examples:

> Quero ver minha irmã que mora em Olinda. Faz um tempão que eu não vejo ela. *(I want to see my sister who lives in Olinda. I haven't seen her for ages.)*

> Eu quero dizer que eu consegui dinheiro ontem. Vou comprar um relógio para mim. *(I want to say that yesterday I've got some money. I will buy a watch for me.)*

Category II (incomplete letters): Some of the letters were messages of affection addressed to someone (addressee). Others contained some exchange of information between two people in which the sender revealed some personal information. However, some elements peculiar to letters were omitted, such as the sender, the greeting, a farewell that closes the text, place and date. Example:

> Mamãe, tenho saudades de você. Volte logo. Só isso. Carinho. Rebeca. *(Mommy, I miss you. Come back soon. That's all. Love. Rebeca.)*

Category III (complete letters): These contained all of the elements that are obligatory in letters: the name of the sender, the addressee, the greeting, the farewell, place, and date. The communicative nature of a letter was clearly identified: questions were asked about how the addressee was; and the sender gave information about him/herself. Example:

> Recife, 5 de maio de 1999. Sue, Como vai você? Eu estou boa. E você? Estou gostando de morar aqui em São Paulo. Minha família vai bem. Meu pai e eu estamos aqui em São Paulo. Minha mãe resolveu ficar em Recife mais um pouquinho. Estou com saudade de todo mundo aí, principalmente de você. Eu gosto de você muito. Lembranças para minha professora Tia Rosa e para os outros professores do colégio. Daqui a alguns meses eu chego de volta. Carinho. George. *(Recife, May 5, 1999. Sue, How are you? I am fine. And you? I like living here in São Paulo. My family is doing fine. My father and I are here in São Paulo. My mother decided to stay in Recife a bit longer. I miss all of you, especially you. I like you very much. Send my love to my teacher Rosa and to all the teachers at school. In a few months I will be back. Love. George.)*

Newspaper Article Production

Each newspaper article was assigned to one of three categories, based on those identified by Albuquerque, & Spinillo (1997, 1998).

Category I (non-newspaper articles): These consisted of comments, opinions or a report of a personal experience about a tragic event. Some of the children produced a text that consisted of telling personal news to someone. These texts were produced in a narrative rather than in an informational style. Examples:

> Hoje em dia, as pessoas estão ficando malucas com o trânsito. Elas não obedecem a velocidade e correm muito e matam o povo. Muita gente está preocupada. Tem que fazer alguma coisa. *(Nowadays, people are going crazy because of the traffic. They do not obey the speed limits and they are running over and killing people. Many people are worried about this. Something must be done.)*

> Era uma vez que eu vi uma batida de carro. *(Once upon a time I saw a car accident.)*

Category II (incomplete newspaper articles): These were restricted to the description of a tragic event (car crash, robbery, disaster etc.) or to the presentation of an event or a theme that was of public interest (election, economy, sports etc.). Texts that corresponded to news headlines were also included in this category. Examples:

> O presidente aumentou tubinho. *(The president increased all the prices.)*

> Brasil é o campeão do mundo *(Brazil is the champion of the world.)*

Category III (complete newspaper articles):[5] These texts consisted of a headline followed by the main topic and information on facts that occurred (what, when, where, who, why). However, these elements were not always simultaneously presented within a single text. It was also observed that children used the indefinite article (*a* or *an*) instead of the definite one (*the*). The texts produced were in an in-

---

[5] *Information is drawn from Teberosky (1990, 1992) who discusses the conventional components that characterize this type of informational text. For a detailed discussion about the prototypical structure of journalistic texts, see Lage (1987).*

formational style resembling the prototypical structure of a newspaper article. Example:

> Polícia invade uma favela. Na noite passada a polícia invadiu uma favela em Recife para pegar armas roubadas nas casas das pessoas. Uma pessoa ficou ferida no tiroteio com as pessoas que moravam lá e os policiais. *(Police invade a shantytown. Last night police invaded a shantytown in Recife to get stolen weapons in people's houses. One person was hit in a shootout between residents and police officers.)*

2.3 System of Analysis Adopted in Task 2

The data were coded in two ways: the number of correct responses and the types of justifications given. Each justification was further analyzed according to the criteria children adopted for identifying each type of text. These were as follows:

Undefined:	No justification was presented or the criteria adopted were not specified.
Social function, character and content:	The criteria adopted were based on the functional aspects of the text (what it is for, when it is used), on the characters presented in the text, and on its content.
Linguistic conventions and structure:	The criteria adopted were related to the linguistic features of the text (linguistic conventions and style) and to its structure (beginning - ending). The use of these criteria demonstrated that the child had some level of meta-textual awareness.

A detailed presentation of the types of justification given by the two groups of children on stories, letters, and newspaper articles is presented in Table 1. On the basis of the justifications given, each child was assigned to one of three levels of meta-textual awareness in relation to each type of text. Thus, the same child, for instance, could be classified in Level 1 in relation to stories but in Level 2 in relation to letters. These are as follows (see also Albuquerque, & Spinillo, 1997, 1998).

Level 1:	Children who used undefined criteria in all of their justifications.
Level 2:	Children who used function, character or content (or a combination of them) in all or in most of their justifications. Children who used undefined criteria or structure/linguistic conventions in one of their justifications were also situated in this group.
Level 3	Children who used structure and linguistic conventions to identify the three texts of the same genre. Children grouped in this level identified the texts correctly.

Table 1. Examples of children's justifications in Task 2 (Identification of genres)

Criteria	Story	Letter	Newspaper article
Undefined	I don't know. It's a beautiful story.	I know. I've seen a letter before. I guess this is a story.	I saw it on TV. I have seen it in the newspaper.
Social Function, Character, Content	It is a story because it isn't true. It is a story because it's about childish things. It is a newspaper article, because something tragic happened to the poor little dog.[6]	Because there is a person who sent a letter to another person to read. She is inviting the girl. So we may guess it is a letter. Because the girl sent her love to him.	It is about a politician. It is important. Everybody must know this, the vaccination, the illness. It is about violence.
Linguistic conventions, Structure	Because you said "Once upon a time" in the beginning. It has the beginning "Once upon a time." And it has the last bit that says how the story ended: "happily ever after."	It is a letter because it has the date and the place. Because it has "Dear." When we write a letter we begin with "Dear" and then we say a lot of things. It is a letter because it begins the way we learned with Miss Andréa. This is the way we learned. It has a farewell and the name of the person.	They say the day to get the medicine. They say the date and that the vaccination is only for children. It has a title (the headline). They say what is happening in the city. And when things happened.

3   RESULTS AND DISCUSSION

3.1 Text Production

The relationship of text categories (i.e., categories of texts produced in each genre) to social groups was explored by means of Kolmogorov-Smirnov analyses carried out separately for each text.

As shown in Table 2, there are significant differences between groups, as regards story production ($p < .01$). This was due to the high frequency of Category III among the middle-class children, whereas the stories produced by street children were basically situated in Category I. This result suggests that the texts produced by middle-class children conformed to the structure that characterizes stories, whereas those produced by street children did not.

---

[6] Some of the justifications in this table are for incorrect identifications.

Table 2. Number and percentage (out of 24 productions) of the categories of text genres produced by children

Categories	Middle-class children		Street children	
	no.	%	no.	%
Story				
I	5	20.8	12	50.0
II	6	25.0	7	29.2
III	13	54.2	5	20.8
Letter				
I	4	16.7	17	70.8
II	11	45.8	29	29.2
III	9	37.5	0	0
Newspaper article				
I	10	41.7	4	16.6
II	9	37.5	10	41.7
III	5	20.8	10	41.7

Significant differences were found between groups in relation to letter production ($p<.001$). This occurred because of the fact that a large percentage of the letters produced by street children were classified in Category I, with none of them achieving Category III, whereas most of the letters produced by middle-class children were in Category II and III. In relation to newspaper articles, significant differences were also documented between groups ($p<.05$). Interestingly, more newspaper articles produced by middle-class children were situated in Category I compared to those produced by street children, and there were many more newspaper articles in Category III among street children than among middle-class children.

As a whole, middle-class children produced complete and well-formed stories. This group of children was also good at producing letters, though most of their letters are not as well formed as their stories were. On the other hand, street children tended to produce texts that cannot be considered stories or letters (Category I), but they were able to produce fairly good newspaper articles. Actually, the percentage of texts that did not correspond to newspaper articles was very low (Category I: 16.6%) in contrast to the high percentage of productions that were classified as well-formed texts (Category III: 41.7%).

3.1.1   Types of Children's Errors when Producing Different Text Genres

Table 3 presents the types of errors children made when producing a text genre. The term "error" is henceforth used to refer to textual choices children made and which did not correspond to the conventions of the genre (presented under Category III for each text genre) requested by the examiner.

Table 3. Frequency of children's errors when producing stories

Types of error	Middle-class children	Street children
Personal experience	2	8
Description of actions	3	0
Song, rhyme	0	2
Passage from the Bible	0	2

As can be seen from Table 3, very few middle-class children interpreted stories as a description of actions or as reports of a personal experience. On the other hand, street children produced a report of personal experience rather than a fictional story. It seems that for these children a story is defined as a real life account, that is, a report of factual events that happened to them. Table 4 summarizes the results with regard to letters. Middle-class children's mistakes did not concentrate on one particular type of error. However, the most frequent error detected among street children was that for them a letter means expressing one's wish, and contains a report of a personal experience.

Table 4. Frequency of children's errors when producing letters

Types of error	Middle-class children	Street children
Personal experience	0	4
Wish	2	12
Message	2	1

Table 5. Frequency of children's errors when producing newspaper articles

Types of error	Middle-class children	Street children
Personal experience	3	2
Comments, opnions	7	2

Inspection of the errors children made with regard to the newspaper article (Table 5) revealed that, instead of producing a newspaper article, middle-class children expressed an opinion about a factual and public event. It seems that they had in mind the typical content that characterizes this type of text. Nevertheless, street children rarely made this type of error. As a whole, the common error street children made was to produce a report of a personal experience, and this was particularly so in relation to stories. Middle-class children, however, did not display any systematic pattern of error.

3.2 Identification of Text Genres

Differences between groups in relation to correct identification of the three text genres (see Table 6) were explored by means of T-test carried out separately for each genre.

Altogether, middle-class children's percentage of correct identification was higher (92.6%) compared to the percentage observed among street children (61.5%). Middle-class children performed significantly better than street children in relation to story and letter identification ($p<.01$). However, no significant differences were found between groups in relation to newspaper articles ($p>.05$), since both groups obtained a high percentage of correct identification. These results indicate that middle-class children were able to identify texts instantiating all three genres correctly, whereas street children experienced difficulties with stories and letters, in particular with letters. For street children, newspaper articles were easier to identify than the other two genres.

Table 6. Number and percentage (out of 72) of correct responses given in text genre identification

| | Middle-class children | | Street children | |
	No.	%	No.	%
Story	64	88.8	41	56.9
Letter	65	90.3	34	47.2
Newspaper article	71	98.6	58	80.5

3.2.1   Types of Children's Errors when Identifying Different Text Genres

We also analyzed children's mistakes when identifying text genres (see Table 7). As middle-class children's mistakes were few, it was not possible to identify any particular pattern of error. On the other hand, street children tended to judge letters and newspaper articles as if they were stories, and to consider of stories as if these were newspaper articles. It is indeed difficult to explain such a result, since most of the justifications offered for their incorrect identifications were based on undefined criteria. However, in some of the justifications given, it was observed that children were influenced by the fact that one of the stories (see Appendix A) included a politician (a mayor) as a character. As this character is often found in newspaper articles, it is possible that children were misguided by the presence of this character, believing that this particular story was a newspaper article.

Table 7. Frequency of errors children made when identifying different genres

Stimulus	Middle-class children identified as			Street children identified as		
	Story	Letter	Newspaper article	Story	Letter	Newspaper article
Story	-	2	6	-	9	22
Letter	5	-	2	33	-	5
Newspaper article	1	0	-	14	0	-

3.3 Levels of Meta-textual Awareness

The relationships of levels of text genre identification to sociocultural groups were explored by using Kolmogorov-Smirnov analyses carried out separately for each type of text genre (see Table 8).

Table 8. Number and percentage (out of 24 responses) of children in each group by text genre

Genre	Levels	Middle-class children No.	%	Street children No.	%
Story	I	0	0	16	66.7
	II	16	66.7	8	33.3
	III	8	33.3	0	0
Letter	I	1	4.2	18	75
	II	13	54.2	6	25
	III	10	41.6	0	0
Newspaper article	I	0	0	9	37.5
	II	24	100	15	62.5
	III	0	0	0	0

There are significant differences between groups, as regards the levels in which children were classified when identifying stories ($p<.01$), letters ($p<.01$) and newspaper articles ($p<.05$). In relation to the identification of stories and letters, as a whole, middle-class children tended to concentrate in Level II and III whereas most of the street children were classified in Level I and none of them reached Level III.

In relation to newspaper articles, it was observed that middle-class children were all in Level II, whereas street children were in Levels I and II with none from either group being in Level III. It is noteworthy that children in both groups concentrated in Level II. This means that, though the differences between groups were statistically significant, they were not as large as they were for stories and letters. Hence, it seems that when identifying newspaper articles, children in both groups tended to show a similar pattern: they never used the structure of this genre and its linguistic features as criteria in their identification. Instead, they used the content, the characters and the social function related to this text genre.

3.4 Talking with Children about Text Genres

Several weeks after the application of the two tasks described above, we met with some of the children again (10 children from each group) and had informal discussions with them about their exposure to stories, letters and newspaper articles at home, at school and on the streets. The conversations, which did not follow a rigid format, revealed that middle-class children were indeed experiencing a home literacy environment similar to that already described by several authors (e.g., Carraher, 1984, 1986, 1987; Purcell-Gates, 1996; Teale, 1986). At school, these children had more contact with stories than with letters and newspaper articles. Street children, on the other hand, had more contact with newspaper articles than with texts belonging to the other genres. Even though illiterate on school standards, these children "read" the news in newspapers placed on the front door of state agents in the street corners through the literate teenagers who interact with them on the streets. They would often watch TV from the window of a pub, of a restaurant or when visiting friends that still lived with their parents in a shantytown. In fact, some of these children listen to many different programmes on the radio everyday.

It is noteworthy that these children are eager to be well-informed about the news in the newspapers. The passage below extracted from an interview with a 9-year-old boy deserves a comment:

> "When I was at school, my teacher used to read stories to us. This was what I liked best about school. Now that I have grown up and that I am on my own, I like to be read the news in the newspaper. It is more exciting than stories and homework. I like to know about people who got killed, as it happens in the movies. Once my friend's brother was shot by the police and his name was in the newspaper. For me he was a hero."

Whereas the vast majority of the news in the newspapers is not directly related to people's lives, several pieces of information in newspaper articles may play an important role in the lives of the street children. As illustrated by the passage above, the newspapers may inform them about people close to them. This is probably the reason why street children associate newspaper articles with personal accounts. On the other hand, it is unlikely that such reports are part of the day-to-day lives of middle-class children.

The most interesting data from our informal conversations were obtained when asking a very simple set of questions: "What is a story? What is a letter? What is a newspaper article?" Although children's responses have not been analyzed in full, it seems important to discuss what these definitions express (see Tables 9, 10 and 11, respectively).

Table 9. Examples of children's definitions of a story

Middle-class Children	Street Children
It is a text that begins with "Once upon a time." It has a title like the "Sleeping Beauty," "The Three Little Pigs," "Snow White." A story is a text. It has to have characters, dialogue. It has to make sense because whoever reads it wants to understand the story. My teacher always says that.	Story? It is when you tell a lie, that is a story. Something that is not true. A newspaper has many stories about people's lives. Sometimes is the story of someone you know.
It is a text that has a beginning, an end and a middle. It begins with "Once upon a time."	A story has pictures, pages, a cover and many, many letters. I like the colours of the pictures. It is something about your life, something that happened to you and to your family.

The responses given by middle-class children indicate that they are aware of the linguistic conventions and formal structure typifying stories. For instance, a child made a remark about the school setting as the origin of their knowledge of stories: *"...My teacher always says that."* On the other hand, street children focus on the content of stories: fictional (*"... Something that is not true"*) or factual (*" ... many stories about people's lives."*). No mention was made by the street children about the linguistic conventions and the structure that is typical of stories. One may wonder whether such knowledge is developed through school activities.

Table 10. Examples of children's definitions of a letter

Middle-class Children	Street Children
It is what they deliver to our home. After we write it we put it in an envelope. We have to say that we miss the person, what we want for Christmas. We may send a letter to Santa Claus.	A letter is when you say "I love you." I don't have a boyfriend. So, I don't send letters or receive them. It is when you send a kiss to somebody. Or a hug.
It is a message that you send to someone. It must have the date, the person's name, I mean, the name of the person who sent it. And the name of the other person.	We send it by post when we cannot talk by phone. If the person does not have a telephone you have to write or send a message through another person. I don't know how to write, so I send my mother a message through my brother. He visits her sometimes.

As attested, for middle-class children, letters are defined in terms of their social function, which is to establish communication between two people who are not in a face-to-face interaction. This group of children is aware of the formal structure of a letter, and of its content (factual and personal) and has a clear understanding of the procedure required to send a letter. In contrast, street children's definitions of letters are more limited. These definitions basically exemplify the fact that letters: (a) are restricted to an affective message addressed to someone; (b) establish communication between two persons who are not in a face-to-face interaction; and (c) are orally produced messages.

Despite the differences between them, middle-class and street children agreed on the idea that letters are for communication between two people who are far from each other.

The definitions offered by children in both groups on newspaper articles (see Table 11) involved information that is factual and of public interest, and information about tragic events. This indicates that the content is a very salient aspect in newspaper articles. Street children's definition also included the headlines of the newspaper, and this suggests that they might have some understanding of the structure typifying this text genre.

Table 11. Examples of children's definitions of a newspaper article

Middle-class Children	Street Children
When you watch TV they talk. They tell you everything that happened.	If I say: "I have news for you." Then I tell you what happened to me.
It has information about the whole world. And about things that happened in your own city.	The newspaper tells what happened to a person.
	We see it on TV or we listen to it on the radio.
They say that somebody died.	They talk about a war, about a car accident.
	They say what happened yesterday: "They crashed" or "The police killed the thief."

4   CONCLUSION

This investigation set out to unveil the types of genre knowledge Brazilian children from different sociocultural backgrounds had acquired as a result of their literacy experiences. The questions addressed and the findings attested are summarized below.

Question 1: What do Brazilian children of different sociocultural backgrounds know about texts? Is their knowledge significantly different?

Most research on the way by which children from different sociocultural groups produce different types of oral and written texts has documented the distinct ways by which middle-class versus working-class children (especially in the American context) use language in a text (usually in narrative texts). Indeed, working-class children are found to use language in ways not valued by the school system. This study attests results which suggest that crude differences may need to be qualified in relation to specific text genres. Rather than described in general as less competent users of language compared to middle-class children, street children are shown to have sophisticated knowledge of a specific and rather advanced text genre (newspaper articles) with which middle-class children are not very familiar. Specifically: With regard to specific text genres (letters and stories), it was noted that middle-class children's knowledge was superior; middle-class children were able to produce well-formed stories and letters, although their letters were not as sophisticated as their stories. When asked to identify stories and letters, middle-class children were significantly more successful than street children. On the basis of the justifications they gave, middle-class children achieved the most sophisticated level of meta-textual awareness in relation to story and letter identification, whereas none of the street children was able to achieve this. Interestingly, street children experienced no difficulties with newspaper articles.

Certain issues that this research did not address are worth considering. We may begin by noting this with regard to the analyses undertaken: The macro-structural categories employed for the description of stories are those proposed by researchers working with story grammars. Although relevant, these categories are too narrow to capture the range of generic resources children of different sociocultural groups acquire in school and in out-of-school contexts. To this end, further research is needed to illustrate whether the criteria used in this study (function, patterns of macro-structural organization, linguistic forms) coincide with or diverge from the criteria employed by Brazilian adults (parents, teachers) who define and negotiate these types of texts along with the children in the context of specific activities (storybook reading, analysis of stories etc.). How often are stories, letters and newspaper articles discussed in middle-class home- and school contexts? How do children's definitions emerge from these interactions? Are there differences in home- versus school-specific ways of defining such text genres? Subsequent research should address these issues and indeed proceed beyond the limited set of text genres selected in this study to unveil the range of genres (reports, science reports, etc.) Brazilian children from different sociocultural groups produce and reflect upon in a variety of contexts.

Question 2: How can such differences in children's textual and meta-textual knowledge be accounted for?

Note that the analyses documented in this chapter required that children, first, use language in the form of a specific type of text (Task 1) and, secondly, focus upon a text, and analyze it in terms of its constitutive or typical features. How can children's different responses to these tasks be accounted for? The findings in our study might be interpreted in terms of the different literacy environments middle-class children and street children have access to in their everyday lives and in terms of the different kinds of experiences with texts these children have in these contexts. The data gathered from the interviews are clearly insufficient to illuminate the complexity of the communicative processes at play in both home and school; the data, nevertheless, provide a first indication as to the literacy environments middle-class and street children live in and to the similarities in the kinds of text genres middle-class Brazilian children are exposed to at home and at school; for street children, streets are the main (perhaps the only one) literacy environment they have, and the experiences with texts (which are not analyzed as objects) provided by the streets are the source of their knowledge about texts.

Meta-textual awareness is an ability that is, to some extent, acquired by children attending school. Usually in classroom-enacted social activities, students are required to revise their texts, to correct a sentence, to look for a specific word in a sentence or in a paragraph – in short, they learn specific patterns of response to different types of texts (Shine, & Roser, 1999). As we noted in our introduction, these activities may constitute frequently-occurring ones in middle-class homes where parents explicitly teach their children about how to read and write. While frequency of occurrence may be a factor to be considered, the texture of such activities is another factor worth attending to. This is hinted at by the following discrepancy with existing findings this study documented. As evidenced by existing research, middle-class children in their homes have a wide range of print material available (including newspapers). Interestingly, this study illustrated that Brazilian middle-class children's knowledge of newspaper articles is not well developed. Apparently, there may be differences in children's access to and use of these types of texts and in the richness of the interaction middle-class and street children have around newspaper-articles. These differences need to be explored.

In light of the above, then, it becomes clear that claims as to the correspondences between "home" and "classroom-bound" contexts focusing on text production and identification need to be further investigated with more data. Data from different cultures could enrich our understanding of the role specific classroom contexts play in children's developing textual knowledge and trace the kinds of textual experiences children bring with them to school. How can school enrich children's limited experiences and knowledge about texts? Through what activities can children's textual and meta-textual knowledge develop? Further research from different cultures can provide interesting answers to these questions.

Finally, further analyses need to be undertaken on street literacy. Although this study has presented some interesting findings on this literacy context, future research is needed to (a) investigate further the kinds of literacy streets promote and how these literacy experiences affect children's textual knowledge; and (b) carry out more detailed comparisons between street versus school literacy. Relevant is the distinction between street children and other groups of children. Street children form a distinctive group that differs substantially from working-class children in that working-class children spend only a limited amount of time on the streets, whereas street children actually live on them. In addition, working class children attend school regularly whereas street children do not, and, unfortunately, the possibility that in the future they will be engaged in the educational system is very low.

In carrying out such analyses, it becomes clear that one needs to pay particular attention to the way this literacy environment is mediated by adults (parents) and is made interpretable to different groups of children and/or by text knowledge children have acquired in school. The role of street literacy needs to be foregrounded because, as Carraher noted, "...being literate is also a "way of being," a way of carrying out social transactions in a literate society" (Carraher, 1987: 95). Current research has begun to reflect this understanding by including within its focus a wide range of contexts and children's experiences with language and texts. As it is by now well-established, it is this access to a wide range of meaning making resources which renders one a literate subject.

ACKNOWLEDGEMENTS

Research supported by a grant awarded to the first author from the Conselho Nacional de Desenvolvimento Científico e Tecnológico (CNPq) of the Brazilian Ministry of Science and Technology. We thank Anna Luiza Martins, Nuênia Souza, Silvana Pimentel and Valéria Quintas for collecting the data, and Eliana Albuquerque for her insightful comments on data analysis. Most of all, we are extremely grateful to the children who shared their knowledge about texts with us.

APPENDIX A: EXAMPLES OF TEXTS READ TO THE CHILDREN IN TASK 2 (TEXT IDENTIFICATION)

Stories

Once upon a time there was a farmer. He had a very naughty little dog. One day the little dog found a snake in the farm and bit its tail. The snake immediately bit the dog and the dog died. The farmer got very angry and cut the snake's tail off. The snake took its revenge on the farmer, and killed some of his cows. The farmer then realized that he couldn't keep up with the snake and decided to patch things up. One day he waited for the snake. When he saw it, he offered it food and asked it to stop killing his cows. The snake agreed and from that day on, never killed any of his cows.

Letters

Recife, 2nd April 1992
Dear Roberto,
How are you? We are all well here. How are things at school? Are you working hard? If you work hard you won't fall behind, and as soon as school is over you can come and stay with us on the farm. There is lots to do here, and you'll have a great time. Peter can hardly wait to have you to play with. We are looking forward to seeing you. Lots of love. Auntie Jane.

Newspaper articles

Man dies at work
The bricklayer S.C., 19, died yesterday afternoon after falling from the 13th floor of Iemanjá Building in the centre of the city. The accident happened at 2pm, and though the builder was immediately taken to the City Hospital, he died before he could receive any medical assistance due to his serious wounds.

ENCULTURATION TO INSTITUTIONAL WRITING

Meaning Making in a Triadic Semiotic Perspective

SIGMUND ONGSTAD

Oslo University College, Norway

Abstract. The project *Genre, positionings, and task ideologies* studied primary school students' task positionings. The basic aim of this chapter is to outline parts of the triadic semiotic framework used in this project and illustrate how this relates to a specific text and its context. This study focuses on second grade students in a Norwegian primary school, where a physical workshop ("verksted") was used to stimulate writing. The theoretical framework functions as a basis for interpretations of a text written by René (aged 8). Videotaped incidents and the final version of the written text René produced allow for a problematizing of school writing as a context for meaning making. The semiotic and communicative approach advocated draws from the work of Bakhtin (1986), Bühler (1934), Habermas (1984), and Halliday (1978). The main idea is that communicators, while positioning themselves by and between the mutual dynamics of *expressivity*, which is connected to form, *referentiality*, which is connected to content, and *addressivity*, which is connected to action. René's text is interpreted in detail from these different positionings. Thus, the close dynamics of a text's form, content and use (or more precisely structure, reference and action) becomes the main focus. The text is interpreted in detail from different positionings. The analyses reveal that writing should be seen as a delicate, simultaneous interplay between expressing, referring and acting, as well as between utterance and genre. The student, René, when writing, is seen as searching for ways to mean by positioning himself between these major aspects. Finally, the notion of validity is problematized in order to relate more adequately to the openness of an interpretative approach. It is suggested that to avoid disciplinary onesidedness, research on writing should validate itself by making explicit its own ideological positionings within this triadic, semiotic communicative framework.

Keywords: genre expectations, school writing, self-positioning, semiotic meaning, writing tasks, triadic theories

1   INTRODUCTION: POSITIONING THE RESEARCH

This chapter problematizes a student's positioning vis-à-vis a general writing task given in a primary school that implemented a process-oriented writing pedagogy. A play-like workshop (Norwegian: "verksted") was used as an activity to stimulate writing. The specific text under investigation is written by René, aged 8, and can be seen as the result of outspoken and implicit task expectations that give a scope for making meaning in the school culture.

In carrying out the interpretations, the discussion positions itself deliberately above the traditional choice between an inductive or a deductive inquiry. Writing research is often squeezed between induction or deduction as ways of reasoning. These two regimes, which are established by scientific disciplines, may obstruct the possibilities for developing a more holistic or general understanding of the many aspects involved in writing. The discussion in this chapter, rather than starting from a given theory applied to prove empirical data or vice versa, follows, partly, the Peirceian idea of *abduction*. This implies giving priority to hypotheses and balances between theoretical and empirical aspects in the processes of reasoning rather than assigning priority to either induction or deduction. The point is not to present conclusive results, but to advocate for, and exemplify how a communicative and semiotic framework could be an explicit part of the research conducted on writing. This approach is chosen because it seems closer to teachers' everyday situation and experiences, while at the same time being anchored in theory.

In light of the above, this chapter, methodologically aims, on one hand, to outline a triadic, social-semiotic perspective within which I situate detailed interpretations of a specific text and its context. On the other hand, on a meta-level the discussion addresses a more overarching issue, as I present a theoretical framework that can clarify and exemplify the dynamic *relationship* between utterance/text and genre/context. Hence, this chapter tries to illustrate how such a shift in research positionings and the teachers' reading of students' texts could be materialized. A short text produced by a student, its contexts and the framework used for the analysis of the text-context interaction are analyzed via the concept of discursive *positioning*, which is outlined in detail in various sections of this chapter. In the last part of this chapter, I interpret and exemplify, ending with a brief evaluation of the framework.

2   CONTEXTUALIZING THE TEXT AND THE CONTEXT

2.1   School Writing or Meaning Making?

The text analyzed in this chapter comes from a larger project entitled *Genre, positionings and task ideologies*, which set out to investigate Norwegian students' task positioning(s) in a primary school in Oslo, Norway (Ongstad, 1996, 1997). The school teachers had decided to offer a workshop to their second-graders every second Tuesday. 25 students were placed on five different "stations" in an activity-room working with clay, fabrics, sandbox, woodwork, and wooden bricks.

We should note that these children came from play and everyday activity in families and kindergartens to be rather rapidly socialized to school, lessons, and classrooms. That writing could follow activity and could actually be about it was for some children beyond their imagination. The first day the following sceptical reaction was videotaped when teachers explained to the children what to do: *You can't* [possibly] *w r i t e about something you have m a d e !* Connecting the two was unthinkable.

The workshop, however, is both different from and similar to children's former experiences. It represents a mixture of routine and freedom. On the one hand, one can register firmness, stability, repetition, regularity and order. The children always find their things by themselves at the beginning of the day and tidy up the room at the end. The workshop takes place in the same room time after time and follows the same procedure. The children often copy each other in what to make, play, build, and write.

On the other hand, one could notice that the workshop-books on which the children write contain different kinds of texts, such as reports and stories. The teachers are open-minded. One can write facts, fiction or faction. The room is no "classroom," but a student-governed site for activity, a variation from the daily routine, with new stations, ideas and experiences each time. One can prioritize to "make" more and write less. There is an air of real freedom, although with risk for regulation. One interesting case is worth noting: In February a stand-in teacher wanted to tell Nils, one of the students, what to do. After a long discussion the stand-in teacher's last argument was that he was the teacher, to which Nils just stated with firm conviction: *We decide what to do, not the teacher!* The supporting reactions from the other kids left no doubt.

Throughout the year, the children's activities and the writing done were video-recorded by the researcher (me). This article then focuses on a text written by René, after having been building with bricks with his friend Anders. The writing was done in his workshop-book after the completion of the physical activity. The relationship between the text and the sequence of happenings that led up to it offers an opportunity to raise and discuss some basic questions about the relationship between genre-related, process-oriented, collective school writing, on the one hand, and subjective textual meaning making, on the other. One can trace the relationship between the genres of work/play and genres of writing and at, the same time, attend to the comradeship between the two boys, René and Anders, while building, drawing, and writing. Further, one can contrast the concrete building and writing with the immanent deeper *meaning* these activities may have had for the students, by analyzing their utterances as well as their body language and their emotional self-positionings. Finally, one can trace, between the lines of René's text, genre-dependent expectations inherent in institutional writing and illustrate how these may function as enculturation to school writing.

I textualized the recording as a sequence of descriptive and impressionistic elements, with the intention to try to get through in writing a feeling of how talk and emotional reactions were connected to the activity itself. One argument for this interpretative choice was to find a form that would be recognizable and hence relevant to both writing researchers and practising teachers (though it should be admitted that hardly any such textualization can avoid the subjectivity of the interpreter).

2.2 A Student Text and its Context

Workshop, class 2x, City School 14, April 1994. The translated excerpt is from Ongstad, (1997: 312-315). The pretext is shortened to approximately 15% of the original Norwegian text before translated into English by me. It should be underlined that the translation of the somewhat impressionistic style is hardly idiomatic. Left-out text is marked with (...) Time in minutes from the start of the video-camera is marked for each new slot. The main function here is to contextualize René's text. This particular focus has governed the excerpt from the original.

2.55.   Whistling. Anders, while conscious and estimating fetching bricks: *Are you going to build a pyramid?* René: *That's not before I've finished this.* Anders' building is built in an Inca pyramide-like style, with square caramel-shaped bricks sized 4x4x2cm. Minutes later, mostly to himself: *That's it.* Looks up, and for a short moment straight into the camera lens. Says, to René, but loud enough for everyone to hear: *The pyramid is finiiiished!* (...)

15.55.   René "play-walks" with his fingers in the staircase he has finished: *I am going to make it like this [you]. Anders, look here then!* Finds a long brick as a connection between the floor and the castle-palace. Repeats: *Look here then, Anders. Look then.* (...)

33.40.   René sits on his knees, now parallel with Anders, both with their backs to their building(s) [which have now grown into one large construction]. They look at each other, but do not say anything. René opens his workshop-book. Catches sight of a drawing he has made earlier, points and says: *Here is my Olympic hill.* Anders bends forward, pretends that the finger is a ski-jumper and makes a sound, *oooeeyy*, while performing a flight, and lands after a mega-jump outside the "hill" (and the book). Smiles satisfied. (...)

34.40.   René makes, just as satisfied, an after-movement as if he inspects the profile of the jumping hill. They look silently straight out in the air, gazing at nothing in particular. (...) René starts counting with a very rhythmic voice: *One, two, three, four, five, six.* Looks for precisely how many rows of bricks there are in what he is drawing. (...)

51.30.   Sol, the teacher, is approaching them. Says calmly: *The two of you should get started with writing and stuff.* René: *Yes, yes, we are writing, and playing a bit.* His voice is a bit "high spirit ascending" signalling a certain emotional state. Says: *Write? We are just drawing, don't you see?* Sol: *Yes, yes, yes.* (...)

60.40.   René is plodding with the Norwegian word *palass* [English: palace]. His pencil is resting a long time on the *s*. They are twaddling again. Mostly René. He disturbs Anders by trying to hit and to direct Anders' pencil. Anders just smiles, he is not annoyed. Laughs. Finds the Indian rubber. Rubs. René turns to his book again. Reads his own sentence: *I have built a palace.* Says suddenly while he grasps the rubber: *I? We. We have together. **We** have built a palace. I and...* Rubs out "I" (...)

72.30.   Annemari (teacher) passes by: *This was rather short writing.* Anders: *I can't make up any.* Annemari: *I have heard that you have been telling and playing. Why don't you write about that? It's OK to have that in the books.* (...) René: *When he was video recording, I made faces. Will I write that up?* (...)

73.20.   They start working again. René: *Is "klosser" [Norwegian] written with two l's?* Repeats the question. Anders: *No.* He takes a look at René's book, and says, half giggling while he stretches the length of the o-sound to the extreme: *It says "kloooser"* [Norwegian]. Laughs. *It says "klooooooser!"* René gets uncertain and changes *o* to *å*. Anders laughs even more, although not sneering or gloating. Says: *It's written with o and double s.* René rubs it out. (...)

74.40.   Anders writes: *While we were drawing, we twaddled.* After the last word, he expresses, almost singing: *That's it. Then we are finiiiiished,* and closes the work content, with a hearable clash. [René later, some other day, added a last sentence, *it was difficul too putugeder.* I will return to this fact later. Since spelling is one of the issues, I have deliberately made up different faults in the English version at various places. A copy of the original text and drawing is cited in the Appendix].

12/4 We have built   12/4 Vi har bygd
a palac it became   et palas det ble
nice we used   fint vi brukte
bricks. I   klosser. Jeg
coperated with   joba samen med
Anders. We twadled   Anders. Vi tula
a bid. René and   lit. René og
Anders livd   Anders bode
thar. it was   dær. det var
difficul too   vanskeli åg
putugeder.   seteisamen.

3   THEORY AND APPLICATIONS

3.1   Outlining the Framework

In surveying writing research, both Nystrand, Green, & Wiemelt (1993) and Ongstad (2002a) noted a clear historical tendency on the part of the researchers to overemphasize specific *aspects* of the writing process, such as control of *forms*, *content* organization and communicative *purpose*. As a result, distinct writing ideologies have emerged, such as *formalism*, *semanticism* and *functionalism*. Although this tendency was more significant, though onesided, in the past, probably due to rather simplistic models of language that prevailed at the time, one could argue that even current research on writing is faced with the challenge to overcome onesidedness and move beyond or integrate issues from competing paradigms (Faigley, 1986; Habermas, 1998; Ongstad, 2002a). Directions such as creative writing, process-oriented writing, different genre approaches, constructivism, socioconstructionism, dialogism, post-structuralism, systemic functional grammar (SFG) may all tend to function partly with blinkers. They tend to chose a corner of the vast field of language and communication that historically has proved to be relevant for writing as a phenomenon.

In the discussion that follows, I present some basic components of a necessarily simplified and more general framework which may be useful to both problematize onesidedness and to suggest ways through which it may be overcome (for fuller versions, see Ongstad, 2002a, 20002b). A central notion this framework builds upon is that of *positioning*. This concept, which has been partly generated from several different frameworks, will be applied to and exemplified by my interpretative positionings of René's text.

According to Bakhtin (1986), Bühler (1934), Habermas (1984), Halliday (1978, 1994), Martin (1997) and Ongstad (1997, 2002a, 2002b, 2004) signs, utterances, texts, discourses, genres, and contexts – in short, all main aspects of communication – are basically seen as triadic. To utter and hence to interpret is a dynamic and never-ending balance between the aspects of form, content and use in any utterance, short or long. Any physical phenomenon has form as it appears to our senses. According to a Saussurean view the verbal sign will use a certain form as a *signifier* for a certain *signified* content. This form is structured and refers to something, and hence these form a complementary, dyadic sign. However, Bakhtin (1986) opposed this view and claimed that in real life communication, in utterances, the expressivity of form, the referentiality of content and a third aspect, the *addressivity* of the action, will form an unseparable triad.

Thus when I, for instance, say or write to my students: *Write!* the form is what one can hear or see, in this case letters and an exclamation mark. Further are all aspects of what it means to write, implicitly referred to as *content*, and finally the exclamation mark helps underline the addressivity and, hence, the utterance as an act I want them to perform. However, for an utterance to make sufficient sense a context or a genre is needed as well. Therefore, at the same time, any utterance will be dependent on the subtle interplay between the said and the unsaid. Accordingly, one should differentiate between the level of utterance/text and the level of genre/context.

Thus, in any act of uttering, two main processes are involved in a parallel way. There is firstly, if we refer to Figure 1, a "horizontal" (A) blending of form, content and function, studied as dynamics (positionings) of structure, reference and action while uttering. Secondly, a "vertical" (B) process, where mentally stored elements, or "meaning potential" in Halliday's terms, work as active resources in so-called theme-rheme processes (Halliday, 1994). These are intricate dynamics of given (theme) and new (rheme) in the utterance as utterers or interpreters unfold them as text aspects, step by step through the text.

According to the proposed framework, then, utterances are, on the one hand, partly being generated by the use of the already stored resources ("upwards" processes). On the other hand, utterances become a potential for future meaning production ("downwards" processes). Although context is not necessarily the same as genre, genres inevitably co-constitute context (Duranti, & Goodwin, 1992; Erickson, & Schultz, 1981; Martin 1997). According to a thought-provoking claim by Freadman (1994), a genre should not be seen as (fully) in a text, nor should a text be seen as in a/one genre itself (cf. Figure 1). Genres are potential and therefore always more than what one can get into one text. Following the same logic any genre, for instance, fairy tales (or systems of genres such as narratives) will function as an advanced, constantly accumulating meaning potential for communication by offering partly-open, partly-closed *pre-balances* (expectations) of form, content, and use, for instance, prototypically and respectively, formulas, patents and recipes.

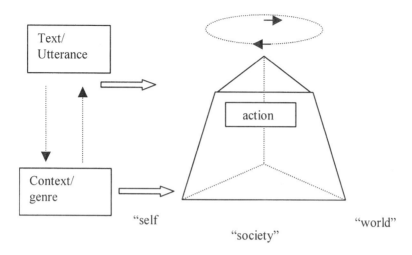

Figure 1. The relationship between the three major aspects on the concrete level of utterance/text (the top triangle) and their respectively corresponding three major aspects of the immanent level of context/genre, constituting the "life world" of any communicator (the "invisible" bottom part).

The above imply that genre cannot be seen as a defined, precise, restricted category (Freadman, 1994; Ongstad, 2002b). Genre is not just a text-type, but rather a way of communicating meaning. While some genres are prototypically rather fixed, a great variety of genres are found in the discursive landscape *in between* the open and the closed. It should be added that the genre system of a culture is constantly shifting, more slowly in traditional societies and faster in more innovative and dynamic cultures. Regarding writing, these shifts occur in the classroom, in education and in society at large, which the introduction of ICT and other new media can exemplify.

In addition, it is assumed that, while communicating, producers and interpreters, consciously and unconsciously *evaluate* all aspects of the produced message. Three major aspects can be distinguished. Firstly, we can relate to form as an aspect emotionally. Our experiences can vary from negative, through neutral to positive. In other words, we consider the utterance as *aesthetics*. This mostly subject-related attitude may be symptomatically present in the *expressivity* of the utterance (Bakhtin, 1986). It is important to bring in this aspect since linguistics tends to leave it out. To better understand writers and readers this aspect is crucial, not the least when we study young children or education in postmodernity, both putting form in the forefront.

Secondly, contents and references can be considered by or evaluated from an *epistemological perspective*. Epistemology represents a positioning of the content aspect of utterances, seen as knowledge (true or false). This aspect is deliberately made dominant in hard sciences. In research on writing it is crucial for understanding how epistemology is related to aesthetics and ethics, since no texts have a clear division between these constitutive aspects of the utterance.

Thirdly and finally, acts can be judged in terms of being right or wrong in some respect (or effective, just, functional and the like). Thus a "norm-related" *ethics* is founded. Ethics has lately become important in studies of communication (Bauman, 1995; Bordum, 2001; Habermas, 1998; Levinson, 1998). Hard sciences tend to leave out this aspect, and, as a result, science has partly failed to take *responsibility* for how epistemologically validated research is used or how the whole discipline *functions* as a tool or a means in the cultural domain. By applying this premise to research on writing, apparently, one advocates that linguistics, applied linguistics and text theory need to address issues concerning where and how the research is ethically positioned. In other words, ethics is here understood in a rather broad sense.

Nevertheless, even if presented separately here, it should be stressed that these three aspects and all other triadic communicational aspects always occur blurred and *together*. They are complemenary, parallel, and *reciprocal* (mutual). Hence, as a reader of this very paragraph you may, for instance, consider consciously or unconsciously the quality of writing (the expressivity) and how it effects your emotionality, how true and valid you think the epistemological claims are and of what help these thoughts are, separately and as a whole. Focusing on this triad actually brings us back to a historical experience in practical communication. In ancient rhetoric, speakers would consider (respectively) the *pathos*, *logos* and *ethos* of their utterances to achieve communicational wholeness.

Both the three main aspects of an utterance, the form/structure, the content/reference, and the use/act, as well as the above-described subjective respective evaluation of each of those aspects, point to *validity* as a problem. Depending on where one positions the research, and accordingly the object, one faces different validity expectations. Regarding the dilemma of choice Habermas holds:

> The validity-theoretical interpretation of Bühler's functional scheme offers itself as a way out of the difficulties of speech-act theory because it does justice to all the three aspects of a *speaker* coming to an understanding with *another person* about *something*. ...... A validity-theoretic interpretation of Bühler's functional scheme further leads to the assumption that with a speech act "MP," S takes up relations *simultaneously* to something in the objective world, to something in the subjective world and to something in the social world (Habermas, 1998: 73,76).

Habermas further holds that in communication we have both to differentiate between and at the same time hold together three basic kinds or regimes of validity. Subjectivity is related to the person's inner world, objectivity to the outer world and normativy/intersubjectivity to society. In the quote above these validities are respectively related to *speaker*, *something* and *another person* (the inner world, the outer world and society form the communicator's "lifeworld").

To summarize (see Figure 2): On the main concepts invoked: Form, content and use are presented as the basic constituents of both utterance and genre (1). Emotionality relates primarily to form, we search for essence in content and efficiency in acts (2). These aspects, when evaluated, consciously or not, establish respectively, aesthetics, epistemology and ethics as separate, but, at the same time, as communicatively related fields (3). These can, respectively, be connected to a further division of a person's *lifeworld* in three major dimensions: aesthetics relates to the expressing self, epistemology to the referred world and ethics to society as kept up by the act of communication (4); however, again, all aspects are mutually related and there is no clear-cut division between them, since they all interact. Validating in these three intertwined fields and dimensions is respectively related to subjectivity, objectivity and normativity (5), but with no clear discursive borders. Again, all aspects are systemically related to each other, although positioning or discursive *focusing* will bring each aspect *mentally* to the forefront, a point that is symbolized with dotted lines.

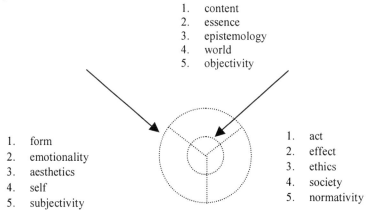

1.   content
2.   essence
3.   epistemology
4.   world
5.   objectivity

1.   form
2.   emotionality
3.   aesthetics
4.   self
5.   subjectivity

1.   act
2.   effect
3.   ethics
4.   society
5.   normativity

Figure 2. The internal relationship between aspects of utterance/genre (1), the core of main aspects when experienced, considered and measured as an isolated phenomenon (2), fields of judgement (3), relation to life-world (4) and basis for validation (5).

Both figures metaphorize that all the presented concepts (and many others) can be related in a general, semiotic, cultural system. However the system is open and can change (over time). Further there is no primacy for particular aspects. Importance and relevance depend on which field the phenomenon in question will be researched from.

In the following only *some* aspects of the system will come into consideration. Still the very presence of the overall outlined framework can help make us stay aware of what we are *not* focusing.

4   INTERPRETATIONS AND EXEMPLIFICATIONS

4.1 Positioning(s) both as Researched Objects and Approaches

In section 4 I focus on how "self" or Habermas' "inner subjective world" as one of the main three aspects in the life world can be connected to a system of *simultaneity* between form, content and use and to their respective philosophical and didaktic fields, aesthetics, epistemology, and ethics. By using Bakhtin's notions, I will see aspects of René's utterance as positionings by means of and related to expressing, referring and addressing, (Bakhtin, 1986) or his *self-positioning* (Ongstad, forthcoming a). The concept of positioning is found among others in the work of Evans, & Tsatsaroni (1994) and especially Harré, & van Langenhove (1997) where it most often refers to utterers' positioning in dialogues. My own use of the concept of positioning is not directly related to the above-mentioned uses of the term, although positioning both for these researchers and me is seen as a relative and a *discursive* communicative phenomenon. My approach relates directly to the triadic view proposed by Bakhtin, Bühler, Habermas, and Halliday, although none of those scholars are using the term "positioning." Nevertheless, they all have accepted the relative nature of communication, and this necessary relativity and openness is what positioning is coined to take into account.

Positioning is in itself an empty and relational concept which can make sense only when combined with a given *focus*, such as self-positioning. To focus on something has some basic, logical implications: Firstly, a focus creates a *figure* and hence a *ground*, which in this case is René's text and its context. Secondly, the figure can only be focused from a *position*, which normally will be tacit about itself and thus, ideological in its nature (Bakhtin, 1986). An ideology is something we think *from* rather than *on* (Ricoeur, 1981). Figure, background and position, then, are logically and inevitably interrelated (Ongstad, forthcoming b). Accordingly, my positioning(s) of René's *self*-positionings can hardly be seen as "objective." The validity depends on what and how I focus, discursively. The disadvantage, seen from the perspective of traditional validity, is that "findings" and understandings cannot lean safely on essential, significant, categories. The advantage though, not the least from the perspective of a practising teacher, is that different kinds of positionings can be interrelated, and be, therefore, in a sense compatible.

A main challenge in applying theories to practice is how a system described in a certain discipline is connected to the particular, to the specific, to the individual, to the unique, to the (always) new. Such particularities have been a major challenge for general sociology, analytic Marxism, the theory of habitus (Bourdieu, 1989), grammar-based approaches (Halliday, 1994), genre approaches (Martin, 1997; Reid, 1987) and even for a general theory of communicative actions (Habermas, 1984). They are all working with or from the general, and face trouble the closer they come to the specific. To stay valid, they need to avoid certain challenges. For instance, a general rule of thumb seems to be that a high degree of significance makes findings less practically relevant and highly relevant general views struggle to obtain high epistemological validity.

This is not just a theoretical problem. It is one of the main challenges for any research-based pedagogy, as indeed for a writing pedagogy. The challenge of balancing them has come to the surface in the Australian genre debate: should one prioritize texts over genres, the student over students, individuality over collectiveness (Reid, 1987)? An ideal answer is of course to cater for both. However, which single model can handle that? Positioning, then, is a concept that tries to bridge such gaps, by refusing to make definite oppositions such as subjectivity versus objectivity, objectivity versus normativity or normativity versus subjectivity, and by accepting the close and dynamic relationship between utterance and genre, text and context. In addition, it accepts and utilizes the almost paradoxical relationship between language and communication that is woven into the triadic framework.

In the following, most words and concepts given in *italics* signal that these particularly marked patterns are *positioned* in relation to the communicative framework above. I focus on different text aspects through framework concepts, and vice versa. As signalled in the title, a specific concern is possible tensions between aspects of the school's collective writing pedagogy and the subjectivities of a student writer.

4.2 René's Text in relation to Genre Patterns

In the following I will prioritize three aspects of the framework, (1) genres, (2) the social dimension in students' activities and writing and (3) writing as form, which of course leave out many other aspects of the framework.

At the *word-level* René's text, apart from its basic problems with double consonants, is rather normal for a boy in the second grade. However, as a genre, it may not be so. The students have been engaging in this kind of writing from August to April and have become familiar with the textual expectations of the task. They report activities, describe objects and solve school tasks. The boys obviously consider themselves finished when reporting is done. Anders has even announced it orally in his exclamation: *finiiiished!* To report has seemingly become a dominant aspect of which genre and writing context he expects this to be.

However, between the lines and in the air there is another unspoken genre-specific expectation: you are supposed to tell, and to tell rather much or at least more than these boys have produced; a text can incorporate or be about something fictive. The teachers often try to stimulate students by asking interesting and interested questions. Since the term used for the building has changed in the building process from a pyramid to a fortress to a castle to a palace, the teacher hints that perhaps there are some fairy tale potentials connected to them. Annemari, one of the teachers, who has registered that the two boys have been playing and twaddling, is perhaps a bit disappointed that the texts are so short. She nevertheless tries to stimulate the boys to write more, by asking questions, for instance, about who lived there. That is an easy match for the boys; it is a mere task and has a straight answer: *René and Anders...*(etc). That René's and Annemari's genre expectations are not quite the same becomes clear when René asks: *When he was video recording, I made faces. Will I write that up?* The little *up* signals that René sees the writing mainly as a report. He does not say *write, tell* or *write about*.

Thus, René's text is at first glance a personal report, which is interrupted by the genre-breaking sentence: *René and Anders livd thar.* This can be interpreted as a schoolish answer on a separate task René can solve fast, although it was intended as stimulation in the spirit of process-oriented writing. Without this context as background, an external reader would have small chances discovering it. The border line between what is genre and what is context is problematic in this case. First, the whole workshop has over time developed into a pedagogical genre, that is, a certain stereotypical way of acting in this educational context. Within this genre, as with

Chinese boxes, one can find other discursive genres, such as the blurred report and/or tell/draw expectation. Secondly, there are the workshop books with more stable communicative patterns. Thirdly, one can find the relative stable patterns of playing at different stations. And looking through René's whole book, one can note clearly a certain inclination to "medieval and royal buildings." So far one can conclude that René's utterance symptomatically contains different genres and diverse reactions to this school's genre expectations.

4.3 The Social Dimensions in René's Activity and Writing

Following the lines through Rene's text in the left handed column of Figure 3, we focus on the *activities* which are being *reported*. The cohesion structures a response or an answer to the tacit task, to *tell* and to *document* what has been done: building, cooperating, twaddling, living, putting together. In one sense, the choices are quite adequate relative to what is found on the videotape. Thus, René is reporting. Still, there is some striking lack of coherence, partly, due to René's response to the blurred expectation and, partly, as a result of some other agendas.

At the surface, pronouns and proper names serve as grammatical subjects and as agents. They are crucial for the construction of the structure of the text: *We have built; we used bricks; I cooperated with Anders; we twaddled; **Anders and René livd thar.*** Focusing on René's text we may run the risk to overlook how important his *social we* really is. The lucky moment when the camera caught his hearable "inner" speech to himself during his writing process opens up a deeper implication:

> "I have built a palace." Says suddenly while he grasps the rubber: "I? We. We have together. *We* have built a palace. I and.." Rubs out "I."

Society, the You-and-I-connection, and the *ethics* of his *solidarity* are hidden in the *social context*. What is more, Anders and René's mateship is filled with deep, non-verbal, embodied, semiotic *meaning*, an almost tacit voice of *togetherness* and *sharing*:

> 33.40 René sits on his knees, now parallel with Anders, both with their backs to their building(s) [which now has grown into one large construction]. They look at each other, but do not say anything.

This is not just a common dialogical you-and-I-connection. The friendly relationship has materialized into *co*-building both as process and product. For René it is very important to *report* exactly that, both *ethically* and considered in relation to a regime of true-false validation of his own utterances. A report should be *correct*. This *subjective* or *individual* strategy is far from any *fictional* narratives in the school's expectation. His respect for a valid and honest positioning seems crucial for how he makes *meaning* in this particular text. It is in this perspective I will interpret his very last sentence: *it was difficul too putugeder*, an utterance to which I return.

4.4 The Value of Form

One of this school's intentions with the workshop activity was to generate *creativity* that could facilitate more and more varied forms of writing even for young, novice writers such as second graders. To let these young students have this freedom and face up to challenges without the teachers being too commanding and controlling, was a quite radical and brave arrangement. However, there are certain other genre expectations blurred into both activities and writing stemming from this intention. One is task and tasks in my studies were seen as genres (Ongstad, 1996). In the activity part, task is play-like and it seemingly gives children relative freedom.

Nevertheless, there is an expectation of *productivity* in both phases of the whole session. For the two boys much time is spent on physical activity, fitting the bricks properly and connecting step by step their separate constructions into one, without planning so at the start; in other words, there was a focus on *form as structure and structuring*. In addition, almost just as much time and energy is put into *referential* drawings of what in the end turns out to be configured as a "palace" (see Appendix). In the boys' minds things have to be structurally *right* and they try to catch the *correct profiles* of their buildings. As genre, it comes close to *descriptive* geometry or architects' professional drawings. Hence, less time is spent on writing, which also is *performed* less *enthusiastically*, more like a normal indisputable duty, a traditional school *task*.

In the following I will trace René's positionings when transforming phonemes into graphemes. In the linguistic sense, both are *forms*. Since there is no safe one-to-one relationship between the two, he runs into problems:

> 73.20 They start working again. René: *Is "klosser"* [Norwegian] *written with two l's?* Repeats the question. Anders: *No.* He takes a look at René's book, and says, half giggling while he stretches the length of the o-sound to the extreme: *It says "kloooser"* [Norwegian] Laughs. *It says "klooooser!"* René gets uncertain and changes *o* to *å*. Anders laughs even more, although he is not sneering or gloating. Says: *It's written with o and double s.* René rubs it out.

For readers with little knowledge of Norwegian language I should make clear that *klosser* is the only word with double consonants (out of nine) in his text he actually has written "correctly" in the final text. He is preoccupied with it though and faces up to the challenge for a while, and from one point of view this is clearly even a *cognitive* matter. However, *correct* spelling is not just *logic*; it is, in fact, a question of *aesthetics*. Anders thinks *kloser* [Norwegian] as a *form* looks hilariously funny, partly because it is not a Norwegian word and partly because, written with a single *s* the quality of the vowel will change from *å* to *o* and because a single "s" extends the pronounced length of the following vowel. René is perhaps a bit puzzled by his mate's strong *emotional* reaction and realizes that he has not mastered the *cognitive* secrets of spelling. Thus, René is *evaluated*, not by his teachers this time (who actually are rather tolerant), but by his mate, and not just *epistemologically*, but more on an *expressive* and hence *emotional* basis.

Furthermore, if we overemphasize the role of verbal language here, we may forget that the two boys actually spent quite a long time making the drawings. To them *form* was indeed important, both during the building and the drawing process (see

Appendix). At least for René it seems fair to conclude that an *aesthetic* drawing was, after all, just as important as correct spelling. Our perspective has benefited from being *semiotic*, not just a verbal and linguistic one.

Adjectives normally express subjective and personal evaluations. In René's text there are just two, (the palace became) *nice* and (it was) *difficult* (to put together). My interpretation is that these two utterances are aesthetic evaluations of his physical activity and are given a deeper meaning or significance. The last sentence has been added later on, probably another day. The video clip clearly shows that it was not there at the end of the writing session reported above. Why did René add the last bit? We will not know. My hypothesis, though, is that when he looked over his text later, perhaps by himself, he needed to communicate a core experience to others, a *pride* over his and Anders' piece of engineering. Much of the pride is expressed in the committed drawing. In spite of the fact that he writes to answer a task, he finds it necessary to express, with an extra utterance, a basic *feeling* about the whole enterprise. However, another question is how much writing potential there can be at the end of the day in writing about personal pride, for an eight year old boy, especially when the school's ideology just as much seems to be more extensive narrative, fictional writing.

4.5 And Taken Together...?

In this chapter, through an example, I have paid attention to genre complexities focusing on the two aspects (Figure 2), form/emotionality/aesthetics/self/subjectivity and the corresponding act/effect/ethics/society/normativity, partly leaving out the third, the referential aspect. Thus, the three different columns in Figure 3, represent different possible readings or positionings or interpretations of *some* main aspects of the text from my position. They can, at the same time, be seen as René's *positionings* positioned by me as a researcher and generated on the basis of the overall framework. Whether he would agree and thus validate the interpretation positively, is not at stake in this example, even if it is relevant in a pedagogical perspective. He is in this respect mainly positioned by my approach.

The left column line is the textline we followed to trace reported activity. This is what the school system implicitly asks for by accepting reports. Mainly verbs (performatives) have this function. The mid column line connects elements of a social dimension – in this case René's perception of the value or the nature of the relation between the boys when building *together*, here symptomatically carried by pronoun and proper names. This dimension is crucial for the dynamics of textual structuring (the theme-rheme shifts of given and new, which I have chosen to bypass in this article; see Ongstad, forthcoming a).

A third dimension, the right handed column line in Figure 3, combines and relates the pleasant outcome of play and meaningful activity, evaluated by adjectives and thus made into aesthetics (*nice and difficult*). These adjectives can be seen as René's overall symptomatic evaluation of their efforts (pride over his ability to master complexity in the building process). I have held this as "an existential bottom line" in his text, which basically is not meant as an *essential result*, a validated truth, but rather an interpretive, an *abductive* claim. The interpretations are part of a discursive blend of *some* social and emotional aspects seen with a third eye by focusing on epistemologies of building, drawing and reporting as communicative utterances.

On the text level, the text, in other words, contains an embodied and simultaneous blurring of elements from *self, world, and society,* or the *lifeworld* according to René there and then, focused from, interpreted by my positioning(s). These very general and immanent aspects have symptomatically come to surface by interpreting the form/structure, the content/reference and the use/action in his semiotic utterances. These major embodied, contextual lifeworld constituents define and balance each other reciprocally and constitute and develop the embodied contexts for each person's *meaning* making. This, at the end of the day, is perhaps the strongest dimension in the gradual unfolding of becoming a writing self, even in seemingly trivial school writing.

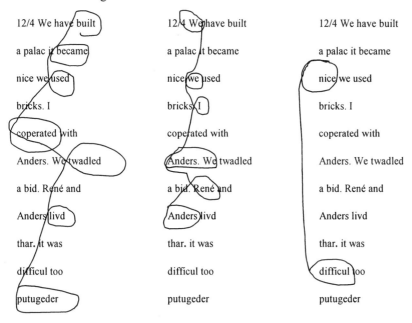

Figure 3. Connecting acts (verbs via the lines in the left handed column), the social relationship between the two boys (pronouns and proper names via line in the mid column), and evaluations of the process (adjectives via the line in the right handed column).

5   SUMMING UP

To summarize, I will turn the perspective around, by letting the text exemplify and illustrate aspects of the framework. René's workshop *utterance* is a *focused* text; this is seen in the light of a given theoretical framework, which *positions* the text *communicatively*. The original text has a visual *form* which can be represented in different ways in different *contexts*: as photocopied by me, as typed in two different languages, as handwritten, with drawing. We can position it *aesthetically* and *emotionally* as spelling or we can *foreground* its *syntactic*, textual *structure* for different purposes and so on.

The text is *referentially about* something or perhaps several things. This content is, on the one hand, very concrete *references* to phenomena and processes of which we can partly check the *epistemological validity* in the *context* I have given. On the other hand, the deeper "content" is abstract and complicated, since we do not have access to the utterer's deeper intentions, partly because we cannot *semantically* say for sure how the syntactic structure (form) could/should be interpreted. We can only work *abductively* and *symptomatically*. These aspects are, nevertheless, important to take into consideration in direct relation to the more linguistic aspects of the text.

The utterance is also an *act* (or a series of several acts). This positioning, by me or by any receiver, is *functional.* Interpreted "cynically," the verbal text is mostly just a plain school answer. Positioned more empathically, it may *express* René's inner *feelings* about the *activity* at school that day. The text can also be read as a *genre*-like, schoolish *answer* which I, as researcher, can *position* as a researched *object*, a figure.

René has himself evaluated some of these aspects *aesthetically, epistemologically and ethically* in different ways, considering among other things the building process and its result, the correctness of spelling and the validity and ethics of what is referred (to), his commitment to mateship and the will to get his final evaluation and meaning through to his readers.

However, by splitting these interpretations and exemplifications in specific textual aspects along three major strands, we cut off the impact and implication of a dynamic, but backgrounded, context, the *genre*(s). Hence, to consider the *form* properly we have to read it against different genres: as a piece of handwriting, a report, a task answer, or a school text. The same holds for the aspects of *content* and *use.* By shifting focus, that is, positioning from structure to reference to action, we may even risk to twist the genre. Thus, we are (as always) dependent on our own genre as researchers to make sense, that is to validate our text. The paradoxical problem is that we cannot know exactly which genre, or whether it is crafted only on the basis of one particular genre.

Furthermore, coming from different research traditions we, as researchers, will tend to choose different positionings, which, as I pointed to, has happened paradigmatically in the past (Ongstad, 2002a). René has used his *embodied meaning potential* to *express* himself both at the level of the *utterance,* and *symptomatically* at the level of *genre.* We may assume that by playing, building, drawing and writing he has even increased his semiotic meaning potential for a next time, absorbing aspects of uttering and genres/contexts. However, by using linguistic theories only we would have run the risk to separate ourselves from what constitutes a text and an utterance *as a whole* and our understanding of *subjective* writers and the significance of meaning in their lifeworld. Accordingly, we need to consider *the paradoxical simultaneity* of these aspects. Actually in doing so, the researcher is forced to come closer to teachers' more open and abduction-like situation in their everyday practice.

The school and the teachers are in the *background*. However, teachers' expectations and their writing pedagogy are brought to the forefront, becoming a figure, by my focusing on the encounter between the explicit text and its tacit and blurred genres. The ideology of the narrative expectation in stimuli questions such as *Who lived there?* [in the palace] hints at a whole new expected genre, the story. It is, however, important to underline that the interpretations are *not* at all a critique of the teachers and the school. This was probably one of the most progressive schools in this field in Oslo. My point is that any pedagogy and ism has blinkers. And for teachers it is crucial to know roughly how different directions and new pedagogies relate to each other, since by leaning heavily on just one something may always escape one's pedagogical focus and leave too much to context.

By presenting the theoretical framework with a deliberately broad scope, the openness may at first confuse readers, since there does not exist a direct operationalization and methodologies that could be derived from the framework. On the other hand, the chances for a more differentiated and eclectic approach are better (Ongstad, forthcoming b).

What moreover seems to be at stake here is a conflict of interests between a tacit collective intention and a concrete different subjective meaning. While most of the directions that deal with institutional writing are preoccupied with form, content, function, interaction and even with semantic/functional meaning, few, if any, seem to pay attention to how form as emotional/existential/expressive *meaning* has become a new postmodern *ideology*: -I am my form, my form is me (Ongstad, 1999a, 1999b). My abductive claim about René's text partly tries to match such a challenge.

For the three major aspects of René's lifeworld, *life, world* and *society* we can suggest the following: Only *symptomatically* can we interpret his *self-positionings*. My suggestion has been that emotionality may be the strongest *self*-element here (marked with the right hand column in Figure 3). *World* is established by serious play and referential communication. The expectation of writing extensively and at length about this "world" is secondary to the direct and inner experience of it. In terms of *society* René is reconfirming *others* by keeping tight connections to Anders, by echoing or parroting the school's discourse, and by being serious about his final statement in the workshop book on behalf of his readers (its logos and ethos). In any case a triadic, communicative, semiotic framework will refuse to make any of the above aspects into *essential categories*. They are all mutually related, and if we want to enter the hermeneutic circle from one of the parts/aspects or from the whole, we will, in any case, run into trouble deciding what is the overall meaning, if any. Hence, what René's inner intentions were we will never know. It is a combination of his and my *positionings* that governs my interpretation that *emotionality* (pathos) is a possible *dominant* in this utterance.

Considering these interpretations we may find it unsatisfactory that a permanent and solid finding is hard to reach within such a framework. By giving priority to the *referential* aspect, this openness of course in principle *can* be reduced to a level that can be handled as statistically significant, and from where one can work along an inductive or a deductive regime. However, the higher the significance we aim for, the less value the findings may have for everyday teaching. The openness of the framework is therefore closer to the risky real situation teachers will find themselves in, there will always be a blind spot behind their back as a direct result of the very focusing. Ideology is what we think from (Ricoeur, 1981). Teachers are in practice in a dilemma between the necessity to react to texts there and then, on the one hand, and constantly being open for the unexpected significance of unfocused, potential meaning, on the other hand.

What are the *weaknesses* with a triadic, semiotic, multifunctional approach? It is potentially time-consuming (thinking and rethinking issues). It is (mainly) non-hierarchical (no specific result is guaranteed). It has to blur kinds of validities (obstruct traditional research models). It is complex in its implications (one has to have some knowledge about a series of research approaches in order to be self-critical). In its broad understanding it risks being simplistic and general (the world is packed into few aspects) (see Ongstad, 1999a; 2001; 2002a.)

However, some of the weaknesses can also be seen as strengths. What a combined framework of Bakhtin, Bühler, Habermas and Halliday actually does is to create a *semiotic* and not just a *linguistic* understanding of uttering/writing, which now seems timely and necessary. It can incorporate body and other semiotics (it takes the body/person/self into consideration, not only the text or the utterance). It stresses the *openness* and *interrelationships* between main communicational aspects (and makes systemness and dialogism relevant). It explains and handles the inevitable dynamics between utterance and genre, text and context, new and given. It avoids unfruitful conflicts between dyadic approaches (for instance, structural and post-structural approaches or single-minded Piaget/Vygotsky oppositions). Most important, though, is that different kinds of students, writing teachers, approaches and ideologies can find a place *within* the framework and communicate over the hedges of different priorities. The overarching, open structure does not *solve* the problems, but it addresses them in a non-excluding manner (Ongstad, 2001). There should be no doubt that my reading of and my "findings" in René's text would not have emerged without the application of the framework, since it opens for a wider range of interpretations than any singular approach, and it helps seeing the possible coherence between the communicative aspects.

Finally, Habermas has claimed that there are different kinds of validities in subjectivity, objectivity and normativity (Habermas, 1998). With his notions it thus seems fair to claim that René validates his work, respectively, with *veracity* (nice and difficult), *truth* (correct drawing and textual concession of twaddling) and *fairness* (positioning comradeship with solidarity, and being honest about crucial feelings). René's text is, of course, lean regarding the ideological criteria of process oriented writing pedagogy, such as productivity, activity, and originality. However, as subjective *meaning* making, is the utterance *"it was difficult too putugeder"* less worthy than the expected productivity? Collective enculturation to school writing has to make room for the need for subjective meaning making within the genres implicitly offered through the task regime.

APPENDIX: TEXTS AND DRAWINGS BY RENÉ AND ANDERS

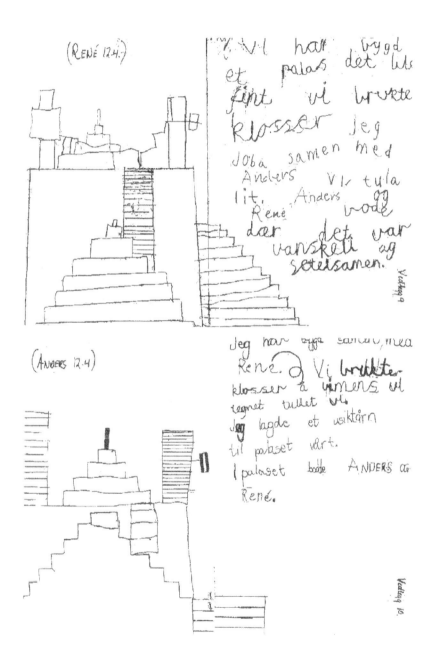

WHOLE-CLASS AND PEER INTERACTION IN AN ACTIVITY OF WRITING AND REVISION

LINDA ALLAL, LUCIE MOTTIER LOPEZ, KATIA LEHRAUS, & ALEXIA FORGET

University of Geneva

Abstract. The perspective of situated cognition provides a conceptual framework for studying social mediation in activities of text production. The investigation presented here concerns two forms of social mediation: (1) whole-class interactions that prepare the students for drafting and revising their texts; (2) peer interactions occurring when dyads engage in joint revision of their drafts. The data collected in three fifth-grade classrooms include observations of whole-class interactions, recordings of dyadic interactions and classifications of text transformations that students carried out during individual and joint phases of revision. The analyses examine the relationships between qualitative indicators of interaction dynamics and quantitative data on text transformations. The findings show that differences in the whole-class interactions are reflected in the students' revisions particularly with respect to the degree of rewriting that they undertake, as compared to simple error correction. Although analysis of the dyadic interactions reveals important variations in the dynamics of the exchanges, two general findings emerge. In the large majority of cases, the activity of joint revision leads to a substantial increase in the number of text transformations, beyond those made by each author individually. Even in cases where no new transformations occur, the authors engage actively in interaction about revision (e.g., they propose revisions of the other student's text, explain revisions made individually to their own text, argue against proposals of the other student, etc.). Implications of the results for future research on writing instruction are discussed.

Keywords: Social mediation, whole-class interaction, peer interaction, revision, writing

1   SOCIAL MEDIATION IN CLASSROOM WRITING

The social mediation of classroom learning can be approached from several perspectives, including sociolinguistic studies of the discourse of teacher-student interactions (Barnes, 1976; Cazden, 1986), research conducted in a neo-Vygotskian conception of scaffolding and joint knowledge construction by teacher and students (Bliss, Askew, & McCrae, 1996; Newman, Griffin, & Cole, 1989), analyses of peer interaction in situations of tutoring (Fuchs, Fuchs, Bentz, Phillips, & Hamlett, 1994; Person, & Graesser, 1999) and in cooperative learning activities (Johnson, & Johnson, 1994; Mercer, 1996), investigations of tools that mediate learning in instructional settings (Salomon, Perkins, & Globerson, 1991).

The emergence of the perspective of situated cognition and learning (Brown, Collins, & Duguid, 1989) provides a broader framework for linking and interpreting the different aspects of social mediation in the classroom. This perspective views learning as a process of participation in a "community of practice" (Lave, & Wenger, 1991) that shares values, norms, ways of behaving and of negotiating meaning. In a classroom "learning community" (Brown, & Campione, 1990), the learner actively contributes to the constitution of the shared culture while at the same time developing new skills that incorporate the forms of social interaction and the tools that are valued in the community. Classroom investigations of situated learning (see the review by Allal, 2001) have examined processes of social mediation primarily in three situations: (a) collective, teacher-led interactions that allow the construction of shared norms, practices and knowledge representations; (b) teacher-student interactions, on a one-to-one basis or a small group, in which expert scaffolding or coaching sustains guided practice on the part of the learner, (c) peer interactions which include collaborative exchanges and confrontation of viewpoints.

Research on writing instruction has gradually integrated social constructivist and situated learning concepts. The writing process approach developed by Graves (1983) emphasizes interactions occurring in writing conferences between teacher and students and interactive peer response and critique. Rafoth's conception of a "discourse community, where writers, readers and texts come together" (Rafoth, 1988: 131) offers a framework for approaching the social construction of written communication. The features of a classroom community designed to foster "literacy apprenticeships," comparable to authentic literacy practices outside school, are defined by Resnick (1990) in the following terms:

> Children work to produce a product that will be used by others ...; they work collaboratively, but under conditions in which individuals are held responsible for their work; they use tools and apparatus appropriate to the problem; they read and critique each other's writing; they are called upon to elaborate and defend their own work until it reaches a community standard (Resnick, 1990: 183).

There is an increasing amount of empirical research on the role of social mediation in writing instruction at the elementary school level. Englert and her co-workers (Englert, 1972; Englert, Berry, & Dunsmore, 2001; Englert, Raphael, & Anderson, 1992) have investigated the practices that allow literacy apprenticeships to be created and to function productively in classroom communities. Kostouli (2000) explored the way in which student learning about a specific genre is mediated by the discourse structure of the writing conference, and especially by the teacher's strategies for creating a coherent goal-structure. Allal (2004) studied the implementation and the effects of an integrated, sociocognitive model of writing instruction that included both whole-class interaction and various forms of scripted peer interaction (O'Donnell, 1999). Several studies found that the quality of students' texts could be enhanced by peer collaboration on joint writing tasks or by reciprocal peer revision of individual work (Daiute, & Dalton, 1988; MacArthur, Schwartz, & Graham, 1991; Saunders, 1989). A study by Zammuner (1995) comparing different conditions of individual and dyadic production and revision concluded that peer interaction was particularly helpful when students wrote texts individually and revised them with a peer who could adopt a detached, critical stance.

The research presented in this chapter is focused on two forms of social mediation studied in a situation of text production and revision: (1) whole-class interactions that precede the students' drafting and revision of their texts; (2) peer interactions occurring when dyads engage in joint revision of their drafts. We will therefore examine more closely some conceptual issues linked specifically to these topics.

1.1 Whole-class Interactions

Interactions of the teacher with an entire class, also called whole-class discussions (Yackel, & Cobb, 1996), can occur before, during or after activities carried out by students in small groups or individually. These collective interactions are considered to be key moments in the constitution of the "taken-as-shared" meaning of norms and practices in a classroom community (Cobb, Gravemeijer, Yackel, McClain, & Whitenack, 1997; Cobb, Stephan, McClain, & Gravemeijer, 2001). There is, however, considerable variation in the terms used to describe the processes involved in whole-class discussions. Cobb et al. (1997) speak of "interactive constitution" of mathematical meaning; Voigt (1994) uses the same term to describe the emergence of interaction patterns; Newman et al. (1989) refer to "collaborative construction" of knowledge in the classroom. In each of these cases, the terms appear to be used in a generic sense to refer to virtually all forms of teacher-student interaction, ranging from the classic IRE sequence (teacher initiation, student response, teacher evaluation) to highly collaborative forms of dialogue. Some authors use terms that emphasize the interdependence of the teacher's and student's contributions, for example: "joint constitution" (Resnick, Pontecorvo, & Säljo, 1997); "joint construction" (Salomon, & Perkins, 1998); "co-construction" (Valsinger, 1988).

In order to analyze the whole-class interactions observed in our research, we have adopted the following conceptual distinctions:

- We use the term *"constitution"* to refer to a continuum of teacher-student interactions. One pole of the continuum corresponds to the classical direct instruction lesson: the teacher presents instructional material, the students listen and carry out any tasks requested by the teacher (e.g., *"Take out your dictionary and..."*). The other pole corresponds to situations in which the teacher formulates open-ended questions, stimulates exchanges and debate among students, who compare their interpretations, assess the adequacy of different procedures, and take initiatives that influence the orientation of the discussion. Any segment of a whole-class discussion can be located on the continuum, somewhere between these two poles, providing that the teacher and the students generally respect their complementary roles and thereby contribute to the progression of the instructional activity.

- We have defined criteria to identify the point on the above continuum where it becomes relevant to speak of *"interactive construction, joint construction, co-construction"* of norms, practices, knowledge and understanding. Our criteria are that: (a) the teacher asks one or more open-ended questions (which may or may not be followed by more focused questions), and (b) several students give a variety of answers and/or examples that are not already available in the classroom context, that is, that are not present in the teacher's question, that have not been previously evoked during the same interactive session, that are not provided by an existing documentary source (blackboard, instruction sheet, etc.). These criteria allow us to identify sequences of teacher-student interaction in which students make significant contributions to the constitution of the ongoing instructional activity.

The research on social mediation of classroom writing activities generally recognizes the importance of whole-class discussions, and sometimes presents analyses of this form of interaction (e.g., Englert et al., 1992), but has not developed an in-depth framework of interpretation, comparable to that proposed by Cobb et al. (1997) for the area of mathematics education.

1.2 Peer Interactions

Following the work by Doise, & Mugny (1984) and by Perret-Clermont (1979) on the role of sociocognitive conflict in conceptual change resulting from peer interaction, Gilly, Fraisse, & Roux (1988) developed a framework for analyzing a wider range of interactive dynamics in dyadic problem solving. Their research showed that students engage in four main forms of "co-elaboration" of their resolution procedures: (1) *agreement (acquiescement)*: one student makes a proposal, the other expresses agreement; (2) *co-construction*: each student makes one or more proposals that are complementary to proposals expressed by the other student; (3) *confrontation of different proposals* by the two students without explicit argumentation about their disagreement; (4) *contradictory confrontation with argumentation* about the reasons for disagreement. In summarizing their results, Gilly et al. (1988) emphasized the idea that sociocognitive conflict, as manifested in the fourth form of co-elaboration, is a powerful learning mechanism but is not the only source of cognitive progress; the first two forms of co-elaboration, which are collaborative rather than conflictual, also contribute to learning.

This perspective provides the foundation for our analysis of dyadic interactions in a situation of joint text revision. Although previous research on peer interaction in writing did not, to our knowledge, make direct use of this classification system, several studies raised similar preoccupations. Daiute, & Dalton (1988) showed that collaborative interaction during joint text production included moments of sociocognitive conflict but was largely constituted of implicit, unresolved negotiation, as well as many playful exchanges. A study by Rouiller (summarized in Allal, 2000) identified several features of productive dyadic interactions: In addition to confrontation of viewpoints, students verbalized the successive steps of co-constructed verifications and reminded each other of the need for joint monitoring of the revision process.

1.3 Revision as a Component of Learning to Write

Revision is generally considered to be a key component of learning to write. It is through revision that students can improve their initial drafts, using the tools and resources of social interaction available in the classroom. Revision also stimulates metacognitive reflection about writing (Rouiller, 2004). Since the processes of revision have been analyzed in detail elsewhere (Alamargot, & Chanquoy, 2001a), we will mention briefly only the main concepts used in the research reported here. As described by Witte (1985), revision can occur at any point in the writing process, namely, prior to drafting (pretextual revision of plans), during the drafting of a text (on-line revision), and after having completed a draft (deferred revision). Revision is a complex set of processes that include "reviewing" (reading and evaluating the adequacy of a text), "editing" (correcting spelling, grammar and punctuation errors, making local modifications and lexical substitutions), and "rewriting" (producing new text material that is added to the existing draft, deleting existing passages in a draft, replacing an existing passage by a newly written one, changing the location of a passage within a draft).[1] We use the term "revision" to refer to these processes whether they lead or do not lead to changes in the existing text; the term "transformations" designates the changes actually carried out (Allal, 2000). Transformations are an indicator that revision has occurred but the absence of transformations does not necessarily imply an absence of revision. When an author reads a passage, finds it satisfactory and leaves it unchanged, the revision process in nonetheless present. Learning to revise entails learning when and how to make transformations, as well as learning when not to make transformations.

2   AIMS OF OUR RESEARCH

Within the framework of a longitudinal study conducted in fifth and sixth-grade classrooms, we are attempting to understand the role of social mediation in text production and revision activities. The present chapter focuses on analyses of data collected in fifth grade regarding: (a) whole-class discussions that precede writing and revision activities and (b) dyadic interactions between students involved in joint revision of individually drafted texts. The principal aim of these analyses is to examine the relationships between the observed processes of social interaction and the characteristics of the texts produced (initial and revised drafts). This purpose is reflected in the following questions formulated for the two directions of analysis. Regarding *whole-class interactions*:

- To what extent are there variations in the teachers' interpretations of the proposed scenario for text production and revision? What types of practices emerge during the whole-class discussions?

---

[1] *We use the terms "reviewing," "editing," and "rewriting" as specified above, rather than as initially defined in the Hayes, & Flower (1980) model of writing. This means primarily that "editing" is not considered as an automatic process but as a process involving varying degrees of intentionality and reflection, particularly in the case of young writers who are still constructing basic language skills.*

- To what extent is there a relationship between the practices developed in each class and the characteristics of the texts produced and revised by the students?

Regarding *dyadic interactions* during the students' joint revision of their drafts:

- To what extent does the activity of joint revision lead to additional text transformations beyond those made individually by the author of each text?
- In what ways do the patterns of interactive co-elaboration of revision vary among dyads?
- How are these variations related to the types of transformations carried out during joint revision?
- To what extent do both members of a dyad benefit from the joint revision activity?
- To what extent are the dynamics of a dyad's interaction and the resulting transformations affected by the homogeneity of the two students' language skills?

The data available at this stage of our research concern two whole-class discussions (of approximately 40 and 20 minutes) observed in three fifth-grade classes and audio recordings of the interactions (approximately 30 minutes) of one dyad per class. On this basis, it is not possible to determine how each class functions as a writing community over the course of a school year or to identify the general parameters of each classroom's micro-culture, as is done in research conducted by Mottier Lopez (2001) in another context. The analyses presented here have an exploratory character, aimed at defining directions of investigation for future longitudinal analyses of the evolution of social mediation practices and of text transformations between fifth and sixth grades. These analyses provide, nevertheless, a first series of insights into the role of social mediation in the development of fifth-grade students' skills in text production and revision.

3   METHOD

3.1 Context

The research was conducted in three fifth-grade classes (students' age 10-11 years) in the public school system of the canton of Geneva. Two classes were in the same school and the third class in a nearby school. The schools are located in a suburban area where the distribution of the school population shows a slight under-representation of families of upper socioeconomic status (around 12% as compared to 18% in the canton as a whole). In the three classes participating in the study, the percentage of children with Swiss nationality varied widely, from only 36% in class 1, to 56% in class 2 (which is close to the canton average), to a much higher level of 75% in class 3. These differences will be taken into account in the interpretation of the patterns of whole-class interaction.

The three teachers participating in the study were volunteers who had already taken part in previous research studies and/or in teacher training activities. As experienced professionals having taught in elementary school classrooms for over 20 years, they have been involved in a wide range of professional development activities in the area of language instruction and in other areas. Their mastery of teaching skills is presumably higher than that of the overall teacher population of the canton of Geneva.

In each class, one student dyad was selected for audio recording. The teacher was asked to choose a dyad whose members were likely to interact in a productive way and to express themselves freely while being recorded. Our analyses of the dyadic interactions are therefore not representative of the dynamics that may occur when dyad members encounter difficulties of oral expression, or other factors which seriously impede productive exchanges.

3.2 Text Production and Revision Activity

Prior to the writing activity, the teacher was asked to form dyads composed of students who had different (but not widely disparate) achievement levels in French and who were expected to work well together from a social and affective viewpoint.

The activity proposed in each class was based on a situation entitled "The life of a star." The activity involved four main phases: (1) each dyad chose a star (in the area of music, sports, cinema, etc.) that both children admired; (2) each member of the dyad then wrote answers to questions from a journalist who was planning to write an article about the star; (3) the draft of the text was revised individually by each member of the dyad; (4) the two members of the dyad compared their texts to discover if they had imagined the star's life in similar or dissimilar ways; they then confronted their respective revisions and jointly completed the revision of each text.

The writing activity was designed with an authentic communication goal so as to encourage students to produce texts as interesting and as well written as possible. The text genre (a written, autobiographical interview) was familiar to the students since the magazines they read often present this type of interviews with stars who talk about their life, past and present. The questions asked by the journalist were expressed as follows:

- When and how did you begin to get involved in your activity?
- What success was the most outstanding of your career and why?
- What problems do you encounter as a star?
- What advantages do you have as a star?

The writing activity took place in class in three sessions. During the first session, the teacher grouped the students in dyads and each dyad made its choice of a star to write about. In the second session, the teacher introduced the writing activity following a scenario prepared by our research team. This scenario proposed collective discussion of ideas which could be included in the texts and the interactive composition of writing guidelines that the teacher wrote on the blackboard. The guidelines concerned text organization (e.g., choice of verb tense, use of chronological organizers, such as *then, later, finally*) and language conventions (spelling, punctuation). The students then produced their individual drafts responding to the journalist's questions. The third session began with a reminder by the teacher of the aims of text revision. The teacher also distributed an individual guide to be used during revision that reminded students to verify four key aspects of the texts: quantity and quality of information provided to the journalist, grammatical agreements, spelling, and homophones likely to appear in this type of text. In addition, the teacher led a collective, interactive revision of a sample sentence containing typical errors for the genre under consideration. The drafts were then revised by the two members of the dyad who marked their proposed transformations on two separate photocopies of the text.[2] These individual revisions were followed by a phase of confrontation and joint revision of each text.

4   RESULTS

The results presented here concern, firstly, the interactions between the teacher and the entire class during the phases preceding the drafting and the revision of the students' texts and, secondly, the interactions between the members of student dyads during the phase of confrontation and joint peer revision. In both cases, qualitative analyses of interactions are combined with quantitative indicators of text transformations in order to answer the research questions presented in section 2.

4.1   Whole-class Interactions

In each of the three classes, a member of our research team observed the whole-class interactions which took place before the students wrote their drafts and, the next day, before they carried out the individual and joint revisions of their texts. All of the indications that the teacher wrote on the blackboard were also recorded. On the basis of these observation notes, a narrative protocol was formulated for each class.

A qualitative analysis was conducted by extracting from the protocols the segments of whole-class interaction which were related to the following aspects of the activity:
- communication context and genre of the text to be written,
- text content and lexical choice,
- text organization and form,
- construction of the writing guidelines (written on the blackboard),
- use of the individual revision guide,
- use of reference materials,
- conception of revision.

---

[2] *Our study had several purposes, one of which was to compare the effects of revision order (author-peer vs. peer-author) on the transformations carried out by each author. Analysis of this variable showed that the order peer-author tended to increase several types of transformations (Allal, & Mottier Lopez, 2002). The recorded dyads in classes 1 and 2 carried out their individual revisions under the author-peer condition and the dyad in class 3 under the peer-author condition. We believe, however, that other factors linked to the dynamics and composition of the dyads, as described subsequently, had a much greater impact on the dyads revision activity than the factor of individual revision order, prior to the joint revision phase.*

For each of these categories, a distinction was made between interaction segments that reflect a process of co-construction, according to the criteria defined section 1.1, and those that do not meet these criteria.

Our presentation here will focus primarily on the variations among the three classes with respect to the practices emerging during the whole-class discussions. It will also seek to determine whether there is a relationship between the practices in each class and the characteristics of the texts produced and revised by the students, as shown in Table 1.

Our observations show that, in all three classes, the teachers follow the main steps of the scenario furnished by our research team; there are no major deviations with respect to the order of the proposed steps or their overall content. There are, however, important differences in the ways in which each teacher interprets the scenario and develops interactions with her class. Of the seven categories used to analyze whole-class interactions, the most salient differences occur for the following three categories.

1. The conception of revision. The teacher in class 2 does not introduce any interactive exchanges about the meaning of the word "revision." In class 1, the teacher talks about revision as a "critical look" at one's draft. She associates revision with exercises that the students have previously carried out, such as the classification of errors or the addition of elements (adjectives, relative clauses) to an existing sentence. In contrast, the teacher of class 3 expresses explicitly the idea that revision is not just correction of errors, but also rewriting. *"In addition, you can add words, make your text more interesting, ... delete words, ... improve the text, change what is written."* She adds a summary of these points to the guidelines on the blackboard. During the interactive revision of the sample sentence, she asks the students to give examples of new ideas that could be added after the sentence.

2. The elaboration of text content. The teachers of classes 1 and 2 lead a collective exchange in which the students propose examples of answers that could be given to each of the journalist's questions. The teacher of class 3 goes much further in the interactive co-constitution of potential text content. For question 3 she proceeds like the other teachers, but for questions 1, 2 and 4, she asks the students to discuss in small groups (3-4 members) what sorts of answers could be given; she then leads a whole-class discussion that draws on ideas developed in the small-group exchanges. This technique leads to very widespread student participation in the whole-group discussion.

3. The construction of the writing guidelines. All three teachers construct the guidelines with their class, but the construction procedures and outcomes are quite different. In class 1, the teacher asks focused questions about verb tense and organizers during the discussion of the text content and writes a few key words on the blackboard. The guidelines are formulated in generic terms *(organizers, spelling, punctuation, ...)*, without any examples. The teacher of class 2 marks some general categories (*verb tense, organizers, spelling,...*) on the blackboard before the students arrive. During the whole-class discussion, she has the students give examples that she writes in the appropriate category (e.g., *Organizers: when, then, since, in addition,...etc.*). In class 3, the teacher stimulates active student participation in the construction of the guidelines and asks for multiple examples to illustrate each guideline. She writes the guidelines in the order of the student suggestions and formulates them in terms of the author's writing/revising activity.

> *I think about spelling*
>
> *I think about punctuation*
>
> *I answer the questions*
>
> *I write in a logical order*
>
> *Organizers: before, since, after, then...*
>
> *I add, I delete, I improve the ideas*

The guidelines in class 3 are the only ones specifying that revision entails rewriting (adding, deleting, improving ideas), in addition to editing or error correction. Although the guidelines are expressed in holistic terms, the multiple examples given by the students, as well as the teacher's comments on the examples, constitute a source of contextualization with respect to the communication goal (*"Is that interesting for the readers to know?"*), the text genre (use of first person pronoun *"I"* or *"we"*), the adequacy of content (*"Is that an advantage or disadvantage?"*).

We will now examine the relationships between the qualitative analysis of the whole-class interactions, which we have just summarized, and the characteristics of the students' drafts and revised texts, as shown in Table 1.

Several aspects of the dynamics of the whole-class interactions appear to influence the students' text production and revision. In class 3, where the teacher encourages a broad conception of revision, we observe significantly more rewriting (adding and deleting of words) than in the other two classes. The revised texts in class 3 are significantly longer than those in classes 1 and 2 (a tendency already observed for the initial drafts, although the difference is not statistically significant). The initial drafts in class 3 also contain fewer incorrect words. This suggests that the students of this class are able to carry out more on-line revision during drafting, which could allow them to focus more attention on rewriting during the subsequent revision activities.

The data in Table 1 also shed light on the specificity of the whole-class discussion in class 2. The teacher of this class never talks about rewriting as an aim of revision but instead provides a very structured approach to editing and error correction. This observation coincides with the fact that the students in class 2 attain a significantly higher rate of error correction than in the other classes.

If we look at the density of transformations (i.e., the number of additions + deletions + modifications + corrections per 100 words), we see that this indicator is very similar for classes 2 and 3 (around 18 transformations/100 words), even though the approaches to revision are quite different (more editing in class 2, more rewriting in class 3). In class 1, on the other hand, the students show a much less active engagement in the process of revision.

Table 1. Characteristics of students' drafts and revised texts, means and standard deviations (in brackets) by class

Characteristics of students' texts	Class 1 (n = 14)		Class 2 (n = 18)		Class 3 (n = 16)	
Drafts						
Nb. words	150.0	(32.5)	144.7	(25.0)	160.2	(25.4)
Nb. incorrect words	26.8	(12.6)	27.0	(12.9)	19.9	(9.4)
% incorrect words*	18.3	(8.8)	18.9	(8.4)	12.7	(6.1)
Revised texts						
Nb. words*	151.1	(33.3)	149.8	(24.1)	173.8	(27.0)
Nb. words added and deleted*	1.9	(2.8)	11.6	(20.7)	20.8	(14.9)
Nb. words changed	11.2	(5.3)	14.8	(8.5)	10.9	(5.5)
Nb. errors corrected*	7.9	(3.9)	10.9	(5.6)	6.6	(4.3)
Density of transformations	8.7	(4.1)	18.5	(16.7)	18.1	(8.7)
% errors corrected	32.4	(13.7)	40.8	(11.7)	33.9	(14.0)

*Univariate analyses of variance show significant differences between the classes for these indicators ($p < .05$).

In the description of the student population (section 3.1), it was noted that the percentage of Swiss students varies substantially among the three classes. Analysis of variance was used to determine the effect of nationality (Swiss vs. non Swiss) on the students' achievement levels in French and on the main characteristics of their drafts. An interesting pattern emerges from the analyses. Being Swiss has a significant positive effect on students' grades in "French-communication"[3] and on the number of words in their drafts. The effect of nationality is not, however, significant for the students' grades in "French-basic skills" and for the number of errors in their initial drafts. This suggests that Swiss nationality is associated with greater language fluency but not with greater mastery of basic language skills. The degree of language fluency of the students in a class, as well as their capacity to "tune in" culturally to the teacher's expectations, could easily amplify the impact of the teacher's strategies for conducting whole-class discussions, thus contributing to the observed contrasts between classes 1 and 3. This tends globally to confirm the idea that classroom interactions are shaped by both teacher and student contributions.

---

[3] *Grades are attributed, on a scale of 1 to 6, for two areas of language instruction: French-communication (reading, oral and written expression) and French-basic skills (conjugation, grammar, spelling, vocabulary).*

4.2 Dyadic Interactions

Our presentation of the dyadic interactions recorded during the phase of joint revision takes into account several sources of information. We first present two types of information concerning the individual members of the dyads:

1) The student's achievement level in French, as reflected in first-term grades, for French-communication and for French-basic skills;
2) The characteristics of the initial draft of each student and the types of transformations carried out individually before the phase of joint revision (as described by the indicators in Table 1).

A third source of information concerns the characteristics of the transformations appearing in the final version of each text after the phase of joint revision. This analysis is based on a multidimensional coding system developed in previous research (see Allal, 2000 for a detailed presentation of definitions and criteria). In the present study, coding concerns the following dimensions: object of the transformation (lexical and grammatical aspects of spelling, text organization, semantics, other), type of operation used to make the transformation (addition, deleting, substitution, rearrangement), optional vs. conventional nature of the transformation, effect of the transformation on text quality (positive, negative, ambiguous).

In addition to the above sources of information, we examine the origin of the transformations in order to determine whether the dyadic interaction led to additional transformations beyond those already made by the author during the phase of individual revision. Table 2 presents the five possible origins of the transformations appearing in the final version of each author's text. Categories 1 and 2 concern the transformations carried out by the author that would exist in the final revised draft even if there were not a phase of dyadic peer interaction. Category 1 includes transformations made by the author but not by the peer during their respective revisions; category 2 includes author transformations that are identical to peer revisions, prior to the dyadic interaction. Categories 3, 4, and 5 concern transformations that occur as a result of author-peer interaction, including suggestions provided by the peer (category 3), modifications of the author's initial transformations that result from discussion with the peer (category 4), and new ideas of transformations that emerge during the dyadic confrontation (category 5). The total for categories 3, 4, and 5 reflect the additional transformations resulting from dyadic interaction in the phase of joint revision, beyond those already carried out by the author in the phase of individual revision (categories 1 and 2).

As shown in Table 2, the phase of joint revision leads to a substantial increase in transformations for both members of dyad 2. In dyads 1 and 3, on the other hand, joint revision increases transformations for one member of the dyad (Sonia, Samuel), but not for the other (Anne, Mourad).

Table 2. Origins of transformations in the texts of three dyads (absolute numbers)

Origins of transformations	Dyad 1		Dyad 2		Dyad 3	
	Anne	Sonia	Stefan	Tania	Samuel	Mourad
1. Author	6	2	0	11	8	6
2. Author (+ peer)	1	2	4	0	5	2
Total	7	4	15	11	13	8
3. Peer	0	4	10	7	8	0
4. Author + Discussion	0	1	1	3	2	0
5. Discussion	0	0	2	7	3	0
Total	0	5	13	17	13	0

A final, but most important source of data results from the qualitative analysis of the dynamics of peer interaction during joint revision. This analysis is essential to understand the processes underlying the transformations described in Table 2. For this purpose, we developed a coding scheme derived from previous research on peer interaction. The basic structure of our scheme is based on the categories of interactive co-elaboration defined by Gilly et al. (1988), but, for each category, we have defined sub-categories that take into account several complementary parameters proposed by Baker (2002) and by Kumpulainen, & Mutanen (1999). The recorded protocols of dyadic interactions are divided into sequences of exchanges pertaining to a same object. Sequences are coded and grouped so as to identify the recurrent patterns of interaction that characterize the dyad. The categories for classifying sequences are defined as follows:

- *Agreement*: one student makes a proposal concerning a given object, the other expresses agreement; successive sequences of agreement can be unilateral (only one student makes proposals), or alternating (proposals are made by both students, with some alternation, across different objects);
- *Co-construction*: with respect to a given object, each student makes proposal(s) that are complementary to proposal(s) expressed by the other student and the articulation of these proposals assures a process of joint construction;
- *Confrontation reflecting disagreement*: with respect to a given object, the students express divergent viewpoints; their disagreement can occur with or without argumentation by one or by both students, sequences of disagreement can lead or not lead to resolution of the divergence.

In addition, there are some sequences that begin with disagreement, but move into collaborative co-construction of the solution. In this case, the sequence receives a double code reflecting the two forms of interaction.

We will now draw together the different sources of information concerning the dyad recorded in each class.

Dyad 1

The dyad recorded in the first class is composed of two girls, Anne and Sonia, who chose to write about the singer Lorie. Their levels of scholastic achievement in French are different. Anne's grades in French-basic skills and in French-communication are higher (5, 6) than Sonia's (4, 4). Their drafts show several differences: somewhat surprisingly, Sonia's text is substantially longer (225 words) than Anne's (145 words) and contains a percentage of incorrect words (13 %) that is not a lot higher than the percentage in Anne's draft (11%). The number of incorrect words in Sonia's text is of course much larger than in Anne's (16 vs. 30 words).

When carrying out their individual revisions, neither of the authors adds or deletes words from her draft. This observation tends to show that they do not consider rewriting as part of the process of revision. With respect to error correction, Anne is considerably more efficient: she corrects 44% of the incorrect words in her draft, whereas Sonia corrects only 7 % of the errors in her draft. The transformations appearing in the final versions of both texts concern only spelling conventions (lexical and grammatical aspects) and are generally carried out by addition or deletion. The effect on text quality is always positive for Anne's draft, whereas for Sonia's draft, 5 transformations (out of 9) are improvements and the 4 others are not (i.e., errors remain after transformation or new errors are added).

During the phase of dyadic interaction and joint revision, less time is devoted to Anne's text, which is shorter and contains fewer errors, than to Sonia's text (approximately 8 minutes vs. 14 minutes). It is Anne who leads the discussion concerning her own text and who asks Sonia to propose her revisions. Two patterns emerge with respect to Sonia's proposals. In a small number of cases, they are identical to Anne's revisions and are quickly passed in review. In other, more numerous cases, they are incorrect and lead to disagreement with arguments expressed by both students, or sometimes only by Anne. In this second situation, Sonia does not insist very long and generally accepts Anne's refusal of her proposals. Anne sometimes suggests consulting the dictionary in order to determine whether Sonia's proposal is correct. These verifications allow her to ignore Sonia's proposals and retain her own initial revisions. The result, as shown in Table 2, is that no new transformations, beyond those already carried out by Anne, are made during the phase of joint revision.

With regard to the joint revision of Sonia's text, the author takes the lead in reviewing the transformations she has made. She describes the transformations with apparent self-confidence, except for a doubt expressed about one instance of spelling. Anne then takes over and begins reviewing her own transformations of Sonia's text. There is rapid agreement, with little discussion, in most cases, including two proposals by Anne which lead Sonia to modify her draft. When disagreement occurs between the two students, it generally concerns suggestions by Anne. The arguments expressed by the two students show different levels of language awareness: Sonia's arguments appeal to tacit knowledge of what she thinks "seems right:"

> *It appears to me better, in my head, with only one "l".*

In contrast, Anne uses linguistic terminology to explain and justify her viewpoint:

The acute "e" accent is wrong because there is a preposition before the verb "to sing."
[in reference to: "ils m'ont aidé à chanté"].

When Anne doesn't find an appropriate argument, she suggests consulting the dictionary. These verifications are carried out collaboratively and constitute the only sequences of co-constructed activity observed for this dyad.

Globally, the interactions in the phase of joint revision have a limited effect on Sonia's text: four transformations are added on Anne's suggestion; one additional transformation is the result of a discussion which leads to an incorrect modification of Sonia's initial correction (see Table 2).

This dyad shows continuous engagement in the task, with almost no "off-task" interactions during the joint revision phase. However, except for the collaborative use of the reference material, the interactive dynamics between the two students do not appear to be very satisfactory. Anne positions herself as the authority of the group; Sonia does not easily accept this authority, especially when modifications of her text are proposed by Anne. This relationship leads to episodes with underlying tensions and overt relational conflicts, which limit the positive effects of the joint revision.

Anne:	*No, that's not the present perfect. That, it's a preposition (...) So you're wrong. You have to cross out.*
Sonia:	*Yeah. OK. I crossed out* (slightly annoyed tone of voice).
Anne:	*But you haven't really done it!*
Sonia:	*...I don't know...*
Anne:	*But you have to cross out!*
Sonia:	*But I crossed out! Stop!* (deeply annoyed tone of voice).

However, Sonia does not in fact make the correction. Instead she crosses out a letter in the word having no relationship to the discussion with Anne. Even in cases of apparent agreement between the two students, Sonia does not always mark the transformation on her draft or fails to mark it correctly. For example, she agrees with Anne that there is only one *"f"* in the word *"professeur"* but only pretends to cross out the extra letter.

Relational tensions between Anne and Sonia appear throughout their interaction and probably explain why no new transformations are elaborated during the joint revision. It is likely that the difference in language skills between the two students (as shown by their grades) contributes to their relational difficulties, but it is also possible that other factors play a role (e.g., their social skills or self-images).

Dyad 2

The dyad recorded in the second class is composed of a girl, Tania, and a boy, Stefan, who chose to write about the master of ceremony of a TV game, Jean-Pierre Foucault. The students' levels of scholastic achievement are the same in both French-basic skills and French-communication (grade of 5). Their drafts are quite

After having revised both texts, the students check them rapidly once again using the revision guide (for example, they pass quickly in review the number of sentences in each paragraph to be sure there is enough information). It is worth noting, in addition, that this dyad does not engage in "off-task" interactions; during almost half an hour all their exchanges concern the revision task or the content of the texts.

Dyad 3

The dyad recorded in the third class is composed of two boys, Mourad and Samuel, who chose to write about the rap singer Eminem. Their level of scholastic achievement is the same in French-basic skills (grade of 4) but Samuel's grade in French-communication is slightly higher than Mourad's (5 vs. 4). Their drafts show several marked differences: Samuel's text is substantially longer (160 words) and contains a higher percentage of incorrect words (21%), as compared to that of Mourad (144 words of which 13% are incorrect).

During the phase of individual revision of their drafts, Samuel added 22 words to his text, while Mourad added only 11 words. With respect to error correction, the two students show an equivalent level of success: 33% of the incorrect words in each draft were corrected by the corresponding author. The transformations appearing in the final versions of both texts concern primarily spelling conventions (lexical and grammatical) but there are 2 transformations of text organization in Samuel's text and a semantic transformation, of varying length, in each student's text. Transformations of both texts are carried by addition and deletion, as well as by more complex operations of substitution. The effect on text quality is always positive for Mourad's text and is most often so for Samuel's text (88% of the transformations are improvements).

In the phase of dyadic exchange and joint revision, much less time is devoted to Mourad's text than to Samuel's text (approximately 3 minutes vs. 26 minutes). It is nevertheless Mourad who leads the discussion concerning both texts. For his own text, he passes rapidly in review the corrections he has already made and Samuel generally expresses his agreement. A single case of disagreement entails argumentation by both students about whether the word "audience" [*public*] is singular or plural. They do not, however, arrive at a shared solution and Mourad retains his own viewpoint. The result, as shown in Table 2, is that no new transformations, beyond those already carried out individually by Mourad, are made during the phase of joint revision.

Although Mourad leads most of the discussion concerning his partner's draft, Samuel seems quite satisfied that so much time is spent on his own text. The dyad's interactions can be classified in two main categories. The first includes sequences of agreement. These sequences are generally initiated by Mourad: He reviews the transformations he wrote on Samuel's text and the author generally expresses his agreement. Samuel points out, however, several transformations he made which do not appear in Mourad's revisions and Mourad agrees. The second category concerns disagreements. In most of these cases, Mourad's proposals are finally adopted and marked on Samuel's text with only a minimal amount of argumentation. There are, however, several cases of in-depth argumentation, including attempts to resolve the disagreement by checking in reference material.

In addition, there are two sequences where disagreement leads to collaborative co-construction of their on-going revision. One example occurs when the two students decide to employ a checking device they have previously learned to distinguish infinitive and past participle forms of verbs (*vendre vs. vendu*). They review systematically the verbs in Samuel's text using this device, expressing simultaneous verbalizations of some verifications and complementary collaborative exchanges about others. The second case of co-construction concerns the collaborative search for a word in the dictionary. In both cases, the object of their co-construction is a revision procedure, rather than new linguistic knowledge.

The overall result of these interactions is reflected in the origins of the transformations of Samuel's text (see Table 2). In addition to the 13 transformations he made initially, 13 more transformations are added during the dyad's discussion: 8 are proposed by Mourad, 2 result from a discussion that modifies Samuel's initial corrections and 3 are new transformations that emerge during the discussion.

This dyad makes relatively frequent use of reference materials (dictionary, grammar checklist, conjugation tables), but does not always find a solution to the problem being discussed. For example, when they disagree about the plural ending of a verb (Samuel has used incorrectly the noun inflection *"s"*; Mourad proposes the correct verb inflection *"nt"*), they look in the conjugation tables and in the dictionary and fail to find the solution, but Samuel finally accepts Mourad's proposal.

This dyad often engages in word play while they look in reference books or analyze an expression or word about which they have a doubt. For example, in one long sequence, they go back and forth between two problems: the confusion between homophones (its [*ses*] vs. it's [*c'est*]) and the spelling of a past participle (annoying [*embêtant*]):

Samuel:	(reading) *"it's very annoying."* But *"annoying"* is a verb...
Mourad:	*Yes, a verb in the simple past tense, uh, ...a present participle.*
Samuel:	*Yeah.*
Mourad:	*Yeah, but there is "very" in front.*
Samuel: *très..].*	*Yeah, that's right; it's not a verb "very"; I very, you very ... [je très, tu*
Mourad:	*Yes, I milk the cow. [Je trais la vache* - a play on words with the homophones "très" and "trais"].

The two boys in this dyad often exchange insults expressed in a playful way (*"you're zero," "what an idiot"*). They engage in frequent word games, including several "off-task" sequences inspired by words they come across while looking in the dictionary. In one such sequence, the word *"grenade"* is a starting point for a succession of references to Afghanistan, Ben Laden, the Red Cross, the Salvation Army. In general, their playful and imaginative mode of exchange seems to foster their task engagement rather than distracting them from the goal of text revision.

5   DISCUSSION

Our discussion of the findings of this study will focus, first, on the whole-class interactions, then on the dyadic interactions and, finally, on the possible relationships between these two forms of social mediation of writing and revision activities.

5.1   Whole-class Interactions

Our observations show that even when teachers follow an instructional scenario, such as the one provided in our research, they introduce a substantial range of variation in the way they implement the scenario. This is likely to be true, we think, for all complex instructional activities which imply a certain co-constitution of the activity's content and meaning through the interactions between teacher and students. It also shows the limits of attempts to influence teaching practice by the provision of curricular materials which will inevitably be interpreted in a variety of ways.

By confronting the observations of whole-class discussions in each class with the characteristics of the students' drafts and revisions, we discover two main differences among the classes. The first concerns the *conception of revision* formulated by the teacher-student interactions. In the scenario provided to the teachers, the proposed instructions evoked a broad view of revision that included rewriting (*"In addition to the correction of existing words, you can add sentences, new words, new ideas. You can also delete words..."*). In classes 1 and 2, however, the exchanges about revision tended to focus exclusively on editing (correction of errors and local improvements, such as enlarging a noun group with an adjective). In class 3, the teacher talked about revision as editing but also as rewriting and she had the students give examples of new ideas that could be added after the correction of the sample sentence. This difference in the whole-class interaction about revision was reflected in the transformations subsequently carried out: a significantly larger number of additions and deletions appeared in the texts of the students in class 3.

The second difference between the classes concerns the overall *dynamics* of the interactions. In all three classes, there was a considerable amount of interactive constitution of the task requirements. For the different aspects of text production and revision (generation of content, construction of the writing guidelines, revision of the sample sentence), the teacher encouraged the students to give a variety of suggestions and examples. In class 3, however, this process went much further in the direction of co-construction of shared knowledge and practices based on student contributions to the whole-class discussion. The teacher of this class had a greater tendency to encourage students to develop their suggestions and explain their proposals. She also fostered intensive student involvement in the construction of the writing guidelines and in the revision of the sample sentence. The consequences of this strategy are, nevertheless, not that easy to pinpoint. The teacher's approach apparently reinforced the students' use of rewriting, but did not necessarily lead to a larger overall amount of revision; the density of transformations (editing plus rewriting, expressed as changes per 100 words) was not higher than in class 2. It is noteworthy that the students of class 3 wrote longer drafts with a lower percentage of errors. The intensive, interactive preparation for writing the initial draft could account for this result in terms of an increased capacity to carry out on-line revision during drafting. In addition, factors linked to nationality, such as greater language fluency and the ability to tune in to the teacher's expectations, probably contributed to the differences between class 3 and the other classes.

5.2 Dyadic Interactions

Our analyses of the dyads' interactions and text transformations show that the sequence of activities – individual revision of each draft, followed by confrontation and joint revision of both texts – had a positive impact on student investment in revision in the sense of increasing the time spent on this task and the number of transformations carried out. In addition, the vast majority of the transformations that were made led to improvement of text quality. Although more extensive revision does not always mean higher text quality (Bereiter, & Scardamalia, 1987; Rijlaarsdam, Couzijn, & Van den Bergh, 2004), spending time on revision can be considered as an important (even necessary) condition for learning about writing and for learning, in the long run, how to make significant improvements in text production.

Our observations raise several questions that need to be further elucidated. A first question concerns the *composition of the dyads*. The literature on group composition (Webb, 1989) shows that learning is enhanced when there is heterogeneity, but a limited degree of heterogeneity, with respect to the relevant skills for accomplishing the task. Groups with members having high and middle-level skills, or middle and low-level skills generally perform better than groups with high heterogeneity (high and low-level skills) or than homogeneous groups. From this viewpoint, the tension and interpersonal conflict observed in the interactions of dyad 1 were probably caused by the large difference between Anne's and Sonia's written language skills. Sonia, the student with the weaker skills, did not want to accept the dissymmetry between her role as help-receiver and Anne's role of help-provider. Affective and social factors linked to self-esteem and identity may have intervened in this case as much, or more than cognitive factors. The productive, dynamic interactions of dyad 2, composed of two students with practically identical levels of language skill, do not at first seem to be consistent with the results of prior research showing the advantages of a certain (limited) heterogeneity. Once again, there may be affective and social dimensions of these students' interactive styles that provided just the right degree of heterogeneity to stimulate their exchanges in a positive way. Finally, in the case of dyad 3, it was quite obvious that social and affective factors were present in their jostling exchanges of insults and in their word games. This coincides with the research by Daiute, & Dalton (1988) and by Rouiller (2004) showing that an attitude of playfulness can stimulate students' engagement in writing and revision tasks. In summary, dyad composition needs to take into account a variety of factors – cognitive, affective, social – that can influence the way students carry out a joint activity. It is obviously impossible for teachers to find the right mix of these factors each time they ask students to do group work. It can therefore be useful to introduce whole-class discussions or other techniques (e.g., the scripted interaction formats proposed by O'Donnell, 1999) designed to improve students' collaborative skills.

A second question concerns the *relations between peer interactions and the outcomes of these interactions* observed in student productions. If we refer only to the transformations of the students' drafts, we could be tempted to conclude that the activity of joint revision was not beneficial for Anne (in dyad 1) and for Mourad (in dyad 3). In both cases, the moment of joint revision led to no increase in the number of transformations beyond those already produced by the author of the text. Analysis of the interactions showed, however, that Anne and Mourad were very actively engaged in reflection about revision throughout the exchanges with their respective partners. Anne verbalized explanations and justifications for carrying out, or not carrying out, different transformations of her own draft and of Sonia's text. Mourad was also very active in the lengthy discussion about Simon's text; he led a major portion of the review and was constantly involved in the search for solutions either by argumentation or by looking in reference materials. In terms of "time-on-task" (Berliner, 1979), Anne and Mourad worked steadily on revision during the dyadic interaction even though no new changes were introduced in their own drafts. To summarize: when new transformations occur during joint revision they are generally a sign of positive involvement in the revision process, but their absence does not preclude active investment in reflection about revision of one's own or one's partner's text. This observation coincides with Rijlaarsdam et al.'s (2004) affirmation that transformations are only the "tip of the iceberg" and do not convey fully the underlying process of revision.

With respect to the question "what are the *effects of the revision activities* carried out in our study on student learning?", we have no direct measures but we can formulate the following interpretations based on our observations:

- Sonia's text improved slightly (in terms of error correction), but she probably failed to learn anything about text revision; most of her energy was spent resisting, and occasionally giving in, to Anne's suggestions.
- The other five students all invested actively in the revision activity. A sizeable number of transformations (13-17) were added to three students' texts, but no new transformations were made on the remaining two drafts. It is nevertheless likely that all five of these students learned something from the dyadic interaction about the aims and the practice of revision.

Although their revision activity was largely focused on the area of spelling (lexical and grammatical aspects), they engaged in practices that elicited a range of language skills: comparison, justification, explanation, use of reference materials. It can be noted, moreover, that exchanges about some aspects of spelling entailed quite a complex coordination of several concepts, as illustrated by the *ta-t'a-tas* example discussed by Tania and Stefan. As other research has shown (Allal, 2004; Bétrix Köhler, 1995; Largy, Chanquoy, & Dédéyan, 2004), the mastery of French spelling, especially the grammatical aspects, the problems of homophony and the presence of unvoiced letters, remains a challenge for young writers throughout the elementary school years. The cognitive resources that the students have to invest to try and solve spelling problems may explain in part why they carry out relatively few transformations concerning text organization and semantics.

5.3 Relations between Whole-class and Dyadic Interactions

The theories of social mediation of learning lead us to expect relations between the representations and the practices constituted during whole-class discussions and the ways students function and interact in small-group situations of peer interaction. In the first part of our longitudinal study, concerning three fifth-grade classrooms, it was not, however, possible to go very far in analysis of these relations. Having recorded and transcribed the interactions of only one dyad per classroom, we are not able to determine whether the differences among the dyads are influenced by the differences among the whole-class discussions that took place in the three classes. In the second part of our study, extended to the same classes in sixth grade, two dyads per class are recorded so as to facilitate the search for influences of whole-class discussion on peer interaction.

We can mention, nevertheless, in conclusion, several hypotheses based on our fifth-grade observations to be explored further in the future. The whole-class discussions we observed included the construction of writing guidelines which could be used for both drafting and revising. Although we observed very few signs that the students explicitly referred to these guidelines, their drafts and the revisions they subsequently made were often highly congruent with the guidelines. This suggests that the interactive construction of the guidelines was more a means of structuring (mentally) the students' approach to writing and revision than a way of giving them a tool used operationally during these activities. This hypothesis could be investigated by comparing a situation in which guidelines are constructed and remain available during writing/revising with a situation in which guidelines are constructed but do not remain available during writing/revising.

A second area of investigation concerns what Newman et al. call the "indeterminacy" of teacher-student interactions. They state that in an instructional dialogue, "the participants act *as if* their understandings are the same" (Newman et al., 1989: 62) while they gradually advance in the negotiation of meaning. This could lead us to look at peer interactions, which follow whole-class discussions, in terms of the elements that reveal discontinuities in the process of co-construction of shared knowledge and practices. For example, although the conception of revision verbalized in class 3 apparently influenced the students' revisions (i.e., they carried out more rewriting than in the other classes), the interactions of the recorded dyad made very few references to text content and the process of transforming content; almost all the students' exchanges were focused on operations of editing. This may show that the initial impact of whole-class discussions is on cognitive processes (in the present case, how to write and revise a text) rather than on metacognitive reflection about these processes. By studying several cycles of whole-class and small-group peer interaction, it would be possible to determine how the co-construction of representations and practices may be extended toward shared metacognitive reflection about the social mediation of learning.

CO-CONSTRUCTING WRITING CONTEXTS IN CLASSROOMS

Scaffolding, Collaboration, and Asymmetries of Knowledge

TRIANTAFILLIA KOSTOULI

Aristotle University of Thessaloniki, Greece

Abstract. The aim of this chapter is to delineate a specific perspective to tracing children's developing understandings of genre writing; this is described as a socially-situated, intertextual process that is mediated by interaction. The discussion focuses on two writing conferences in two 5th grade Greek classrooms (characterized by a working-class and a middle-class student population, respectively), and attends to the discourse strategies used by participants, teachers and students, for the construction of the thematic and interactional structure of these units. The analysis provides evidence on the discourse processes through which children of different sociocultural groups *gain access* to literacy learning and considers how the learning contexts created through talk within each writing conference may in fact, limit or facilitate children's access to learning opportunities. To attain this aim, I proceed as follows: Rather than analyzing conference discourse through a pre-established set of descriptive categories, attention is directed to the way by which the teacher and the children navigate through discourse patterns and varying perspectives to reflect upon narrative texts and construct a "shared" pool of the criteria that make a school narrative text effective (according to communicative standards co-constructed within each classroom community). The questions I raise are the following: How does the teacher cooperate with the children and how do all participants manage to coordinate their varying resources and construct a "shared" perspective toward meaning making? Is this construction possible in all cases and on what factors does it depend? The conferences under investigation point to two distinct styles of knowledge construction, i.e., scaffolded versus collaborative learning. While, on the theoretical front, these two styles seem to be differentiated in rather clear-cut terms, the data reveal a more complicated picture. This chapter illustrates how scaffolding attempts made by the teacher are taken up (or rejected) by the students (and vice versa) and how, through these processes, the teacher and (some of) the students, as active participants in these classroom contexts, negotiate their divergent understandings of the nature and functions of writing.

Keywords: writing conferences, literacy events, reading events, genre learning, scaffolding, collaborative learning, re-contextualization, intertextuality

1   SOCIAL INTERACTION, DISCOURSE AND LITERACY LEARNING IN
                        CLASSROOM CONTEXTS

1.1 On the Negotiation of Meanings

Teaching and learning have been traditionally defined in very limited terms, as two
causally-related decontextualized processes which are, respectively, associated with
the presentation and acquisition of certain, "objectively-defined," pieces of information (see also Edwards, & Mercer, 1987; Edwards, & Westgate, 1994). Interestingly,
students' learning processes, though examined in classrooms, i.e., in contexts of
interaction where many different participants are involved, have been presented as
emerging independently of these interactions; the learning outcomes attested were
basically attributed to individual learner factors (ability, motivation, attention, etc.).
However, as shown by subsequent research developing out of Vygotsky's work
(1978), interactions may, in fact, play an important mediating role, facilitating some
students and excluding others from gaining access into learning opportunities
(Crabbe, 2003; Gutierrez, 1994; Lee, & Smagorinsky, 2000).

    Research proposals developed within several distinct fields (such as those of so-
ciocognitive psychology, interactional sociolinguistics, and educational ethnography) seem to converge on a different set of premises on situated language use; these
have redefined both the nature of school classrooms and classroom discourse (from
static descriptions through the I-R-E categories [Sinclair, & Coulthard, 1975] to the
co-construction of meanings in classroom emergent contexts) and the roles teachers
and students undertake in this dynamic process of meaning negotiation. According
to this approach, school classrooms, rather than seen as static contexts within which
curriculum is simply implemented and school knowledge is transmitted to students,
are re-interpreted as learning communities whose culture gets co-constructed by all
members, each contributing according to their own degree of expertise. The acquisition of school competencies is described as a locally-situated process (i.e., a process
which does not exist independently of specific classroom contexts) and an interac-
tively-accomplished one (mediated by the interactions co-constructed by teachers
and students around texts) (Cazden, 1986, 1988; Marshall, 1992; Mercer, 1995,
1996; Moll, 1990; Santa Barbara Classroom Discourse Group, 1995). Variously
referred to as activity types (Russell, 1995), writing events (Basso, 1974) or literacy
events (Barton, & Hamilton, 2000), these sequentially emergent interactive units
mediate learning processes. What draws researchers' interest are issues such as
these: Given the divergent perspectives that participants may bring to a given classroom, how are common understandings (i.e., intersubjectivity) attained? How is
classroom culture built through interaction?

    Apparently, the adoption of this perspective entails certain, quite important im-
plications with regard to the way one should analyze the teaching and learning of
literacy through the reading and writing events that are constructed in real classrooms. I single out two, which I summarize as follows. First, if written texts and the
negotiations around them are part of the many resources that contribute to the construction of the classroom culture, apparently, learning to write in classroom con-

texts can no longer be seen as a process that simply involves the appropriate use of lexico-grammatical forms. This should rather be seen (in line with Rogoff, 1990) as a collective accomplishment involving children's gradual "appropriation" of a certain, contextually-dependent set of semiotic resources (i.e., genres and interactional patterns) this community values as important for making and indeed for displaying meanings. The second issue concerns the intertextual construction of literacy practices. According to current sociolinguistic research, the classroom should be revisited as a dynamic, communicative environment, consisting of a series of evolving learning contexts (Bloom, & Egan-Robertson, 1993). Apparently, given intertextuality, any interactive unit, such as a reading event or a (teacher- vs. peer-led) writing conference can only be understood as a component in a series of units that interrelate toward developing a "shared" perspective towards classroom knowledge. But how do such units relate to each other and how do their linkages shape children's developing understandings of classroom literacy? Interestingly, although it is acknowledged that the interactive contexts constructed around written texts constitute important structures that mediate students' school-situated learning, information is still needed on the characteristics of talk that shape the texture of such events, and contribute to the construction of classroom literacy.

Integrating the classroom-situated learning of literacy practices (the Santa Barbara Classroom Discourse Group, 1995) with concepts developed in various strands of research on genre literacies (Johns, 2002), this chapter presents results from a program that has been implemented in a number of Greek primary schools with the aim to foster Greek children's genre writing. I suggest that, in unveiling the construction of classroom-based literacy practices, we need to proceed beyond the analysis of isolated units toward delineating a broader approach to genre writing as an intertextual process of meaning making. According to this approach, children's appropriation of school literacies is seen as a socially-situated and interactively-emergent process that is shaped both by the types of genres employed, the kinds of units constructed as well as by the kinds of intertextual linkages students and teachers establish as they negotiate new and redefine given notions around writing. These issues are explored through the analysis of two writing conferences, constructed along with a series of units in two elementary school classrooms.

1.2 Writing Conferences as Social Units: Basic Premises

The role of writing conferences has been widely recommended in process-oriented L1 and L2 writing pedagogy. With the shift of research attention to the social nature of writing, detailed analyses have been undertaken on how different social factors help students become more effective writers (see Ferris, & Hedgcock, 1998 for an overview); these include, among others, the comments made by teachers versus peers on fellow students' texts [Ferris, 1995a, 1995b, 1995c, 1997], and the types of feedback given (oral vs. written, content- vs. form-based) (see Paulus, 1999). The shift of attention to writing conferences (mainly used in reference to one-to-one teacher-student writing interactions around the student's text) has brought about a whole new perspective on the social factors that shape children's developing under-

level of competence. Following upon Wood et al. (1976), some of the strategies (cited in Hogan, & Pressley, 1997: 16) cited are the following: *Offering explanations, Inviting student participation, Verifying and clarifying student understanding, Modelling of desired behaviour (Making thinking visible), Modelling of question and comment generation, Inviting students to contribute clues.* These strategies are gradually removed as the child gains confidence and competence in performing various tasks.

Undoubtedly, building upon such a clear-cut catalogue of strategies, practical suggestions can be made with regard to the way teachers may help children appropriate new knowledge. I argue, however, that these proposals, by focusing on the local level (i.e., by singling out individual strategies), tend to align with more static and rather individualist approaches to literacy learning. In the discussion below I illustrate how scaffolding relates to classroom-situated literacy learning; classroom learning is seen as a collective accomplishment that arises out of the negotiation of various types of information proposed to the classroom conversational floor; these pieces of information, in terms of their status, may be given to some and new to other participants. Before I outline this proposal, certain clarifications are necessary.

Let me begin by addressing the relation between collaboration and scaffolding, which are differentiated in Gregory's scheme. To clarify their interaction, I accept that these strategies are part of the many different resources participants use for the construction of any interactive unit, including writing conferences. Collaboration pervades conversational interaction, with turn-taking being the basic expression of one's collaboration with his/her interlocutor (or responsivity to him/her). Can we, in light of this, proceed to suggest that collaboration necessarily leads to the construction of a "common" or "shared" perspective towards knowledge? Conversely, can scaffolding be seen as opposed to collaboration? As to be noted below, scaffolding cannot be implemented otherwise but through the collaborative interaction of all participants involved. To capture these nuances, I introduce a distinction between collaboration (the co-construction of an activity but not necessarily of new elements that would be added to the "common" perspective constructed towards knowledge) and the symmetrical co-construction of knowledge, taken to apply in cases where participants operate with similar agendas, goals and expectations on language use. The issue therefore is this: How is the co-construction of a common perspective attained in classrooms, given the asymmetries of knowledge and the divergent resources participants bring to classroom interactions (Linell, & Luckman, 1991; Markova, & Foppa, 1990, 1991)? Establishing certain pieces of information (which were previously assumed to be unknown to a community of learners) as part of the community "shared" or "common" knowledge is not a straightforward process but rather one that arises out of negotiations undertaken in a series of interactive units. How does this negotiation proceed?

To clarify this process, I suggest that relevant inquiry should be directed not toward cataloguing scaffolding strategies – or, more aptly, the strategies assumed in a given instance to scaffold children's development – but toward tracing the *scaffolding processes* co-constructed by participants; these would involve negotiations around the status of information introduced into the classroom negotiation floor. As to be indicated in the analysis below, scaffolding is *sequentially* created at various levels (within any unit, within an interaction, or a series of interactions) in a step-wise fashion; attention should therefore be directed to (1) the scaffolding attempts made by the teacher, (2) children's response patterns or types of uptake, and (3) teacher's re-application of new or already-used scaffolding strategies. This sequence captures the basic feature characterizing all types of conversational interaction – their dialogic nature. As proposed by Schegloff (1984), each utterance signals participants' understanding of the previous turn (and the information it conveys), while, at the same time, it contributes information which may (or may not) extend the "common" knowledge base built gradually through the interaction. However, steps 2 and 3 may not immediately follow step 1. Thus, a notion introduced by the teacher at the beginning of a unit may be initially rejected, only to be taken up by students and be appropriated at a later point within the same or in a subsequent interaction. According to the proposal I develop, scaffolding is situated at the following three levels:

- *Local level of scaffolding sequences*: This level captures the sequences through which participants respond to and shape each other's meanings.
- *Intra-textual/intra-unit scaffolding*: Themes and issues raised in a specific unit may be taken up and used as a scaffold for the development of other units in the same interactional event.
- *Global level or intertextual scaffolding*: Information which is presented in one interactive unit or literacy event may be singled out and used as the scaffold through which a new literacy event may be constructed.

I focus on the final level, which, however, cannot be presented as developing independently of the other two. All of these interrelate to define classroom learning.

The proposal I make on classroom learning is as follows: While learning has been, in general terms, described as a process during which participants integrate new information with given information (i.e., information which has been presented and negotiated in preceding turns, or units), I suggest that, given the collective nature characterizing the negotiation of information in classroom interactions, research interest should not focus on how new information gets attached to a static body of given information. After all, who regards this information as new and given? Is it the teacher or the students? And can we suggest that for all students the same piece of information constitutes given information? In light of this, then, it emerges that what should be of interest are the processes by which different participants, during the construction of any new unit (such as a writing conference) single out, and reach consensus on which pieces of information are indeed shared by all, which are shared to some degree, and which constitute new information. In other words, presenting the construction of any new unit (i.e., of a writing conference) as the process during which new information gets added to previously-introduced pieces of given information negates both the multiplicity of perspectives offered by many different participants (and which may or may not be taken up by the others), while it construes of given knowledge as a homogenous construct accessible to all different participants. I suggest that in the construction of any such unit, what is important is how participants redefine and re-negotiate information assumed to be given or shared by all classroom members, before new information gets attached to it.

Integrating these different lines of research into a unified perspective, I indicate that the way by which different pieces of information are used across classroom contexts is an indication of the learning processes that take place in classrooms.

2   DATA AND METHODOLOGY

2.1 Genre Literacy in the Greek Educational Context

The writing philosophy that prevails in the Greek primary school educational system builds on a specific approach, informed principally by the expressive framework. By focusing on the act of writing itself, text production is basically defined as the purpose-free expression of one's thoughts. In a typical unit within the nationally-enforced language-teaching syllabus, written text production as an activity tends to follow the presentation of a text (which is usually a literary text or a constructed, non-authentic piece of language) and the grammar section containing exercises to be completed. While the written texts produced (within the maximum allocated time of 15 minutes on a syllabus-set topic) are read by the teacher, any discussion and/or revision (in their form or meaning) are clearly discouraged.

Running against this line of research, a sizeable amount of language teaching research (Charalambopoulos, & Chatzisavidis, 1998; Kostouli, 2002) has put forward suggestions toward the implementation of a different writing pedagogy. Drawing from current sociocultural approaches to language learning and teaching (Leont'ev, 1981; Ochs, 1988; Vygotsky, 1978), these proposals basically suggest a re-conceptualization of writing as the genre-specific construal of meaning. The main premises capturing what Michaels (1987) refers to as the "writing system" (i.e., the set of overall values and implicit norms that shape children's orientation toward written text) acknowledge the following (see also Kostouli, 2002):

- Writing is situated within units which contain multiple-draft production and revision in interactive situations (such as writing conferences and peer interactions) in which text-shaping variables (such as communicative goals, audience and text structure) are negotiated.
- The selection of the materials to be used and the specifics of writing assignments (audience, topic, and genre) are determined by the teacher in co-operation with the children. No time limitations are imposed to children for completing their writing tasks.

2.2 Data

The data discussed in this chapter come from two school classrooms, one with a predominantly middle-class and one with a working-class student population (assessed through parents' level of education), within which this alternative philosophy has been implemented. To trace the paths or learning trajectories children followed within and across classrooms for the construction of classroom literacy, I took two steps. First: I identified the sequences of units constructed within each classroom during the course of the school year. Each sequence contains a number of literacy events and activities. Secondly, I traced the relationships between events within each sequence as well as the relationships between sequences. As indicated in the discussion below, it is through the analysis of the historically-situated meanings (i.e., the relationships established over-time between and among texts and contexts) that we may capture children's developing understandings of writing situated within the social life of the classroom. The data analyzed in this chapter are extracted from a sequence consisting of two reading events, and a whole-class writing conference; these units were co-constructed by two female teachers (who had attended courses for about two years regarding the implementation of this alternative philosophy) in cooperation with 5th grade (11-year old) children attending primary school in Thessaloniki, Greece. The sequence of units is as follows, in which each unit represents a two hour event:

Day 1	*Reading Event 1*	Interpretation of various, authentic narrative texts.
Day 2	*Reading Event 2*	Reading and analysis of various narrative texts and fairy tales.
Day 3	*Text Production*	Children produce a first draft of a narrative text: a fairy tale story or a report of a personal experience.
Day 4	*Writing Conference*	Discussion on some of the texts children produced.
Day 5	*Re-writing session*	Children are producing the second draft of their text.

2.2.1   Learning, Interaction and Re-contextualization Processes

Level 1: Reading and Writing Events as Mutually Contextualizing Units. While the relationship between reading and writing has been basically discussed in textual terms (for a recent survey, see Belcher, & Hirvela, 2001a), in the present case, attention is directed to reading and writing *events*; these are defined as sequentially emergent activities through which participants introduce and negotiate their (possibly different) perspectives on writing and narrative texts in particular; the perspectives offered for discussion need to interrelate, and contribute towards the version of the "shared knowledge" that is constructed in each classroom under investigation.

Building upon the social interactionist perspective (Luke, & Freebody, 1997), I suggest that the relationship between the information each interactive context introduces and the common perspective, i.e., the literacy culture, that is co-constructed in each classroom should be seen as mutually constitutive. I take that reading and writing events provide indices to the version of literacy the members of this specific classroom community co-construct. Alternatively, we may get access to the literacy culture constructed within each classroom community by attending to which parts of this sequentially developing perspective are displayed in the series of interactive units participants create.

The issues attended to are as follows: How do reading and writing events relate to each other? What notions of genre literacy are foregrounded through the reading events and writing conferences constructed? The analyses of the linkages established point to intertextuality – a notion which is analyzed as a social construction. The issue therefore is this: Are writing conferences contextualized (i.e., relate [in terms of their thematic and interactional structure] to proceeding (immediately or more distant) interactive units? Does each unit within the conference project new information which is taken up and explored in subsequent units?

Level 2: Units within the Conference. The writing conferences under examination consist of a number of thematic units and sub-units, within which participants discuss different narrative texts with the aim to construct a coherent structure of assessment criteria; through this set students may assess the communicative effectiveness of any narrative text. The first unit (or thematic field, as mentioned below) once completed, may function as a contextual resource of given information (i.e., as a "shared" pool of storytelling criteria) participants may draw upon and use in the subsequent unit for assessing the effectiveness of the second text. Does this happen? Analysis illustrates how this different level of contextualization occurs.

3   DATA ANALYSIS

3.1   The Thematic Structure of the Conferences

Following Erickson, & Schultz (1981), I refer to the writing conference as a whole as an *interactional occasion,* while the term *cycles of activity* (Dorr-Bremme, 1990) is retained for the instructional and non-instructional phases of such conversational event, characterized by specific participation frameworks, and pursuit of certain goals (De Fina, 1997; Gumperz, 1982a, 1982b). Although cycles of activity may help analysts delimit the units constituting this sequentially-emergent literacy event, still these units are too general to help us capture the details by which meaning is co-constructed. To this end, a lower-level unit was deemed necessary to be introduced; this is the thematic field. Following Maynard (1989), the thematic field (TF) is defined as an interactional structure consisting of a series of turns which refer to a specific topic (see Brown, & Yule [1983] on the difficulties in identifying topics); in this case, the thematic fields are delimited by the specific texts classroom members attend to. Figures 1 and 2 present the thematic structure of the writing conferences constructed in the working- and middle-class classrooms respectively.

Depth of thematic fields	Macro-propositions summarizing the themes discussed
Thematic Field 1	First story
11-42	General impression: short text, lack of action, lack of built-up agony, lack of details, abrupt ending
43-49	Characters (names)
50-65	Discussion on the fact that this text lacks built-up tension, agony, fantastic elements
66-74	Discussion on characters' emotions, details
75-91	Events, action
Thematic Field 2	Second story
92-117	Reading the story
118-137	General impression: problematic plot, beginning and ending, repetition, characters, punctuation problems
138-170	Plot, episodes
171-198	Agony, fantasy, characters, action, details, type of ending

Figure 1. The thematic structure of the writing conference in the working-class classroom

The discussion in this chapter focuses on the first two thematic fields constructed in each of the two conferences analyzed. As Figures 1 and 2 illustrate, each thematic field consists of smaller units. Ideally, each of these units would introduce a different frame or a new way of orienting towards the developing knowledge base of storytelling criteria. The content of each unit is summarized via a macro-proposition. A diagram is constructed which illustrates the underlying organizational structure of the conference. The issues raised are as follows:

- *On the thematic nature of writing conferences:* What are the criteria teachers and students negotiate and/or establish when reflecting upon narrative texts in these two classrooms? How do the participants use the information introduced in preceding reading events for the construction of the thematic structure in each of the writing conferences? How does knowledge about writing and story genres develop from unit to unit within each conference?

- *On the interactive dimension:* What role does the teacher and the children undertake in this continuously evolving process of meaning negotiation? Do the participants in both classrooms approach the conference with varying presuppositions and, if so, how do they manage to construct a specific perspective toward narrative texts?

- *On learning:* How can children's learning be traced over the units constructed? Attention is directed to the relationship between the thematic structure of the conference, the way its sequence of units unfolds, the Discourses or frames of orientation toward information each unit presents and the interactive roles participants undertake. Does the sequential construction of thematic development correlate with the progression from scaffolding to collaborative or independent participation? Through what strategies is this transition signalled?

Depth of thematic fields	Macro-propositions summarizing the themes discussed
Thematic Field 1	First story
24-41	General impression: the elements identified and which do not make the text effective are: character's inadequate presentation, vagueness, sentence structure
42-55	Identification of the genre this text instantiates
56-81	Story beginning, repetitions, vague points, characters, scenes
82-95	Discussion of the genre (is this text a story?)
96-157	Traditional vs. Contemporary stories: Points of differentiation
158-165	Applying the distinction to the text under examination. Is this text a traditional or a contemporary story?
165-218	Turning this text into a traditional story
Thematic Field 2	Second story
261-275	Reading the text
276-293	Discussion on the features that make the text vague
294-307	Details that should have and/or should not have been mentioned
308-312	Problems in the order of sentences
313-318	Reference to a related (in terms of its content) movie

Depth of thematic fields	Macro-propositions summarizing the themes discussed
319-330	Discussion on the details that are mentioned in this story
331-340	Emotions – feelings – vagueness
341-364	Plot – action
365-421	Identifying the genre – Proposals
422-430	Classroom management unit
431-519	Conclusive remarks – what we need to do to make the text better

Figure 2. The thematic structure of the writing conference in the middle-class classroom.

3.2 The Interactional Aspect: On Dominance

Usually, the interactional role assumed by the teacher versus the students in a conversational interaction is indicated through the realization of dominance, analyzed in terms of its quantitative, topical, and interactional dimensions. Quantitative dominance is assessed through the number of words spoken by each speaker (see Itakura, 2001) – this measure indicates the "space" each speaker occupies in the sequence of utterances created (Linell et al., 1988, cited in Itakura, 2001: 63).

Table 1 illustrates the patterns of teacher versus student participation in total and within each unit comprising the thematic structure of each writing conference. This detailed analysis is illustrative for helping us respond to an important question: How can we trace students' learning? Attending to the interactive trajectories participants followed when constructing storytelling criteria within and across units provide parts of the answer to this question.

A detailed analysis of the interactive patterns attested in Table 1 indicates a complicating picture that does not corroborate the linear progression we expected participants would follow in their negotiation of meanings, i.e., from scaffolding to the independent construction of thematic units. To summarize findings which are outlined below, in the working-class classroom the learning trajectory followed consisted of both textual and interactional dimensions; children made a transition from the use of fragmented criteria to the appropriation of a limited set of criteria introduced by the teacher. This transition was attained with the teacher's scaffolding role prevailing throughout all units. In the middle-class writing conference, students proceeded from the use of highly contextualized language to acknowledging and building upon the teacher's criteria situated on a highly advanced level, a secondary Discourse (Gee, 1990). The teacher and the students collaborated in a variety of ways, with children controlling the interaction in some units to other cases in which the teacher assumed a more dominating role.

Table 1. Dimensions of quantitative dominance in the two classrooms for two stories: Number of turns per unit, and percentage of students' turns

	WORKING-CLASS CLASSROOM				
	STORY 1			STORY 2	
UNITS	No. Turns	% Student turns	UNITS	No. Turns	% Student turns
1^α	192	40.10	1^β	261	22.60
2^α	94	12.77	2^β	119	26.05
3^α	78	30.77	3^β	561	3.19
4^α	67	17.91	4^β	285	15.79
5^α	261	24.90			
TOTAL	692	27.46	TOTAL	1226	17.05

	MIDDLE-CLASS CLASSROOM				
	STORY 1			STORY 2	
UNITS	No. Turns	% Student turns	UNITS	No. Turns	% Student turns
1^α	245	77.96	1^β	261	13.03
2^α	83	46.99	2^β	131	67.94
3^α	263	83.27	3^β	160	59.38
4^α	150	30.67	4^β	81	91.36
5^α	570	40.18	5^β	54	44.44
6^α	69	27.54	6^β	103	42.72
7^α	437	53.09	7^β	77	71.43
			8^β	173	66.47
			9^β	491	53.97
			10^β	111	17.12
			11^β	776	46.26
TOTAL	1817	53.66		2418	48.51

Textual Units, Interactive Patterns and Learning Processes: Comparing the interactive construction of teacher and student roles across the two writing conferences in question indicates that the two writing conferences point to distinct styles of knowledge construction. One would suggest that the writing conference in the working-class classroom points towards an asymmetrical interaction, with the teacher dominating over the children, (72.5% over 27.4%, respectively for thematic field 1 and 84.2% over 15.1% in thematic field 2), while in the other conference, the teacher and the children seem to cooperate in the co-construction of storytelling criteria. The data are as follows. In thematic field 1: teacher: 46.3% compared to 53.6% of the children and in thematic field 2: teacher: 51.4%, students: 48.5%. Further analysis of the data suggested that certain qualifications had to be made.

Firstly: A detailed analysis of the students' interactive role indicated that the children cannot be treated as a collective. Counting the number of children who participated within each thematic field and unit yielded a very interesting picture. In both classrooms, a similar pattern emerged; some children emerged from their interactive behaviour as the central partners, others were more peripheral participants, and others played the role of the hearers. In the working-class classroom, Tasos (uttering a total of 197 words [60.9%]), and Angeline (uttering 88 words [27,2%]), emerged as the dominant participants, followed by four other students who contributed to the discussion and two others who contributed minimally (just a few words) to the discussion. In the second classroom, more children participated in the construction of meanings. In the middle-class classroom, 4 children were identified as the central participants (Bill [383 words, 32.6%], Angeliki [222 words, 18.9%], Maria [204 words, 17.3%], and Alexander [99 words, 8.4%]), 3 as peripheral participants (between 2-3%) and the rest (12 students) as overhearers.

It seems therefore that, depending upon children's interactive role, within each writing conference two different learning contexts were created, one constructed for and by the central participants and the other by the over-hearers. However, the contributions of the central participants across the two classrooms were different.

As to be shown, with regard to the working-class classroom, central participants consistently build upon the scaffold provided by the teacher. Given the interdependent relationship of participants' interactional styles, it is worth asking if children's subordinate role emanates out of the dominant role the teacher undertakes and imposes on them right from the beginning or whether this dominant role was assumed by the teacher due to the difficulty children faced in creating and sustaining a coherent thread in their discussion of texts. In the middle-class, a different picture appears, with the teacher emerging as a more dominant participant as the interaction progressed. How can we account for this development? The notion of intertextuality helps us move beyond a simple presentation of the participants' strategies to outline the factors influencing participants' interactive role in the construction of the two writing conferences under examination.

3.3 On the Intertextual Construction of Meaning: Retrospective and Prospective Contextualization Processes

As noted, research conducted on (mostly L2) writing conferences tends to analyze these units as autonomous, i.e., as units which are developed and completed within a specific lesson, with no attention given to the resources (prior knowledge, interactional history etc.) children and teachers draw upon and bring to the construction of the writing conference in question.

In this study, writing conferences in both classrooms are situated within a series of units which were constructed as steps in attaining a general goal: to establish a certain school-valued perspective of reflecting and talking about narrative texts. It was intended that the two reading events and the writing conference would develop as mutually contextualizing units; information presented in one such interactive context is expected to be taken up, negotiated and get extended in subsequent ones. But has this goal been realized in the two classrooms under investigation? To trace whether a thread of "shared meanings" is constructed over time in both classrooms, I focus on each writing conference and attend to the kinds of criteria co-constructed in the first thematic field, which is expected to be built in both a prospective and a retrospective manner – this unit is expected to display students' (but also the teacher's as well) current understandings, partial understandings or misunderstandings of the pieces of information introduced in preceding units, while it would act as a structure providing new information to which the subsequent units of the same conference will relate and expand.

In light of the above, then, several questions arise: What are the kinds of information participants use for the construction of storytelling criteria? Do they draw upon and to what extent do they exploit notions introduced in preceding units and events? What role does the teacher versus the students play in this process? Are there differences in the way children from the two sociocultural groups re-contextualized previously introduced information? Apparently, we cannot simply assume that children appropriated all notions introduced in one interactive unit and employed them immediately for the construction of the next. While reading events may function as the co-text participants may draw from, proceeding beyond static construals of the co-text, I argue in line with Korolija (1998) and Korolija, & Linell, 1996) that the preceding reading event should not be seen as a ready-made and always accessible body of given information that interlocutors use for the construction of any new current unit. Reading events as cotexts should rather be interpreted as providing participants with a source of past "jointly constructed" resources that participants may use for the construction of current or future literacy events. It is necessary therefore that we attend to the elements the participants themselves and indeed the children "selected and displayed" (Schegloff, 1984) in their comments, i.e., which aspects of the cotext they are making relevant for the construction of any current thematic unit. The criteria presented in each reading event, and the participants (teacher versus students) who made direct and indirect reference to these criteria are presented in Tables 2 and 3.

Table 2. The criteria singled out in Reading events 1 and 2 in the working-class classroom

| | Reading event 1 | | | | Reading event 2 | | | |
| | Teacher | | Students | | Teacher | | Students | |
Narrative criteria	no.	%	no.	%	no.	%	no.	%
Plot (direct)	0	0	0	0	0	0	0	0
Characters	0	0	0	0	0	0	3	4.8
Protagonist	0	0	0	0	10	16.6	7	11.2
Emotions (indirect reference)	9	42.8	8	80	25	41.6	31	50
Events (direct reference)	0	0	0	0	6	10	3	4.8
Beginning-ending (direct)	12	57.1	2	20	19	31.6	18	29.03
Message (direct)	0	0	0	0	0	0	0	0

Interestingly, while it is expected that participants in the middle-class classroom (compared to the working-class children) would be more actively involved in the social construction of intertextuality, drawing upon, redefining and extending the criteria depicted in Table 3, this pattern is not noted. Furthermore, differences were noted with regard to the intertextual connections each teacher made; the teacher in the working-class classroom made frequent and direct references to a number of criteria, such as plot and feelings, which as we can see from Table 2, they were actually not introduced directly or were mentioned indirectly in previous units. Interestingly, it was only at the very end of the conference that the middle-class teacher proceeded to make some intertextual projections to the criteria presented in Table 3. These differences in the role of teachers is instrumental since they too contribute to the construction of the two distinct learning contexts suggested earlier. What effect does the teacher's role have on students' genre learning? As to be indicated below, the different routes to literacy learning established in these classrooms are, in fact, shaped by the depth and extent of intertextual connections made between the various different units constructed within each classroom.

Table 3. The criteria singled out in Reading events 1 and 2 in the middle-class classroom

	Reading event 1				Reading event 2			
	Teacher		Students		Teacher		Students	
Narrative criteria	no.	%	no.	%	no.	%	no.	%
Plot (direct reference)	3	6.66	0	0	0	0	0	0
Characters	12	26.6	3	12	2	16.6	0	0
Protagonist	1	8.3	3	12	0	0	0	0
Emotions (indirect reference)	15	33.3	18	72	8	44.4	9	56.2
Events (direct reference)	5	11.1	0	0	0	0	0	0
Beginning- ending (direct reference)	3	6.66	6	24	8	44.4	7	43.7
Message (direct refrence)	6	13.3	0	0	0	0	0	0

3.3.1   Co-constructing the Criteria

A detailed analysis of the information negotiated within and across units indicated that the working-class central participants, firstly, faced considerable difficulty at exploiting previously-introduced information for the construction of the conference, and, secondly, at sustaining, through interaction, a coherent and constantly accumulating thread of given and new information on the topic focused upon, without the scaffold provided by the teacher. Consider (1), illustrating the ways thematic field 1 is constructed; in both classrooms, this field is initiated with an open question by the teacher: *"What do you think about this text?"*

Excerpt (1)
1. Student: short/
2. Teacher: One by one (.) I want you to raise your hands ((xx)) anyway

3. Stavros: Aaa they were very short (.) and it did not have ((xx) agony
4. Teacher. very good/ anyone else/ tell us Dimitri/
5. Dimitris: Aaa (.) just as Stavros said it was very short (.) and not very big =
6. Teacher: yes it was short and small this is the same thing exactly it tell us (.) Angeline
7. Angeline: it does not tell us how he found them =
8. Teacher: =Great
9. Angeline: = if something happened to him
10. Teacher: all these things are missing. (.) they are not there it is important/ tell us Vangelis.

(a sequence follows in which Vangelis explains that this text reminds him of the movie "Home alone")

11. Tasos: it does not have all the details it should have had
12. Teacher: great/ it does not have ((extended reference to themes), right?
13. Tasos: and he ends the story very quickly (.) he does not explain us how he got lost/
14. Teacher: great/
15. Tasos: what happened and he got lost/
  ....
16. Teacher: ... by the way about the story characters can you tell me something about the characters in here
17. Student: it has none (.) only the kid (.) and not his name

In the above excerpt, a distinction needs to be drawn between *content-oriented* turns (turns which contribute some new pieces of information to the discourse or the knowledge base created thus far) and *non-content oriented* turns (turns which either repeat information or perform the task of discourse management). Children offer new information (often in mono-syllabic words) in some turns (1, 3, 7, 9 11, 13, 15, 17) or present criteria in a very contextualized manner (turns 7, 9 and 11, 13). While both Angeline and Tasos point to the notion of plot, they do not have the metalanguage to explain (mainly to the other children who are overhearers) what they mean.

In general, it seems that in constructing the various units within the first thematic field, the teacher and the children operated with distinct perspectives on how to reflect upon a narrative text and comment on its effectiveness. Interestingly, a number of turns within this thematic field contain children's utterances which repeat previously-introduced pieces of information or contain clarification requests issued by the teacher (they are series of turns in which the teacher tries to understand children's points or illustrate that what the children said is not directly relevant to the topic in hand). Indeed, partial understanding is explicitly acknowledged by the teacher at the end of the thematic field, when she asked the question "*so what is a plot? Have we all understood what a plot is*? and received incorrect replies and silence.

(2) is an illustrative example of the difficulties the teacher and the working-class central participants faced for understanding each other's perspectives. The teacher begins by foregrounding the theme: "*tell me what I should write down from the comments we have made so far. Tell me about the action*"; this way, the teacher introduces new information via a notion – action – that has not been used in the previous units.

Excerpt (2)
1. Chris: they are short.
2. Teacher: they are what?
3. Chris: short

4. Teacher: they are short so in other words they do not have (.) short plot I should write short plot anything else tell me
5. Achilles: it does not have agony
6. Teacher: it does not have agony
7. Peer: well done Achilles
8. Teacher: by the way can you tell me (something) about the emotions the narrator presents us in this
9. Student. None
10. Stavros: It does not have fantasy.
11. Teacher: No fantasy right.
12. Angeline: It does not tell us if something happened to him since he was alone
13. Teacher: great. This is in the plot (9.) by the way about the emotions

In excerpt (2), the teacher begins by suggesting that the children summarize the information or the knowledge they have gradually built during the construction of preceding units. The teacher summarizes (in turn 4) the first (inadequate according to her standards) child contribution to the conversation, by subsuming it under the category of the "*short plot*", i.e., under a term that constitutes new, unfamiliar information to the children (see Table 3). The unfamiliar status of this piece of information is signalled by the children, who do not take it up and develop it further. After another child's contribution to the conversational floor, the teacher returns to foregrounding another criterion, the criterion of narrative evaluation, realized through characters' feelings. The children provide a monosyllabic answer. It is interesting to note that even this criterion, which was discussed in preceding reading events, and should constitute given information for the children, is not taken up by the children neither is it elaborated. Thus, while through the strategies employed (summarizing previous turns, questions, etc.), the teacher tries to help children move into contexts for practicing advanced literacy skills, for this group of children making the shift from the type of discourse they are used to be operating with (analyzing narratives through everyday terms) to notions belonging to a secondary Discourse, (to use Gee's (1990, 2001) terminology) requires a great deal of abstraction – an element of advanced literacy.

Situating a set of utterances under the category of plot involves understanding both the nature of this notion and being able to trace its instantiations in various texts. The teacher in her turns makes an attempt to scaffold children's transition from common, everyday understandings of stories to a new, school-valued way of reflecting upon these texts. The two participants, however, seem to operate with largely distinct perspectives on how to comment upon narrative texts. What kinds of information do these children use when re-writing their texts to make them effective according to these criteria? This is an issue I will return to in the conclusion.

In light of the above, we may now attend to the patterns of knowledge construction noted in the middle-class classroom, where children were active participants in the construction of the sub-units defining the first thematic field.

Excerpt (3)
1. Eftixia: Miss, I did not like it that much/ ((because)) it does not have any names and it does not have many full stops/ in other words in some sentences (xx))
2. Teacher: Yes/
3. Eftixia: with different topics
4. Teacher: with different topics/ yes go on Maria/

5. Maria: Miss (.) in the first sentence it says (.) one day when to the roof of my apartment building I saw a cat who was miaowing and my mother called me and I could get near to her/I mean Miss he could have written
6. Other student: ((xx))
7. Teacher: Go on (.) first Maria talks first and then
8. Maria: He could have written that he did something with the cat and then his mother called him and he could not get nearer to it in other words that he tried to get near the cat but then his mother called him and he could not get any closer to her
9. Student: ((xx))
10. Teacher: So its meaning? As a result the meaning (.) it is not clear/ go on Anggeliki/ ((Once)) yes (.) and kids speak louder ((xx))
11. Aggeliki. Miss I did not like it because what he wants to say he puts it in one big sentence/
12. Teacher: in one big sentence/
13. Aggeliki. Yes (.) he wants to say something without describing it he puts it in one big sentence/ it is as if he writes a summary

(3) is an excerpt of Thematic field 1 in the conference constructed by some of the central participants in the middle-class classroom; thematic field 1 consists of 9 units. (3) captures a part of the first subunit, which is collaboratively built by 4 girls, with the teacher inserting positive evaluative comments and performing echo-repetitions. The children cite excerpts from the text and discuss them – a strategy within which the working-class children in the other classroom were not familiar. This group of dominant middle-class children seems to comment on the text on the basis of a certain set of criteria which are understood and shared by the central participant group but which, however, are left implicit for the other children.

In general, throughout thematic field 1, the central participants assume a dominant role; this is indicated even more clearly at a later point by the way children responded to an attempt made by the teacher to initiate a new thematic unit by suggesting this: *how would we characterize this text*? This attempt at a new topic initiation is aborted by the teacher herself after just 4 unsuccessful turns to establish it as a new theme. The children dismiss this question, carrying on their discussion along the previously-invoked theme, and presenting their justifications on what they liked in the text under analysis. 6 subunits are created, all being initiated by the children. The rest of the children collaborate, performing various functions, such as "adding information," "drawing conclusions," "agreeing with yes-no answers." The teacher's interactive role is limited to echo repetitions, a strategy which basically re-affirms children's common-sense ways of reflecting upon the text under examination and the criteria proposed for assessing its effectiveness. By assuming a subordinate role which basically ratified children's implicitly-conveyed set of storytelling criteria, the teacher reinforced the division between central and peripheral participants; in fact, the teacher made no attempt to help peripheral participants join the conversation, contribute to it or (just) make sure that the conversation carried out is clear and understood by all students. Interestingly, as a result of this pattern, the learning routes middle- and working-class children followed were quite distinct; in the working-class classroom, through the scaffolding role undertaken by the teacher, a pool of storytelling criteria – small and fragmented though it may be – can be identified (see 3.4. below); in contrast, middle-class children's consistent use of a highly contextualized way for describing texts has not led to the identification of any such small but clear-cut set of terms the rest of the children could draw upon.

A more detailed analysis of the teacher's versus the students' role in the middle-class classroom indicates considerable variation from one thematic field to the next and indeed from unit to the next within the same thematic field. Consider units 1a, 4a, 6a (10b is an non-instructional unit, concerned with various issues of classroom management) in which the teacher undertakes a very dominating role. How is this variation to be accounted for? As (4) illustrates, this group of children too (i.e., the central participants) faced considerable difficulties at appropriating genre-specific terms and inserting them into their discourse. This is where the teacher assumed a more dominating role.

Excerpt (4)
1. Teacher: Good so we say that it does not have plot the plot is all the things you said in other words the fact that he did not have any money (.) the fact that you mentioned that he did not have any money how he got on the bus how he got off the bus in other words what does this text not have?
2. Student: Rhythm
3. Student: Fantasy
4. Teacher: In other words the =
5. Bill: = agony
6. Teacher: = agony in other words the character does not meet here what in the previous text
7. Bill: difficulties
8. Teacher: difficulties so here what does this text not have?
9. Student: adventure
10. Teacher: difficulties or obstacles but does he tell us how the kid is feeling?
11. Student: no

3.4 Tracing Learning

Although the data reveal interesting similarities and differences in the texture of the writing conferences constructed across the two classrooms, the data cannot provide us with information on the learning processes that take place through these units. To account for this, and in light of the patterns noted, the following set of questions need to be raised. With regard to the working-class classroom: What are the effects of teacher's scaffolding attempts in the working-class classroom? On the middle-class conference: How can we account for the increasingly dominant role the teacher undertook in the middle-class classroom?

As noted, the effects of scaffolding attempts made by a teacher can be attended if we trace the way the children took up (if they did) notions introduced in preceding units. No single strategy – such as reformulations, questions, open questions or use of re-cycling units – may be effective for scaffolding children's understandings of knowledge – of narrative criteria in this case; its significance can only be appreciated if examined on the intertextual level. Consider the case under examination: Given that the information presented or negotiated in thematic unit 1 is re-introduced in thematic unit 2 and the writing conference and reading events form sequential components in an intertextually created web of meaning-making, it is reasonable to expect that children's gradual appropriation of the teacher's secondary Discourse notions would be increasingly reflected on both the interactional and the textual level.

The clarify the kinds of knowledge built through the retrospective and prospective intertextual linkages established by the teacher and the students, I outlined the types of information negotiated by participants throughout the thematic units constructed. To make this differentiation, I drew upon Gee and distinguished between turns conveying information in everyday commonsense ways or in primary Discourse terms (types of discourses children are socialized in during their preschool years and pointing to everyday experiences) or in a secondary Discourse terms (incorporating genre-specific metalanguage). Tables 4 and 5 illustrates the different perspectives by which the teacher and the children operated in each classroom.

Table 4. The types of information conveyed in the working-class classroom conference

Types of information	Participants' turns	
Text 1	Teacher	Students
Theme introduction. Primary discourse	4	-
Theme introduction. Secondary discourse	4	-
Theme development. Primary discourse	51	32
Theme development. Secondary discourse	9	1
Text 2		
Theme Introduction. Primary discourse	3	-
Theme Introduction. Secondary discourse	2	-
Theme development. Primary discourse	64	23
Theme development Secondary discourse	5	10

On the basis of the textual and interactional evidence attested thus far, we may conclude that the teacher in the working-class classroom played a very dominating role with the intention to help children appropriate a genre-specific set of criteria for commenting upon texts. What did students learn? What specific criteria did they appropriate? The specific criteria introduced and carried across thematic fields are presented in table 5.

Interestingly, this group of working–class children failed to appropriate certain certain criteria (plot, action), despite the teacher's frequent intertextual references. Their appropriation would require a more extended period. The criteria appropriated (characters, character's names, number of characters mentioned) do not diverge from notions children themselves employ in their everyday discourse when referring to story characters.

The picture is different in the middle-class classroom (see Table 6) in which we have no indication of children's appropriation processes, since the teacher started using genre-specific criteria only at the end of the conference.

Table 5: Criteria generated during writing conference in the working-class classroom

Criteria mentioned by the children	Criteria introduced through various teacher strategies (mostly questions)
Thematic field 1	
The text is.... Short, no agony, short and brief, context-bound attempt to define a criterion (twice occurring), the text has no details, it ends abruptly, it does not contain fantastic elements, no details[1], no agony, no fantasy, no adventure.	What are the characters in the story, what are the characters' names, characters' feelings/reactions, plot, events.
Thematic field 2	
No typical introduction, no punctuation, no happy ending, repeated reference to self, repetition, no fantasy, no agony, no adventure, no reference to a lot of characters, no character names, context-dependent attempt to define a criterion (character's feelings, emotions), characters, character names	(re-introduction of) plot, (introduction of) obstacles as an essential constituent of plot.

Table 6. The types of information conveyed in the middle-class classroom conference

Types of Information	Participants' turns	
Text 1	Teacher	Students
Theme Introduction. Primary discourse	3	9
Theme introduction. Secondary Discourse	-	-
Theme development. Primary Discourse	45	30
Theme development. Secondary Discourse	-	-
Text 2		
Theme Introduction. Primary discourse	4	-
Theme introduction. Secondary discourse	2	-
Theme development. Primary discourse	161	127
Theme development. Secondary discourse	6	1

4   CONCLUSION

While writing conferences have been analyzed in a number of ways, the aim of this chapter was to illustrate that these should be revisited as socially constructed events

---

[1] *The term 'no details' is used by the children as a general criterion, although in a very extended discussion, the notion of details had been made specific: details refer to plot, events, number of characters involved in the story.*

which are created anew each time, depending upon the participants involved and the difficulties facing each time. While in both classrooms under investigation, a common set of texts was employed and a common goal was posited, the reading and writing events constructed were distinct, reflecting participants' own difficulties with written language and their own levels of academic achievement. The analysis of the gradual way by which the thematic and interactional structure developed indicated that the co-construction of a writing conference is a demanding process which involves the coordination of many different perspectives toward a common thread. By attending to the way participants in each classroom community negotiated the interactive and thematic structures established, we were able to attend to the construction of different learning contexts – one by the teacher and the dominant group and the other by the overhearers. The reasons for the creation of these learning contexts were different. While in the middle-class classroom, the teacher reinforces the perspectives of the dominant group of children, excluding and not bringing into the conversational floor the rest of the children, in the other classroom, the primary learning context is built by those children who were able to pick up and respond to – though unsuccessfully most of the time – the teacher's perspective. Interestingly, the teacher herself realizes this divergence and the different learning contexts created and she gradually (mainly in the second thematic field) lowered her demands and introduced in the discussion terms and notions familiar to the children's discourse.

Further research would need to address in detail the way by which children negotiated through their language their relationships, claimed a position in the units constructed and asserted their power. What seems to arise, however, from the above analysis is that clear-cut and crude demarcations between middle-class versus working-class children may not always be very helpful in accounting for interactional differences in classroom contexts. Mechanisms within the classroom help create further distinctions which need to be explored in subsequent papers. Why is it that some children were more dominant than others? What are the factors mediating this process? Further analyses of classroom situated processes would need to indicate how writers construct their gendered identities through their participation in contexts for negotiating writing.

A second point worth raising concerns the analyses and the many routes we need to follow (in light of evidence such as the one attested in this chapter) for tracing the relationship between the conference talk and the revisions children introduce in their texts. As the data revealed, not all children had access to or were able to gain access into the learning opportunities constructed in their classroom. It is interesting to trace however, the revisions and changes the dominant groups of children in both classrooms introduced in their texts in comparison to those who adopted the role of the overhearers. Although learning may occur even in cases when it is not displayed, such data would help us trace the relationship between the learning contexts constructed in one and the same writing conference and the way these affected how children defined revision and the changes they introduced in their texts.

APPENDIX

Transliterated excerpts of some of the Greek examples attested

(1)

1   Teacher: Loipon (.) pos sas fanike (.) afto to paramiθi?
2   Student: Sindomo/
3   Teacher: Enas enas (.) θelo na sikonete çeraki ((xx)) telos pandon/
4   Stavros: Eee (.) itan poli sintoma (.) ce δen mas ((xx)) aγonia/
5   Teacher: Bravo/ Allos/ Pes mou Δimitri/
6   Δimitris: Eee (.) opos eipe o Stavros itan poli sintomo (.) ce poli micro diladi =
7   Teacher: Ne itan sintomo ce micro to iδio praγma (.) afto akribos/ Γia pes mas eee (.) Angelina?
8   Angelina: Δe leei pos tous vrike =
9   Teacher: = Bravo =
10   Angelina: =An epaθe tipota/
11   Teacher: Leipoun ola afta ta praγmata (.) δen iparçoune/ ine vasiko/ pes mas Vageli?/
12   Tasos: ((Δen eçi)) oles tis leptomeries pou prepei na eçi mesa/
13   Teacher: Bravo/ Δen eçi ((δiarkeia)) etsi?
14   Tasos: Ce to telioni poli γriγora (.) δen eksiγi pos çaθike/
15   Teacher: Bravo/
16   Tasos: Ti eγine ce çaθike/
17   Teacher: Bravo/ Afto/ Ine poli apotomo to telos/ Malista/ Γia pes mas ((xx))
18   Student: Ti na po?
19   Teacher: Eçi poli ((plousio))/ Episis eee (.) γia tous iroes? Mporeite na mou peite kati γia tous iroes? Eδo pera =
20   Student: Δen eçi kanena (.) mono to peδi (.) oute to onoma tou/

(3)

1.   Eftiçia: ciria emena δe mou poliarase/ ((γiati)) δen anaferei onomata çe δen eçi arketes teleies/ δilaδi se ((kapjes)) protaseis ((xx))
2   Teacher: Ne/
3   Eftiçia: Me δiaforetika θemata/
4   Teacher: δiadoretika θemata/ Leγe Maria/
5   Maria: ciria (.) stin proth protasi leei .hh otan mia mera piγa stin taratsa tis polikatikias iδa mia γata pou niaourize çe me fonakse i mama mou çe δen boresa na tin plisiaso/ δilaδi kiria θa borouse na γrapsei/
6   Student: ((xx))
7   Teacher: ela lipon (.) prota θa milaei i Maria ce meta/
8   Maria: Θa borouse na γrapsei oti kati ekane me ti γata ce meta ton fonakse i mama tou ce δen borese na tin plisiasei δilaδi prospaθise na tin plisiasei (.) alla ((ton fonakse I mama tou)) ce δen borese na tin plisiasei/
9   Student: ((xx))
10   Teacher: Opote to noima tou? Opote to noima tou δilaδi (.) δen ine safis/ leγo Angeliki/ ((Mia fora)) Ne (.) ce na fonazete peδja perisotero osi ((xx))
11   Angeliki: Emena kiria etsi δen mou arese ce poli γiati oti θelei na pi to vazei olo se mia protasi/
12   Teacher: se mia protasi/
12   Angeliki: ne (.) θelei na pi kati çoris na to periγrapsei to leei se mia protasi/ Ine san na kanei perilipsi/

Transcription conventions
(.) break in the flow of speech less than 0.4 of a second
= latching of utterances

((xx)) unclear speech (for a) bracketed material indicates a suggested hearing.

PRIOR KNOWLEDGE AND THE (RE)PRODUCTION OF SCHOOL WRITTEN GENRES

An Analysis of British Children's Meaning-making Resources

DEBRA MYHILL

University of Exeter, United Kingdom

Abstract. This chapter draws on recent research on genre literacy to investigate aspects of British children's school writing, as revealed in the texts produced by children at different age levels and sociocultural groups. Specifically, this chapter explores the way developing writers' prior knowledge shapes their learning about how to produce written texts in school and become confident writers. The discussion singles out different constituents of the notion of prior knowledge; this is conceptualized in terms of both sociocultural conventions for organizing meanings (or formal schemata) and register choices, as well as knowledge of visual design and text layout. The discussion builds upon the premise that detailed textual analysis of written texts can reveal important information on the types of prior knowledge with which children approach genre writing in the school context, and illustrates some of the difficulties children face in the production of genres which constitute advanced school literacy tasks. Evidence is discussed of how some children use the semiotic meaning-making resources from their out-of-school literacy experiences in ways that can be effective (or ineffective) according to school standards. Furthermore, the discussion takes into account the extent to which this prior knowledge is acknowledged in the British school context, especially in its examination and assessment processes. Finally, the chapter highlights the role curriculum requirements and pedagogical practices play in establishing school writing as little more than sociocultural reproduction of culturally valued genres.

Keywords: Prior knowledge, school written genres, schemata, genre writing pedagogy, children's writing, connectives, text layout, visual literacy

1   INTRODUCTION

In accounting for children's writing in schools, the issue of the resources children have available and draw upon to communicate through spoken and written texts in school is of great importance. Writing is inherently more difficult than talking: whilst talking in everyday situations is mostly an unplanned activity (at least in terms of the linguistic forms chosen), writing is an activity which demands not only the communication of ideas but also the presentation of these ideas in school-appropriate ways. Thus, learning to write in school is learning how to combine linguistic forms, with textual (organizational) structures and, as shown below, visual design and layout resources to create texts which would be regarded as powerful in the school community. This is fundamentally a learned activity that is shaped through both deliberate instruction and individual experiences of text and of life. These two learning processes are not independent but may, in fact, inform one another.

However, young developing writers in school may be differentially positioned in terms of their "acculturation" into the ways language may be used to express different forms and purposes through written texts (Wyatt-Smith, & Murphy, 2001). Children whose home background has socioculturally prepared them for the production of written genres (usually, middle-class children) may be advantaged. Martin (1985) argues that pedagogical practices which simply create opportunities for writing in school privilege those children who may already have access to ways of making meaning which are valued in school. While teachers may be eager to help all children become active members of the culture they inhabit (Hammond, & Derewianka, 2001), all too often actual practice may favour those who are already initiated. This advantage may arise not only out of middle-class children's frequent encounters with texts and different text types, but may also be due to the fact that middle-class speech patterns for conveying meanings (compared to the spoken forms used by less privileged groups) are closer to the structures expected in written discourse (Kress, 1994).

It is interesting to note, however, that whilst most commonly employed pedagogical practices – genre literacy included – tend to begin with and focus upon what children "can't do" in their writing, far less consideration has been attributed to what they "don't know." It is a well-known premise that children's prior knowledge shapes the way by which children approach the construction of a text and being aware of the extent of a child's prior knowledge enables effective pedagogical decisions to be made.

Indeed, this is what genre pedagogy set out to attain. Practitioners of this tradition advocated the explicit teaching of genre as a mechanism that would empower minority children. As this chapter indicates, however, teaching genre may not necessarily lead to empowerment (i.e., to the creative exploitation of the taught set of resources); children may be led to the social reproduction of the specific forms taught to them rather than to the creative use of a community-valued system of certain written discourses. What are the factors which mediate this process? Foucault claimed that *"every educational system is a political means of maintaining or modifying the appropriation of discourse, with the knowledge and power it carries with it"* (Foucault, 1972: 227). Building upon this claim, one could argue that effective instruction may, in fact, have differential results to children, with some benefiting from it more than others. Given this, I claim that children's learning may, in fact, be strengthened by more secure understanding of a developing writer's prior knowledge, which is constructed through children's experiences of texts and of life. It is necessary therefore that we begin with children's prior knowledge. What does this prior knowledge consist of? Components of this construct are identified in this chapter.

1.1 Prior Knowledge

Prior knowledge, as a significant pedagogical concept, is central to the theoretical perspectives of both socioconstructivists and cognitive psychologists. Different theorists, however, have ascribed different terminology to the mental organization of prior knowledge – usually referred to as frames, scripts, scenarios (Brown, & Yule, 1983; Tannen, 1993), mental models (Johnson-Laird, 1980) and schemata (Bartlett, 1932). As Brown, & Yule argue, these different terms are *"best considered as alternative metaphors for the description of how the knowledge of the world is organized in human memory and also how it is activated in the process of discourse understanding"* (Brown, & Yule, 1983: 238). Hayes, & Flower (1980) described writers' prior knowledge in terms of stored writing plans, mental maps of different types of writing which the individual writer can draw upon when embarking upon a written task. However, by being more concerned with the cognitive process of writing, Hayes and Flower are less specific about how these writing plans are established; in addition, mainly due to the fact that this work draws principally upon competent writers, little information is available on the nature of these stored writing plans in developing writers. Important is the distinction discussed by researchers such as Carrell, & Eisterhold (1988) and Swales (1990) between *content* schemata, which draw upon an individual's direct experiences of life, and *formal* schemata, which depict an individual's knowledge of text structuring patterns. Together, these schemata assist in the formation or reproduction of a genre. Considering this issue from an L2 perspective, Hedge notes how, for some writers, the experience of reading may help them develop schemata for writing: some good writers, *"who may not necessarily have had any formal instruction in discourse types, start writing with the appropriate 'schema' in their heads"* (Hedge, 1988: 94). Tannen sees this interaction between prior knowledge and present experience as central to the meaning-making process: *"the only way to make sense of the world is to see the connections between things and between present things and things we have experienced before or heard about"* (Tannen, 1993: 15). According to Edwards, & Westgate, the learner constructs knowledge and understanding through *"an interaction between what is already known and new experience"* (Edwards, & Westgate, 1994: 6). Apparently, and given the fact that learning to write is *"acquired through culturally specific, formal and informal systems of pedagogy"* (Luke, 1988: 17), pedagogical approaches to writing need to acknowledge and properly incorporate this notion. Mercer suggests that pedagogical practices, and specifically those concerned with the teaching of writing, should be seen as *"a developmental process in which earlier experiences provide the foundations for making sense of later ones"* (Mercer, 1995: 33). Nutbrown (1994) argues that explicit consideration of children's schemata in the classroom is a valuable way of making connections between theory and practice. In a different line of research, prior knowledge is conceptualized in terms of generic competence. The notion that people interact with written genres is at the heart of contemporary genre theory (Derewianka, 1996, Kress, 1994; Martin, & Rothery, 1986; Swales, 1990) and both theoretical and pedagogically-oriented research on literacy (Czerniewska, 1992; Morgan, 1997; Wray, & Lewis, 1997) frequently draws on genre theory to inform the way texts are produced and understood. Genres are

interpreted as socially constructed forms, communicating meaning in culturally specific ways. Derewianka describes genres as *"different types of text which are used in
a particular culture to achieve specific purposes"* (Derewianka, 1996: 7), underlining a recognition that genre production is not simply about replicating a fixed sequence of text structures, but, more significantly, about using language to express
the sociocultural values represented by, and embedded within, those text structures.
The text structure and the linguistic choices are the medium, while genre, as Swales
(1990) points out, is a broader concept than text type, and represents a *"class of
communicative events,"* with common communicative purposes, through which particular social meanings and values are expressed. Genres operate within *"socio-
rhetorical networks"* (Swales, 1990: 9) or discourse communities, which share
common goals. An understanding of *"the processes of generic production is one
aspect of knowledge of cultural and social production"* (Kress, 1994: 222): learning
to make meanings through specific community-valued genres is, in part, at least,
learning about sociocultural representation. The Australian critical literacy movement foregrounds cultural representations as an explicit focus for the study of texts
and advocates that attention be directed to the *"cultural and ideological assumptions
that underwrite text"* (Morgan, 1997: 2) and to how these assumptions differently
position readers and speakers. In this account, grammatical forms are interpreted as
part of the textual resources which are used to express content, ideology and cultural
positionings. The use of the passive voice in scientific texts, for example, is more
than a convention: by removing the agent and by foregrounding the scientific topic
as subject, these texts reflect a cultural view of Science as objective and empirical,
and, more subtly, they position the claims of a piece of science writing as uncontest-
able, as universal truth.

The different terminology used to capture prior knowledge may help us realize
that this construct might consist of many different components. It is interesting,
therefore, to discuss how each of these components may be used to help us account
for the difficulties children face in writing. So, the basic question is this: What does
prior knowledge consist of? How do schemata and genres relate to each other?

This chapter explores two different manifestations of schemata in British children's writing. Firstly, the discussion considers children's prior knowledge of formal
text schemata, that is, knowledge of the socioculturally-shaped text patterns children
deploy for representing experience in the form of specific text types, and the linguistic choices associated with these patterns. Secondly, it considers children's prior
knowledge and social experience of the way visual design and layout features may
combine with verbal systems to construct a more complex, multi-modal unit and
indicates how these experiences influence children's endeavours in school literacy
practices.

2   GENRES AND MEANING-MAKING PRACTICES IN THE BRITISH
SCHOOL CONTEXT

In the UK, the teaching of writing is framed by a statutory National Curriculum for
English which adopts an eclectic theoretical position, incorporating both process and

genre approaches to writing, as well as a conservative emphasis upon the use of Standard English and technical accuracy in spelling, punctuation, and grammar. Since 1998, the primary school writing curriculum has been heavily influenced by the introduction of a National Literacy Strategy (DfEE, 1998), which specifies term-by-term teaching objectives for literacy, in an attempt to improve standards. The Strategy has been extended into the secondary school curriculum since 2002. A programme of national testing and public reporting of results accompanies the National Curriculum: children are tested upon their achievements in English at the ages of 7, 11, 14 and 16.

The National Literacy Strategy (NLS) reflects the influence of genre theory and it recommends that all primary school children be explicitly taught the characteristic features of six text types (report; recount; explanation; instruction; persuasion; and discussion). In the secondary school, the focus on text types evolves, rather ambiguously, into an emphasis upon the purposes for writing, framed in terms of four writing triplets (to imagine, explore, entertain; to persuade, argue, advise; to review, analyze, comment; and to inform, explain, describe). In the classroom, the realization of the NLS has led to explicit teaching of linguistic and textual features such as connectives, simple and complex sentences, the use of imperatives, and how texts open and close. There is extensive guidance material available for teachers to support the teaching of text genres: this material has been sent to all schools and is available on the Department for Education and Skills website. Some of the material has been directly mediated through in-service training days or through additional support from advisory teachers. Teachers are free to select any text which represents a given genre, although where teachers lack confidence (or time) they are likely to use the guidance materials more heavily. Pedagogical strategies for teaching genre include the use of reading as a model for writing; guided or shared reading, which analyzes the typical genre characteristics of the text; shared writing of the genre being taught; and independent writing, where learners attempt to create their own texts in the genre under study. The approach, in practice, is very linguistically-oriented, with more attention to grammatical structures than to how these grammatical structures create meaning. However, teacher subject-knowledge of the grammatical terminology and of the text features is not always secure and this has meant that, in many cases, children are taught about generic features in a somewhat decontextualized way. Thus, although the pedagogical principles are founded upon *"explicitly analyzing the textual features of an instance of a generic form"* (Morgan, 1997: 67), the genres and their values remain un-explicated and uncontested.

As the Australian line of genre literacy research has illustrated (see Cope, & Kalantzis, 1993), school writing has typical genres of its own; although these genres may partially mirror genres found outside of school (of course, the extent to which this is done is the object of empirical research), these are, nonetheless, very specific and intrinsically related to the context of school and to the wider context of examination. A significant factor in school genres is that they emphasize an asymmetric power relationship between the teacher and the writer, with the teacher not only knowing the conventions of the genre, but often also acting as the determiner of the topic or title to be considered, and as the arbiter of the finished piece of writing. School, therefore, represents a specific type of discourse community in which teachers and examiners as expert members of this community work with novices. The assessment system used by this discourse community reflects a specific sociocultural view of what schooled literacy is, and is a key mechanism of acculturation into that forms and patterns valued in this community (Wyatt-Smith, & Murphy, 2001). Indeed, Cook-Gumperz maintains that schooled literacy is *"validated through test performances"* (Cook-Gumperz, 1986: 41). In the UK, the testing regime is not only more frequent than in most other countries, but it is also heavily politicized and used for purposes of public accountability.

This study attests a number of issues that have arisen from the application of genre pedagogy in the British context, focusing in particular on the way by which this pedagogy accommodates children's prior knowledge. The analysis illustrates that, if such knowledge is downplayed, curriculum requirements and pedagogical practices can, unintentionally, establish school writing (for some children, at least) as little more than sociocultural reproduction of a specific set of genres which are valued in this community. What are the factors, then, leading some, but not all children, to reproduce generic meanings? Why is it that some children are able to proceed beyond a given set of choices and negotiate generic meanings in more dynamic ways? In short, as to be indicated, although genre literacy pedagogy, as implemented in the British context may be concerned with the empowerment of students, this process is mediated by matches between children's prior knowledge, on the one hand, and the expectations associated with the school context, on the other.

To attain this aim and capture all of its implications, both students' texts and classroom processes should be analyzed. However, due to space limitations, this chapter focuses on children's texts only. The texts examined range from more to less effective according to school expectations; the differences attested reflect the different types of prior knowledge children bring to the writing task. Prior knowledge, as used here, is not only knowledge acquired in out-of-school, and home contexts but also knowledge a writer has accumulated from different sources (including school) and has available prior to performing a certain writing task. This knowledge is mediated by classroom interactions taking place between the teacher and the students. I attend to the end result of this process, and analyze the linguistic, textual and multimodal dimensions of the texts produced by different children. Information from classroom processes is provided when necessary to back up the claims I make.

The texts cited are drawn from three different data sets of British children's writing. The data on 16-year olds' writing are drawn from a stratified sample of 280 examination scripts for the General Certificate of Secondary education in English (taken by 16-year olds). Texts written by 11-year old children are from a second data set; this is a stratified sample of 600 examination scripts for the national key stage 2 English tests (taken by 11-year olds). This data was collected as part of national evaluations of pupils' performance in writing. Both data sets were analyzed quantitatively and qualitatively using the same analytical coding frames, which captured numerical data about linguistic and textual features, and qualitative data about the content and textual organization of the samples. The third data set is a small corpus of British children's writing, across the age range from 5 to 18, collected in small-scale research investigations into children's understanding of genre. These texts were analyzed qualitatively and included information about the teaching context which had elicited the writing, and pupil background information.

The aim of this chapter is not to present quantitative evidence but rather to clarify, from the information gathered from these sets of data, the notion of prior knowledge, and some of its constitutive dimensions and trace the routes children follow when using this knowledge to perform various school writing tasks. However, the descriptions offered, undoubtedly, point to the need for further systematic analysis to be undertaken on how British children from different sociocultural groups apply their different sources of prior knowledge to the construction of texts.

3   CHILDREN'S KNOWLEDGE OF GENRES AND SCHOOL EXPECTATIONS FOR WRITING: MATCHES AND MISMATCHES

3.1 Children's Experiences of Narrative and Non-narrative Genres

In the UK, children of every age are overwhelmingly more likely to select the narrative option in the national tests in English (QCA, 2002). This may, in part at least, be due to far stronger prior knowledge of narrative written genres than any other genres. Young writers' schemata for narrative are usually constructed through a broad set of cultural experiences of narrative. Fictional narratives are perhaps the only form of text which is widely available for every age, from pre-school stories to be shared in the home or the nursery, to adult narratives to be accessed by mature readers. Primary school text books often reformulate factual information into narrative forms (e.g., Usborne Books; science stories). Even children's experience of video and television is highly supportive of narrative understanding (Smidt, 2001). Many children will experience time shifts, or flashbacks in televisual form before they encounter these strategies in a written narrative text, having, thus, employed various semiotic systems to scaffold their understanding of the narratology. Television, too, has a strong tendency to present factual information in a narrative form: wildlife documentaries often study the natural world through anthropomorphic narratives. The BBC natural history documentary *Wildlife on One,* screened in the UK on 09.07.02, described the activities of "Mr and Mrs Dunlop, the foxes"; and programmes such as *Crimewatch*, with the very serious intent of catching criminals, present narrative vignettes of authentic crime events. Many popular computer games, played by both children and adults (such as *Tomb-raider*) are structured upon an unfolding narrative adventure. Given that narrative, in western societies at least, is a powerful, and readily accessible cultural form, it is reasonable to expect that all children approaching narrative written genres will bring to the task some kind of (though not necessarily the same) prior knowledge of the narrative form.

However, children's schemata for non-narrative genres appear to be less well-developed (QCA, 1999): analysis of writing in the UK national tests indicates that weaker writers, in particular, have a tendency to revert to narrative (QCA, 2002). A similar tendency by African American children to rely on narrative strategies for constructing expository discourses is recorded in Ball (1992). Children are less likely to read non-narrative texts, other than special interest books or magazines, and many of the non-narrative genres they are asked to write in school exist outside of school primarily as adult genres (newspapers; campaign material; written speeches; argument writing). Their experience of producing these genres is limited, or even non-existent: children writing a letter of complaint, for example, are unlikely ever to have been in the position of the receiver of a letter of complaint, and may well never have written one. Such genres are principally mechanisms by which adults exercise power; grammar is crucially involved in this process, which is why, for example, it is more reasonable to expect that adults writing a letter of complaint to a shop will probably use the verb "purchased" as a way of asserting their authority, when most teenage writers would employ the more commonplace "bought."

The nature of children's prior knowledge of written genres (i.e., formal schemata) create problems for children in tackling written tasks. On the one hand, children's cultural experience of narrative forms may favour the production of narrative genres over non-narrative ones. Negotiating openings and endings in non-narrative texts is an area of relative weakness in many developing writers (QCA, 1999). Closure in narrative is easier, because children have more models available to them through their richer prior knowledge of narrative: at its simplest level, a narrative usually has a problem which needs resolution. In contrast, non-narrative genres are characterized by more variety in ways of managing closure. News articles rarely have a neat resolving conclusion, because of the dangers of the editorial cut of the final few lines, and the cognitive demand of synthesizing and summarizing an argument in the absence of secure prior knowledge of this genre is considerable. It should be noted, however, that children's prior knowledge, even of narrative, is often in terms of content and ideas, rather than in terms of explicit linguistic signalling. This difficulty is particularly evident in the construction of non-narrative texts. For example, the signalling of the organization of a narrative text may not be linguistically explicit, since it can be achieved through simple chronology; non-narrative texts, however, may need more sophisticated linguistic signalling of information sequencing; this is a task children find more difficult to manage (Myhill, 1999).

3.2 Sociocultural Silences: Reflections on Content Schemata and Register Choices

In this section, I consider how one aspect of children's prior knowledge – their knowledge of formal schemata – influences their writing; this can be noted by attending to writing tasks, the production of which demands knowledge which children are not expected to have. This seems to be particularly evident in the construction of non-narrative (non-fiction) texts, where children are often asked to write in genres which they may not have encountered in their reading, and are unlikely to have experienced as writers.

The letter in Figure 1 is written by an 11-year old in response to a writing task which asked children to invite a famous celebrity to a school fund-raising event. The child, not a confident writer, struggles with many aspects of the task. Beginning with register choices, we may note that the student is uncertain about the form of address to use when writing to someone known to you, but not known by you. This is compounded by her social language experiences of references to royalty which reinforce her understanding of her title as "The Queen": most conversational exchanges and television broadcasting about the monarch do indeed tend to refer to her as "The Queen". The writer is unlikely to have seen any letters to the queen, and clearly does not know accepted forms of address to royalty.

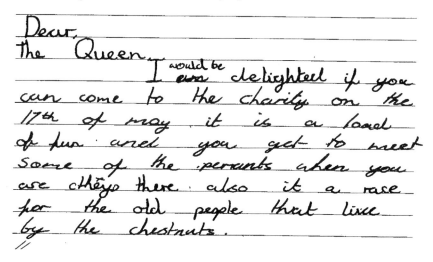

Figure 1. A letter written by an 11-year old: Ineffective linguistic and textual choices.

However, other children tackling the same task struggled similarly with the appropriate form of address, even though other celebrities were chosen. For example, if David Beckham is the chosen guest, should he be addressed as David, David Beckham, or Mr Beckham? Many of these young writers had little sociocultural knowledge to support them in this respect. This writer is also uncertain about the tenor to adopt: she attempts some formality in the opening sentence (*I would be delighted..*) but slips into her own speech patterns later (*it is a load of fun*).

Focusing on the information structure, and the balance writers need to negotiate between given and new information, we note that the writer is uncertain about the information she needs to assume as given and the information she needs to provide for her reader. She relies heavily on given information; the writer draws upon her knowledge of school events (fun; meeting parents; races) but does not understand the need to provide contextual information for her distant reader (what charity is the event for? What would the role of the guest be? Who are the old people who live by the chestnuts?)

By contrast, the writer of the letter to the editor in Figure 2 below, who is also eleven, is very comfortable with adopting the appropriate tone and providing the relevant information for his unknown reader.

```
Dear Editor,
I am writing to you because I have just been in-
formed that the bus that takes the Broad Hills
```

```
children to Bere Efford CP School will be with-
drawn after Easter, which means no transport for
the children. I think this is idiotic and have
several reasons for believing this.
```

[letter continues for three paragraphs]

```
I hope you see my point of view and join forces
with us to save the school bus.
```


```
Yours sincerely
```

Figure 2. A persuasive text written by an 11-year old (middle- class):
Effective linguistic and textual choices.

In terms of the information sequencing, the following can be said. The letter opens with a clear statement of the issue the letter is addressing, describing the nature of the problem. The writer does not assume his reader knows the contextual details and summarizes them succinctly. The opening paragraph also gives a direct statement of his position in relation to the transport problem. The closure of the letter is particularly controlled: having argued why the school bus should not be withdrawn, the writer tacitly assumes he has successfully argued his case and invites the editor to share his viewpoint. The letter also manages a move from authoritative assertion in the opening to a more conciliatory tone in the closing invitation.

Regarding register choices, the tone is formal and detached throughout: several lexical items indicate the increased formality by shifting from the more common-place vocabulary item to a more sophisticated choice (*informed* rather than *told*; *withdrawn* and not *taken away* or *stopped*) and structures such as *"several reasons,"* and *"I am writing to you"* support the formal tone.

This piece of writing does reveal the way by which prior sociocultural knowledge can influence developing writers' attempts at producing a text which can be judged effective according to school standards of effectiveness. This writer, from a middle-class family, brings to the task sociocultural literacy knowledge which seems to support his understanding of the task demand. Kress (1994) argued that in middle-class professional spoken dialects are closer to written structures than the spoken dialects of other classes and that, as a consequence, *"the difference between the syntax of speech and that of writing is far less for such groups than it is for groups whose dialects are little if at all influenced by the structure of writing"* (Kress 1994: 3). It is likely that the oral discourse patterns of a middle-class family have translated into written understanding in this piece. This may be true of lexical items, such as *"idiotic," "withdrawn,"* and *"informed,"* but also of the general structure of argument and how arguments are articulated. This would include understanding the need to balance assertion with conciliation, and the need to justify claims made (*"several reasons"*). I would argue that the difference lies not at the level of the sentence but rather at the global structure.

Comparing the two text samples, however, certain differences should be noted. The influence of the task itself should be singled out. Writing a letter of complaint about the removal of school transport facilities may be closer to children's own experiences and interests than writing an invitational letter to a celebrity, the task for the writer in Figure 1. This difference in the relative authenticity of the two tasks (adding another way of reflecting upon children's prior knowledge) may, in part, account for some of the differences in the written texts.

But what about other types of tasks children encounter mainly in school and indeed in secondary school? Consider the genre of explanation or science report. In reporting about phenomena, children usually employ everyday concepts; school requires that one incorporates in his/her description a specific vocabulary and specific ways of information presentation. It is worth noting to how children manage these tasks.

3.3 Prior Knowledge: Local Forms versus Global Structures

We can get a clear indication of weak writers' limited nature of prior knowledge by attending to the texts such writers produced after a series of lessons focusing on specific genre elements. I am interested in tracing writers' inability to move from linguistic forms to the textual global forms defining a genre. I consider advanced literacy texts; it is hypothesized that children would not be equipped with rich prior knowledge (and especially formal schemata) of these text types; it is not expected that children would have the opportunity to either encounter frequently outside of school the written genres required in school, or to experience in their homes the oral discourse patterns which advantage the production of these written genres (Martin, 1985; Wells, 1986). If genre features (from linguistic forms to textual structures) are negotiated in classroom lessons, would all children be able to use these and to what degree?

One teaching technique introduced within the NLS strategy is an emphasis upon deconstructing how different written genres work in order to give all children access to those genres. In principle, this is a determined attempt to compensate writers who approach writing with limited prior knowledge of the expected forms, and to reduce the ways in which school writing can simply act as a mechanism for social reproduction, based on home literacy experiences. However, in practice this is not always successful, unless the teacher attends to the level of prior knowledge brought to the task by the children in his/her classroom.

From the data, we noticed that children followed two main routes. The first is mere obedience to using linguistic forms without any accompanying understanding of how meaning is being communicated through the genre. Morgan calls this *functional literacy*: the writer is explicitly taught and subsequently masters the sub-skills of writing, and where *"form, understood as good form, a form-following, is all, and function is left to tag along"* (Morgan, 1997; 59) Where the teaching focus is upon genre characteristics, this can result in superficial adherence to typical linguistic structures of the genre, but with no attendant structuring of meaning to cohere with the form. The second is creative use of the linguistic forms within general structures.

The two routes are exemplified in Figures 3 and 4 versus 5 in the use of connective devices; these reflect, respectively, dependent obedience to certain instructions as to the use of these forms or independence from a given set of choices.

Deer Hunting

Some people think that hunting is really really bad or cruel to animals because it bad to see, If kids see it because it could be a bad influence. you would not like it if it was done to you. Another group who agree with this point of view are anti-hunt people. hey say that hunting (knowen as killing) is helping the deer population. If there was a weak deer in the chain, there would not b e any more weak deers.

On the other hand the idea that they claim the hunting might be banned because when you try to help the population you might kill a strong deer. But on the other hand young deer will run quickly so you won''t be able top kill it. But on the other hand if it is banned there will be weak deer, won't there.

Figure 3. Ineffective argumentative text (written by a 12-year old, working class).

The text in Figure 3, written by a 12-year old, shows inappropriate use of discourse markers; while such markers help the writer signal his/her point of view, and signpost the direction of the argument to the reader, in Figure 3, it seems that the writer has simply obeyed the requirement to use these markers; the text, as it is structured, does not indicate that the writer had reached a clear understanding of the way discourse markers could be used to signal the structure of the argument produced. Note that adverbial phrases such as "on the other hand" do not mark a contrary statement, and the actual line of reasoning is extremely difficult to follow.

The teaching of isolated linguistic forms such as connectives that signal a genre is not sufficient: the writer's lack of knowledge of how to structure and develop an argument (writing at text, paragraph and sentence levels of discourse) overrides the potential benefit of using appropriate discourse markers. Apparently, such writing reflects children's own definitions of the genres they are asked to produce. How is the "argumentative genre" (which the text in Figure 3 instantiates) defined by this child? This seems to be equated with the listing of claims rather than with an integration of these according to certain ways of topical progression (see Connor, 1996). The text presented in Figure 4 seems to reflect a similar tendency on the part of the writer: obedience to taught structures. The text was produced following a series of lessons addressing the NLS teaching objectives for year 6, Term 1 (DfEE, 1998) which consider connecting words and phrases and how points and paragraphs are connected in different types of texts. Obeying the most heavily emphasized aspect of the teaching of connectives, the use of ordinal connectives (*first, second, last*), the writer selects inappropriate sequencing conjuncts for the explanation genre. Instead, the writer needs connectives which signal range rather than order (*one way, another way, a further way etc.*).

Where electricity comes from.

Electricity can come from lots of things, the first is a nuclear power station were nuclear energy is used to make electricity.

The second is when coal, oil or gas is burnt in a power station, this is the most common way of making electricity. Another way is using big and small wind turbines which turn a generator and that makes the electricity.

The last way of making electricity is hydro electric power which is using water coming through a dam. The water coming through the dam turns the generator which makes the electricity.

Figure 4. Ineffective use of connectives in a science report explanation (10-year old, working class).

This can be contrasted with the 11-year old writer below, partially quoted earlier in Figure 2, who has used connectives with considerably more competence to signal the line of argument through the letter, and to negotiate his relationship with his implied reader.

Dear Editor,
I am writing to you because I have just been informed that the bus that takes the Broad Hills children to Bere Efford CP School will be withdrawn after Easter, which means no transport for the children. I think this is idiotic and have several reasons for believing this.

Most importantly, the road is far too dangerous for children to walk on. There are blind corners, muddy roads and lots of places where farmers use the roads to transport animals.

Also, tractors and trailers use the road and carry hay bales, silage and other objects which aren't very secure and could fall on top of the children and damage them. This would cost the Council even more because their family will sue them for compensation.

Thirdly, I want to know whether the Council would let their own children walk the roads at the crack of dawn and then be home late at night on such dan-

gerous lanes. Yet young children are expected to
walk when the bus is withdrawn.

Lastly, I have a suggestion to make. It is that if
it costs so much money to pay for a 48 seater bus,
why not provide a 15 seater minibus for the children
which would be cheaper and also a more practical
size to transport the children.

I hope you see my point of view and join forces with
us to save the school bus.

Yours sincerely

Figure 5. Effective use of connectives in a persuasive letter (11-year old, middle-class).

4   CHILDREN'S USE OF VISUAL DESIGN FEATURES IN THEIR TEXTS

Another constituent of prior knowledge children may explore through the production
of written texts is reflected on the way children make use of text layout and design.
Social experiences of texts outside of school are increasingly non-linear and dominantly visual, rather than dominantly verbal (Kress, 1997; Kress, & van Leeuwen,
1996). Many public texts which children encounter in the streets, such as signs and
advertising hoardings, combine the verbal with the visual. Indeed, some signs now
operate almost exclusively through symbolic representation – think, for example, of
the number of public toilets which now indicate male and female only through a
symbol. Print advertisements, whether on public display on hoardings or in magazines, make heavy use of image and connotation to convey meaning, and the verbal
content is interrelated with the image. Indeed, Kress argues that written language is
no longer the dominant mode of meaning-making, and that *the visual has reached a
position of equality in many, and a position of dominance in some"* (Kress, 1997: 5).
The exploitation of new forms of literacy, such as text messaging, in commercial
sectors recognizes new ways of making meaning, especially amongst young people.
This forty-something writer arranged to meet her teenage son outside a local garage,
called "GR8 Autos": my ignorant reading of this name literally reproduced the
graphemes (Gee-Arr-Eight Autos). My teenager took great satisfaction from my text
messaging illiteracy, pointing out the correct reading of the name (Great Autos).
However, it is not simply public and commercial texts which construct meaning in
visual and verbal forms. Many of the books children read, either at home or in
school, disrupt conventional notions of text linearity, and do not require left-to-right,
top–to-bottom reading directionality. Books for young children have always made
considerable use of a co-valent relationship between pictures and words. In addition,
twenty-first century literacies for older readers, including adults, make increasing
use of different ways of constructing meaning in print form. Non-fiction texts, in
particular, often choose to represent information in non-linear structures. In many of
these texts, the principal verbal information on the page is contained within boxes
highlighted through the use of coloured print or coloured backgrounds and is

strongly supported by pictures, photographs, diagrams and other visual design features. Conventional notions of text linearity are subverted and information on the page can be read in any order: the eye can move randomly from one text box to another. Many of the books for both younger and older readers, commonly found in classrooms and school libraries, exploit the potential of layout possibilities to abandon left-to-right directionality and deploy multi-modal techniques for presenting information. Popular series such as the Dorling Kindersley *Eye Witness* series, Usborne *Illustrated World History* series, Kingfisher *I Wonder Why* series, and Scholastic *Horrible Histories* series make heavy use of visual and verbal textual interplay. Indeed, the Eye Witness series breaks with traditional text conventions, not just in presenting information in a format which can be read from different entry points to the page, but also by frequently disrupting the notion of a page. Instead, the text is sometimes designed over a double page spread as a single visual unit with the only concession to left-right directionality being the heading at the top left hand corner which summarizes the focus for the double-page spread. Kress (1997) argues that young children's awareness of the inter-relationship between the verbal and the visual in creating meaning is evidenced by their understanding of generic forms and their ability to reproduce forms such as newspapers with multi-modal features.

Theorists are increasingly conceptualizing writing as more than the representation of verbal language in graphemic form: indeed, Sharples (1999) advocates the theorization of the act of writing as one of "creative design" in which text layout and visual features are as important as verbal representations. Publishers recognize the sociocultural significance of these new forms of text design – indeed, the publisher's blurb on the back cover of a non-fiction text commonly found in school libraries, *Tales of Real Escape,* states that *"vivid illustrations, fascinating photographs, and lively maps and diagrams accompany this exciting collection of stories,"* information which explicitly foregrounds the visual over the verbal. Kress, & van Leeuwen (1996) argues that a literacy curriculum for the twenty-first century should acknowledge this multi-modality in meaning-making to ensure that all children acquire reading skills and strategies which will realistically equip them for the texts they will meet in out-of-school contexts. Indeed, Kress has been and is very critical of pedagogical and assessment practices in which *"the page is not considered as a meaningful or significant element in writing"* (Kress, 1997: 86).

However, much of the writing required in school and tested in examinations has expectations of highly conventional, linear, left-to-right text reproduction, and this expectation intensifies as the child grows older. Secondary school writing is dominantly continuous prose, apart from the occasional labelling of diagrams, or the permission to use illustration. Examination writing, which determines students' life chances, is almost exclusively linear and continuous prose. In terms of meaning-making in writing, children's prior knowledge of real non-fiction texts does not help them meet the demands of writing certain kinds of genres (such as expository or argumentative genres) in school; arguably, they have to learn that meaning-making through some types of written texts produced in the classroom or in examinations (in terms of the type and range of the visual resources allowed to be employed) is different from meaning-making in other contexts.

It is interesting to note that when approaching non-fiction writing tasks, some student writers tended to rely exclusively on the verbal system only while others drew upon visual design and layout means – usually by indicating where visual material might be positioned. The writing sample in Figure 6, is produced by an 11-year old in a national examination; this student is writing an information leaflet for visitors to a park.

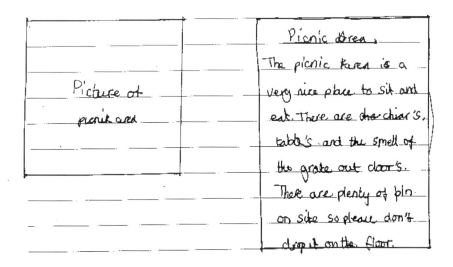

Figure 6. Extract from an information leaflet text, produced by an 11-year old.

The writing extract in Figure 7 is by a 16-year old in a public examination for English: the task was to write a persuasive piece, informing parents of the dangers of allowing their children a television in their bedrooms. Interestingly, the assessment scheme for this paper gives no marks for the appropriate use of visual text, and the research report on children's performance in the test (QCA, 2002) refers only to traditional prose features, such as sentence boundaries, full stops, connectives and paragraphs. The child's multi-modal response is invited by the task but not acknowledged by the test. It is worth inquiring into the reasons leading this child to this choice, although, due to lack of relevant data, no definite answer can be given. What does this integration of verbal and visual elements reveal? Does it illustrate writer's awareness of multi-modal resources or does it express his/her attempt to increase the force of his/her argument by adding extra material?

Consider now Figure 7. Like the text of the 11-year old student discussed in Figure 6, this student too recognizes that graphics can support the verbal information, and both writers demonstrate that they understand the potential interplay between verbal and visual structures. The full pieces of writing for both these writers observe top-to-bottom, left-to-right directionality and are principally in continuous prose. Arguably, the most appropriate response to this task would have been to follow the principles of the non-fiction texts available in schools, described earlier, and to reduce the amount of continuous, linear prose. Given the assessment criteria and the emphasis of the National Curriculum for English upon written prose, it is unlikely whether an examiner would have given him credit had he produced the text in a non-linear mode. Indeed, the examination report (NEAB, 2002) makes no reference to any visual or graphic representations, noting instead children's ability to use persuasive features such as rhetorical questions and emotive language.

Why is this selected? Is it because the writer thought this choice would make the text more effective? It should be noted that there is a clear difference between the two texts cited in Figures 6 and 7 and this pertains to the way the argument is conveyed by the textual dimension of the multi-modal text. The textual component of this 16-year old's text is an effective persuasive essay, with the graphic presented as an extra. In contrast, note that the verbal component of the text cited in Figure 6 is not as strong.

However, whatever movies are shown, television, as you will know, can be educational, but the reality is that much of it is pure fiction and is of harm to your child. Reading is of much more benefit than TV, and so should be encouraged. Independent research has proven that TV watching raises stress levels and decreases your child's concentration span, whilst reading promotes concentration and reduces stress. However, many adults ignore such research, and pass it off as rubbish. You assume that a TV will give your child a sense of responsibility; but can you afford to be so foolish?

Insert colourful graphic showing TV watchers and non TV watchers concentration spans

As you read this, research is taking place into a link between TV watching and attention deficit disorder. Giving your child a TV in their room will not only dent their education, but will also effect their health.

Giving your child a television in their room may increase their freedom, but it **will** damage their health and education. At the end of the day the decision is up to you; but do you want to disadvantage **your** child's hope of success in life?

Figure 7. A persuasive text by a 16-year old (middle-class): Integrating visual and verbal information.

4.1 Creative Exploitation of Visual Design/Layout Resources

Though visual design and layout information is not explicitly acknowledged, there are children who seem to employ the visual component of their sociocultural knowledge creatively in the construction of meaning in their written texts. Consider the recipe written by the 8-year old writer of Figure 8. The piece was written in a lesson where the teaching focus was on writing instructions. Attention had been given to the use of imperatives in instructions, the importance of clear sequencing of the instructions, and how diagrams and illustrations could support the written text.

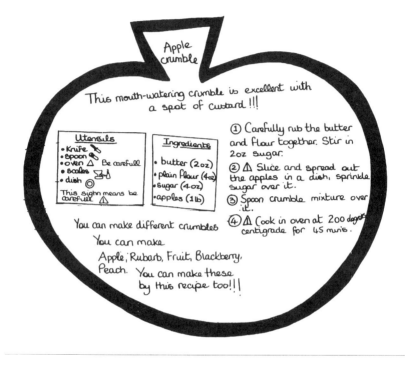

Figure 8. Integrating textual and visual information in an instructional text (written by an 8-year old, middle-class).

Although we do not have direct access to this child's prior knowledge, this writer draws from the information presented in the school through the teacher's explicit teaching about the genre features of instructional texts, but she has overlaid the textual component with her awareness of the way visual elements may enhance the force of a text – the recipe constructed is not a text but a multi-modal semiotic text. The writing demonstrates not simply a clear grasp of certain textual and semiotic/multi-modal features but the student's ability to use them productively, i.e., to attain further aims. From the text produced, this writer shows that s/he knows that recipes are not simply instructions: they are in part persuasive texts, designed to encourage the reader to try the recipe. The visual layout of the recipe, inside the apple outline, is a persuasive device, and the sentence which precedes the instructions, (*"This mouth-watering crumble is excellent with a spot of custard!!!"*), is a persuasive enticement. This highlights the advantage conferred upon those with sociocultural prior knowledge of written genres: they are not reduced to simple reproduction of certain instructions on generic meaning, but they can recreate genres with a fuller understanding of how form and meaning interrelate to communicate with the reader.

5   CONCLUSION

Children's in-school experiences of writing may be seen as a process of acculturation into schooled writing practices:*"when children learn to write, they learn more
than the* system *of writing. They learn about the* social practices *of language"*
(Czerniewska, 1992: 2). In the UK in particular, with its emphasis on formal testing
of writing throughout the curriculum, there is a tension between describing genres as
cultural forms, but teaching them as static, fixed and unchangeable forms. The
teaching of writing, more so than the teaching of reading, is prone to this tendency.
Genre-based pedagogies for teaching writing are frequently founded upon the principal aim of deconstructing for the learner the linguistic and textual structures which
characterize a given genre with the view that the ability to reproduce genres is a
form of *"empowerment through appropriation"* (Morgan, 1997: 66). However, critics of this approach argue that it is a reproductive model, not a critical productive
model: children are taught to conform to and replicate the demands of the genre,
rather than to consider the values the genre embodies. It involves *"an increasing
loss of creativity on the child's part, and a subordination of the child's creative
abilities to the demands of the norms of genre"* (Kress, 1994: 11).

   This criticism seems to apply to the writing pedagogy implemented in the UK
which is principally founded upon pedagogical assumptions that do not take children's prior knowledge (or lack of it) into account. Attention to the linguistic aspects
of genres has often been reduced to singling out linguistic forms in specific texts or
addressing notions of correctness, themselves culturally contested (e.g., Standard
English; comma usage). As this study illustrated, pedagogical practices (emanating
from teachers' reduced confidence in and knowledge of this approach) can, unintentionally, establish school writing as little more than sociocultural reproduction of
certain genres valued in this context. Less attention seems to be directed towards
exploring how children learn to make and interpret meaning through text types or
genres valued by specific discourse communities. Inherent in this is the need to recognize the significance of the various schemata for writing which children bring to
writing tasks, including the semiotic resources for meaning-making which derive
from out-of-school literacy experiences. Langer, & Nicholich (1981) argue that eliciting and organizing prior knowledge enables new learning to be more meaningful,
and activates schemata onto which new knowledge can be mapped. But, equally,
addressing what developing writers "don't know," the sociocultural silences, should
be a pedagogical priority.

   While this chapter draws upon the notion of schemata (formal and content schemata) as the metaphor for the mental organization of prior knowledge, in light of the
evidence suggested I would argue that we need to proceed beyond proposals on
prior knowledge as a static set of expectations which children bring to text production. This notion should rather be used in reference to a constantly evolving set of
strategic resources children have available regarding text production.

   Analysis of classroom pedagogical practices are important to help us capture the
processes facilitating or hindering developing writers in learning how, through their
texts, they may negotiate prior knowledge with the information presented in the
classroom lessons. I expect that from this negotiation children would come to under-

stand how to communicate meaning with their implied reader(s). In addition, this information should be brought to teachers to inform them about the way teachers can engage in a more critical exploration of linguistic and textual structures with all students. It is necessary that we help teachers develop strategies to assist all children in learning how to the balance the expectations of the school context with their own social and cultural experiences of written genres.

STUDENT WRITING AS NEGOTIATION

Textual Movements in French High School Essays

CHRISTIANE DONAHUE

University of Maine-Farmington & Associated member of the THEODILE research group, Université de Lille

Abstract. This chapter develops out of a broader study of 250 texts which were produced by 11th-13th grade students from both the US and France and were collected over a five-year period. The students were asked to create argumentative texts in which they explored questions about social issues after having read various (full or excerpted pieces of) published texts on these issues. The texts produced by the students are analyzed not as constellations of a stable set of linguistic-textual features, but as the result of a dynamic set of social and rhetorical negotiating moves in the discursive spaces of the school situation. The discussion explores a few of the interesting points of the tension between convention and creativity that have been located in six French students' texts. Student writers use what M.L. Pratt calls "literate arts" to construct their texts. We can localize these arts in the identification and description of students' movements of *"reprise-modification"* (François, 1998). This concept is a natural extension of Bakhtin's dialogics, with each utterance acting as "a link in a chain." Attention is directed to the identification of those textual movements with which students play with reproduction, reprise of the expected, but also proceed to the invention of the new, and modify the texts they encounter in the act of appropriating school discourse. The writer's work between the common and the specific is part of the essential nature of school writing. As proposed, this analysis permits a better understanding of how average students' texts interact with readings and with both cultural and educational commonplaces, working from the already-said and respecting – at least some but rarely all of – the limits of school expectations. This insight into students' discursive activities subtly changes the way we read students' work.

Keywords: Discourse analysis, Bakhtin dialogics, argumentative discourse, *reprise-modification*, literate arts, textual movement, negotiation, secondary school discourse, convention, style

1 INTRODUCTION

Discourse analysis has developed in the past few decades many interesting methodo-logical frameworks for exploring the texts produced in different kinds of situations, including school situations. Part of the extensive work in this domain has been con-ducted in contrastive rhetoric, research in this field is concerned with capturing overall text differences between different cultures, identifying linguistic and textual features associated with specific genres, exploring reader expectations and discourse patterns, raising, through these topics, the possibility of linguistic relativity (see

Connor, 1996, for a thorough overview of these questions). Text linguistics has offered a "descriptive apparatus" (Connor, 1996: 12) for this kind of analysis, allowing
for careful identification of certain features such as theme-rheme construction, use
of connectors, deixis, various modes of enunciation, and so on.

Generally, and in spite of highly developed work by U.S. researchers including
Berkenkotter, & Huckin (1988) and Swales (1990), such analysis has been largely
marginalized in the field of composition (as this is known in the North American
context). This is probably due to the fact that composition research and discourse
analysis, though focusing on academic and school writing, tended to proceed along
distinct and even parallel-running research lines, with little interaction noted between the two fields. This may be, partly, because discourse analysis – at least in its
initial developments – has been mainly concerned with identifying and counting
frequencies of specific textual features in order to describe patterns in text production and text reception. Indeed, this orientation has been criticized by composition
theorists, such as Flynn (1995, cited in Charney, 1996) and Schilb (1990), for its
failure to provide ways of understanding larger and complicated issues related to the
ideological nature of text production and interpretation. Highly-publicized debates in
the field targeted "whether empirical methods have any legitimate place in composition studies, and, if not, how we are to achieve intellectual authority without them"
(Charney, 1996: 567).[1]

Some lines of research in composition theory have focused on school writing as
a form of initiation into the shared conventions, values, or ways of speaking of specific academic groups – in part, their genres (Bartholomae, 1985a; Bautier, 1995;
Bizzell, 1992; Brice-Heath, 1983; Rose, 1989; Shaughnessy 1977; and of course
preliminary traces in Bernstein, 1958 and Labov, 1978). Much of this research has
indicated that students' ignorance of or resistance to these shared conventions and
world-ways constitute very interesting areas of inquiry indeed.

In recent years, discourse analysis has broadened its scope of inquiry to include a
variety of approaches that illustrate how texts function in interaction with their social and cultural contexts. Perhaps the most valuable recent developments have been
inspired by Bakhtin's work on meaning-making. Bakhtin's perspectives on language, genre, and the historicized meanings of utterances provide a richer and more
comprehensive theoretical framework for thinking about the way texts function in a
variety of social contexts. This framework enables us to look at texts – utterances, in
Bakhtinian terms – not as collections of individual features but as complex and dynamic moments of interaction with other texts, in the largest sense. This perspective
enables us to move towards understanding how a particular discourse, as the production and interpretation of culturally recognized and ideologically shaped representations of reality (Ivanič, 1998), functions in an intertextually constructed web of linguistic and discursive choices. When applied to the study of student writing, this
perspective offers vitally important insights, for it allows us to locate and describe
different moments of a text's makeup.

---

[1] *Rare works such as the 2002 "Discourse Studies in Composition" collection, edited by Ellen
Barton, & Gail Stygall, are beginning to explicitly bridge the gap.*

Drawing from the Bakhtinian perspective, in this chapter, I offer a reading of a small set of French students' texts. Situating the inquiry within the general field of school discourse, this chapter undertakes a detailed analysis of some of the specific, concrete ways school discourse is instantiated in a few French *lycée* student texts. The way of reading and analyzing students' texts that is developed strives for meta-consciousness of the part of the analyst, who is conceptualized as a particular kind of reader (even more so when the analyst is also a teacher). Culler (1982) suggests that to interpret is to articulate an experience of reading. This does not mean that we cannot be systematic and rigorous in our reading. As Paltridge reminds us, both the production and the interpretation of texts are not individual performances but processes which themselves are informed by preceding events, performances, and interpretations (Paltridge, 1997: 11). In studying a text, researchers, as indeed all people, bring with them their own ways of seeing and recognizing. I suggest that this should be included in our description (much as ethnographers have begun including this acknowledgement of the interpretative nature of their descriptive work). In this sense, I propose that my reading of the students' texts be seen as a dialogic moment made up of multiple factors.

This chapter, therefore, seeks to provide a sampling of both systematic description and multi-layered contextual interpretation of students' texts, which are seen as arising not out of the use of a stable set of linguistic-textual features but out of a dynamic set of social and rhetorical negotiating moves employed in the discursive spaces of the school universe. The analysis seeks to develop a principled way of exploring the traces of the various ways this group of student writers, much like other writers, manages intertextuality. The discussion illustrates how these students work with words, expressions, styles, and structures from a given prompt text, while creating a new text of their own.

2 BAKHTIN, DIALOGISM AND AUTONOMY IN FRENCH SCHOOL WRITING

Student writers are often depicted in French scholarship as working their way towards autonomy – in fact, this is presented as the goal to be achieved. A recent French conference sponsored by the Institut National de Recherches Pédagogiques (INRP) explicitly announced this as its theme: "ways to develop autonomy in student writers." Leading French sociolinguist Elisabeth Bautier (1996) suggests that one of the major unsettling changes French students face as they make the transition into secondary education is the teachers' expectation of student autonomy in study and writing skills. Other researchers, like Barré-deMiniac et al. (1993), suggest that student autonomy is one of the markers that differentiate successful students from those who struggle, even well before high school. This focus on autonomy is not a question of encouraging students to have a singular voice, to be individuals, or to benefit from group work-shopping in individual ways, nor is it a focus on autonomy *vis-à-vis* the texts students read and write about. Rather, it is a focus on secondary students' ability to produce texts independently, alone, in on-demand situations, without relying on peer review, group processes or even revision as part of the writing process.

This emphasis may be partly understood as arising out of the structure of the *Baccalauréat* exam.[2] Students in France must pass this exam as autonomous writers in order to receive their secondary education diplomas and thus gain access to post-secondary studies. Once there, students will not be supported in their writing. I would like to claim, however, that no writer writes alone in the way imagined by the French demands. In fact, the writing valued by the French system enables us to see students' ability to negotiate with context and with the voices represented in the texts students encounter in their reading, with the institutional requirements that shape aspects of language use in the texts they are writing, and with the generic expectations that influence their acts of making meaning. The claim I put forward, i.e., that student writing be seen as an act of negotiation, is not new; Bartholomae (1985a) and Bizzell (1992) were among the first to introduce and explore this negotiation in detail. The proposal I make that creativity and convention be conceptualized as forces working against each other in a text, prevails in current research as well. Ivanič (1998), for example, analyzes academic writing through Fairclough's notions of manifest intertextuality (i.e., actual signaled intertext), on one hand, and interdiscursivity, on the other (a notion which echoes conventions, styles, and genres from other texts).

Important work conducted in the French context (in the fields of educational science, genre theory and cognitive psychology) interrelates this perspective to student argumentative text writing (see, for example, Alain Boissinot's *Les textes argumentatifs* or several publications from the *Institut National de Recherches Pédagogiques* Press). In reviewing studies of student texts, Connor (1996) singles out many lines of work on argumentative discourse across cultures; within these are studies focusing on cross-cultural constructions of effective arguments and patterns for introducing and using sources. What interests me is neither a classification of "cultural" or other features in a set of texts, nor an explanation of the student-subject, i.e., the producer of the text and the processes involved in the construction of him/herself, but the text itself and what my interaction with it – a potentially reproducible interaction – allows other readers to see about the way the text in question works as both "written by" and "writing" the situation.

---

[2] *After a fairly unified curriculum for the first nine years of school, French students enter the lycée, the last three years of school and move towards tracks of education based on interests and aptitudes: technological/pre-professional, vocational, and general tracks. The last group of tracks offer students areas of concentration: literacy and language, science and mathematics, and economics/social sciences are the most prevalent options. All of the technological, pre-professional, and general tracks lead to the Baccalauréat exam, a lengthy comprehensive exam which weighs subject areas differently in the scoring depending on the student's area of focus. Writing plays an omnipresent role in students' experiences, from start to finish. Testing and assessment are largely done through written essays and oral presentations. Writing is included in every discipline. Writing ability along with broad cultural literacy are key to success on the Baccalauréat. Comprehensive information about the French educational system can be obtained from the Ministry of Education's website and Maria Vasconcellos (1993). Le système éducatif. Paris: Editions la Découverte.*

2.1 Theoretical Notions

This chapter sets out to identify some of the features by which the negotiation process described above may be instantiated. I suggest that to do so, we need to integrate several theoretical and methodological perspectives developing out of work that is carried out in both discourse analysis and composition theory. The student texts considered here are read in terms of the dialogic elements they display; I emphasize their various forms of intertextuality, and integrate three terms: *reprise-modification* (François, 1998), *literate arts* (Pratt, 1990), and *textual movements*, in my attempt to describe and interpret these dialogic elements. These three concepts create a model which suggests that in analyzing texts as products and in capturing the process of reading we need to bring out their essential dialogic nature.

Dialogics: A Bakhtinian line of research has extensive implications for shaping our understanding of school writing. The discussion builds on the premise that

> [...] there can be neither a first nor a last meaning; [anything that can be understood] always exists among other meanings as a link in the chain of meaning, which in its totality is the only thing that can be real. In historical life this chain continues infinitely, and therefore each individual link in it is renewed again and again, as though it were being reborn (Bakhtin, 1986: 146).

The language choices students make are historicized. What might be said is always already built on what has been said; the language, as Bakhtin argues,

> has been completely taken over, shot through with intentions and accents [...]. All words have a "taste" of a profession, a genre, a tendency, a party, a particular work, a particular person, a generation, an age group, a day and hour. Each word tastes of the context and contexts in which it has lived its socially charged life [...]. Language is not a neutral medium that passes freely and easily into the private property of the speaker's intentions; it is populated, overpopulated – with the intentions of others (Bakhtin, 1981: 273-274).

As the student writer learns "to use discourses which already exist," his/her text is constituted through "the unique way in which s/he draws on and combines" these discourses (Ivanič, 1998: 86). This process, we will see in the student examples, is often most affected by the immediate history of the text the student has just read.

Since writers select among a shared set of lexical, grammatical, and syntactic resources, the texts they produce are constituted by new uses of already-inhabited language. Theoretically, in outlining the various factors that limit the choices a writer has available in the process of constructing a text, we may distinguish one set of factors that are associated with convention (and include norms and practices, like the genre of the text, the cultural context within which the text is produced, the values of the discourse community [Ivanič, 1998: 41], the subject matter, or the linguistic features of a particular language), from another set encompassing those factors that allow for more play or individual freedom, capturing the stylistic or creative choices an individual writer makes within the limits of the situation. Bakhtin's dialogics may, in fact, serve as the umbrella frame for both convention-driven choices and choices that resist, move beyond, unsettle or disrupt convention.

The notion of dialogism has been further developed by French linguist Frédéric François (1998) in his concept of *reprise-modification* as the fundamental discursive movement at work in all forms of discourse. *Reprise-modification* means, literally, re-taking-up-modifying. It is realized on the textual level, and can be revealed in all aspects of linguistic structure, from words to syntax to text structures. It can also be revealed in the slippery in-between spaces of text construction, the moments not always localized in one or another specific word, phrase, or genre. *Reprise-modification* thus involves reproducing words, phrases, utterances, passages in a variety of ways that simultaneously modify them. This concept is a natural extension of Bakhtin's dialogics, with each student utterance acting as "a link in a chain," both built on the history-in-use of words and looking towards their reception by readers or speakers (Bakhtin, 1986).

Dialogism should not be seen as neutral or cooperative. M.L. Pratt (1990) uses the term *literate arts* to describe dialogic moments which are, in fact, the site of contact and contest. She uses the example of a South American native's letter about Spanish massacres and oppression, written and sent to King Philip of Spain hundreds of years ago but not read until the 20th century because the culture of the time could not accommodate the heterogeneous text supplied by the native. Using the frame of interaction between cultures as a "contact zone," she suggests that successful literate interaction is almost always carried out in situations of unequal power and negotiation; the term of "literate arts" is used in reference to strategies for success.

A notion closely interrelated to dialogism is that of *intertextuality*. As Paltridge (1997) points out, several literary theorists have been influential in developing the notion of intertextuality, including Foucault, Barthes, and Bloom, although he credits Kristeva with introducing this notion as Bakhtin's challenge to static, homogeneous views of genre which was seen as independent of social and historic contexts. Many theorists have built upon this Bakhtinian frame to argue that genres are flexible expressions of shared group values and that utterances reflect accumulated meanings while creating new text (Hanks, 1989 cited in Paltridge, 1997: 11).

The Bakhtinian frame described above provides us with a way of reading student texts that foregrounds values other than traditional originality. Bakhtin argues that utterances are double-voiced; he uses the term "ventriloquy" to express the power of dialogic overtones (cited in Ivanič, 1998: 48). Discursive movements like "copying" become necessary steps in text construction; the nature of the copying becomes quite interesting, and cultural differences in its value become apparent (Ivanič, 1998: 3-4). In fact, we can think about copying as one strategy along a continuum of strategies of reprise-modification: copying, quoting, paraphrasing, summarizing, referring to, linking outward from a single word, indirectly suggesting, referring to through connection to a cultural commonplace, echoing through association, stylistic allure, or implied assumption, and so on. These have been presented in other studies (see Folman, & Connor on originality of content conceptualization, in this volume) as moving from less to more original, though this linear path may seem insufficient. The theoretical frame provided by Bakhtin and François indicates that any one of these strategies can be more or less "original."

According to this entire dialogic perspective, then, written text production cannot be operationalized as the acquisition of the set of static conventions shaping meaning in texts but as a dynamic negotiation that involves the writer in the process of moving with and against given resources, adopting, bending, and diverting available textual patterns and resources to attain his/her communicative ends. This process is a factor in the evolution of convention itself; rather than showing a "smooth progression towards possession" of academic discourse, student texts show diverse forms of negotiation (Donahue, 2002b: 68; Ivanič, 1998: 52). These forms are henceforth referred to as forms of "textual movements." These movements are not seen as constituents of an inventory of strategic structuring steps (as Swales [1990] has suggested in his categories of text moves used in the introductory paragraphs of academic articles), but as ways of naming modes of discursive progression (not necessarily linear) in a text. Textual movements (also referred to as "literate arts" by M.L. Pratt) as dialogic moments can be subsumed under the general notion of *reprises-modifications* defined above. We localize the discursive arts in the identification and description of students' movements of *reprise-modification*, textual movements which play with reproduction, reprise of the expected, invention of the new, and modification in the very act of appropriation. This chapter considers particular examples of *reprises-modifications*, ones related to working with a prompt text, but all of the other possible reprises are at the horizon of the discussion.

School expectations: Multiple factors, of course, influence the construction of a given text, such as genre expectations, language parameters, institutional norms and scholastic expectations, both stated and implied. Some of these influences are crucial to the discussion, in particular those related to the school situation as a discourse community. Given the utopic connotations Harris (1997), Pratt (1990) and others have suggested we tend to attach to the notion of community, certain clarifications are necessary. The notion of community is quite problematic; it implies relative homogeneity, a sense of belonging, implied standards of cooperation, shared goals and projects, shared conventions and world-views, a shared language and so on. In this view, texts are produced and interpreted against criteria defined and imposed by certain discourse communities, and student writers must adopt the valued practices and conventions of the community in order to be heard. The term "community" invites monolithic perspectives and images of a nurturing space with clear boundaries, welcoming initiation. However, most close looks at particular communities bring out as much difference as they do shared elements.

In addition, while the metaphor of the discourse community offers a way to understand why students might express themselves in conventional ways, it does not account for the reasons student texts exploit these same conventions in various ways. In fact, students joining the school community are often not in the evoked situation at all. Pratt's (1986b) term of "discursive spaces" might be preferable to that of "discourse communities," precisely because it frees us from the apolitical innocence and apparent stability of "community" while allowing us to talk about at least temporary groups that student writers join in order to successfully navigate through their studies.

Students' texts produced in a particular school situation, or class do share certain identifiable strategies for making meaning, but these texts are far from interchangeable. Their discourse is neither some part of full-blown academic discourse, nor just an immature version of that discourse, but constitutes its own genre. Learning this discourse means learning the activities and conventions associated with it, though not being wholly assimilated by them. Students' texts offer us concrete traces of the negotiating acts of this "bridge" discourse, thus allowing us to capture, at least for a moment, the dynamic interaction between text and school as context.

The school genre studied in this paper is an essay which is defined via a specific set of parameters in the French classroom. It is essentially interpreted as a response to an excerpt taken from a respected author. Dozens of assignments collected during the study from French classrooms, descriptions of successful essays in privately-published student help books and textbooks, and official descriptions of student essays in government-produced curricular materials all call for essays with a *brief introduction*, *a development* in a thesis-antithesis-synthesis structure, *use of examples* from literary, historical, and current events sources but not from personal experience, a *generalized voice*, which makes an argument in the sense of a logical discussion of the various points and counterpoints of an issue, and *a conclusion-synthesis*, which establishes the student's stance on the issue presented – again, without personalizing that stance. The essay should be concise, detailed, well reasoned and clearly formatted; it should show the student's "culture générale" (cultural literacy) and control over language, syntax, and grammar.

3   DATA AND METHODOLOGICAL FRAMEWORK

3.1 Describing the Methodological Framework

The work detailed in this chapter has developed out of a descriptive analytic study of 250 student texts and a sub-study of 40 of these texts, from the US and France, collected during a five-year period. The students were in 11th-13th grade, responding to questions about social issues after having read a published text, texts, or an extracted piece of a text related to these issues.

If, in light of the discussion in the previous section, text construction and reception are best conceptualized of as dialogic and heterogeneous, based on context, reader interpretation, and layers of meaning, the methodology to be used for describing and analyzing these students' texts must match this complex openness. "One of the aims of the conversation analyst," Paltridge points out, "is to avoid *a priori* assumptions about analytical categories and to look for phenomena which regularly and systematically occurs in the data" (Paltridge, 1997: 14). Halliday (1985, cited in Paltridge, 1997: 3) suggests that "selective analysis," choosing and developing data for the purpose at hand, is effective. The larger studies I have done have favoured offering a comprehensive multi-layered perspective that combines both quantitative and qualitative analysis; for the purposes of this shorter discussion I restrict the analysis to certain features of *reprise-modification* that exemplify the work going on between the student text and the prompt text.

The focus is directed on exploring the methods students employ for "appropriating" a discourse, i.e., taking full ownership, integrating oneself into the discourse through a sort of acculturation (see Bartholomae, 1985a; Bautier, 1995; Bizzell, 1992; Harris, 1997). The term selected, however, *reprise-modification,* is presented as a more useful, all-encompassing term, with less baggage attached to it and less implied agency than that of "appropriation." It allows us to see that student writers are truly both creating and being created by the words, phrases, styles, patterns they use to write, as has been suggested by Ivanič and others.

The methodological framework developed for this interpretive analysis is grounded in functional linguistics, literary criticism, and composition theory but combines them in ways no one of them would develop alone.

Systemic functional linguistics as represented by Halliday (1985) (see for a discussion, Ivanič, 1998: 39-40) offers tools for capturing the situational and cultural-historical contexts of meaning-making in order to emphasize that meaning is not an individual choice. Paltridge (1997) points out that in the examination of any written text, meaning is grounded in the contexts of culture and situation. The sociolinguistic perspective offers ways by which we may link the text findings to larger social issues and explore specific features of intertextuality; from the sociolinguistic perspective I employ the notion that language is a means of expressing social identity (for a further analysis on this, see Ivanič, 1998) and that genre users are working with an overall communicative "budget," which may include routinized models of socially relevant communication and social stocks of knowledge that vary from individual to individual (Paltridge, 1997: 21).

Several perspectives from literary critics have provided complementary strands of theoretical thought, one capturing the way genres work within various discourse communities (such as those of school-based discourse community) (see, for example, Genette, 2002) and the other exploring how analysts might read such a discourse (see Culler, 1982; Eco, 1989; Jauss, 1978; Starobinski, 1970). From this perspective we can learn how a reader who is a teacher might rethink his/her relationship with student writing, becoming, at least provisionally, another kind of reader.

Developments in composition theory have allowed us to consider issues concerning students' process of initiation into school-based writing. Specifically, the social constructionist perspective provides very valuable insights into the development of writer's identity (see Bautier, & Rochex, 1997; Ivanič, 1998). Though this perspective has questioned the concept of a unified self and emphasized the social influences that create many different identities, it has not paid sufficient attention to the fact that the individual still does, must, exist – some real thing must be the site of the social influences. Various notions have been proposed by researchers. Goffman uses the notion of the "performer" (Ivanič, 1998: 22). François (2002) describes the biological "*sac de peau*" (skin-enclosed being) (personal communication).[3] In order to keep both the social emphasis and the reality of individuals in play, I prefer to focus upon the various textual *movements* between the more social and the more individ-

---

[3] *I am well aware of the ongoing debates about the constructed self, biological bases for language development, nature/nurture and so on. What I am positing is a necessary and intricate relationship between the social and the biological.*

ual, between the more convention-tied and the more creative choices made by a
writer. However, I would argue that we cannot clearly identify particular textual
features as belonging to one category or the other.

3.2 Locating Dialogic Elements in Students' Texts

In the larger study conducted (see Donahue, 2002a, 2002b, 2002c), the overall set of
features recorded included word choice, construction of subject positions with first,
second and third person in the singular/plural and with passive voice, integration of
other voices (paraphrase, quote, definition, etc.), local and global coherence devices
(deixis, explicit connectives, built-in shared assumptions, larger organizational patterns), argument strategies (examples, natural logic, assertions, placement of thesis),
and so on. These features were chosen during an initial holistic reading of all of the
texts. The quantitative study identified potential patterns of text function and construction but left unanswered many questions about the interrelationship of linguistic
choices, context, subject matter and structure. A subsequent close reading of a subgroup of the essays enabled an account of multiple factors occurring and influencing
each other (and thus the reading of each essay) simultaneously. The categories presented here are specifically those which help us locate dialogic features in terms of a
writer's response to another text (in this case to a prompt text) but potentially to
other texts students encounter; that is, a few of the integrated features of what students take, modify, and reproduce à leur compte from both the text read and the dynamic context. These categories, however, fit into and are supported by larger overall patterns of various indicators which tend to move together to create certain effects. What is most important in this particular analytic-interpretive approach is that:
- the interpretation offered is not a statement about "the" way to consider each
  text but one way of reading student texts among others;
- this way (represented partially here) includes a re-synthesis of the various individual textual components broken out by the analysis – this has been one of the
  greatest handicaps to some versions of discourse analysis in the past, such as
  text studies focusing on an isolated coherence device or on a single form, such
  as a pronoun's presence or absence in a student's text.
The specific categories considered for this chapter include:
- reprise word-for-word,
- reprise through paraphrase,
- reprise of assignment language,
- reprise of stylistic allure or atmosphere,
- reprise of political perspective,
- reprise through use of examples, and
- reprise through use of commonplaces
"Commonplace" is used here in the rhetorical sense, to name the ready-made molds
into which arguments, thoughts, experiences are often poured (François, 1998).
They may be the cognitive commonplaces of concepts or the linguistic commonplaces of utterances, both authorized by an institution or a culture as pre-articulated
ways of apprehending or expressing common experiences (Bartholomae, 1985a: 17).

The essence of a culture, the collective memory of that culture as described by Paltridge (1997: 20), is generally reflected in its commonplaces, its highly distilled versions of common wisdoms; students who end their texts with neat statements about
education as the solution to all of our problems or who reflect on how an experience
has changed their lives by describing the pre-self and the post-self of the experience
are using these commonplaces, unexamined or naturalized ready-made ways of seeing and explaining experience; these allow members of a culture both to express
experiences and understandings in a shared way and to come to understand their
own experiences as, in fact, shared, not unique. Commonplaces are sometimes close
to clichés and stereotypes, expressions along a continuum of possibilities for processing ideas, beliefs and lived moments.

4   STUDENT TEXTS IN THEIR CONTEXT

The texts analyzed in this chapter were written in the late 1990's in French classrooms, by students preparing to take the French portion of the *Baccalauréat* exam.
The students worked on a particular kind of essay, an *étude d'un texte argumentatif*
(study of an argumentative text), which was introduced in 1996 and already modi-
fied in the French national program by 2001. The essay was designed to offer students the opportunity to work on the production of an "argumentative" text; this task
required that students respond (through a series of short answers) to the perspective
outlined in the prompt text, and then produce a written essay developing, critiquing,
or extending the argument in some way. In the study under examination, the essays
read by the students were excerpts from larger works, *La vérité en marche* by Emile
Zola and *Les yeux ouverts* by Marguerite Yourcenar (a translated paragraph from
Yourcenar and from Zola is provided in Appendix A, to give the sense and flavour
of each author's style). Each excerpt was approximately 700 words long, a full sin-
gle-spaced page of text.

The Yourcenar text was a short piece taken from a series of interviews with the
author. The subject of the excerpt is solitude. The interviewer, Mathieu Galey, asks
Yourcenar whether she feels alone, even when surrounded by others, in the way
great writers often do. Yourcenar's response is first an affirmation of the solitude we
all feel, solitude when we are born, when we die, at work, in sickness. She counters
this with the assertion that she feels no more alone than other human beings, although she is physically alone at certain points of the day – early in the morning,
late at night, as she works on ideas…Yourcenar follows this with a development of
the many ways in which she is not alone. She points to being visited frequently,
sharing her everyday life with her daily contacts (housekeeper, grocer, gardener,
village children) and reaching out to other circles, friends with shared tastes and
concerns. Yourcenar's final point is that those who welcome others are rarely alone,
and that class and culture do not count in these relationships, that humans are constantly overcoming the effects of class. Yourcenar's rhetorical strategies include
parallel cumulative syntax, rhetorical questions, concrete examples used to evoke
abstract commentaries, images used to connect to conceptual claims. The Yourcenar

essay question asked students to consider whether in our day and age, the effects of social class and culture can be easily overcome.

The Zola text is an excerpt from one of Zola's exhortative pieces, a direct call for the youth of his generation to move towards a just society. He calls this the "great need" or "great duty" of the next generation. The piece is written in 1901 and is specifically designed to reach out at the start of a new era. In a play back and forth between the older generation and the younger generation, with a lexical chain of equivalencies for age and youth, past and future, ends and beginnings, Zola details the work that has been accomplished (science, generosity, productivity, honour in battles for justice and free speech and thought) and outlines the struggles to face ahead (a greater freedom, a stronger justice, tolerance, truth, and humanity). He uses layer upon layer of rhetorical strategy: repetitions of syntax and phrasing, direct address with the informal "tu," strong patterns of contrast between good and evil in point-counterpoint, the imperative, sentences that shame the listener (*we will only be ready to die if we know you will carry on; aren't you ashamed that we (older ones) are more impassioned than you about what should be your great need?*), imaginary dialogue that puts words in the mouth of the reader/listener, and connections to shared experiences with this intended recipient. The essay in response to Zola was to describe the "great need" or the "great call" awaiting the current generation, developing and carefully organizing the essential aspects.

4.1 An Introductory Example

Before launching into the interpretation of the six texts studied here, I would like to describe one of the texts in order to establish the stylistic flavour of this particular kind of French high school essay. This is not to suggest that all texts produced are similar nor that this text is "representative" (which it is not) but rather to give a sense of the work involved in these particular school artifacts. A full translation of this text, as well as a sample of a student's Zola response, is offered in Appendix B.

Text 1 (#77)[4] Christine D. / Travail d'Ecriture (all grammatical errors are left intact)

Alors que certaines personnes, comme M. Yourcenar dans "*La solitude pour être utile*", pense que "La classe (…) ne compte pas; la culture au fond très peu", d'autres ne tolèrent pas les différences et s'enferment dans leur univers. De nos jours, y a-t-il eu une évolution des esprits pour réellement dépasser ces distinctions entre individus? C'est ce à quoi je répondrai personnellement après avoir développer mon argumentation.

Premièrement, le temps passe et les nouvelles générations délaissent de plus en plus leur culture. Ainsi, les structures sociales, les manifestations religieuses ou intellectuelles qui définissent différents groupes tendent à se mélanger, se confondre pour occuper une place discrète dans les relations avec les autres. Mais ceci n'est pas spécifique à l'année 1996. Déjà avec le « melting pot » américain, le mélange de différentes civilisations se mettaient en place.

De même, les esprits évoluent. On accorde moins d'importance à la classe sociale des personnes qui nous entourent. Notamment à l'école les élèves ne sympathisent pas

---

[4] *All numbers in parentheses refer to the numbers assigned in the larger study of 250+ student essays.*

qu'avec d'autres élèves issus d'un même environnement culturel et social. Au moment de la récréation, les plus jeunes se préocupent plutôt de savoir lequel lance la balle le plus fort ou laquelle saute le mieux à l'élastique.

Cependant, la sensation d'insécurité dans laquelle se trouve certaines personnes les place dans une peur irrésonnée de l'inconnu. Alors elles ne souhaitent avoir des relations qu'avec des personnes de même éducation. Ainsi, les français dévisageraient un écossais s'il portait un kilt et se promenait dans les rues de la ville.

Par ailleurs, à travers l'acquisition de biens et de services, les individus expriment avant tout un besoin d'identification sociale. Par exemple, une personne achète une grosse voiture et par là même affiche un « rang social élevé », par conséquent, certains voisins sont intimidés et les relations entre-eux deviennent donc très réduites.

Parfois, les distinctions sont involontaires. Exepté quelques rares cas, des études récentes sur le choix du conjoint ont démontré que l'homogamie (c'est-à-dire un mariage avec une personne ayant des caractéristiques socio-économiques semblables) est dominante aujourd'hui. Aussi 77% des agriculteurs se marient entre agriculteur.

Malheureusement donc, volontaire ou pas, même en 1996, les différences de classe et de culture sont difficilement dépassées. Cependant avec l'évolution de la société, on peut espérer que dans quelques années, ces dissemblances n'existeront plus.

This student essay comes from the Lycée Julliot de la Morandière, Granville, académie de Caen. This lycée is a large, comprehensive public school, including college preparatory, pre-professional and vocational-technical programs. About 80% of the students pass the *Baccalauréat* exam annually.

The school's population is fairly representative of various socioeconomic groups and most of the students are interested in pursuing higher education. In particular, the vocational-technical program represents a real possibility for improving students' socioeconomic status; children of working-class families can move to higher status as technicians or in middle management. The student writer of this essay was in the vocational-technical program, in her penultimate year of studies. At the end of this year, she would face the French essay portion of the Baccalauréat exam.

The explicitly scholastic nature of the essay is already obvious from the title, *"Travail d'Ecriture"* (Writing Work). The essay is handwritten, which is the norm for French school work, often even in university-level studies. The essay's format clearly delimits the introduction, body, pivot-sentence between the two parts of the body, and conclusion with double spaces.

The essay's introduction is comprised of three sentences. The first presents an outline of the pro-con type: *"Yourcenar thinks... but others think..."* This announcement is followed by an explicit reprise of the assignment's language and finally by a statement by the student, *je répondrai personnellement (I will personally speak to this).* This statement, while atypical, does establish the presence of the student. And yet, it does not provide the student's actual perspective, the "thesis" as American teachers might call it. It only suggests that such a perspective will eventually be given.

The essay's overall A/B structure after the introduction is divided into two parts: the presentation of the student's interpretation of Yourcenar's ideas (*newer generations let go of their cultures and people are evolving*) and the presentation of potential ("others") opposition to her ideas (*some still have unreasonable fears of the unknown, need social identification, homogamy is still prevalent today*).

After the introductory sentence in each part, presented in italics in the text above, ideas are developed through a series of the assertions mentioned above, followed by generalized cultural, historic, or statistical examples: religions are mixing, children in the schoolyards play together regardless of class membership, people buy fancy cars to show their affiliation, a large percentage of agricultural workers still marry among themselves, and so on. The A/B structure is supported by frequent explicit connectors, in particular time frame connectors such as *premièrement; avant tout (first, first of all)* and contrastive connectors such as *alors que; mais; cependant (while, but, however)*.

The relationship between the Yourcenar text and the student's essay is one which was fairly typical of the French students' essays in the larger study. Once the point of the essay, the general focus, is established, the content of the prompt text itself often becomes far less relevant. In this example, in fact, Yourcenar's text is no longer directly mentioned at all. The elements discussed in the essay might have originated from thinking about the prompt text, but the text itself is no longer the focus of the student's work.

In addition, in this particular example, the assignment does not relate directly to Yourcenar's actual main theme of solitude. The issues of "class" and "culture" appear only briefly at the end of her short excerpt. The prompt text thus becomes a literal point of departure.

Although observing the classroom situation of production was not part of this study, the texts offer clues about what was covered in class or in other related readings. For example, the student here cites the infrequency of intermarriages between agricultural workers and other social classes, a specific example used in several of the students' essays in this group and not likely to have been spontaneously generated by so many students.

The concluding paragraph, in traditional French school style, presents the "thesis" in an even-handed way: *on the one hand, class and cultural differences are difficult to overcome, but, on the other hand, as society evolves one can hope…* This kind of balanced perspective (as opposed to a forceful thesis) is quite typical of French student essays.

5   FORMS OF REPRISE-MODIFICATION

The sample analyzed above contains examples of some of the features that are frequently found in French student writing, some more specific to this particular assignment, and others related to the individual student's response. Our sense of the shared (the conventional) and the individual (the creative) is generally sharpened when we look at groups of essays in response to a prompt; the generic limits on the text and the elements of individual "style" are easier to draw out.

The two groups of texts presented here are selected from the largest sample and analyzed in detail because they offered the most interesting examples, in my judgement, of the specific kinds of reprise-modifications discussed in this chapter. As already noted, the analysis is not meant to provide definite conclusions on the strategies this specific age group of students adopts in their writing but rather to outline the basic elements of the dialogic way of reading student texts. The texts analyzed do their work in multiple ways, but I will look primarily at how they draw certain features, information, and other textual, linguistic, and stylistic elements from the prompt texts they read. All of them are built with the most essential textual movement of *reprise-modification*, which takes multiple forms, from simple reprise of the actual language the student is using (here, French) to complex reprises of cultural thought patterns or intimate genre structures.

The very nature of the two questions posed in the assignments studied, *"speak for your generation"* (in response to Zola) or *"speak about overcoming the effects of class and culture in this day and age"* (in response to Yourcenar), invites a response built on commonplaces and other reprises. All six essays instantiate what Bartholomae (1985a) might call "approximations" of academic discourse. In "Inventing the University," Bartholomae suggests that students often must begin their integration into university discourse, their appropriation of it, by simply repeating the words of the text in front of them, slowly moving from that "mouthing" to a recreation of their own text. But he argues that what students produce in this evolutionary process is an approximation of academic discourse, a semblance which moves slowly towards a "true" habitation of the discourse. I would argue two points here to nuance this perspective: (1) average[5] students' texts, rather than approximations of some future-expert discourse, are legitimate moments of a "bridge" discourse, moments of negotiation, always temporary, always a use of the available that adopts, chooses, rejects, transforms in order to communicate within the situation at hand which is itself a provisional situation and not a long-term integration into an academic universe, and (2) this progressive (but not linear) evolution occurs in all of our integrations into new discursive situations. This is the way intertextuality works. Every textual movement identified here is one version or another, along a continuum, of the dialogic movements to which readers and interpreters respond: dialogic in that they are versions of re-using, re-inventing each word, phrase, and utterance put into play. Each movement identified is not closer to convention or further from it; each utterance can be more or less original in its own right, depending on its use rather than its nature.

In the texts described, the movements in question are: heavily influenced by the language of the assignment, built on cultural commonplaces frequently circulated in the media, the students' daily circles, and school settings, and supported by examples based largely in literary and sociohistorical contexts. They use occasional personalized examples transformed into generalized ones, overall structures organized along present versus past binary lines, and build on (assumed) shared values and perspectives, sometimes in ways that seem to recreate stereotypes.

---

[5] *"Average" is used here in descriptive ways, as opposed to statistical ways – to indicate that we are looking at student texts which are not far outside of the norm, neither outstanding nor judged as problematic by readers who are teachers. This means that the student texts studied had received a grade of B-C or, in France, 9-13/20, and were collected from classes of students in schools which equally fell in the national norm for middle-ground schools, neither elite nor troubled.*

5.1 Reprise-Modification of the Language of the Assignment

The introductory paragraph in each of the essays presented here is invariably tied to the wording of the assignment, along the lines of, for example, *"We can ask ourselves, then, whether in this day and age it is possible to overcome the effects of class and culture,"* in response to the assignment described above, *"consider whether in our day and age, the effects of social class and culture can be easily overcome."* These explicit *reprises* place the texts squarely in the domain of school writing and ensure the student writer's place in the conversation that the assignment proposes.

5.2 Reprise-Modification of the Prompt Text's Theses

The Yourcenar texts show *reprise-modification* of Yourcenar's politics (as well as the politics and values, upper-middle-class, of the educational system). The arguments tend towards compromise, a middle-of-the-road "let's all get along" message represented by an articulation of the "good" (read, liberal-humanist) point of view, the kind of message educators tend to favour. One student says *"If the differences of class and culture have softened over the years, with the relaxing of social and cultural barriers and the fact that individuals are getting closer, we still note that, to a fair degree, important differences subsist and unfortunately the class system remains in place"* (Text 2: #52). There is some shared confusion across texts about culture-as-ethnic group versus culture-as-arts and aesthetics, although on the whole the texts portray fairly common versions of class and culture: class represented through economic stratification, culture represented through differences in nationality or ethnic group.

The students writing in response to Zola congratulate the previous generation, as does Zola, and criticize war as does Zola. The concluding paragraph in all six essays tends towards a doubtful commentary on the practicality of the proposed solutions, in particular because of weak human nature. One essay says, for example, *"The problems of lack of solidarity, intolerance, and racism are due to a lack of knowledge about others and a lack of maturity among people which prevents them from overcoming their frustrations..."* (Text 6: #104).

Texts also reproduce and modify the fairly liberal-humanist values of anti-discrimination, social welfare, and education. The arguments tend more towards social critique and cast doubt on human nature's ability to pull off change. The great needs identified are in no way surprising, at least not to this reader. They seem quite part of l'air du temps, the news, current events, "les discours qui courent" (current hot topics), perhaps even other classes the students share. But for the student writer discovering these concepts, they may well, of course, be new. The interesting factor in reprise-modification is that we never quite know the degree to which the reprises are simply mouthing as opposed to taking on for oneself the perspective (content) or the phrasing (ways of expressing) in question, even when the reprise is word-for-word.

5.3 Reprise-Modification of the Atmosphere of the Prompt Text

Some of the texts operate with a kind of intellectual-affective *reprise-modification*, constructing a dialogue with the prompt author by recognizing the value of the author's perspective in the same gentle way that the prompt text appeared to respectfully present a balanced perspective. Yourcenar is presented first by giving her credit for being a thoughtful, intelligent, or caring individual: *"On the subject of solitude, the author opened up the theme of the relationships she maintains with people around her and declared that she gave «only modest attention to class and culture»"* (Text 2: #52). Only then are the counterpoints presented, as if to imply that Yourcenar might be a better person than the rest of us: *"But we wonder whether today it is easy to overcome barriers of class and culture or whether there are barriers between different social milieux"* (Text 2: #52).

This affective reprise only goes so far, however. The three texts did not reproduce Yourcenar's use of the first person, for example. She often presents herself directly, as in: *"I have many friends in the village; the people I employ, and without whom I would have trouble maintaining my large property which is after all fairly isolated, and lacking the time and the physical energy needed to maintain the yard and house, are friends."* The French school norm to avoid first-person, narrative, self-reflective writing appears to override Yourcenar's influence in personalizing the arguments. Yourcenar talks of herself, the students do not even thought they are technically invited to. These students, in 11th grade (the students writing about Zola were in 12th grade) and not in the elite track of French secondary studies, may be relatively more convention-tied.

5.4 Reprise-Modification of the Prompt Text's Stylistic Allure

We can trace specific stylistic features of the prompt texts in the students' texts. From Yourcenar's style, students borrow, take on and appropriate a tone of reasonableness and the assignment's allure of compromise. One student, for example, says *"In addition, through the acquisition of goods and services, individuals express above all a need for social identification"* (Text 1: #77). The word "need" suggests that the writer feels the individuals in question might be justified, and the term "social identification" is positive in its implication that groups of disparate individuals can seek out inclusion. In another example, the writer says *"Sometimes, the distinctions (class-based) are involuntary"* (Text 1: #77). The use of the word *involuntary* is connected to a sense of understanding and recognition of social factors beyond the individual's control. The assignment suggests that Yourcenar allows only a modest role for the effects of class and culture, and queries whether we can easily rise above these differences; the student in Text 1 is equally moderate in her perspective, suggesting that *"unfortunately, voluntary or not, even in 1996, class and culture differences are difficult to overcome. However with the evolution of society, we can hope that in a few years, those dissimilarities will no longer exist."* In addition, the student voice of the archi-spectator, historicized and reasonable, dominates this essay. The student claims that her description of cultural problems is *"not specific to 1996"* and that the American melting pot model is a good example. She thus demonstrates a reasonable perspective, recognizing historicized features of the discussion at hand.

Some texts work with a series of auto-reprises in the variant definitions of culture: culture appears as social structure, as religious or intellectual groups, as civilization, as ethnic groups, and as social environment – all variants on a theme, subtly building the overall notion. In Text 2, the notion is built through repeated terms like "open" and "closed," the repeated binary of social progress and improvement tempered by frustration at the continued and evolving ways discrimination occurs: *"Even though culture (in the sense of arts and cultivation) has been opened up only recently to all social classes, it still stays more privileged for members of the upper class. In this way, this culture stays open to everyone but the lower classes only get a glimpse"* (Text 2: #52). At the same time, the student's text coheres with a quite typical present-past binary, which is a frequently used academic structure. In other eras, the student says, social class limited people's options. Now, things are improving. However, the remaining problems are becoming worse. Society may evolve, she argues, but individuals do not, and the bourgeois still innovate (her term) new methods of exclusion. This binary thread parallels the binary Yourcenar constructs as she weaves back and forth between recognition of solitude and counterpoint development of ways in which she is never alone.

The Zola texts show a strong *reprise-modification* of the stylistic patterns of Zola's speech (the tone, syntax, urgency, rhetorical strategies including heavy use of the imperative, exhortation, and repetition for emphasis – all of the stylistic aspects described earlier). In response to Zola, students put into play several kinds of stylistic reprise, while there is essentially no reprise of specific content (themes, arguments, ideas). The terms representing big abstract notions are repeated often, in particular the words "violence," "racism," and "intolerance;" parallel sentence structures emphasize the rhythm, such as in this passage:

> "It is true that our society knows great uneasiness due to a forgotten element. The forgotten great value of tolerance. [...] We can find the remedies. [...] In particular for the examples close to home, like homeless people that we ignore out of "habit," or in front of whom we look away in shame. Well, be shameful! But do not stay indifferent. Dare to look at the problem in order to find in our hearts the solution. Do not turn away from the more distant examples, either, like the war in Bosnia which flows from incomprehension among peoples. Be honest with ourselves and get interested. Stop closing ourselves behind our pride..." (Text 4: #101)

The *"osons...soyons...oossons..."* (dare be stop...) or *"...un oubli. L'oubli..."* (...a forgotten element. The forgotten...) are powerful syntactic structures that resemble those seen in Zola's text. The rhetorical question-answer format is frequently repeated as well: *"Do you believe this massacre would have happened? Of course not!"* or *"How many conflicts are the result of this misunderstanding [...]? All!"* These various rhetorical strategies appear throughout Zola's text, an oratory piece with ringing syntactic force.

5.5 Reprise-Modification of Structure

Texts do their work by shadowing the underlying structure of prompt texts – the organization, the order of information, the pattern of concrete examples used to construct supported versions of abstract concepts. Text 6, for example, picks up on the structure of Zola's piece in particularly strong ways. For example, the assignment did not ask for solutions, only an articulation of the generation's great needs. But Zola provides solutions in his text – rise up, get involved, pursue justice, remember your fathers' pain – and so does this student:*"Each individual's attitude must change. For example in the combat against extreme poverty carried out by Albert Jacquart,"* or *"It is through informing people and raising their awareness that we can banish intolerance."* He also introduces these connections with explicit parallels, such as *"Zola says..."* *"and so we, youth of today, also must..."*

Text 2 presents the notion of class in a series of variant implied definitions, much the same way that Yourcenar implicitly develops the notions of solitude and interdependence. Yourcenar builds her definitions on the assumption that "alone" is equivalent to "without others' physical presence" and offers various examples of the few times she is actually alone and the many times she is not: the delivery man stops for a glass of wine, the friends with shared interests call. This use of concrete examples to build a sense of the notion of "not alone" is the approach the student writer uses in Text 2 to build the notion of "class" when, for example, he describes parents preventing their children from attending dances with other children of a different class.

5.6 Reprise-Modification through Commonplaces

Texts appear to be crafted in step with the already-said and the to-be-said of larger social debates. The proposed solutions are commonplaces, the primary one being a liberal-good citizen worldview in which education is the ready-to-hand solution for our problems ("education is the solution" or "youth will show us the way"). In particular, the kernel notion that intolerance will be overcome by education and open mindedness, clearly a perspective both Yourcenar and Zola would support, reappears as a central guiding mold for students' thoughts. One student suggests that men are at their worst when they choose to remain ignorant; another argues that lack of knowledge about the other leads to intolerance and racism.

The texts rely equally heavily on doxic values: democracy, equality, antiviolence. The central themes of liberty, justice, humanitarianism underlie all three Zola essays. Text 4 points out that charity begins at home; Text 6 points to the importance of change starting from within. Again, the subject matter and the question invite these commonplaces. And they are for students, for us all, the place to start, a culturally available way of talking about the subject at hand. We would perhaps be hard put to design assignments for students that do not call on these available forms, forms students inhabit for as long as they need them in their academic apprenticeship.

5.7 Reprise-Modification through Examples

The texts are constructed with strategies that allow student writers to reproduce-modify the personal by speaking "around" personal experiences without actually telling their own stories. Several examples fall into the category of "suspiciously non-personal," as in the student who talks with rancour about how some bourgeois families invite only closed, elite circles of students to their dance parties. Others are clearly local experiences: games at recess as the great social equalizer among young, still-innocent children, encounters between the Parisian elitist and the resident of public housing, or possession of material goods as an indicator of wealth – the big car, the nice house.

Traditional academic examples are offered as well. Some are sociohistoric, such as marriage statistics, shared metaphors such as the "melting pot" image, etc. Others are literary, series of references to famous figures or authors making statements that support the student's claims: *"The stupidity of mankind resides in his willingness to remain ignorant, and according to Einstein, «two things are infinite: the universe and human stupidity, although about the universe, I'm still not absolutely sure»"* (Text 4: #101), or *"Tolstoi affirmed that «wealth is a crime because it assures the dominance of those who have over those who do not»."*

Only one student offers an explicitly "local" example, citing lines from the popular rap group "Assassins," although even this reference is not made personally (as in, "I hear in the words from this song…"); instead, he says *"This is what brought 'Assassins' to show their discontent in one of their most piercing songs, «the African is my brother, the Muslim and the Jew I respect their prayers»"* (Text 6: #104).

5.8 The Unstated, the Implied

As in much published writing, including the two pieces represented here, students build their responses at least partly on unstated assumptions. Text 1, for example, constructs its argument based on the non-explicit themes of the innocence of children, of education as potentially removing innocence, of innocence as robbed by capitalism. Culture in this essay is ethnic, in fact it is the equivalent of ethnocentrism, although this equivalence is again only implied. The assignment is implicated in this result, as culture is presented by the assignment itself as an obstacle to overcome.

In the negotiations students carry out, none argues completely outside of the realm of the expected. No one makes the case, for example, that the poor have a culture or that cultural difference *isn't* something to "overcome."

One essay is built on the assumption that we don't want war, we don't want intolerance (Text 4: #101), since the text calls for banishing intolerance and discusses the sad results of war; another sets up a very subtle reference to the "veil" we need to remove because it obstructs our view; cultural references to veils are a flashpoint in French culture for larger issues of immigration and racial tension (Text 5: #102). These subtle references create a real sense of assumed shared values with readers.

Of course, shared assumptions can lead to stereotype as well. The student author of Text 6 demonstrates one of the ways in which this can happen when he describes the cause of juvenile delinquency, linking working parents' absence to the inevitable lack of authority figures in children's lives, leading them inevitably to search for alternate authority figures in local drug dealers.

6   INTERPRETING MOVEMENTS, LOCATING THE RESISTANCE

Any reading of student work (or of any other texts) is first and foremost an act of interpretation, however rigorous or analytic this interpretation might be. In light of this, therefore, it is clear that my aim is not to propose the "correct" understanding of the movements described above, nor a rigid classification, but to suggest a possible way of exploring these – a reading which will help us see how these various explicit moves instantiate elements of both the common or conventionally constructed set of thoughts, expressions, utterances and the new, the individually creative uses of these shared elements. Even more crucially, the focus was directed to identifying some aspects of each student writer's play between these two forces. I call this play "style" in the tradition of François (2002) and Starobinski (1970). We might also call it "voice," which is neither the deep, true voice of the expressivist self nor the fragmented voice of the socially constructed self, but a slippery voice-as-style located in the student writer's work as s/he moves across and between the shared and the specific. This focus on the play, through *reprise-modification*, with language and discourse permits a better understanding of how average students interact with readings and with both cultural and educational commonplaces, working from the already-said and respecting (at least some but rarely all of) the limits of textual expectations.

Available research has suggested that the negotiations student texts carry out represent students' "postures;" both the limits imposed and the individual freedom allowed to student writers have been discussed in terms of how students create their identities as a writer or construct school-based selves (see Bautier, & Rochex, 1997; Ivanič, 1998). Student texts thus represent discursive positions or provisional postures adopted by or assigned to student writers: the "writerly" or the "integrative" posture are among those described by Bautier, & Bucheton (1997), as are the "positivist" or "cooperative" posture described by Ivanic (1998). Several postures may be taken up in a single text.

While Ivanič, Bautier, & Bucheton emphasize the role of the student writer as negotiating an identity, here we have seen the text itself as a site within which we can observe the traces of this negotiation process. No closed inventory of any of these postures is posited, since these postures may recombine and shift constantly[6]. Student writers in particular both desire and resist the central discourses they are acquiring, working with shared convention as they have taken it and it has taken them, partly because they are in the relatively narrow position of needing to learn the rules operating in a discourse that they have not necessarily chosen to acquire.

---

[6] *These kinds of discursive postures need to be clearly distinguished from existential positions, the lived positions that students and other human beings inhabit. There may well be crossover between the two but not necessarily; among other things, language is not the only way to construct an identity.*

From the analysis presented in the previous section, it becomes clear that students in constructing their texts are influenced at multiple levels by the prompt texts they read. This is, of course, what the literacy contract of a working text is all about – entering the academy, entering the literate world – entering the conversation, the already-said, the to-be-said. It is interesting to see, however, the ways by which average texts bend and divert the imposed or suggested frames and arguments. Some such patterns are outlined below:

- All of the six texts use the literate art Pratt (1990) would call "transculturation": taking part of what a dominant culture claims but using it to different ends. Text 3 weaves in Yourcenar's perspective respectfully, but then develops opposition to her: *"Yourcenar says..." "...she "reasons well..."* But *"Others (we) say..."* and *"Yourcenar is right for herself but not for 'us'."* She succeeds where others – almost an implied "real" people, everyday people like the student – can't. This is a subtle rejection of Yourcenar that retains just the right amount of respect.

- Five of the six texts function by using what Pratt would call the "literate art of mediation" for subject matter that can't normally be expressed in the school situation. The students writing in response to Yourcenar may not feel free to critique bourgeois values. The school situation, an implicit locale for reproducing bourgeois values, is not the first place to be making a case for communism or for pure capitalism, for example. No student text resists Yourcenar with passion, questioning, for example, her claim that her maid is as important to her as her sister...The texts present an expression of unusual awareness of the role of schools in questions of the reproduction of class and bourgeois cultural values, as when one text suggests that the lower class tries to internalize the norms and the values of the middle-class through schooling that copies this milieu today, in order to educate children. Another text links the upper class with a more complete "culture" in the sense of cultivation. These are concepts a student could choose to talk about as a student, as the recipient of such social engineering, but it would be difficult. Yourcenar's text allows students to indirectly comment on the situation.

- Texts offer subtle shifts in emphasis, extending the argument presented in the prompt text. Text 5 steps further than Zola by claiming that we must preserve the values established by the previous generation (as says Zola) but we must go further, intensify our efforts. This subtle shift is a mild critique and a creative introduction of a newer perspective. Text 4 frequently explicitly works at integration into the academic conversation through auto-reformulations. The writer adds, for example, clarifying notes ("racism, that is") and parenthetic appositives ("They [the fathers]..."). This phenomenon is relatively rare in student writing, although academic authors permit themselves such asides and reconsiderations without hesitation.

- Texts are constructed with multiple responses when only one is called for. Text 6 retranslates "grande besogne" into "social problems," by lumping them all under the rubric "environmental problems." *"These are all forms of environment,"* the student says, *"a term which is not limited to air, water and space but regroups lots of other criteria – social, cultural, communicative, religious..."*

This approach cleverly allows for the essay to develop multiple points. In addition, they are not the types of "great needs" evoked by Zola. While he remains resolutely abstract and largely positive, calling for youth to pursue justice and democracy, this student and the two others discussing Zola identify specific problems and call for resolution of those problems. The examples are almost always from current situations or local issues – ghetto housing, drug dealing, immigration, children inadequately supervised – although again no personal experiences or examples appear.

7   CONCLUSION

This chapter set out to illustrate through the description of various movements of *reprise-modification*, or various literate arts, that texts and even students' texts are, in fact, constructed partly with the already-said and partly with the new; community-shaped expectations are not rejected, but neither are they bought into wholly. Texts do their work through the process of negotiating patterns, forms and values that are generally institutionally accepted, although quite often not specifically identified or applauded by teachers. Students are not being "taught" explicitly much of what they are picking up on: the cultural commonplaces, the stylistic reprises, the unstated assumptions. These effects are perhaps the most interesting ones to us as we think about teaching students to write.

Succinctly, by tracking these discursive arts – localized in *reprises-modifications* in a small corpus, the following tendencies were noted:

- texts do show traces of interaction with, influence by, more than just the "ideas" of the prompt texts the student authors read;
- community expectations and norms about content, structure, argument support can override the influences of the texts students encounter in their readings;
- cultural and educational commonplaces are both a way of expressing ideas about a theme but also a possible strategy of resistance;
- the individual interpretation/appropriation of words, expressions, structures can be the interaction that bends and diverts expectations and negotiates a place for a student's text to be heard.

These descriptions help us understand students' texts in a wider perspective as an act of negotiation. By identifying some of the ways in which the student writer's text produces meaning, we are led to developing a broader picture of school discourse, seen as a dynamic point of encounters between various elements: student-situation-history-context-language-institution.

This insight into students' discursive activities can change the way student work is read, with long-term effects. A Bakhtinian-informed dialogic perspective suggests, for example, that commonplaces are a necessary place to start, even to be. Writers work along a continuum, moving back and forth among the most obvious of reprises (i.e., the quote) to the most unstated (the commonplace). In between, writers might reprise-modify through paraphrase, example, or definition. Elements like stylistic allure or rhetorical echo are another axis of this continuum.

Inhabiting the thoughts of others, a necessary element for discourse construction, means cohabiting with the writer's own thoughts – an "other" who can even be one-self at another point in time. One of the problems with the expressivist position has been just this: it implies that writers can inhabit themselves first so that they are then more able to inhabit the ideas of others. But the "self – others" frontier is, as we can see from the student texts explored here, not clearly demarcated. There is no real way to tell what a student actually believes in his/her essay. We get the *feeling* that some are more sincere because their examples seem local or their passion seems real. But is it just that, a feeling? Would different readers get a different feeling? What rhetoric is at work? This is partly why the analysis presented here has focused on the texts themselves and not the student writers, who can not be directly deduced from their texts.

That said, the perceived influence of text and situation on the students' writing, described above, and their presentation of "self" – "perspective," suggests that it would be interesting to use the analytic method described here to follow students themselves, developmentally for example. We could follow a group of students over time, as Nancy Sommers has done with students at Harvard, to see whether they develop a (roughly) consistent perspective or are in fact as flexible as these prelimi-nary (isolated) results suggest. We could compare different social groups longitudi-nally and try to identify when various student writers pick up different negotiating strategies, whether some strategies seem to consistently appear before others, and what seems to encourage their acquisition. We could continue the cultural analysis begun in this study, and compare the strategies students from different cultural groups use when engaging in dialogic interactions with various genres constituting their school discourse. In such an inquiry, the methodological apparatus used in this chapter would provide an alternative to the traditional methodological requirements of cross-cultural contrastive research and could encourage researchers from different methodological perspectives to engage in fruitful dialogue about what each brings to our understanding of student writing in various cultural settings. Such a dialogue could be a challenging next step.

In any case, the students' texts produced and analyzed in this chapter show a fairly successful simultaneous sharing and striking out, a way of negotiating be-tween commonality and individuality, a way of performing the ongoing tension be-tween the two, creating the negotiation which is students' "bridge" discourse. The proposed receptive-interpretative way of reading these texts foregrounds such nego-tiations and opens the door to collaboration between discourse analysis and compo-sition theory.

APPENDIX A

AUTHOR'S TRANSLATION OF A PARAGRAPH FROM ZOLA AND YOURCENAR

Emile Zola:

Oh youth, youth! I beg you, dream of the great need which awaits you. You are the future worker, you will throw down the foundations of this next century, which, we believe firmly, will resolve the problems of truth and equity, posed by the century now coming to a close. We, the old, the older ones, we leave you the formidable weight of what we have searched for, many contradictions and obscurities perhaps, but surely the most impassioned effort any century has ever made towards enlightenment, the most honest and well-founded documents, the very foundations of this vast edifice which is science that you must continue to build for your honour and your happiness (in French, *honneur et bonheur*). And we ask you no more than to be even more generous, even more free-spirited, to surpass us by your love for everyday life, by your efforts put fully into your work, this fecundity of men and earth which will finally know how to make a harvest of joy overflow, under a shining sun. And we will fraternally give up our place for you, happy to disappear and to rest from our completed labor, in the happy sleep of death, if we know that you will continue and that you will carry out our dreams.

Marguerite Yourcenar:

I don't see the writer as more solitary than others. Look at my house: there is a continual coming-and-going of people, as if the house were breathing. It is only in rare periods that I feel alone, and even then, not completely. I am alone at work, if being surrounded by ideas or beings born from one's mind is being alone; I am alone in the morning, very early, when I watch the sunrise from my window or from the terrace; alone in the evening when I close the door to the house while I look at the stars. Which means that in fact I am never alone.

But in everyday life, again, we depend on other beings and they depend on us. I have many friends in the village; the people I employ, and without whom I would have trouble maintaining my large property which is after all fairly isolated, and lacking the time and the physical energy needed to maintain the yard and house, are friends; otherwise they wouldn't be here.

APPENDIX B

TRANSLATION OF SOME STUDENTS' TEXT SAMPLES:
Text 1: #77 Writing Work by Christine D.

While some people, like Margeurite Yourcenar in *Solitude in order to be useful*, think that "Class does not count, culture counts very little," others do not tolerate difference and close themselves into their universe. In this day and age, is there an evolution in people's thinking that will really allow us to overcome these distinctions between individuals? This is what I will respond to personally after having developed my argument.

First of all, time passes and new generations leave their culture more and more. Thus, social structures, religious and intellectual manifestations that define different groups tend to mix and become one and so occupy a more discreet place in relationships with others. But this is not specific to 1996. Already with the American "melting pot" the mix of different civilizations was happening.

In the same way, people's minds evolve. We assign less importance to the social class of those around us. In particular at school students don't get together with only other children from the same cultural and social environment. At recess, the youngest children are more preoccupied with who throws the ball the farthest or jumps rope best.

However, the feeling of insecurity in which some people find themselves puts them in a state of unreasonable fear of the unknown. So they just want to have relationships with people with the same education. So, the French would look askance at a Scotsman walking around the streets of Paris in a kilt.

In addition, through the acquisition of goods and services, individuals express above all a need for social identification. For example, a person buys a big car and by doing so, shows off a "high social level," consequently certain neighbors are intimidated and the relations between them are thus very limited.

Sometimes, the distinctions are involuntary. Except for a few rare cases, recent studies about choosing a mate have shown that homogamy (that is, a marriage with someone with similar socioeconomic characteristics) is dominant today. And so 77% of agricultural workers marry in their own group.

Unfortunately, then, voluntary or not, even in 1996, the differences in class and culture are difficult to overcome. However with the evolution of society, we can hope that in a few years, these differences won't exist any more.

Text # 4: #101, Writing Work by Aude B.

Our generation is the inheritor of the legacy of our ancestors who, by their experiences, arrived at great values. We must fight to preserve them. This contract is our "great duty." It is the same one as our ancestors, except that our duty is to intensify it, as forgetting certain values is the cause of many of our society's evils.

It is true that our society knows great uneasiness due to a forgotten element. The forgotten great value of tolerance. Unfortunately, it is not yet universal because the capacity to tolerate is not innate in humans. Our parents were aware of this, so much so that they ceaselessly fought to acquire the foundations of a coexistence among humans, so different and yet united. How many wars occurred? How many conflicts are the result of this misunderstanding of the other? All! The second world war is a sad example. An unprecedented example of intolerance and incomprehension which brought about the exclusion of an entire race.

Indeed, intolerance inevitably brings on exclusion of a man, a social class, a race, an ethnic group. But let us not allow ourselves to hide behind fatalism. Each of us can take away a stone from the wall of exclusion. Given that talking about this scourge is a way of recognizing its presence, we can find the remedies. In particular for the examples close to home, like homeless people we ignore out of "habit," or from whom we look away in shame. Well: be shameful! But do not stay indifferent. Dare to look at the problem in order to find in our hearts the solutions. Do not turn away from the more distant examples, either, like the ethnic war in Bosnia which flows from incomprehension among peoples. Be honest with ourselves and get interested. Stop closing ourselves behind our pride. As Flaubert says, "the height of pride is to disdain oneself" and indeed, indifference and pride push us to disdain others. We end by forgetting respect.

This respect is the foundation of tolerance. We must know how to respect each person's ideas. We must respect what people, and in particular youth, believe. Because in a society where everything is unstable, where we can no longer find our reference points, faith in an idea gives hope and will. Of course, there are always false prophets who exploit the absence of reference points in order to lie to young people. They hide behind false values that eclipse the older ones. This is the way dictatorships are founded. However, there is a remedy: communication allows us to annihilate these falsehoods but also to understand each other's motivations. This communication is translated by a kind of intellectual charity. And as Clémenceau tells us, "There is much to say against charity. The most serious reproach is that it is not practised." In addition, intellectual charity is an exchange of knowledge that allows us to understand better.

Given that intolerance is linked to incomprehension, we have the responsibility to learn. Knowledge and culture give us the keys to understanding. Instruction enriches us and helps us to accept behaviours or ideas that are not our own. Do you believe that if the Colombs had bothered to study the Indians, this massacre would have happened? Of course not! The stupidity of man resides in the fact that he is willing to remain ignorant, and according to Einstein, "Two things are infinite: the Universe and human stupidity; but as far as the Universe is concerned, I have not yet acquired absolute certainty." This stupidity and this ignorance are found as well in the example of colonizers who, wanting to impose their culture, ended up bringing about the detriment and impoverishment of the colonized's culture. It is by this detriment that, once again, false prophets and dictators were able to exploit the situation.

Tolerance is the foundation of a balanced society. It is obtained by respect for others and understanding of others. Even more, it is up to us, inheritors of a heavy past, to learn and to communicate so that we can accept our neighbours' differences. But we must prove ourselves worthy of our heritage. Only I am afraid that in order to accomplish this task, we will have to hold out against huge faults. And is that really within the reach of human nature?

Aude B., 101, Travail d'Ecriture

Notre génération est l'héritière du legs de nos ancêtres qui, par leurs expériences ont aboutit à des grandes valeurs. Nous devons lutter afin de les préserver. Ce contrat est notre "grande besogne". Il reste le même que nos ancêtres, seulement, notre devoir est de l'intensifier car l'oubli de certaines valeurs est la cause de bien des maux de notre société.

Il est vrai que notre société connait un grand malaise dû à un oubli. L'oubli d'une grande valeur qu'est la tolérance. Malheureusement, elle n'est pas encore universelle car la faculté de tolérer n'est pas innée chez l'homme. Nos parents en ont pris conscience, si bien qu'ils n'ont cessé de mener un combat pour acquérir les bases d'une coexistence entre êtres humains différents et pourtant unis. Combien de guerre ont eu lieu? Combien de conflits résultent de l'incompréhension de l'autre? Tous! La seconde guerre mondiale en est un triste exemple. Un exemple inouï d'intolérance et d'incompréhension qui ont mené à l'exclusion de tout un peuple.

En effet, l'intolérance entraîne inévitablement l'exclusion d'un homme, d'une classe sociale, d'une race, ou d'une ethnie. Mais ne nous cachons pas derrière la fatalité. Chacun de nous peut ôter une pierre du mur de l'exclusion. Etant donné que parler de ce fléau c'est en reconnaître la présence, c'est que nous pouvons trouver des remèdes. En particulier pour les exemples qui nous touchent de près, comme les personnes sans-logis auxquels nous ne faisons pas attention par "habitude", ou bien devant lesquelles nous détournons le regard par honte. Eh bien: ayons honte! Mais ne restons pas indifférents. Osons regarder le problème pour y trouver en son coeur les solutions. Mais ne méprisons pas les exemples plus lointains, comme les guerres ethniques en Boznie Herzégovine qui découlent de l'incompréhension entre plusieurs peuples. Soyons honnêtes avec nous-mêmes et intéressons-nous. Cessons de nous renfermer derrière notre orgueil. Car pour Flaubert "le comble de l'orgueil est de se mépriser soi-même" et en effet, l'indifférence et l'orgueil nous poussent au mépris de l'autre. Et l'on finit par oublier le respect.

Ce respect est la base de la tolérance. Il faut savoir respecter les idées de chacun. Il faut respecter ce en quoi les gens, et surtout les jeunes croient. Car dans une société où tout vacille, où l'on ne trouve plus ses points de repères, la foi en une idée donne l'espoir et la volonté de tout. Certes, il y a toujours eu des faux prophètes qui profitent de cette absence de points de repères pour mentir aux jeunes. Ils se réfugient dans des fausses valeurs qui occultent les anciennes. C'est le fondement de toute dictature. Cependant, il existe un remède: c'est la communication qui permet à la fois d'anéantir ces duperies, mais aussi de comprendre les motivations de chacun. Cette communication se traduit par une sorte de charité intellectuelle. Et d'après Clémenceau: "Il y a beaucoup à dire contre la charité. Le reproche le plus grave qu'on puisse lui faire, c'est de ne pas être pratiquée." Par ailleurs, la charité intellectuelle est un échange de savoir qui permet de mieux comprendre.

Etant donné que l'intolérance est liée à l'incompréhension, nous avons la tâche de nous instruire. Le savoir et la culture nous donnent ces clefs de la compréhension. L'instruction nous enrichit et nous aide à accepter des comportements ou des idées qui ne sont pas les nôtres. Croyez-vous que si les Colombs avaient daigné étudier les Indiens, un tel massacre aurait eu lieu? Bien sûr que non! La bêtise de l'homme réside en ce qu'il se complaint à rester ignorant, et d'après Einstein: Deux choses sont infinies: l'Univers et la bêtise humaine; mais en ce qui concerne l'Univers, je n'en ai pas encore acquis la certitude absolue." Cette bêtise et cette ignorance se retrouvent aussi dans l'exemple des colonisateurs qui, en voulant imposer leur culture, ont abouti au détriment et à l'appauvrissement culturel de peuple colonisé. C'est par ce détriment, que de nouveau, des faux prophètes et des dictateurs, ont pu profiter de la situation.

La tolérance est le fondement d'une société équilibrée. Elle s'obtient par le respect et la compréhension de l'autre. En outre, c'est à nous, les héritiers d'un lourd passé de nous instruire et de communiquer afin d'accepter les différences de nos voisins. Encore faut-il se montrer digne de notre héritage. Seulement, j'ai peur que pour accomplir cette tâche, il faille braver de gros défauts. Et cela est-il à la portée de la nature humaine?

WRITING FROM SOURCES IN TWO CULTURAL CONTEXTS

SHOSHANA FOLMAN & ULLA CONNOR

The Academic College of Tel Aviv Yaffo, Israel, & Indiana University, U.S.A

Abstract. This research investigates writing from sources in two educational contexts as it specifically relates to the academic task of constructing a high school research paper. In order to look closer into this issue, the following research questions were asked: (a) What are the synthesizing styles of writers composing from sources in two different cultural contexts and to what extent do they differ cross-culturally? (b) How do the similarities and differences between the two samples reflect the "nature" and "context" of the task? To answer these questions the research papers of thirty English-speaking senior high school students in the U.S. and the research papers of forty Hebrew-speaking senior high school students in Israel were analyzed using a Taxonomy for Research Paper Evaluation, especially developed for this study. To analyze the data, t-tests, size of effect (d) and the sum of absolute differences statistics were conducted. The results show that the composing styles of both samples were low on synthesizing, showing preference for alternative styles of composing from sources. The results also suggest that while the research paper is a universal norm-based product defined by the international academy, the products of the two cultural groups were situated at different points along the approximative systems of research paper writing. In light of this interpretation of the findings, theoretical and pedagogical implications are drawn for mainstream literacy acquisition.

Keywords: Writing from multiple sources, intercultural rhetorical differences, synthesizing styles, discourse synthesis, context, cultural context, taxonomy, writing assessment, research paper, norm-based products, research paper evaluation, high-school writing tasks, approximative systems, literacy acquisition

1 INTRODUCTION

The central role of the research paper assignment within educational systems has been particularly acknowledged in the professional literature in the last twenty five years. The research paper has been found to be one of the most common end-of-high-school and college-level writing tasks that students encounter across the curriculum (Curtin, 1988). It was also found to be an ecologically valid task both in school and beyond (McGinley, 1992).

As a reading-writing task, the research paper has been found to induce critical thinking, inquiry and learning (Greene, 1995; Nelson, 1990a). It has also been found to emphasize the importance of decision making on the writer's part, from selecting a focused topic and sources to developing and organizing structure and thesis.

Writing a research paper presupposes procedures and reporting conventions of a given academic community. It has been found to entail the most complex constructive processes that students are expected to perform (Bereiter, & Scardamalia, 1983).

Synthesis of information from many sources, inherent in composing a research paper, has also drawn the attention of the research community. Researchers have found that the multi-source discourse synthesis is one of the most cognitively demanding academic learning tasks. In order to "transform source texts to create new texts," writers organize textual meaning, select information on the basis of a relevance principle, and make connections between the information they select from sources and the content they generate from prior knowledge (Spivey, 1990: 257; see also Young, & Leinhardt, 1998). Thus, this task, like more basic tasks of writing from sources, such as arguing in response to letters to the editor (Wolfe, 2002), entails drawing on source texts for relevant information and integrating this information with the processor's previous knowledge in order to construct a new conceptual framework (Ackerman, 1989; Bereiter, & Scardamalia, 1983; Bracewell, Frederiksen, & Frederiksen, 1982; Flower et al., 1990; Greene, 1993, 1995; Kanz, 1989a, 1989b; Kennedy, 1985; McGinley, 1992; Nelson, & Hayes, 1988; Sarig, 1991a; Sarig, & Folman, 1993; Spivey, 1988, 1990, 1997; Spivey, & King, 1989; Stein, 1989). Such synthesis displays the processor's ability to assess critically both the source texts and previous knowledge (Kanz, 1989a; McGinley, 1992; Nelson, & Hayes, 1988). The processor's ability to synthesize often predicts performance on high-level literacy tasks, such as summary writing and paraphrasing.

Findings from the studies of discourse synthesis show that good writing consists of many features, such as identification and incorporation of high-level intertextual material, connectedness and organization (Spivey, 1984; Spivey, & King, 1989), awareness of rhetorical structure, appropriate rhetorical stance and original material (Ackerman, 1989, 1991), and, most importantly here, critical approach to the source texts (Greene, 1995; Kanz, 1989a; McGinley, 1992; Nelson, & Hayes, 1988).

A survey of research-paper writing in the U.S. has shown that the research paper has a well documented status in the English curriculum of 84% of the college freshman composition programs and 40% of the advanced writing programs (Curtin, 1988; Nelson, & Hayes, 1988). Yet, only in the mid-eighties has the research paper come to the fore in studies on writing pedagogy.

The purpose of the present study is to examine research paper writing in two cultures, namely the American and the Israeli. In order to address this issue, we asked the following research questions:

• What are the synthesizing styles of research-paper writers composing from sources in two cultural contexts, and to what extent do they differ cross-culturally?

• How do the similarities, and differences between the two samples reflect the "nature" and the "context" of the task the students responded to?

2   METHOD

In order to investigate the issue of writing from sources in two educational settings, as it specifically relates to the academic task of constructing a high school research paper, the following study was set up.

2.1 The Samples and Research Contexts

The American Sample and Research Context. The sample of the American research papers consisted of thirty papers written by twelfth-grade students from a suburban high school in Indianapolis, Indiana. All research papers were submitted as partial fulfilment of an advanced (honours) end-of-high-school English course (English 6). These papers were submitted at the end of the Fall semester (n=25) and at the end of the Spring semester (n=5) of the same academic year. The papers were photocopied for us, after the course instructor had scored them.

The school from which the U.S. data came is a large suburban high school in a Midwestern city of one million people. The county is racially integrated with a majority of white students. However, being in an integrated area, the school has a substantial African-American population. In addition, some Vietnamese and other Asian residents live in the county. The socioeconomic level of the students is mixed, ranging from upper-middle class to middle and lower class. The teachers in the school are local residents, and teacher turnover is low. The senior-year students were 17-18 years old.

In the U.S., the research paper was a requirement of a senior year English one-semester course. The U.S. students in this study were given guidelines concerning the following features: (a) *the process of topic selection* ("... talk with an adult about something that affected him or her as a young person. This topic should be of interest to you and researchable"); (b) *the scope of the paper* (fairly limited to 6-9 pages); (c) *reliance on source materials expected* (at least three appropriate sources); (d) *the suggested timetable and progress stages* (selecting material, drafting and revising the research paper); and (e) *the criteria for evaluation of the research paper* (three different scores translatable into letter grades) were designated for research process and format: content, written style and correctness, and research process as represented by the product.

The scoring of the American research-paper sample sets was done by the course instructor, using a 0-5 holistic criterion-referenced evaluation scale, which the students had received, at the beginning of the course.

The Israeli Sample and Context. The sample of the Israeli research papers consisted of forty research papers written by twelfth-grade students from a suburban high school in central Israel. All of the research papers were submitted in partial fulfilment of the Israel Ministry of Education and Culture's matriculation requirements in sociology. This sample consisted of research papers submitted in the Fall (n=24), and in the Spring (n=16) semesters of the same academic year. We were given special permission to analyze these research papers, photocopies of which were deposited in the high school library after they had been scored by an external examiner.

The policy of high school upper-grade research paper approval in Israel has a built-in selection apparatus. According to this policy, only students whose mark is B or above can opt for the research paper as an end-of-high-school project. Research paper writing adds to the matriculation points in the area of study in which the research paper is written. The high school from which the Israeli data came is also a large centrally-located suburban high school, with a student body of 1,200. The school draws its student population from suburban middle to lower-middle classes, with an ethnic composition mix (of about 60% of the students of a Sephardic origin and 40% of them of an Ashkenazik origin) typical of other comprehensive high schools in Israel. The teachers in this school are local residents and the turnover among the social science and humanities teachers is rather low. The senior-year students were 17-18 years old.

The research paper is defined in Israel as an *independent study,* the primary objective of which is to summarize or clarify a well-defined issue. The research paper in this study was, therefore, not expected to be scientifically innovative, but rather to show dedication and genuine ability to carry out an independent study. (*Guidelines for Research Paper Writing* [1991], Ministry of Education and Culture. Israel).

In Israeli schools, one teacher assumes responsibility for the research papers written in his/her school. This teacher is in charge of giving general oral guidelines for research paper writing (one session). S/he is also responsible for referring students to two main sources of information on research paper writing which are found in the school library: The Ministry of Education and Culture (1991) *Guidelines for Research Paper Writing*, and an additional two-page instructional pamphlet, prepared locally, which mainly relates to research technicalities, such as format, scope and editorial matters. The teacher in charge also initiates and supervises the various administrative phases of getting the *topic, outline* and academic *advisor* approved by the Ministry of Education and Culture. The academic advisor, who is an expert in the content domain of the research paper, is usually selected by the student.

Once the topic is approved, the students are guided almost exclusively by their academic advisors. Most of the advisors guide their students at the outline stage and then direct them to work on their own, meeting with them only after the first draft has been completed. Thus, there is no real instruction and guidance as to the conceptualization or the realization of the research paper.

Even though Israeli students write research papers in various content domains, the Israeli research papers selected for this study were all on sociological topics (for one matriculation point in sociology). This content domain was selected in order to match the sociological-existential topics of the American sample of research papers, thus meeting the methodological requirement for consistency in specific subject matter. Interestingly enough, when the topics of the two sets of sample research papers were compared, they were found to be remarkably similar.

The external examiner is usually a teacher (in another high school) in the subject area from which the research paper draws and for which the student gets credit. The marking system prevalent in Israel is a holistic one. The examiners usually receive a six-criteria guiding sheet on the basis of which they determine the grade for the research paper. Students receive one matriculation point for writing their research paper.

2.2 Some Methodological Considerations for Cross-cultural Comparisons

We claim the compatibility of these two sample sets of products (the American and the Israeli) by showing our close adherence to three basic methodological guidelines recommended by Purves (1988) as methodological directives for carrying out valid studies of contrastive rhetoric.

- *"The language (native or foreign) in which the writers are writing must be defined."* In this study each of the sample populations composed their research papers in a naturalistic non-laboratory setting, writing in their native languages (i.e., English and Hebrew).
- *"The education of the writers should be similarly defined and described."* In this study the populations were twelfth-grade high school students within the educational systems being considered.
- *"The settings in which the writing occurs should be as similar as possible."* In our study the task is defined in both research contexts (American and Israeli) as an end-of-high-school research paper. The research or term paper (used in both cultural contexts synonymously) is defined as "...a particularly demanding constructive act... [in which] a writer must locate, read, select and organize material from various sources to form an original synthesis" (Nelson, 1990b: 1).

Thus, disregarding differences in the pedagogical framework for composing the research papers in each of the cultures, students in both contexts probably opted for topics which were of interest to them as an age group. However, while both sets of research papers related to the same content domain and shared similar form requirements, they differed in scope: the Israeli research papers were between 20-40 pages (a minimum of 15 pages was required), whereas the American research papers were between 6-12 pages. This difference in scope had a direct bearing on both the depth and breadth of the survey of the literature, and possibly on the core of the papers as well.

Table 1. Methodological comparison between the American and the Israeli samples

Criteria for comparison	American context	Israeli context
	Major Similarities	
Language of writing	both Mother tongue (English in US; Hebrew in Israel)	
Education of writers	11-12 years of schooling	
Writing task	Research paper	
Set-up	Naturalistic	
Subject matter of task	Sociology – General existential issues	
	Major Differences	
Explicit in-class writing instructions for research paper	Senior course in English composition	Independent study
Specified guidelines for scope	6-9 pages	A minimum of 15 pages
Specified criteria for evaluation	3-set criteria	6-set criteria
Guidance in content domain	No specified guidance	Academic advisor
Task reward	Partial fulfilment of a senior course in Englishcomposition	One matriculation point (high school exit exam) in Sociology

2.3 The Scoring Instrument: A Taxonomy for Research Paper Evaluation

The instrument used for the evaluation of the two research paper samples was developed especially for this study. The instrument is a criterion-referenced *taxonomy*. It consists of five major category-clusters (presented in the left hand column below), sub-divided into 18 categories (with sub-categories, which are outlined in the Appendix), scored on a 1-5 scale.

Each of the five main category-clusters relates to what we believe are state-of-the-art requirements of the research paper as gleaned from the professional literature on the research paper as a learning task and from the data collected from this study. A brief description of the theoretical underpinnings for the main category-clusters follows.

Drawing mainly on Spivey (1990), as well as on work by Greene (1993), about connections between prior knowledge, source texts' content and target texts' content, we constructed the first category-cluster, which is labelled *"Content-Conceptualization."* This category-cluster, and even more specifically, category 1 – "Scope and Depth of Topical Theoretical Knowledge" – captures both the content schemata of the new target text (which is the product of the connective inferences between the information writers select from sources) and the content they generate from their own previous knowledge (see also Ackerman, 1991).

TAXONOMY FOR RESEARCH PAPER EVALUATION

Content-Conceptualization	1	Scope and Depth of Topical Theoretical Knowledge
	2	Originality of Content Conceptualization
	3	Synthesized Topics of Discourse
	4	Content Accuracy and Reliability
	5	Evaluative – Judgemental Observations (Attitude) toward the Issue at Stake, the Bibliographical Source Texts and/or Results
Rhetorical-Textual Realization	6	Genre of the Research Paper
	7	Hierarchical Textual Relations and Level of Elaboration
	8	Relatedness of the Bibliographical Survey to the Paper's Core
	9	Coherence and Connectedness of the Various Textual Sub-structures (Chapters, Sections, Macro-structures and Micro-structures).
Communicative – Considerateness	10	Explicitness of Task Representation and Genre Representation
	11	Explicitness of Voice and Stance
	12	Explicit Connectedness at Various Textual Levels
Linguistic Realization	13	Clarity and Communicativeness of Discourse
	14	Appropriate Word Choice and Phrasing
	15	Adherence to Academic Register
The Research-Paper Procedural Imperatives	16	Employment of Research Instruments
	17	Adherence to the Research Paper Style Sheet
	18	Data Processing and Analysis

Category 2 in the same cluster "Originality of Content Conceptualization" draws on Spivey's (ibid) guidance about transforming texts to create new texts.

We constructed Category 3 – "Synthesized Topics of Discourse" – to reward students for the ability to analyze, synthesize and integrate ideas of others within their own projects, especially in light of findings about students' intuitive tendencies to "stay close both locally and globally to the source text when composing the target text" (Nash, Schumacher, & Carlson, 1993).

We constructed category 4 – "Content Accuracy and Reliability" – thus delimiting the complete liberty that a writer may take in his/her transformations of source texts into target texts. Following Greene (1993), and Lu (1987) among others, we also included (within the category cluster) Category 5 – "Evaluative-Judgemental Observations (Attitude) toward the Issue at Stake, the Bibliographical Source Texts and/or Results."

The second category-cluster – *"Rhetorical-Textual Realization"* in general, and Category 6 in particular draws on Meyer, & Rice's (1977) top-level structures as they relate to expository writing. According to their system, the most sophisticated (i.e., cognitively demanding) top-level structure is "Problem and Solution" and the least sophisticated one is "Addition."

In the same way, Category 7 – "Hierarchical-Textual Relations and Level of Elaboration" – and categories 9, "Coherence and Connectedness of the Various Textual Sub-structures (Chapters, Sections, Macro-structures and Micro-structures)" and 12, "Explicit Connectedness at Various Textual Levels," draw on some leading mental models of text processing (in reading), which have been applied to writing as well (Kitsch, & van Dijk, 1978).

According to Giora (1985), pragmatically well-formed texts are hierarchically structured. Thus, one of the criteria for the evaluation of the well-formedness of text is the hierarchical structure of information, as it is represented in the surface structure of the text (see also Folman, 1997).

The third category-cluster *"Communicative Considerateness"* mainly draws on work by Folman, (2000), and van de Kopple (1985), and has been operationalized by Barton (1995) and Greene (1995). Categories 10, 11 and 12, capturing "Explicitness of Voice and Stance" and "Explicit Connectedness at Various Textual Levels" are typical of the kind of information tapped by this cluster. "Explicitness of Task Representation" in this cluster and "Connectedness at Various Textual Levels" are related to the use of meta-discourse. Meta-discourse helps make the text as explicit as possible for the reader.

The fourth category-cluster, *"Linguistic Realization,"* draws on the requirements of the discourse community, i.e., the target audience (Bizzell, 1990; Folman, 2000a, 2000b). As Greene puts it: "...Writing an essay that contributes a unique perspective requires that [students] adapt and restructure information from different sources to meet their goals within the bounds of *acceptable academic discourse* and the directives of the literature on *discourse communities* (the underlining is mine) and the requirements they put forth..." (Greene, 1995: 187).

"The Research Paper Procedural Imperatives" – category-cluster five – draws primarily on the literature related to the construction of the research paper (see for example, Birenbaum, 1995, as well as various style sheets, such as *The APA style sheet*, 1995).

It may seem that some of the taxonomy's categories are scored on scales that in-dicate discrete qualities and some others are scored on graded typical scales. Yet, both the former and the latter constitute graded scales which move from low score – 1 on the scale to high score 5 – on the same scale. Thus, even in cases such as that epitomized in category 6, where it seems that the scale is made up of discrete value-qualities, the lowest score on the scale, which taps the additive genre, is regarded by scholars in the field as the lowest genre of expository writing, whereas Problem-Solution is regarded as highest – hence the scale of scores.

As for the reliability of the taxonomy, reliability analysis for each sample showed the taxonomy to be a highly reliable instrument, with Cronbach Coefficient Alphas of .94 and .87 for the American and Israeli sample, respectively. Reliability analysis of the taxonomy across samples was considerably high, with Cronbach Coefficient Alpha of .91. Reliability analysis of the taxonomy's category-clusters across samples was fairly high with Cronbach Coefficient Alphas of .80; .71; .80; .87; .66 for category-clusters one through five respectively.

3   DATA ANALYSIS AND RESULTS

The products were analyzed by the researchers, each marking research papers originally written in her native culture. To establish inter-rater reliability approximately one third of the American research papers were analyzed by both researchers (working independently). Inter-rater reliability calculated using Pearson Product Correlation Coefficients, was found to be impressively high (.98), and statistically significant (at the p=0.0001). Table 2 shows means and standard deviations by category for each sample.

Table 2. Means and standard deviations (in brackets) by category for the American (n=30) and the Israeli sample (n=40)

Category	American		Israeli	
01	1.73	(1.08)	3.38	(1.08)
02	2.27	(1.11)	2.38	(0.59)
03	2.23	(1.16)	2.58	(0.84)
04	2.67	(0.88)	3.33	(0.83)
05	2.20	(1.19)	2.15	(0.80)
06	2.30	(1.15)	2.08	(1.10)
07	2.33	(1.03)	2.78	(1.03)
08	2.40	(1.40)	2.23	(1.40)
09	2.77	(1.04)	3.33	(0.89)
10	1.57	(0.86)	2.65	(1.39)
11	2.20	(1.30)	2.55	(1.15)
12	2.30	(1.18)	3.28	(0.88)
13	2.33	(1.45)	3.58	(1.01)
14	2.70	(1.02)	3.40	(1.03)
15	2.90	(1.16)	3.68	(0.86)
16	1.27	(0.74)	2.65	(1.23)
17	3.53	(1.04)	3.23	(1.07)
18	1.10	(0.31)	2.15	(1.39)

Table 3 displays the means, standard deviations and size of effect results for the sample category-clusters.

Table 3. Means, standard deviations, comparisons and effect size results for the American (n=30) and Israeli (n=40) samples by category-cluster

Category Clusters	Descriptives		Test results	
	American	Israeli	t	d
Content Conceptualization	2.22 (0.90)	2.76 (0.57)	2.87**	.73
Rhetorical-Textual Realization	2.45 (0.92)	2.60 (0.78)	0.71	.18
Communicative Considerateness	2.02 (0.96)	2.82 (0.95)	3.46***	.84
Linguistic Realization	2.64 (1.06)	3.55 (0.85)	3.93***	.95
The Research Paper Procedural Imperatives	1.96 (0.51)	2.67 (1.01)	3.81***	.93
Total	2.26 (0.77)	2.85 (0.59)	3.58 **	.87

* p < .05, ** p < .01, *** p < .0001

The taxonomy's category-clusters were formed for two main reasons: First, the sample size did not yield enough observations for each category in each cell to allow for a valid t-test, and second, comparisons of category-clusters allowed for collapsing differences on a category level into global (factor) differences between the samples.

On the whole, the results show significant differences between the two samples in overall performance on the research paper assignment. Both scored relatively low, with means of 2.26 (45.20%) for the U.S. group and 2.85 (57.00%) for the Israeli group. Beyond these generally low mean scores, the results showed significant differences between the two samples in performance on category-clusters 1, 3, 4, and 5, with means ranging between 2-3 score average, and with the exception of a slightly higher mean for the Israeli group on cluster 4. For cluster 2, however, even though the means for both samples ranged within the same average score of 2-3, no statistically significant difference was found between the two samples.

Table 4 presents the distribution of score frequencies for a low (1+2) and a high (4+5) scoring categorie.

Table 4. Distribution of score frequencies and sum of absolute differences (Σ) for each category in the taxonomy, by the American and the Israeli sample

Category	Score categories				
	Low (1-2)		High (4-5)		Σ
	American	Israeli	American	Israeli	
1	73.33	17.50	10.00	42.50	111.66
2	73.33	67.50	10.00	5.00	21.66
3	72.67	57.50	13.33	15.00	37.74
4	43.33	15.00	13.33	40.00	57.67
5	66.67	60.00	13.33	0.00	40.00
6	83.33	82.50	13.33	15.00	3.23
7	63.33	32.50	13.33	22.50	61.67
8	56.67	55.00	30.00	25.00	13.34
9	43.33	12.50	26.67	45.00	61.66
10	83.33	50.00	3.33	37.50	68.33
11	66.67	50.00	20.00	17.50	38.34
12	66.67	12.50	16.67	40.00	108.33
13	60.00	20.00	36.07	75.00	81.00
14	50.00	17.50	30.00	50.00	65.00
15	43.33	12.50	36.67	67.50	61.60
16	90.00	35.00	3.33	27.50	110.00
17	10.00	27.50	43.33	52.50	53.34
18	100.00	67.50	0.00	27.50	65.00

Table 4 shows significant differences in performance between the two samples in most of the Taxonomy's 18 categories, excluding categories 2 (Originality of Content Conceptualization), 3 (Synthesized Topics of Discourse), 6 (Genre of the Research Paper), 8 (Relatedness of the Bibliographical Survey to the Paper's Core), and 11 (Explicitness of Voice and Stance).

4   DISCUSSION OF RESULTS FOR STUDIES 1 AND 2

The overall quality level of the essays, as assessed by the Taxonomy for Research Paper Evaluation, proved to be low. The statistically significant difference between the overall scores of the two samples, though informative (t=3.58**), relates to the difference between two mean scores, both showing values below the cut-off point of the passing mark (2.26 and 2.85 when the passing mark was 3.00, which equals 60%). Interestingly, however, the significant difference between mean scores is consistent for all category-clusters, the Israeli mean score always ranging somewhat higher than the American score, except in the case of category-cluster 2, "Rhetorical-Textual Realization." For this category-cluster no statistically significant difference was observed between the two samples.

On the basis of these observations which drew on the data analyses we will attempt to answer the first research question: *What are the synthesizing styles of research paper writers composing from sources and to what extent do they differ cross-culturally?*

The data show that the students' products in both samples were low on synthesizing. This overall trend of the low amount of synthesized discourse was inferred from the students' performance in category 3 ("Synthesized Topics of Discourse"), which explicitly measures synthesizing skill. In addition, categories such as 2 ("Originality of Content Conceptualization"), 6 ("Genre of the Research Paper") and 7 ("Hierarchical-Textual Relations and Level of Elaboration"), which tap various aspects of alternative styles of composing from sources, are also relevant in this respect. Students' writing typically included only one or more source texts in an unsynthesized chain. Sometimes, students synthesized some previous knowledge with (or without) a source text. The low level of synthesizing was also obvious in the students' preference for additive and descriptive text organization. Furthermore, writers tended to opt for a flat, non-hierarchical style often characterized by discontinued short passages.

In order to show how scores in these four categories affected our conclusion regarding the synthesizing styles, we shall look closer at one sample paper entitled "Silent Cries" (written by one of the American students), which dealt with child abuse.

Both readers agreed that the synthesizing style (category 3) of the paper could be best characterized by "topics of discourse presenting one or more source texts in an un-synthesized chain form" (2 on the 1-5 scale of category 3). Following are some examples of this synthesizing style as observed in "Silent Cries":

In this paper we first read that *"child abuse is an old sin... Primitive people had a custom which called for the killing of the third or fourth child...."* This historical perspective on child abuse was based on one source text, Dale Rogers' *Hear the Children Crying* ([1987]. New Jersey: Fleming H. Ravell Co.). The writer next describes various manifestations of emotional abuse in a long paragraph drawing on only one source text, Joyce Price's *Emotional Abuse of Children May Plague 10% of Homes*, (Washington Times, 5 Jan. 1988, pp. D4 and D5). The writer next discusses sexual abuse, drawing again on one source text, David Hechler's *Battle and the Backlash* (1988. Lexington, Mass.: Lexington Books).

This example illustrates a writer's text in which hardly any of the topics of discourse are based on a synthesized generalization of knowledge gained from several source texts. The writer cites one source text at a time (apparently synthesized with some of the writer's previous notions on the topic). This barely synthesized discourse makes the text sound more a summary than a synthesis, in other words, "the originality of content conceptualization [can be] characterized as "borrowed – paraphrased or summarized" (2 on the 1-5 scale of category 2).

This style of barely synthesized text also makes the text sound more descriptive and exploratory (i.e., 2 on the 1-5 scale of category 6) than argumentative.

In addition, the "barely synthesized style of discourse" is manifested in "the Hierarchical Textual Relations and Level of Elaboration", category 7. The textual relation of "Silent Cries" can be best characterized as non-hierarchical or as exhibiting minor hierarchical relations on the paragraph level (2 on the 1-5 scale on category 7). This is a fairly low score on this category, indicating lack of global relations between the various structural units and suggesting a low level of synthesizing ability on the part of the writer.

Moving away from this concrete example, it should be pointed out that beyond the limited synthesizing style cross-culturally, minor differences were observed between the samples. Differences were inferred from each of groups' scores: the American writers used more borrowed, paraphrased or summarized style than the Israeli writers (category 2 – 73.33 and 67.50, respectively), while the students in Israel had considerably higher scores than the American writers in the discontinued, scattered hierarchies' category (7.45 and 23.33, respectively). These figures indicate some minor cross-cultural differences within the low-synthesizing ability style observed for the two cultural groups.

The answer to the first research question has a close bearing on the answer to the second research question: *"How do the similarities and the differences between the two samples reflect the nature and the context of the task that students responded to?"* These results, we would like to suggest, mainly reflect the writing syllabuses and the pedagogical practices of each of the educational systems. Even though the end results seem to be similar for both groups in terms of the performance related to synthesis, the pedagogical processes leading to them are perhaps different. Whereas in the U.S., the instruction in writing in the mother tongue seems to be fairly "institutionalized" in the high school syllabus, writing instruction in Israel is not systematic. Nevertheless, the syllabus of the American senior "English 6 Research Paper Writing" course showed little evidence of pedagogical attention to issues such as writing from sources and developing abilities to synthesize text in writing.

These observations suggest that even in educational systems in Israel and in the U.S. where writing instruction has a "respectable" standing within the school curriculum, synthesizing skills are not explicitly taught (Curtin, 1988; Stahl et al., 1996). Such a conclusion may be read between the lines of current research on discourse synthesis, which highlights mainly the naturalistic (Spivey, & King, 1989;

Spivey, 1984, 1990) and intuitive synthesizing skills of students of various age groups (Sarig, 1991a, 1991b). These results underscore the complexity of the task even for college level students (Spivey, 1984; Young, & Leinhardt, 1988) and obviously for younger students (Raphael, & Boyd, 1991). This recently growing research on intuitive synthesizing skills calls for more research on specific features of synthesis that need more pedagogical attention. For example, "... such information would help to determine how much instruction may be needed to enhance elementary students' beginnings of discourse synthesis" (Raphael, & Boyd, 1991: 38).

The results of our study suggest that students are reluctant to engage in synthesizing procedures, which require a great deal of effort. Instead, students seem to engage in activities common to many school writing assignments, which reward students for reproducing information (Applebee, 1981). For some students this practice encapsulates their entire writing education (Flower et al., 1990; Nelson, 1990a). Raudenbush, Rowan, & Cheong, observe that "...there is a widespread perception that U.S. schools are comparatively ineffective in cultivating conceptual understanding of academic subjects" (Raudenbush et al., 1993: 524). The observation is based on a large scale assessment conducted by the U.S. Department of Education. This assessment demonstrates that although U.S. students perform adequately on tests of basic skills, they perform comparatively poorly on tasks that involve problem solving, critical analysis and flexible understanding of subject matter..." (U.S. Department of Education, 1991: 32-41; see also Stedman, 1996). The findings of our study which suggest little synthesizing may also be partially ascribed to a prevalent task representation of the research paper both in Israel (*Guidelines for Research Paper Writing* [1991]. Ministry of Education and Culture, Israel) and the U.S. (Nelson, 1990a, 1990b; Nelson, & Hayes, 1988). In Israel, the research paper is conceived of as a comprehensive, often linear and additive summary of the most available literature on a given topic. Similarly, in the U.S. writing about the research paper task representation of one of her subjects, Nelson stated that: "she seemed to assume that the aim of the research paper assignment was to test her ability to assemble and reproduce information" (Nelson, 1990b: 15). Apparently, this is a common assumption (see also Schwegler, & Shamoon, 1982).

In addition to the similarities in synthesizing styles, some other similarities emerged in the comparison between the samples. Fairly prominent among these similarities was the students' *inadequate differentiation between the bibliographical survey of the literature and the core of the research paper.* This rhetorical cross-cultural trend is suggested by the frequent high scores observed for both groups for category 8, i.e., "Relatedness of Bibliographical Survey to the Paper's Core" on the low to intermediate levels of the scoring scale (56.67 and 13.33 for the American sample and 55.00 and 20.00 for the Israeli sample). Thus, students in each group did not show awareness of the fact that a bibliographical survey is only one, introductory, component of a research paper. For many students, the entire research paper was merely a survey of the literature. They failed to deal with other important components of research paper writing such as research hypotheses, research methods, and techniques for gathering and reporting information and for presenting results in an effective and interesting manner. Some students seem to regard the research assignment as little more than an exercise in gathering, assembling and citing chunks of material from library references in academically acceptable ways (Nelson, & Hayes, 1988).

Another similarity between the groups was the *low level of evaluative-judgemental observations (attitude) toward the issue at stake, as well as the bibliographical source texts and/or results.* Surprisingly, although the research paper is regarded a reading-writing-to-learn assignment which fosters "critical literacy" (McGinley, 1992), both groups exhibited a low level of evaluative-judgmental attitude towards the issue at stake and towards the bibliographical source texts and results. This trend may be due to many factors. For example, a number of educators have observed that a legacy of essayist literacy has led students to see texts as complete, self-contained, and objective, not open to challenge. As a consequence, students often become "deferentially literate," politely observing what other authors have accomplished in their writing. This sociocultural heritage has its corollaries in the reverence felt by Jewish people towards the Hebrew Scriptures.

The effort to maintain an objective voice was also observed for the two samples. This trend was suggested by the non-significant differences in frequencies of the two samples for the characteristic of explicitness of voice and stance-category 11. The high frequencies on the low end of the scale (particularly high for the American sample set – 66.67 and considerably high for the Israeli sample set – 50.00) showed that both groups of writers avoided using explicit voice and stance.

The inadequate explicitness of voice and stance seems to have emanated from a conditioning to regard the research paper as an endeavour requiring distance and objectivity (McCormick, 1990). This line of thought is supported by the instructor's deletions of all the "I"s from the American research papers and from the Israeli researcher's observations that the prevalent academic writing pedagogy in Israel advises students to avoid the first person in academic writing in order to maintain academic objectivity and distance.

Thus, there were similarities between the two groups of students in their writing styles. Yet, the results suggest cross-cultural rhetorical differences in four areas.

First, there were *differences in scope and depth of theoretical knowledge which have direct bearing on content accuracy and reliability* (categories 1 and 4 of the taxonomy). Differences in task definitions, requirements and representations resulted in major differences in scope, depth and theoretical knowledge presentation favouring the Israeli sample over the American one. These differences seem to affect the level of accuracy and reliability of the content of the research paper samples.

The distribution of frequencies for category 1, i.e. "Scope and Depth of Theoretical Knowledge," show high frequencies of scores at the low end of the scoring scale for the American sample (73.33) and moderate frequencies at the intermediate to high end of the scoring scale for the Israeli sample. This difference in performance may be explained by the fact that the Israeli high school students regarded the research paper as a scholarly endeavour calling for reliance on learned sources. The American high school students, on the other hand, conceived of the research paper more as a term paper for which they should draw on not many more than three sources. Sources would not have to be learned sources, but popular journals were acceptable.

Significant differences in performance between the two samples were observed for category 4, namely "Content Accuracy and Reliability." The results showed moderate frequencies on the low and intermediate levels of the scale for the American sample, 43.33 and 43.33, and moderate frequencies on the intermediate and high levels of the scale for the Israeli sample, 45.00 and 40.00. These differences may be due to the American students' heavy reliance on impressionistic-popular sources rather than on more reliable source texts and the Israeli students' reliance on more academic sources and instruments for data elicitation and analysis.

Second, differences in linguistic realization, mainly displayed in (a) limited explicit coherence and connectedness at the various textual levels; (b) clarity of communicative discourse; (c) word choice appropriateness and phrasing; and (d) adherence to academic register.

Significant differences between the two samples consistently favouring the Israeli sample were shown in the frequencies observed for categories 10, 13, 14, and 15. These results were due more to the high frequencies on the low end of the scoring scales observed for the American sample (see for example frequencies of scores for categories 10 and 13), than to the high frequencies on the high end of the scale for the Israeli group (see for example, category 10, but also category 15).

As each of the cultural groups wrote in their mother tongue, differences in performance may be ascribed to a more serious attitude of the Israeli group who received extra credit towards matriculation from writing a research paper. The serious attitude resulted in a more careful academic style, which was more meticulously phrased and worded. The American papers were not always coherent or well-phrased.

Third, there were differences in the way students coped with research paper procedural imperatives, such as (a) employment of research instruments, (b) adherence to research paper style sheet, and (c) data processing and analysis. Among the most surprising differences between the American and Israeli samples, favouring the Israeli sample, were the differences observed in coping with the research paper imperatives. Since the American group had received explicit classroom instruction in this specific area it seemed fairly unlikely that the Israeli group would do better in this respect. This was not, however, the case. In category 16, "Employment of Research Instruments," high frequencies on the low end of the scoring scale were observed for the Americans (90.00), whereas for the Israelis, high frequencies were observed on the moderate level of the scale. In category 17, "Adherence to the Research Paper Style Sheet," high frequencies were observed on the intermediate and high level of the scale for the Americans whereas for the Israelis, high frequencies were observed on the high end of the scoring scale. In category 18 the highest frequencies (100.00) were observed on the low end of the scale for the Americans, with fairly high frequencies on the low end of the scale for the Israelis as well. The American group perhaps considered the research paper a less demanding task (which could earn them only some semester credits) than the Israeli group, which could earn one matriculation point for writing the paper.

Fourth and last, cross-cultural differences emerged in communicative considerateness, reflected mainly in the explicitness of task representation and genre representation.

Results for category 10, "Explicitness of Task and Genre Representation," showed frequencies favouring the Israeli sample, with considerably high frequencies on the low end of the scale for the American sample (83.33) and considerably lower ones for the Israeli sample (50.00). Other frequency distributions, which also favoured the Israeli sample, were observed for category 12, "Explicit Connectedness at Various Textual Levels."

We interpret these results to mean that the U.S. students did not have to define their audience and task explicitly because they were writing for their teachers. The Israeli students, on the other hand, wrote for an outside anonymous examiner and had to be more explicit in their task representation.

This interpretation of the results concurs with Nelson, & Hayes (1988) interpretation of their study: Students find the aims of the research paper similar to those of many school sponsored tasks: to provide proof of learning and to demonstrate skill in producing correct prose. Their intended audience is usually a teacher who does not expect to learn anything from students' writing but instead will evaluate it as an examiner would looking for errors in form and content, and ignoring the writers' ideas and interpretations.

5   INTERPRETATION OF THE RESULTS

Our findings suggest that the research papers of the two samples analyzed have not yet reached the norm expected of research papers by an international academic community, as realized in the Taxonomy for Research Paper Evaluation.

Yet, literacy education – or any other epistemological process – needs to be viewed as a series of approximative processes geared towards meeting the objectives and norms set by professionally respected authorities in a given discourse community (Folman, submitted).

Thus, we propose to regard the cultural samples of this study as situated at different acculturation stages along the approximative system of the research-paper task-performance.

The two cultural groups in this study function within the international academic community, which sets the criteria for acculturation. The groups' acculturation advances to completion as they further approximate the advanced stages of task performance. As these stages of acculturation are completed, the "markedness" of "situated literacy" is transcended, and progress towards a more international literacy is made.

The markedness of each of the cultural samples is a product of a certain interaction between the local sociocognitive variables and the local educational system variables. Together these constitute the building blocks of one's culture.

The research-paper profiles emerging from this cross-cultural research show some differences between the two samples. Most of these differences are related to the pedagogical framework, requirements and expectations and, to a certain extent, to the task representation of the research paper.

Beyond these contextual differences, two very important discoursal features seem to characterize the two research paper samples: low level of discourse synthesizing and low level of critical thinking skills. The limited skills exhibited in both of these features were textually realized in the limited ability to make independent decisions about orchestrating source texts, integrating them with personal views, and reconceptualizing them to form and support the original thesis. It is this area that educators need to emphasize in both countries. As Stotsky states: "Without these skills the research paper may justify the often voiced claims against it, as a learning task perpetuation" (Stotsky, 1991: 212).

6   LIMITATIONS AND RECOMMENDATIONS FOR FURTHER RESEARCH

In our research, U.S. research papers were compared with a corresponding sample of Israeli research papers. The major differences shown between them have contributed to our conclusion that each of these samples represents the "educational contexts" that have given them rise. Given the differences in the size and composition of the populations sampled, it is likely that the Israeli sample is more representative of the Israeli research paper population than the American sample.

In addition, it should be noted that since most American high school students enrol in a research-paper senior English course, most American students write a research paper, and those who do not write a research paper in their senior year do it at another point in their high school career. In Israel, however, research paper writing is done on a voluntary basis. Therefore, the natural selection of students who opt for this task may affect the sample of research papers and not necessarily reflect the population as a whole. Beyond this limitation, the sample is likely to represent the population of research paper assignments written in Israel.

In order to overcome these limitations, research paper samples should be selected from various areas of the United States, representing different socioeconomic and cultural populations. In addition, even though the naturalistic set-up for research paper writing (adopted in this study) has been recommended in the literature, a similar design should be replicated in a more controlled set-up. Identical research paper requirements should be given for both sample populations. Further, similar studies adopting the same research design should be replicated in other content domains, possibly with larger sample populations.

ACKNOWLEDGEMENT

A Hebrew version of this article was first published in *Megamot – Behavioral Sciences Quarterly, Vol, 38*(2) [published by the Henrietta Szold Institute, Jerusalem, Israel]. The authors wish to thank Puah Shai for granting permission to publish the English version of this article.

APPENDIX

TAXONOMY FOR RESEARCH PAPER EVALUATION
I. CONTENT-CONCEPTUALIZATION

1. SCOPE AND DEPTH OF TOPICAL THEORETICAL KNOWLEDGE

- Very poor content schemata (reliance on personal knowledge and/or popular newspaper articles).
- Inadequate content schemata (scant reliance on source texts).
- Mediocre content schemata (some reliance on learned source texts).
- Satisfactory content schemata (satisfactory reliance on learned source texts).
- Very rich content schemata based on multiple source texts (impressive reliance on source texts, primary and secondary sources).

2. ORIGINALITY OF CONTENT CONCEPTUALIZATION

- Borrowed-cited.
- Borrowed-paraphrased or summarized.
- Transformed in part – mixed with borrowed material.
- Fully transformed (showing in-depth analysis).
- Very original (showing thorough, deep understanding).

3. SYNTHESIZED TOPICS OF DISCOURSE

- Topics of discourse presenting previous knowledge in a gist form.
- Topics of discourse presenting one or more source texts – in an unsynthesized chain form.
- Topics of discourse synthesizing some previous knowledge with one (or without any) source text.
- Topics of discourse synthesizing previous knowledge with two source texts.
- Topics of discourse synthesizing previous knowledge with more than two new sources.

4. CONTENT ACCURACY AND RELIABILITY

- Inaccurate and unreliable.
- Vague, elusive and too general (no evidence presented).
- At times accurate single viewpoint presentation of the content.
- Fairly accurate and reliable.
- Accurate and reliable (variety of viewpoints presented)

5. EVALUATIVE - JUDGEMENTAL OBSERVATIONS (ATTITUDE) TOWARD THE ISSUE AT STAKE, THE BIBLIOGRAPHICAL SOURCE TEXTS AND/OR RESULTS

- No evaluation or judgement whatsoever – neutral voice.
- Indirect implicit judgemental observations.
- Some evaluation or judgement of a central issue.
- A basically thorough evaluation or judgment of a central issue.
- A full-fledged evaluation or judgement.

II. RHETORICAL-TEXTUAL REALIZATION

6. GENRE OF THE RESEARCH PAPER

- Additive (addition)–collection (ideas related on the basis of some commonality).
- Descriptive (attributes, specifics, explanations or setting) and exploratory.
- Comparison (differences and similarities between two topics).
- Antecedent/consequent – causal relationship between topics.
- Problem - solution; question and answer.

7. HIERARCHICAL TEXTUAL RELATIONS AND LEVEL OF ELABORATION

- Flat – non-hierarchical relations between structural units; non-elaborated text.
- Non-hierarchical or minor hierarchical relationships on a paragraph level.
- Discontinued scattered short hierarchies.
- Tree relations between structural units (more than 3-level hierarchy – moderate elaboration). Considerable theoretical depth.
- Global tree relations between structural units – more than 4-level hierarchy – high elaboration (for the whole paper). Impressive theoretical depth.

8. RELATEDNESS OF THE BIBLIOGRAPHICAL SURVEY TO THE PAPER'S CORE

- Completely unrelated – or no distinction between the two (the entire work is a bibliographical survey), popular sources used to substantiate thesis, no source texts used.
- Poorly related. No direct relationship between thesis and sources.
- Indirectly related. Some connectedness between thesis and sources.
- Fairly related. Learned sources mostly used to substantiate thesis.
- Tightly related. Clear thesis-support development.

9. COHERENCE AND CONNECTEDNESS OF THE VARIOUS TEXTUAL SUB-STRUCTURES (CHAPTERS, SECTIONS, MACRO-STRUCTURES AND MICRO-STRUCTURES)

- Totally incoherent, disconnected, disjointed.
- Barely coherent and poorly connected.
- Indirectly (implicitly) connected; some coherence suggested.
- Fairly connected and coherent.
- Tightly connected and perfectly coherent (most or all macro- and micro-structures, sections and chapters are properly connected, establishing a chain of topics of discourse).

III. COMMUNICATIVE – CONSIDERATENESS

10. EXPLICITNESS OF TASK REPRESENTATION AND GENRE REPRESENTATION

- No meta-discourse or other markers describing the way the task is represented.
- Vague and implicit allusions to task and genre representation.
- Some scattered remarks about task representation and genre representation.
- Moderate explicitness of task and genre representation.
- Detailed meta-discourse describing the way the task and genre are represented.

11. EXPLICITNESS OF VOICE AND STANCE

- No explicit voice or stance markedness.
- Some allusions to the writer's voice or stance.
- Some remarks showing presence of voice or stance.
- Marked yet often inconsistent voice or stance.
- Explicit and clear markedness of a consistent voice and stance.

12. EXPLICIT CONNECTEDNESS AT VARIOUS TEXTUAL LEVELS

- Low level of explicit connectedness (at all discourse levels).
- Explicit connectedness on the paragraph level.
- Explicit connectedness on the paragraph and within section level only.
- Fairly explicit connectedness (at all discourse levels).
- Very explicit connectedness (at all discourse levels).

IV. LINGUISTIC REALIZATION

13. CLARITY AND COMMUNICATIVENESS OF DISCOURSE

- Very unclear and uncommunicative discourse (grammatical and other technical problems).
- Vague, not always clear discourse.
- Complex, unfriendly discourse.
- Clear and communicative discourse.
- Very clear and communicative discourse.

14. APPROPRIATE WORD CHOICE AND PHRASING

- Very poor word choice and phrasing.
- Fair word choice and phrasing.
- Fairly appropriate word choice and phrasing.
- Good word choice and phrasing.
- Most appropriate word choice.

15. ADHERENCE TO ACADEMIC REGISTER

- Inappropriate register constantly used.
- Constant flunctuations in register.
- Occasional fluctuations in register.
- Mostly adheres to academic register.
- Constant adherence to academic discourse.

V. THE RESEARCH-PAPER PROCEDURAL IMPERATIVES

16. EMPLOYMENT OF RESEARCH INSTRUMENTS

- No use of any instruments (questionnaires, interviews, observations, experiments, etc.).
- Use of improper instruments.
- Use of weak instruments (unvalidated, not directly tapping the variable assessed).
- Use of acceptable instruments.
- Use of valid and reliable instruments.

17. ADHERENCE TO THE RESEARCH PAPER STYLE SHEET
- Complete failure to adhere to the research paper style sheet regarding citation rules, footnotes, bibliography, manuscript format, etc.
- Some adherence to the research paper style sheet.
- Moderate adherence to the research paper style sheet.
- Satisfactory adherence to the research paper style sheet.
- Complete and accurate adherence to the research paper style sheet.

18. DATA PROCESSING AND ANALYSIS
- No evidence of employment of a data-processing method.
- Some evidence of employment of a data processing method.
- Evidence of employment of a data processing method and its analysis.
- An almost complete presentation of the data processing method.
- An explicit description and presentation of data processing and its analysis.

FIRST AND SECOND LANGUAGE USE DURING PLANNING PROCESSES

Evidence from Second Language Academic Writing

ORNA FERENZ

Bar Ilan University, Israel

Abstract. This chapter analyzes language planning processes undertaken by student writers when producing an academic text in English as L2. While the use of first versus second language in L2 writing has been investigated principally in relation to cognitive factors, more recently this language choice has been analyzed as the outcome of institutional and social setting factors, identifiable as part of a writer's social writing network. This network assists students in their process of acquiring academic discourse. Additional factors that influence this process is the writer's social motivation and the identity s/he wishes to project. Since acquiring and producing disciplinary language is a means of projecting a number of valued academic images important to the student's academic network, it is worth inquiring whether there is a correspondence between the writer's use of disciplinary language, the identity the writer wishes to project, the composition of his/her academic network and writer's use of L1 vs. L2 during the activity of planning an academic paper in English as L2. Although through the academic network the writer is exposed to academic language and genres, the relationship between the writer's social network and choice of language, L1 vs. L2, during planning has yet to be investigated in detail. This chapter examines this relationship through qualitative analyses of data obtained from sociolinguistic interviews with L2 graduate students. As shown, the academic network is an important factor that shapes language choice, and ultimately, writers' more versus less successful attempts at producing academic texts in English.

Keywords: second language writing, planning processes, discourse community, social writing network, writer's identity, language usage

1   INTRODUCTION

Recent research exploring various aspects of second language (L2) academic writing (Montes-Alcala, 2001; Zimmerman, 2000) has shown that the production of a text in English as L2 cannot be seen as the simple process of just translating ideas from one language to another. Such a task requires that one integrates disciplinary knowledge with genre-appropriate conventions and interrelates text strategies for rendering meaning with the use of disciplinary-appropriate linguistic choices; all these choices interlock to help the writer project an identity as a member of the academic community. When considering tasks where second language is used, the types of language choices involved in shaping text production may be explored in terms of the extent to which the writer relies on his/her first language and/or the use of English as a second language. A knowledge gap in one language may be filled by the other language. However, when knowledge exists in both languages, it is reasonable to expect that some other type of interaction may occur between the languages (Wolff, 2000). This chapter sets out to investigate the way by which novice academic writers draw upon their knowledge of their first language and of English as L2 during the process of planning an academic text in L2 and illustrates the range of social factors which shape such a choice.

Traditionally, planning processes in both L1 and L2 writing are examined in cognitive terms (Chenoweth, & Hayes, 2001; Manchon et al., 2000) with numerous studies investigating the impact writers' differing levels of L2 proficiency and differences in the type of task performed, for instance, narrative versus expository texts (for a survey, see Wang, 2003), have on writers' planning processes and language use. In this chapter I outline a broader perspective, which situates planning in the context of making social meanings; in this process, the writer attempts to accommodate cognitive factors with the expectations of the communities (where the writing is taking place) and the more local social settings (writing networks) developed within such communities. This shift of emphasis aligns with more general developments noted in current research on language use, which is no longer investigated as a cognitive process only, but is also examined as an integral part of social and sociocultural factors; among these factors we may situate the writer's social network. A social network (Wellman, 1997) refers to the web of relationships people establish within a group or with different groups or members of groups. Relevant research has suggested that academic social networks may assist students in their enculturation (Bazermann, 1988) and socialization (Gee, 2001) processes, shaping their path towards becoming members of an academic discourse community. This process involves acquiring the conventions of academic discourse, learning how to use appropriately the language of the discipline and how to render linguistic choices in discipline agreed-upon forms. Of importance in this process is the writer's social motivation and wish to project a specific social identity.

For non-native English academic writers, the appropriate use of English in academic discourse is not just important but in fact necessary for securing one's membership into the global academic discourse community. Not only must such writers be able to produce linguistically correct English, but also follow at the micro- and macro-level of their academic text the conventions set out by their discourse communities (Swales, 1990). As to be shown in this chapter, the writer's academic social network is an important language source, becoming a factor in the writer's more versus less successful attempts at producing academic texts in English. Through his/her academic network the writer is exposed to disciplinary language and conventions, and this, in turn, may influence his/her choice of language, L1 or L2, during the planning process. However, the relationship between a writer's social network and language use – L1 versus L2 – during planning has yet to be investigated in detail. This chapter addresses this relationship by analyzing (mostly qualitatively) data obtained from sociolinguistic interviews with L2 graduate students.

2   FROM DISCOURSE COMMUNITIES TO SOCIAL WRITING NETWORKS

The concept of academic discourse communities (e.g., Bawarshi, 2000; Beaufort, 1997, 2000; Herndl, & Nahrwold, 2000; Swales, 1990) has been used to identify a group of people, novice and expert writers and researchers, who communicate with agreed-upon types of discourse (articles, reports, etc.). According to Ivanič (1998), full members of a discourse community employ specific, conventionally established ways of making and interpreting meaning. The intellectual projects and the objects of study in a discourse community tend to be unified in terms of the goals being set and the philosophy underlying their analysis. Student writers may initially participate in a discourse community as peripheral members, becoming gradually (though not necessarily) full members. Enculturation into the discourses of the community is mediated by teaching and learning processes, undertaken by the student writer and the local discourse community members (Beaufort, 2000), who facilitate novices' gradual acquisition of content knowledge, the learning of field-specific value systems and definitions, of disciplinary language as well as the use of the reading and writing strategies employed among the "expert" discourse community members (Beaufort, 1997).

However, despite its initial usefulness, the concept of discourse community has proven to be definitionally problematic (Beaufort, 1997) for several reasons. Identifying, for instance, the members constituting a specific community may be quite a difficult task (Beaufort, 1997). Also problematic is the fact that the notion of discourse community refers to a global concept but does not elaborate on the immediate social factors – the micro communities – which are important in shaping developing writers' academic writing skills. More recent investigations have shifted their focus to the immediate local community members (Casanave, 1995; Eckert, 2000), such as thesis advisors and departmental professors, who are directly responsible for students' enculturation (Bazerman, 1988) and socialization (Gee, 2001) into the discourse community.

Developments in many different research fields suggest a more effective methodology – through the framework of social network theory – to investigate a writer's personal relationships with the members of his/her local discourse community (Boissevain, & Mitchell, 1973; Gunnarsson, 1997; Milroy L., 1987; Milroy J., 1992; Milroy, & Wei, 1995). Social network research identifies the people with whom an individual interacts, the extent of interaction, and the type and quality of relationships among all network members. A social network serves as a norm-enforcement mechanism associated with specific interactional, textual and linguistic resources which provide some of the norms for communication.

Communication within a network involves transactions and the exchange of messages among members of the network. In academic networks, this transaction may take the form of an academic paper; this is usually structured according to certain parameters or conventions the academic network sets on the writers in terms of topic, content, genre, discourse organization, lexical choice, and syntax. The extent to which a participant is willing to adopt the norms of an academic network might be an indication of the writer's self-identification as a network member. A student writer wishing to be initiated into an academic discourse community may attempt to conform to this set of conventions. The extent of the conformity may be evidenced in the student's writings (Beaufort, 1997); alternatively, this textual evidence may be used as an indication of the type of academic network the student writer is attempting to associate with (i.e., a professional academic network, a departmental or class academic network, and so on).

As to be illustrated in this chapter, important aspects of the processes shaping text production, including the planning process, may be constrained by these norms. Planning has been investigated by Gauvain (2001), who focuses on the steps a writer needs to make towards accomplishing a writing goal, and Alamargot, & Chanquoy (2001b) who define planning as an activity comprised of strategic procedures and practical goals. A similar perspective is offered in Esperet, & Piolat's (1991) proposal on planning as the formation of the textual, semantic, syntactic and lexical aspects of production – a proposal which differs from Hayes' (1996) conceptualization of planning as problem-solving. Integrating these insights with social factors, i.e., community-specific notions, I suggest that we view academic planning as a process leading to a unit of social action, the research paper in this case, through which academic network members communicate (Koku at el., 2000; Purcell-Gates et al., 2002) and negotiate their understandings of specific issues which are of importance to the community. According to this perspective, then, planning is not an individualistic process through which a writer, as an individual, attempts to develop and structure his/her own ideas but rather a socially-shaped process by which a writer, as a social actor, attempts to shape a text in ways that conform to the norms of his/her academic network.

In analyzing social writing networks, I incorporate issues from identity theory and social identity theory (Degenne, & Forse, 1999; Hogg & Terry, 2000; Hornsey, & Hogg, 2000; Stets, & Burke, 2000). Social identity theory argues that individuals have multiple possible identities, defined by group membership and constructed through social cognitive processes associated with the group (Hogg, & Terry, 2000). Indeed, part of the socialization process is the development of a social identity (Hornsey, & Hogg, 2000). A social identity differs from a personal identity in that a personal identity refers to the unique and individual characteristics that distinguish people from each other. Social identity is acquired through a process of identity activation (Stets, & Burke, 2000), involving the selective application of group features to the self. In this manner, a person's social identity may change from context to context when the situation makes different social identities salient. Furthermore, while group membership assigns a certain social identity to people belonging to that group, it is up to each group member to construct or foreground specific aspects of this social identity at the expense of others. One strategy through which a writer may foreground the social features s/he wishes to identify with is the language s/he uses during the process of planning and writing a text.

3   SOCIAL WRITING NETWORKS AND LANGUAGE USE

In this chapter, language is discussed in two different ways. The first one is associated with the use of specific vocabulary items, syntactic structures or disciplinary-appropriate forms. The second one captures the choice of L1 versus L2. Choices at both levels can be a means of group identification, used to single out current group members and identify outsiders who might fit into the group (Milroy, 1987). In other words, linguistic choices identify the speaker in terms of his/her social identity and are, thus, role defining and role-linked. I suggest that the choice of L1 versus L2, like social influence, be seen as an outcome of social network influence upon the individual (Milroy, & Milroy, 1992).

A first step to analyzing the factors affecting a writer's use of L1 versus L2 is to identify one's network and the language in this social network. Networks are composed of the many different people with whom an individual interacts. A network's composition, therefore, is determined by identifying its members and their hierarchical relationship (superior, equal, or inferior) with the focal individual studied. When several network members are found to be related to each other, as, for example, through work or academic interests, these are proposed to form network sub-groups, called *cliques*. Cliques are cohesive social groups that may apply social pressure upon their members to assure conformity to the clique. This pressure may aim towards unifying identities, behaviour or language usage (Coupland, 2002). Cliques tend to have their own language, labelled the *in-group* language (Nida, 1992; Nida, & Wonderly, 1971). A person may have a network where different languages are used so that no one is dominant. However, when a group of people in a network uses the same language, there may be pressure to use the in-group language; this in-group language is a symbol of belonging and a means of internal communication (Nida, 1992).

Therefore, pressure to use a specific language must be considered within the boundaries of the interplay between the individual and the different network members (Milroy, 1992). It is expected that the same factors that determine social influence among network members will also determine language usage (Pasch, 1997). It is worth investigating, therefore, whether the number of relationships an individual has with the people who employ specific discourses will be reflected in his/her making greater usage of that language.

When studying the writing networks of graduate students, it is of interest to identify whether their networks contain cliques, whether these are academic or non-academic cliques, and the clique's in-group language. As concerns L2 academic writing, there may be a conflict between the clique's in-group language and the writer's target language – a conflict which may interfere with novice writers' attempts to produce academically appropriate L2 written texts. Thus, identification of in-group language within a writing network may lead one to locate a source that may potentially influence language producers in their use of language when producing a text

As with any social pressure, an individual's use of the in-group language (which points to its acceptance) may be connected to several self-motivational factors, such as the writer's identity, his/her desire to be identified as a group member, his/her desire to maintain or change social relationships, as well as to accommodate the listener or reader in order to establish common ground (Finlayson, & Slabbert, 1997; Giles, & Smith, 1979; Gumprez, & Hernandez, 1971). It is reasonable to expect that the greater an individual's desire to be recognized and accepted as a member of the writing network group, the greater will be his/her attempts to adopt the group's behaviour and characteristics. As far as language usage is concerned, the individual will probably attempt to use the language preferred by the group. This is a desired behaviour when the goal is L2 academic writing and the in-group language is disciplinary English.

Furthermore, a person desiring to maintain or change social relationships within a group may use language in an attempt to establish common ground or indicate similar interests with the listener or reader (Ivanič, & Camps, 2001). By using the same language, i.e., the textual and interactional discoursal patterns employed by the members of a social network, the person is projecting similar interests or experience as the reader, inviting the reader to interact, thereby maintaining social relationships.

Identity can be a factor in itself when considering a writer's choice of a specific language; indeed, the desire for group membership can be seen as connected to identity. When a writer attempts to project an academic identity (Hirvela, & Belcher, 2001), s/he may be more motivated to desire academic group membership. On the other hand, by changing language usage the individual also indicates a change in the identity s/he wishes to project, which may result in changes in the network relationships.

Another closely-related attribute that should be considered is the projection of valued academic images (Angelova, & Riazantseva, 1999). The term "valued academic images" signifies the attributes considered important or of value to a discipline or to an academic writer. There may exist a difference between the academic images valued by a discipline and those valued by an individual writer. An attempt should be made to discern if the writer values the same academic images as the academic discipline. However, this sharing of valued academic images is possible only if the writer has access to information on disciplinary valued academic images; this information may be accessible to student writers through their social writing networks. When investigating academic social writing networks, accessibility or inaccessibility to valued academic images may affect language usage as well since the writer may attempt to project an academic identity that is not in keeping with disciplinary acceptable images.

The final factor to be considered is the language sources available to the writer from the social writing network, since exposure to language, whether academic, disciplinary, or non-academic, will influence the writer. A student writer may be exposed to disciplinary language through a variety of sources: reading and writing texts, attending lectures, engaging in conversations with academic and non-academic individuals. In terms of participants engaging in English academic writing, these sources must also be considered in language use, i.e., use of English, non-native English, and L1 (other than English). It is expected that a writer with multiple academic relationships will have more access to academic language than a writer with minimum or no academic relationships. The lack of appropriate language sources within a writer's social writing network disenables the writer from achieving his/her desired identity as a member of the group (Hirvela, & Belcher, 2001). An example of this may occur when a writer desires to project the image of a researcher, yet his/her social writing network has no academic relationships. In such a scenario, while the writer may realize the need to adopt a more disciplinary academic language, s/he may not have the appropriate language resources.

If the social writing network contains an academic clique, then, it is worth investigating whether there may be an association between identity, desire for group membership and use of the in-group language. However, a problem may occur when identity, group membership, and use of the in-group language conflict. The in-group language may also form an obstacle to the acquisition of academic English if the in-group language is either non-academic English or another language. Consider the case of Miriam, who identifies herself as a researcher, but does not have a writing network with an academic clique; as the data documented, she encounters problems with her planning, with how to go about writing each paragraph and what types of information to include in each paragraph.

Analyzing social writing networks as sources of disciplinary information and linguistic knowledge allows us to consider whether the social writing network provides negative language influence or positive exposure to desired academic language. Negative language influence refers to a preponderance of native language or non-academic English language usage among network members, which, in turn, has two effects: the writer is not exposed to the target language – in this case disciplinary academic English – and social influence is applied upon the writer to incorporate the in-group language rather than the targeted language. Desired academic language usage, on the other hand, is the incorporation of academic English as practiced by local members of the writer's disciplinary discourse community.

4   METHODOLOGY

4.1 Participants

Six advanced M.A. and Ph.D. L2 writing students consented prior to data elicitation to participate in the study. All names have been replaced with pseudonyms. Sara and Rachel were Ph.D. students in the process of developing their thesis proposal, Miriam and David were M.A. students either writing their M.A. thesis or having just completed it, and Leah and Judith were non-thesis M.A. students. The students received no compensation for participating in the study. The students were chosen according to their self-identification with an academic network, ranging from virtually nonexistent to almost complete identification. A further criterion included two representatives from one of three possible graduate student identities: Ph.D. students, M.A. students with thesis, and non-thesis M.A. students. Miriam, David, Leah, and Judith were participating in an advanced academic EFL writing course at the time of data collection. Acceptance into the two-hour per week Master's writing course was based on the Bar Ilan English as a Foreign Language Placement Exam, consisting of a 2000 word text with reading comprehension questions and an expository writing task. Of the six participants, only Sara is a native Russian speaker who has lived in Israel for over ten years, and the rest are native Hebrew speakers.

Sara and Rachel were Linguistics Ph.D. student at the time of the study. Their advisors for the M.A. thesis also served as their Ph.D. thesis advisors as well. Both participants studied in a department which is staffed by faculty who are native English speakers and teach their courses in English. Sara teaches English language courses at the same university, and she is surrounded by colleagues who are either native English speakers or proficient non-native speakers. Among the Linguistic Department students are other native Russian speakers as well as Hebrew speakers, and Sara's university unit employs both native Russian and native Hebrew speakers. Both Sara and Rachel's ambitions were to be academics.

Miriam was a Psychology M.A. student. She completed her M.A. thesis under the supervision of a native English-speaking advisor. Miriam's university department contains both English- and Hebrew-speaking faculty. Miriam also worked at a local hospital as part of a research team. Her academic goals were to complete a Ph.D. and become a psychology researcher.

David was a Computer Science M.A. student. He was in the process of writing his M.A. thesis under the supervision of a native English-speaking advisor. David's professional goal was to complete his M.A. to advance his promotion in the government office where he worked.

Leah was a Communication M.A. student. She was not writing a thesis although one of her academic goals was to complete a Ph.D. some time in the future. Leah is a professional translator from English to Hebrew and journal editor. She studied and worked in an all-Hebrew environment with some English available through text sources.

Judith was a Clinical Social Work M.A. student. She, too, was not writing a thesis, and she had no academic goals that would require writing a thesis. Her professional goals were related to her academic field. Both her academic and work environment was in Hebrew except for some academic texts in English.

4.2 Data Collection

Data collection consisted of sociolinguistic interviews, conducted in both Hebrew and English. Each session was audio recorded in the researcher's office. All sessions were divided into two parts. (1) A short introductory conversation in the form of a *semi-structured interview in English*. Questions were asked about participants' (a) language background and attitudes, (b) self-identification as an academic writer, (c) perception of their academic network and its norms, (d) perceived membership in academic network. (2) *Directed conversation on planning process* and language choice; these conversations were in the form of semi-structured interviews in English and Hebrew to elicit participants' attitudes and rationales for accommodation or non-accommodation to network norms during planning. An attempt was made to ask brief questions and provide participants with sufficient time to respond while limiting the researcher's participation. Issues relevant to EFL planning and language use were elicited through multiple questions in order to triangulate respondents' answers. In addition, participants were asked to complete a post-interview question-naire aimed at verifying explicit language use within their networks. Participants were asked to identify the people with whom they speak at home, work and univer-sity, the languages they use, and to estimate the extent to which each language was used on a regular basis.

The use of interviews to elicit retrospective accounts of planning activities and processes was chosen with the aim to mitigate criticism that has been levelled at previous research which relied on the use of think-aloud protocols for eliciting in-formation on complex cognitive processes, such as writing (Connor, & Kramer, 1995; Janssen et al., 1996), due to the extra burden imposed by think-aloud proto-cols upon L2 writers (Bosher, 1998). Since not all planning activities, processes and language choices during planning are immediately available and at a conscious level for many writers, the use of think-aloud protocols was ruled out. A final reason de-termining our decision to use interviews rather than think-aloud protocols was to capture the effect of language choice during the elicitation process as a factor that may influence the data participants are able to convey.

4.3 Data Analysis

Interview data was analyzed along various parameters that allowed us to capture the internal constituency of the social writing networks students formed, the type of planning in which they engaged, and the factors involved in their decision-making processes. Analysis of social writing networks consisted of identifying the extent and depth of participants' social writing networks, the use of L1 versus L2 in the networks, and the ways participants identified themselves vis-à-vis their networks.

Regarding planning: Early research into writing (e.g., Flower, & Hayes, 1981a, 1981b) identified planning as the initial component of the writing process. As the disciplinary field developed, planning has been identified as a process of establish-ing a goal and the steps needed to accomplish the goal (Gauvain, 2001). Following Hayes (1996), the view adopted in this study is that establishing goals and the steps needed to accomplish the goals is not limited to the initial part of the writing process but may occur anywhere before and during writing, and even during revision. This is in keeping with Alamargot, & Chanquoy's (2001b) definition of planning as an ac-tivity containing strategic procedures and practical goals. These goals may be con-tent-related, disciplinary-related, language-related, and so on. Since planning activi-ties may occur at any point in the writing process, two phases within which partici-pants undertake planning have been identified from the data. These phases are used for discussion purposes in order to differentiate between similar activities that occur several times in the writing process. The first phase is *pre-writing planning*, repre-senting planning activities that occur before the writer transfers ideas onto a writing medium. While L2 writers develop text in a writing medium, planning activities continue; this phase of planning is identified as *on-line planning*. It is expected that during planning, writers would be focused on developing ideas and information while in the writing phase they are focused on the formulation of some selected ideas and pieces of information over others. In terms of the language, L1 vs. L2, expected to be used: the writing phase is expected to be (and necessarily so) oriented toward L2 use (since this is the language the academic paper should be written in); in the pre-writing phase, however, the writer has options, since the processes s/he engages in are for self-communication. The choice of L1 over L2, then, during the pre-writing planning raises a number of interesting questions regarding the function of L1 and L2 during planning, the sociocognitive factors influencing language choice, and the impact pre-writing language use has on language use during the writing phase.

Analysis of linguistic decision-making processes identified six main language-related areas: linguistic, discourse, textual, syntactic, and lexical planning (Esperet, & Piolat, 1991), and the decision to use L1 or L2. Each of the planning processes was found to be associated with specific activities, outlined below.

Linguistic planning can occur during the pre-writing phase and during the process of writing. In the pre-writing phase, linguistic planning is mainly concerned with macro-propositional development, in terms of message contents, segmentation, and order, while in the writing phase the main concern is with micro-propositional development. Activities occurring during linguistic planning consist of idea development and organization.

Discourse planning is concerned with the overall text organization and text coherence. As such, this type of planning is shaped by content development and the writer's purpose. This type of planning includes, among others, the selection of discourse schemata and other structures appropriate to writing task and writer's purpose, ordering of ideas, and so on. Participants' discourse planning indicated audience awareness at this planning activity.

Textual planning may occur at two levels, i.e., at the macro-textual level, involving the planning of textual sections (e.g., introduction, methods, discussion), and constitutive moves (e.g., thesis statement), and at the micro-textual level, focusing on paragraph structures (e.g., topic sentence, middle, concluding sentence). It was found that idea organization is an activity that is affected by textual planning.

Syntacic planning is thus not independent of but attends to decision-making at the level of sentence structure (e.g., simple, compound, complex – a choice which has implications to the types of connectors, discourse markers, grammar, and punctuation used), and the ordering of components within the selected sentence structure. Syntactic planning attends to choices made at the discourse and textual level. Problems with L2 syntactic planning may arise in response to the lack of L2 syntactic knowledge or gaps in that knowledge, and they may impact on syntactic processing, requiring targeted strategies to overcome the potential obstacles. These strategies may include interlanguage transfer of L1 syntax to L2. In such a situation, the writer essentially utilizes L1 syntax in L2 writing. Another possible strategy is overgeneralization or oversimplification of L2 forms, which may interfere with or disturb linguistic and discourse planning. Recalling and applying syntactic knowledge was the most common activity associated with syntactic planning.

For research-based academic writing, lexical planning involves deciding on discipline-specific vocabulary. It should be noted here due to the conventionality characterising research writing, some processes may lead to pre-selected vocabulary (the connectors, modals and discourse markers used, among other elements). The ease with which L2 writers perform lexical planning may be dependent on a number of factors, such as lexicons adequate for the task, lexical access, and in case of difficulty, successful lexical retrieval strategies, as well as lexical selection processes. The activity associated with lexical planning was considering word choice.

5   RESULTS AND DISCUSSION

5.1 Participants' Planning and Language Choice

The types of planning participants undertook (before writing began and on-line writing), and the language used by each participant for each type of planning are outlined in Table 1.

Table 1. Choice of language (L1 vs. L2) during planning before writing and on-line writing

	Planning before writing	Language choice	Planning on-line	Language choice
Sara	Idea development	L2	Idea development	L2
	Idea organization	L2	Idea organization	L2
	Word choice	L2	Syntax	L2
			Word choice	L2
Rachel	Idea development	L1 / L2	Syntax	L2
	Idea organization	L1	Word choice	L1 / L2
Miriam	Idea development	L2	Syntax	L2
	Idea organization	L2	Word choice	L1/L2
	Word choice	L1 / L2		
	Audience awareness	L1 / L2		
David	Idea development	L1	Idea development	L1
	Idea organization	L1	Syntax	L2
			Word choice	L1 / L2
Leah	Idea development	L1	Idea development	L1
	Idea organization	L1	Syntax	L2
			Word choice	L1 / L2
Judith	Idea development	L1	Syntax	L1 / L2
	Idea organization	L1	Word choice	L1 / L2
	Word choice	L1	Audience awareness	L1 / L2

As it is clearly illustrated in Table 1, Sara's planning consists of idea development, organization, and word choice while her on-line planning involves idea development and organization, syntactic structure, as well as word choice. In both instances Sara uses her L2, English, throughout, *All in English. Russian would interfere if its really connected with my studies, I won't be able to do it in Russian any more.*

Rachel's prewriting and on-line planning differ slightly from Sara's. Rachel focuses on idea development and organization during planning, and on syntax and word choice during on-line planning. In terms of the language chosen, she uses her L1 and L2 for prewriting planning and L2 for on-line planning, *when I plan the thesis, I think, I activate both L1 and L2, my L1 is Hebrew and my L2 is English.* Miriam's planning has additional objectives. Her planning and language usage is L2 for idea development and organization, and L1 / L2 for word choice and audience awareness. Her on-line planning and language usage consists of L2 for syntax and L1 / L2 for word choice.

David's planning is aimed at idea development and organization, and his on-line planning occurs when idea development, syntax and word choice decisions take place. He uses L1 for the planning and L1/L2 for on-line planning. Leah plans for idea development and organization in L1 while during her on-line planning she uses L1 for idea development, L2 for syntax and L1/L2 for word choice. As for Judith, her planning consists of idea development and organization and word choice, utilising L1. Her on-line planning involves syntax, word choice and audience awareness, for which she uses L1 / L2.

The data indicates that participants undertook different types of planning activities for the pre-writing and writing phases. All of the participants utilized linguistic planning in the pre-writing phase for the purpose of developing and organizing propositions. During the writing phase, David and Leah reported limited linguistic planning, in the form of idea development. This aspect of linguistic planning resembles a novice writer's approach to knowledge telling (Bereiter, & Scardamalia, 1987). Discourse planning, the application of a discourse schema in order to achieve writer's purpose, was indicated by Miriam and Judith. Miriam activated discourse planning in the pre-writing phase in order to structure her idea organization according to academic discipline's discourse expectations; Judith activated discourse planning in the writing phase in order to guide her word choice since she was concerned that a non-professional reader may not understand the professional jargon she was using. Textual planning at the macro- and micro-textual level was noticeable in both the pre-writing and writing phases since idea organization was guided by it. As anticipated, syntactic planning occurred during the writing phase for all participants since it is necessary for sentence formulation. Lexical planning occurred in both the pre-writing and writing phases. During pre-writing, lexical planning was utilized by Sara, Miriam and Judith whereas during the writing phase it was utilized by all of the participants.

If we consider the choice of L1 versus L2 as a pattern according to participant, we see that Sara uses English throughout, reflecting her disciplinary language acquisition in English only. On the other hand, Rachel, who also acquired her disciplinary language in English, uses both Hebrew and English in her planning process, *the research questions mainly I think about them in my L1…when I get into the micro, eh, planning. For example, when I think about, eh, propose, propositional things, like speech acts, um, words, lexical, um lexical accents, lexical fluency, um the little things, the lemes, the lexemes, there I think I use my English because it it activates my L2 because I read about it in English, I read about the literature in English, I try to think in English in order so that it will sound more fluent. I try not to translate words.* This may be due to either accommodating the people with whom she speaks or for cognitive ease, such as in the organizing idea stage. Miriam appears to favour mostly English use for English language papers, *I think in English because everything I read is in English. Everything. That's the reason why psychology student doesn't go to learn English. Because anything we read since the first year in the first degree is English. So you start, and I not native speaker, um, you start thinking English in the subject you learn about it in English.* David explicitly states that he uses only Hebrew for cognitive ease throughout the planning phase, *It is easier to think in Hebrew. Now, eh eh, afterwards when you come to write the work then you take the idea. You can't write straight off the idea. You need to learn it, the explanations and reasons, and plan all the points which is basically the plan for all of the chapters that will be in the thesis.* Leah also uses Hebrew only, *The idea in Hebrew, and the the translation to English... First I think of the ideas and second I think of how to write it correctly,* but in her case Hebrew stores procedural knowledge, discourse knowledge, rhetorical knowledge, disciplinary knowledge and lexis. Judith began with Hebrew and attempted to continue with English. However, restricted English disciplinary lexis led to obstacles in idea development, necessitating return to L1 to achieve satisfactory idea development, thus her L1 usage is also attributable to cognitive ease, *I try to plan in English and then I saw it is not as good so later I planned in Hebrew and translated it and it was better for me.*

Several observations come to light when reviewing the above information on the relationship between language use and types of planning undertaken. To begin with, participants' language use is at times conscious choices that they make in order to achieve immediate and long-range planning goals. For example, the use of L2 may be related to a goal of fluency while the use of L1 may be for cognitive ease. Furthermore, all participants continue to plan even while writing their texts. Thus, it appears that higher-level and lower-level planning operations are not allocated to either before-writing planning or on-line planning, but rather they are carried out according to participants' needs. For the most part, they all plan for various aspects of writing, such as idea development and organization, before writing, and once they begin to write, they continue with on-line planning, which tends to focus on language issues, such as locating and selecting appropriate lexis or recalling and applying L2 syntax. However, three of the six participants, Sara, David and Leah, continue to undertake high-level operations along with low-level operations while on-line planning.

Another aspect that emerges from the data is the combined use of L1 and L2 for some of the planning functions, in particular word choice. For example, Miriam states that *when I know what I want to write and I miss a word [in English], I know in Hebrew what I want in English. I can't I can't say that the whole process is to translate from Hebrew to English, it's not.* Similarly, Judith feels that *I think I would begin in English and I didn't know it, and I switched to Hebrew. I recognized the missing word in Hebrew I thought in English but the missing word would be in Hebrew, I guess.* This may indicate that participants possess several lexicons storing lexis in either L1 or L2, and that when writing in L2, they may not always be able to access their L2 lexicons either due to a gap, retrieval problems or external L2 lexicons. Thus it may be possible to state that the use of L1 serves as compensation for working memory limitations. In this manner the two languages can be at work at the same time (Woodall, 2002).

Inconsistency among language usage during planning, both pre-writing and during writing, appears to be the norm. This is evident in both higher-level operations (idea generation and idea organization) and lower-level operations (syntax, word generation and selection). For example, David, Leah and Judith used L1 for higher-level operations, while Sara and Miriam used L2 and Rachel used both L1 and L2. During lower-level operations, Sara, Rachel and Miriam used L2 whereas David, Leah and Judith used L1 and L2.

Reasons for these patterns of language usage may be attributed to cognitively demanding tasks and writer's attempt to reduce cognitive overload, as with David. It may also be a result of disciplinary knowledge, language, discourse and rhetoric storage. With Leah and Judith, these are stored in L1, thereby necessitating the usage of L1 during planning for recall and application (Leah: *I translate it [texts] from English to Hebrew*). On the other hand, Sara stores this knowledge in L2 as evident in her planning entirely in English. Other participants, for example David and Miriam, store their disciplinary knowledge and language in both L1 and L2 (David: *The base is Hebrew because the organizational thought is according to Hebrew. But by then it doesn't matter. The moment that it has organization, the moment of coming to write and needing to formulate then I switch to English because you need to connect the sentences*). A third perspective may be due to motivation, such as with Miriam. She desires an identity of L2 researcher and thus utilises L2 during

5.2 Accounting for the Findings

5.2.1 Participants' Social Writing Networks

In the two Ph.D. students' networks, there is clear emphasis on relationships with other academics, such as professors and fellow students. Analyzing Sara's network requires that we trace the relationships she establishes with people (her thesis advisor, two professors, one graduate student, spouse, co-worker), as well as the range of written and oral resources (such as texts and lectures) she employs for communicating with these people; the depth of both indicates that Sara had greater academic than non-academic ties. Sara's comments are illustrative: *mainly I speak with, ok, these people who I mentioned, right, Wright and Smith, uh, I took courses, right, I took course with them and took their courses, and eh, sometimes if we thought we had a specific problem with [thesis advisor] Fields maybe, he would refer me to one of the other teachers and, or if I felt that this teacher is an expert in that particular field, so I felt that I could probably go and ask his advice*. From among her non-academic ties, she indicates that she has her spouse's support in achieving her goals. Similarly, Rachel's writing network has strong academic ties. Her network consists of ties with her advisor, at least two professors, at least two graduate students, and access to academic texts and lectures. Of interest is Rachel's lack of non-academic ties. This is telling in that it emphasizes the significance Rachel places upon her academic goals; in other words, Rachel does not consult with anyone who is unable to assist her with her academic writing, *Mostly when I'm doing my seminar papers and I'm writing, I'm at home. And I'm the most proficient person in English at home, so, so I don't ask someone from my family to check.* The emphasis placed on relationships with academics is a possible indication of Sara and Rachel's desire to be identified as a member of the academic group, as reflected by the number of professors and graduate students with whom the two writers consult and discuss their writing.

A distinct difference is noticeable in the social writing networks of the M.A. participants. The networks of Miriam and David, the M.A. with thesis participants, differ from both the Ph.D. networks and those of the M.A. without thesis, Leah and Judith. Compare David and Leah's network ties: David consults *with my thesis advisor, I speak a bit with people at work. Regarding the text itself with my thesis advisor.* On the other hand, Leah discusses only with people *at work, at work, only at work.* Thus, is appears that Miriam and David's networks consist of only one academic relationship, with their thesis advisor. Leah and Judith, on the other hand, have no academic relationships. As for non-academic network relationships, both David and Leah have co-workers as cliques in their networks.

Several issues arise from the data. The first is that there does appear to be an association between a student's academic status and type of relationships, or ties, in the student's writing network. Both Sara and Rachel, as Ph.D. students, have multiple ties with local members of their discourse community. Miriam and David, M.A. students with thesis, have only one academic tie with a member of their local discourse community, their thesis advisor. Leah and Judith, on the other hand, nonthesis M.A. students without thesis, have no academic ties. If this association is consistent, then it appears that the more committed a student is to entering an academic discourse community, as identified by their academic status, the greater the social writing network of academic relationships required to assist the student in furthering his/her academic identity and goals.

The second issue relates to social control and pressure. As the data illustrate, individuals experience social control and pressure when they desire to belong to a group. The social control and pressure is exerted by the group upon the individual, among other things, so that uniformity and cohesion is attained between the group, (i.e., in terms of the discourses or texts employed and the conventions by which communication is carried out within it) and the individual. For example, Sara believes that her relationship with her advisor has influenced her writing: *I think that over the years of our cooperation, and, right, and I'm his student, of course, he has certain expectations, probably, at this point, it's probably automatic but maybe in the past, he's very organized and very structured, so I know that I really have to have my ideas outlined in a clear cut way, the thesis, right, that's what he talks about a lot, right, the thesis statement, then he wants me to be close to the data, and I really have to show how the data supports, eh, my thesis, right. So I do have some expectations, he wants me to write clearly.* Related to this is the type of relationships people make in networks. Although a number of interlocking factors (whose nature can be revealed by further analyses) may shape one's desire to belong to a group, I would argue that a person would prefer to establish more ties with members of his/her desired group. In other words, some conclusion may be drawn about the type of group an individual desires to join by identifying cliques within the person's network. In the case of Sara and Rachel, both women have academic cliques – a feature that signals their desire to join this group. David and Leah, on the other hand, have non-academic cliques which consist of co-workers. It seems that the principal group they desire to be identified with is the one formed by their work colleagues. Interestingly enough, Miriam and Judith have no cliques in their networks.

The third issue relates to academic status and the enculturation and socialization process into the academic network. The enculturation and socialization process is a lengthy undertaking that consumes considerable resources of local members of discourse communities. From the six writing networks analyzed, there appears to be an association between a student's academic status and local discourse community members' support and assistance in this process. This association appears in the writing networks of Sara and Rachel, which both have strong multiple relationships with academic sources. They meet with their thesis advisor on a biweekly basis and with other professors several times throughout the semester. A weaker version appears in the networks of Miriam and David who have only one tie with an academic source, their thesis advisor, thus possibly indicating their academic department's position regarding allocation of resources to M.A. students with thesis. And, given that Judith and Leah have no academic ties, it appears that their very status as M.A. students without thesis already indicates their lack of interest in gaining entrance into an academic discourse community.

The analysis presented above delineated six different writing networks and several conclusions were drawn regarding the participating students' academic identity, desire for group membership, and the way such groups shape members' processes of enculturation and socialization into the network. Drawing upon this information, I analyze the extent to which the writing networks influence the participants' choice of Hebrew versus English language usage during the activity of text planning.

5.3 Writing Networks and Types of Language Resources Available

Based on the post-interview questionnaires, an analysis was undertaken of the languages, L1 or L2 or both, used in each participant's writing network (see Table 2); both English and Hebrew were used in both academic and non-academic contexts. Sara and Rachel are exposed to only English-based academic sources. Miriam is exposed to sources employing both academic English and academic Hebrew, with some non-academic English coming from her spouse. On the other hand, David's language sources range from academic English to academic Hebrew to non-academic Hebrew. Leah and Judith's academic language sources involve limited exposure to academic English while the rest is academic Hebrew. In addition, the two women are exposed to non-academic language sources.

Table 2. L1 and L2 as Resources in Participants' Writing Networks

Language resources	Sara	Rachel	Miriam	David	Leah	Judith
L2 Academic	Texts, lectures, advisor, professors, students	Texts, lectures, advisor, professors, students	Texts, lectures (lexical terms), advisor	Texts, advisor	Texts (only 10%)	Texts (only 80%)
L2 Non-Academic	Co-worker	None	Spouse	None	None	Neighbour
L1 Academic	None	None	Lectures	Lectures	Texts (90%), Lectures	Texts (20%), Lectures
L1 Non-academic	None	None	None	Co-workers, spouse	Co-workers, friend	

In order to distinguish the influence L1 and L2 might have on each of the participants' networks, further analyses were undertaken to identify the relationship between cliques and participants' desired identity (see below Table 3). Sara and Rachel's networks contain academic cliques, David and Leah's networks contain co-worker cliques and Miriam and Judith's networks have no cliques. The presence of cliques signifies social pressure towards conformity. Thus, it could be suggested that Sara and Rachel experience social pressure to conform to academic expectations while David and Leah experience pressure to work-oriented conformity.

The identification of cliques in participants' writing networks enables the classification of in-group language (Table 3, see Social Identification). The in-group languages were identified from participants' post-interview questionnaires. Both Sara and Rachel have academic English as their in-group language, Miriam and Judith have no in-group language, and David and Leah have professional Hebrew as their in-group language. These in-group languages correspond to the language sources and cliques listed above.

The presence of in-group language may encourage or discourage the acquisition of disciplinary English writing. In the case of Sara and Rachel, the in-group language encourages writing in English, since it aids the participants in unifying with clique members. However, for David and Leah, their in-group language most likely discourages the acquisition of academic discourse-related English writing, since it would require that participants relinquish their social identity with their cliques. Another problem occurs with Miriam. Although Miriam and Judith do not have in-group languages, in Miriam's case this may actually become an obstacle. According to the analysis of her self motivational factors, she describes her desire to be a researcher in the field of Psychology as follows: *well in psychology you can't do anything without second degree, um, besides if you need to, if you want to do research, you need second degree because you don't get the tools in the first degree and also you don't, no one considers you as a researcher without minimum, eh, second degree, and today also, eh, with third degree.* In order to achieve this, she will at some point need to position herself within a writing network that will encourage and support her goals in terms of the discipline and its language.

Table 3. Language influence (L1 vs. L2) in participants' networks

	Sara	Rachel	Miriam	David	Leah	Judith
Cliques	Academic	Academic	None	Co-workers	Co-workers	None
In-group language	Academic English	Academic English	None	Professional Hebrew	Professional Hebrew	None
Social Identification	Academic	Academic	Academic	Professional	Professional	Professional

In order to verify the influence the in-group languages may have on the participants, the self-motivational factor of desired group membership was also considered (see Table 3, Social Identification). Sara, Rachel and Miriam desire academic group membership. Their comments are interesting. Sara: *I hoped that I could get a[n academic] career in this*; Rachel: *Maybe be a lecturer in one of the colleges, here at the university*; Miriam: *I like research. I mean, my, um, um, specialite, specialisation in psychology is research.* Therefore, Sara's and Rachel's language sources and in-group language complement their goals and encourage the development of research-based L2 academic writing. Miriam, as noted above, appears to currently lack sufficient language sources and appropriate in-group language to achieve her goal. This may eventually interfere with her research-based L2 academic writing, since her writing network does not provide her with sufficient support and models exemplifying the type of behaviour expected in disciplinary writing.

In contrast, David, Leah and Judith desire professional group membership. David attests the following: *When you work in the public sector then if someone has an engineering degree he can receive a research rank. Whoever has a three year degree can not get unless he does a M.A.*; Leah: *I needed reinforcement for work, my work, because I am a professional editor, an editor of a newspaper;* Judith: *I'm using it at work. I'm a therapist so you need to know more, and I want to go to psychotherapist school here.* As such there appears to be no conflict between the in-group language and group membership. However, David is undertaking an M.A. with a thesis written in English. Since his in-group language is professional Hebrew, this may discourage the development of his English language writing skills to a disciplinary-appropriate level since doing such would require David to separate himself from his co-workers' clique. Furthermore, his writing network does not provide him with sufficient language sources by which to model appropriate English writing behaviour, *Because of what can be seen at work. You write a document, once again, I don't think that English and Hebrew, to write English or to write Hebrew, is significantly different.*

To review, there appears to be an association between the languages which participants have at their disposal as resources during writing academic texts, the cliques
formed, the in-group language, the self-motivational factor of group identification,
and the extent participants' writing networks were influential regarding language
choice and usage. This influence may either encourage or discourage research-based
L2 academic writing. While Sara and Rachel's networks seem to promote their academic writing, David and Leah's networks seem to promote a more non-academic
approach to writing. In other words, it seems that David and Leah's networks did not
encourage the development of research-based L2 academic writing. As for Miriam
and Judith, their network does not provide sufficient resources for the type of writing under study.

Let us now turn to the next part of the discussion in which I present information
on participants' language usage during their L2 planning processes.

5.4 Social Writing Network and Language Use during Planning

A correspondence between social writing networks and language use during planning is evident (see Table 4). One of the hypotheses set out for investigation concerned the amount of interaction a participant had with people using a specific language in a given context (local academic community), and the prevalence of this
language during the process of planning a research paper. It was assumed that the
more a participant interacted with people using a specific language, the greater the
prevalence of this language during the participant's planning processes. This hypothesis was borne out.

As Table 4 illustrates, Sara and Rachel interacted with people from the same
academic discipline, who emphasized academic English language use. As a consequence, their language use during planning reflects this language. In contrast, David
and Leah interacted with non-academic co-workers, emphasizing professional Hebrew language use, and their language use during planning shows an increase of
Hebrew dependence. The extent of influence the network has upon the writer in
terms of language use is also a reflection of the identity the writer wishes to project.
Research has found that writers' identifying with local academic discourse communities will entail a different writing process and lead to the production of a different
textual genre than writers who do not identify with their local discourse community
(Gunnarsson, 1997; Mische, & White, 1998). Three of the participants (Sara, Rachel
and Miriam) desire an academic identity. If we compare Sara, Rachel and Miriam's
language use, we notice that they utilize English to a greater extent then David,
Leah, and Judith, who do not desire an academic identity. It may be said that a student writer's language use is a reflection of his/her social identity and role which, in
turn, is determined by the proportion of academic to non-academic relationships
(Deem, & Brehony, 2000).

Among the participants desiring an academic identity, there is clearer focus on
English use in contrast to participants desiring a non-academic professional identity.
David and Leah's networks are professional in nature and promote the use of profes-
sional Hebrew. Likewise, David and Leah indicate that they use more Hebrew in

their planning. As for Miriam and Judith, these writers' language use is an outcome of their desired identity. Miriam identifies herself as an academic and emphasizes the use of English during planning, whereas Judith identifies herself within her profession and utilizes Hebrew to a greater extent. Thus it is noticeable that the desire to become a group member is an indicator among these participants' use of their networks' in-group language.

Table 4. Correspondence between language use and writer's network environment

	Language Use in Planning		Desired Identity	Writing Network	In-Group Language
	High level operations	Low level operations			
Sara	L2	L2	Academic	Academic	Academic English
Rachel	L1/L2	L2	Academic	Academic	Academic English
Miriam	L2	L2	Academic	None	None
David	L1	L1/L2	Professional	Co-workers	Professional Hebrew
Leah	L1	L1/L2	Professional	Co-workers	Professional Hebrew
Judith	L1	L1/L2	Professional	None	None

6   CONCLUSION

The writing process and its components such as planning have long drawn the attention of researchers in both L1 and L2 research. Most analyses, however, building upon the distinction between "skilled" versus "less skilled" writers, have suggested that writers' expertise and task (the production of a narrative versus an expository text, for instance) shape writers' choice to select L1 while composing in L2. Situating the analysis of planning within a social framework, this chapter set out to illustrate that this is, in fact, a socially shaped decision. Through the data collected and the analyses performed, I inquired into the extent of influence social factors – which are conceptualized in the notion of a writer's social network – have upon writers' use of their first versus second language (English) during the process of second language text planning. All participants were graduate students, producing an academic paper in English as L2. The data indicated that four of the six participants used the in-group languages of their networks while planning. The other two participants used a language appropriating their identity during writing. Since all of the participants were planning for an English academic paper, it may be said that their social writing networks had a positive or negative language influence, depending upon whether the network emphasized academic English or non-academic Hebrew use. Other factors that influenced language use included need for cognitive ease, storage of disciplinary knowledge in one or two languages, and motivation. Thus, it appears that language use during planning is a reflection of both cognitive and institutional, social factors.

As a first and most direct implication of this study one could be led to suggest that students intending to write an academic paper in a second language should expand their networks to include academic cliques proficient in the target language; however, the nature of the network relationships established would need to be further analyzed: What is the frequency of the pertinent comments (i.e., comments made by a professor about the way one should go about writing a paper) in student-professor interactions and how such comments are gradually appropriated by the students? How does the activity of planning a paper appear and how is it negotiated in the interactions a student enters with his/her friends and other members of his/her writing network? Since it is through their relationships with other students and professors that students learn the conventions of disciplinary writing and language use, attending to the actual interactions would provide us with a wealth of information into this process.

COLLABORATIVE WRITING GROUPS IN THE COLLEGE CLASSROOM

CAROLE H. McALLISTER

Southeastern Louisiana University, USA

Abstract. This study analyzes college writing by focusing on texts produced over the course of a single semester by students working under 3 different conditions: independently and in permanent versus changing groups. Focusing on collaborative writing groups (i.e., on groups whose members share full responsibility for the production of a text), this study aims to (1) measure the efficacy of using collaborative writing groups (over other conditions) in a college level composition class and (2) determine how issues related to group cohesion (whether students remain in the same group for an entire semester or for the duration of a writing project) shape writing improvement. The method employed for gathering and analyzing data integrated two social scientific research paradigms: a process-product quantitative design, which measured student writing performance and writing improvement vis-a-vis group cohesion (students' attitude, retention and absentee rates); and a qualitative design, which described participants' impressions of the social and interactional processes involved in collaborative writing groups. Participants were approximately 150 college freshmen at a mid-sized, public university, enrolled in 6 sections of a second semester freshman composition course; 2 instructors, and the author. For an entire semester, two sections wrote the majority of their assignments in permanent groups, two sections wrote in groups that changed with each writing task, and two wrote independently. Groups consisted of 4-5 students, heterogeneously mixed. Results show that collaborative writing groups are efficacious; all students significantly improve their writing; retention rates for group classes are significantly higher than individual classes; and students enjoy writing more in (permanent and changing) group classes. From researcher observations, and from analyses of participants' comments (as noted in the transcripts of tape-recorded sessions) it was observed that permanent groups engaged in more dialogic collaboration, while changing groups used more hierarchical collaboration. Although there are benefits to all groups, students in permanent groups approached and constructed the activity of writing in line with a more process-oriented pedagogy.

Keywords: writing groups, shared texts, collaborative writing, college composition

1   ON COLLABORATIVE WRITING: THEORETICAL FOUNDATIONS

The thesis that all acts of making meaning, such as teaching and learning, arise out of socially constructed contexts pervades current research on the social nature of writing and collaborative learning. While collaborative learning theory has radically reshaped both theoretical and pedagogical approaches in a variety of fields, including writing, DiPardo, & Freedman (1988: 120), drawing from Freedman's national survey of 560 "successful" writing teachers, suggest that teachers are "deeply divided as to the efficacy of the small-group approach." In fact, the issue as to whether collaborative learning is a valid, viable approach for a college composition class is still under considerable debate in the field of composition (Casey, 1993; DiPardo, & Freedman, 1988; Randolph, 1997). One of the common concerns voiced is that students will not engage in extensive writing or learn as much about writing as they would if writing independently. They would spend more time socializing in their groups than they would working directly on their task. Indeed, according to Moffett (1968), one of the main proponents of this theme in composition research, a writer's autonomy is the crucial element that differentiates writing from speaking. In learning to write "…the most critical adjustment one makes is to relinquish collaborative discourse, with its reciprocal prompting and cognitive cooperation and go at it alone" (Moffett, 1968: 87). As a result, in the typical composition classroom, the act of writing remains the domain of individual writers who tend to work alone in their attempt to express their "originality" or "inner selves" through their texts.

Researchers from different traditions disagree, arguing against the traditionally silent composition classroom. Among the many interrelated, though parallel-developing, research strands that attest to the value of collaborative learning are the social constructionist framework (e.g., Vygotsky, 1978), which suggests that all writing be conceptualized as a collaborative act of making meaning, some lines in composition research (e.g., Beaven, 1977; Bouton, & Garth, 1983; Bouton, & Tutty, 1975; Bruffee, 1978, 1983, 1984; Elbow, 1973), research on ESL writing (Liu, & Hansen, 2002), which has incorporated the premises of collaborative learning theory into the construction of "peer response" groups, and research on writing in the business community, which usually refers to collaborative writing as "shared-document" production (e.g., Bosley, 1989). For Bruffee (1983), the collaborative classroom provides the appropriate source for knowledge and meaning.

> This necessity to talk-through the task of writing means that collaborative learning… is not merely a helpful pedagogical technique incidental to writing. It is essential to writing….Like any other learning or problem-solving activity, writing becomes essentially and inextricably social or collaborative in nature (Bruffee, 1983: 571).

Collaborative writing groups offer students an opportunity to participate in the act of making and negotiating meanings through writing, to bring in different resources and use them to resolve the many different issues arising during the production of a text. From a different research strand, ESL writing, we may draw interesting information; teachers who have tried some form of collaboration in the composition classroom, usually peer response groups, attest to the intricate relationship between talking, writing, and learning about this process. In fact, peer response groups, which have been developed to provide support to process-oriented pedagogies, are currently recognized as an important component of L2 writing instruction. Getting through multiple drafts (from student, peer, and self) one builds audience awareness; makes reading-writing connections clearer; and builds content, linguistic, and rhetorical schemata through multiple exposures to different texts or to different versions of the same text. Furthermore, collaborative writing is what students can expect when they leave the classroom (Ede, & Lundsford, 1990; Faigley, & Miller, 1982). Acknowledging the impact of collaborative writing in the business world (Begoray, 1994; Bucha, 1994; Cross, 2000), business writing classes have introduced the production of "shared-documents" (Bosley, 1989), though the validity of this pedagogical practice is current questioned (Belanger, & Greer, 1992; Graves, & Noll, 1999; Sormunen, & Ray, 1996; Winter, & Neal, 1995).

It is interesting to note in this regard, however, that in contrast to useful research insights that have been documented over the past decade by L2 writing research, few of these findings have been actually used to invigorate analyses of students' writing in the field of college composition. Indeed, these two research strands, though addressing issues mutually beneficial, seem to run along distinct lines. Note, for instance, that L2 writing research, which has incorporated peer response activities in ESL writing classes, attests evidence on the beneficial effects these activities have on motivation, attitude and even on students' writing quality (Liu, & Hansen, 2002). Different, but equally important, issues may be drawn from research conducted in Psychology concerning group dynamics and from educationally-oriented work on cooperative learning; the results support the positive value working/learning cooperatively has as opposed to working independently (Deutsch, 1949a; Helmreich, 1982; Helmreich et al., 1978, 1980, 1986; Johnson, & Johnson, 1991; Ringelmann, 1913; Slavin, 1983; Triplett, 1898). Interestingly, little of this research has been focusing exclusively on groups whose task is the shared production of a document writing collaboratively (Lemon, 1988). From the few studies conducted, important themes emerge which may be employed profitably when designing future research. Thus, of great interest are findings on how students describe their learning experience in collaborative writing groups (Gergits, & Schramer, 1994; Tebo-Messina, 1993); how gender impacts roles in collaborative writing groups (Morgan, 1994); how collaborative writing group members negotiated and were impacted by difference (Goodburn, & Ina, 1994); and how collaborative writing transformed social relations in a classroom (Hulbert, 1989). A small case study using a four-person group examined the discourse of a freshman-level collaborative writing group and found it effective (Randolph, 1997).

Within the field of college composition, research attention has focused mainly on the use of peer response groups (Beaven, 1977; Bouton, & Garth, 1983; Bouton, & Tutty, 1975; Bruffee, 1978, 1984; Elbow, 1973), presented under the headings of "teacherless writing groups" (Gebhardt, 1980; Hipple, 1972; James, 1981) or "helping circles" (Macrorie, 1970, 1984; Moffett, 1968; Murray, 1968; Peckham, 1978; Putz, 1970; Spear, 1988; Trimbur, 1985; Wagner, 1975). It should be noted, however, that these peer response groups have not been conceptualized as representing a context which promotes cooperative learning, and positive goal interdependence. Rather than fit either a cooperative or competitive learning situation, these groups seem to operate in a "mixed-motive" situation (Deutsch, 1949b): the basic focus of the group is on critiquing the work of an individual; the group offers assistance, but knows that ultimately each member is competing with one another for the best rank from the teacher-examiner.

This competitive climate seems to run counter to workplace reality, since collaborative writing is what students should expect when they leave the classroom (Faigley, & Miller, 1982; Ede, & Lundsford, 1990). Acknowledging the pervasiveness of collaborative writing in the business world (Begoray, 1994; Bucha, 1994; Cross, 2000), business writing classes have began to focus on the production of "shared-documents" (Bosley, 1989), though, as noted above, concerns have been raised on its validity (Belanger, & Greer, 1992; Graves, & Noll, 1999; Sormunen, & Ray, 1996; Winter, & Neal, 1995). With the increased use of email and co-authoring via computer, collaborative writing can become faceless interactions. Indeed, some question whether computer co-authoring can produce the same results as face-to-face collaboration (Mabrito, 1992; Perreault, & Moses, 1992). Apparently, these issues need to be addressed by subsequent research.

This study, which focuses on college writing, questions the pedagogy which assumes that college composition classes need to focus solely on teaching the individual student how to write, and provides support to an alternative pedagogy which is informed by collaborative learning theories; as proposed, students in a language-centred classroom learn how to write by engaging in the process together. The more specific purpose of this study is to measure the way group conditions shape the process of writing. Research from group dynamics as well as cooperative learning suggest that groups would develop more trust and cohesion the longer they work together, and engage in more dialogic collaboration. Is this type of collaboration more appropriate than a hierarchical, task-oriented collaboration for the type of work involved in producing a written text? Are permanent groups more appropriate than changing groups for writing collaborative assignments? Establishing two group conditions (collaborative writing groups vs. changing groups) and differentiating writing performed in groups from writing done independently, the discussion seeks to unveil the efficacy of using collaborative writing groups in a college composition class and attests interesting results on the way group dynamics shape the process of writing, and determine the quality of the produced texts.

2   METHOD

2.1 Participants and Data

The participants in this study were approximately 150 college freshmen at a mid-sized, public, open-admissions southern university, enrolled in 6 sections of a second semester freshman composition course, the two instructors, and the author. Each teacher had one section randomly designated as using either permanent groups, changing groups, or independent writers.

For an entire semester 2 sections wrote the majority of their assignments in a group that remained permanent; 2 sections wrote in groups that changed with each writing task, about every 3-4 weeks, and 2 sections wrote all their work independently.

Before being placed in groups, students had been given an overall rank from one to four (1-4) on the basis of their writing ability (determined from scores on ACT, first-semester composition class, and preliminary holistic score on diagnostic essay). Then the groups were randomly selected and heterogeneously (according to gender, and writing ability) composed of 4-5 students. Each group contained at least one good, two average, and one poor writer.

The method employed for gathering and analyzing data integrated two social scientific research paradigms: (1) a qualitative design that documented participants' impressions of the social and interactional processes involved in and shaping learning in collaborative writing groups, such as use of verbal and nonverbal language. Data was gathered and analyzed from the perspectives of the researcher, the students, and the teachers and (2) a process-product, quantitative, design that measured student writing performance and writing improvement vis-à-vis group cohesion (students' retention and absentee rates).

2.1.1   Guides for Participants

Students received a guide to different feedback strategies based on Ruben, & Budd (1975) (and suggested by George, 1984; Johnson, & Johnson, 1989; Ruben, & Budd, 1975; Spear, 1988). This guide provided "criteria for useful feedback," such as "descriptive rather than evaluative," "specific rather than general," "solicited rather than imposed." The focus of their classroom experience was collaborative writing – learning in a discourse community – learning to write with as well as to listen and to respond to different voices.

The students' course information sheets listed a few characteristics of cooperative learning groups to foster discussion of group learning. They also showed how subjects working in groups would be evaluated. The model for evaluation was derived and adapted from Beard et al. (1989): students' grades were based on both their contribution to the writing process (based on peer, teacher, and self evaluations) – 50%; and the overall grade on each product (e.g., essays, research paper) – 50%.

Copies of "Descriptions of Common Roles in Interpersonal and Group Communication" and "Role Behaviour Recording Form" were distributed and redistributed throughout the semester as a guide for both peer and self-evaluation. The description of roles gave the students a working vocabulary of terms: *task-oriented* roles, such as coordinator and information-giver; *relation-oriented* roles, such as encourager and follower; and *self-oriented* roles, such as blocker and avoider (Ruben, & Budd, 1975).

Guidelines for responding to the texts themselves were presented orally by each teacher; also, students took notes from the blackboard as well as from their texts, *Writing Across the Curriculum, St. Martin's Guide to Writing, and the St. Martin's Handbook.*

2.1.2   Writing Assignments

This was a second semester composition class using a writing-across-the-curriculum text. All the following writing assignments were condition-generated, i.e., written in permanent or changing groups or by independent writers. The first assignment intro duced students to research methods. Students began with a scavenger hunt for research articles, followed by writing summaries of these articles, a synthesis of their summaries, and a possible thesis for a research paper.

The next paper (500-750 words) was based on a critical study of two or more fairy tales or myths. Students received 6 topic suggestions from the instructor.

The research paper (5 pages) was a group-generated topic springing from the research they had collected. Students worked together both in and out of class.

The fourth project was an analysis (500-750 words) of a short story using critical readings accompanying the text.

During the last week of the semester all six sections wrote an essay collaboratively: *"Define the main idea and sub-ideas of the course; compare and contrast how your readings contributed."* This essay was produced in two hours (see Appendix A for samples of group-written essays; see Appendix B for researcher's observations on group processes while writing).

2.1.3   Forms of Evaluation

Students were required to keep a *journal*, often writing the last few minutes of class twice to three times a week, documenting their response to group work, (reminded to) using the descriptors mentioned above (see Goldstein, & Malone [1985] for the significance of journal-keeping as a method of strengthening collaborative writing). Following observation guidelines, offered by Johnson, & Johnson (1991), Ruben, & Budd (1975), and Spear (1988), both instructors kept a journal of their observations of group work.

Upon completing each writing project, students were also asked to complete a *peer assessment form* in which they rated their own as well as their peers' performance on a 5-point scale. The criteria used evaluated the types and value of members' participation in group processes, leading to the text product (Johnson, & Johnson, 1991; Morgan et al., 1989; Ruben, & Budd, 1975).

From mid-semester on, students produced independently a graded, in-class *evaluative essay* (following every major writing project), in which they critiqued the collaborative writing experience and evaluated their groups' performance.

During the beginning of the semester, *I observed* each of the sections three times each, following all of the groups as unobtrusively as possible and taking notes. Near mid-semester, I spent three sessions as a non-participating member of one specific, randomly chosen group in each of the six sections. In addition to *note-taking*, the sessions were *tape recorded.* After mid-semester when the changing group condition shifted in their structure, I followed one student (per section, randomly chosen) whose group I had joined previously to her or his new group (see Appendix A2). I stayed with the same permanent group as before. I returned twice during the last three weeks of the semester to observe and to record group behaviour (see Appendix A1).

At the end of the semester I randomly selected 4 students from each collaborative section for an in-depth, hour-long *personal interview*. The students knew these interviews were voluntary and confidential, held in my office during the last week of classes or finals week. I also interviewed the teachers.

After the semester ended, I collected grade reports for each participating section, which included students' grades, *withdrawals*, and *number of absences*.

3   RESULTS

The quantitative data represents the results based upon the following: the frequency of types of comments coded according to Bales' Interaction Process Analysis (see Appendix C) from tape-recorded conversations of groups at mid-point and the end of the semester; evaluations of students' writing scored on the diagnostic and the final essays; percentage of students successfully completing course (withdrawal from course comparisons); and the number of student absences. The qualitative data is derived from my observations partly as participant-observer and partly from transcripts of taped conversations. Observations of permanent and changing groups are reported at three different times within the semester – early, middle, and end.

3.1   Quantitative Analysis: Writing Impovement vis-à-vis Group Conditions

3.1.1   Initial Equivalency of the Group

Since this is not a true experiment involving random assignment of subjects to conditions, it is important to establish that there were no major differences between the various classes before the classes began. For every student participating in this research, I obtained the grade in English 101 (prerequisite course) as well as their ACT score in English. Each of these measures was analyzed in a 2 (teacher: A or B) X 3 (class condition: permanent, changing, or independent) Analysis of Variance (ANOVA). There were no significant effects on either measure. Thus, from this analysis it appears that at the beginning of the semester there were no differences in the basic writing abilities of the classes of students.

3.1.2   Group Cohesiveness

"Group cohesiveness" is intended to capture the degree to which individuals are attracted/drawn to the group as well as the ability of the group to keep its members. One indication of such cohesiveness would be the number of students who remained in the class as opposed to those who withdrew. Class withdrawals and completions were obtained for students in each of the three class conditions. The three groups were then compared in a 2 (completion status: completed or withdrew) X 3 (class condition: permanent, changing, or individual) Contingency Table. There was a significant difference among the class conditions with respect to completing or withdrawing from a class, $X^2 (2) = 9.129$, p < .05.

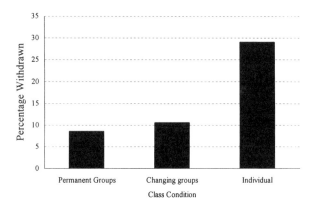

Figure 1. Percentage of students withdrawing from the class for each class condition

Another indication of a group's ability to hold its members could be seen from class attendance. It would be expected that attendance would be higher in classes using groups than in individual classes. The number of days absent and present was collected for each student in each of the three conditions. The three class conditions were then compared in a 2 (attendance: present or absent) X 3 (class condition: permanent, changing, or individual) Contingency Table. There was a significant difference among the class conditions with respect to attendance, X^2 (2) = 97.092, p < .001. As can be seen in Figure 2, the absences in the individual conditions are two to three times those in the permanent group and changing group conditions with the permanent group and changing group conditions being virtually identical.

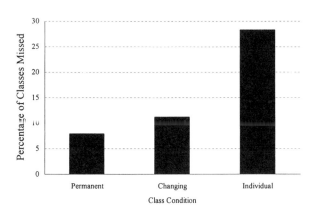

Figure 2. Percentage of classes missed during the semester for each class condition

In summary, both indices of the power of the groups to maintain their membership show the same pattern. The individual condition showed significantly higher withdrawals and absences than the two group conditions with both the permanent group and the changing group conditions at the same levels.

3.1.3   Analyzing the Product

Research by McAllister (1985) demonstrated that graders' awareness of conditions (handwritten vs. typed) could alter their perceptions of essays; therefore, all essays were typed and coded to maintain student anonymity and keep graders blind to experimental conditions.

Eight (8) English faculty blind to experimental conditions were trained as holistic raters before scoring the diagnostic, group, and independently written essays. Each essay was rated by at least 2 graders (a 3rd grader was used when scores varied by more than one point per essay on a 6-point scale). A holistic scoring method based on Cooper (1977), Myers (1980), and White (1986) was employed.

Final Group Product. A final group paper was written by students in all classes. It had been expected that the best papers would be produced by the permanent groups who had been working together on group papers throughout the semester. Lower quality papers were expected for students in the individual condition who were working on their first group project of the semester. Each group project had been holistically graded on a six-point scale. This measure was analyzed in a 2 (teacher: A or B) X 3 (class condition: permanent, changing or individual) ANOVA. There were no significant effects. Thus, even though the conditions differed in their group experience, there were no differences in the writing quality of the group product.

Independent Student Essays. Each student in each condition independently produced two essays that were each graded holistically on a six-point scale. The first essay was a diagnostic essay that served as a pretest while the second essay was the final exam essay that serves as a post-test. Essay grades were analyzed in a 2 (essay: pretest or post-test) X 2 (teacher: A or B) X 2 (student sex: male or female) X 3 (class condition: permanent, changing, or individual) Mixed Model ANOVA. There were two significant effects. First, there was a significant difference between scores on the pretest and the post-test, $F(1,94)=52.89$, p<.001.

As can be seen in Figure 3, the grades on the post-test (final) are higher than the grades on the pretest (diagnostic). This effect shows the improvement in writing that occurred during the semester for all three conditions. However, this effect was qualified by a significant essay X class condition interaction, $F(2, 94) = 3.93$, p < .023. This interaction means that the gains that occurred were not happening equally in all conditions. As can be seen in Figure 3, although all groups show a gain of the post-test over the pretest, the largest gains occurred in the permanent group condition. In other words, individuals in all conditions showed improvement in their writing over the course of the semester, but with the permanent group showing the significant, dramatic improvement.

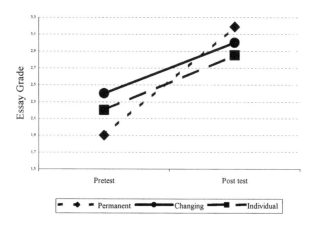

Figure 3. Individual grades on diagnostic (pretest) and final (post-test) essay

3.1.4 On the Interaction Processes: Documenting Participants' Perspectives

Tape recordings were made of one group discussion in each class of the permanent group condition and the changing group at mid-semester and at the end of the semester. Many different frameworks have been developed in fields such as sociolinguistics to trace the processes by which people interact. In this study, my attention is not on the interaction as such; I focus on how participants perceived the way a specific style of interaction (dialogic vs. hierarchical collaboration) was created through the contributions each member made towards the completion of the writing task the group had undertaken. To this end, my attention is directed to the comments made by participants in the course of the interaction as well as to comments made by participants when reflecting on the interaction after its completion. Comments are scored according to Bales' (1950, 1965) Interaction Process Analysis, a coding scheme devised for observing and analyzing group behaviour (see Appendix C). Each comment was placed in one of the twelve categories representing positive or negative reactions, attempted answers or questions in socio-emotional and task-area areas. Examples of "socio-emotional positive responses" include a student's comments upon reading a group member's work: *"Oooh, I like what you wrote on transformations; I want us to use it in the paper! My own transformations suck!"* Here she has raised another member's status within the group. On the other hand, she also produced "negative socio-emotional comments" toward a group member who had missed meetings, such as refusing to re-schedule a meeting to meet his needs with a solid *"NO!" We're not changing; we're leaving it that way!"* "Task-area comments" include a person asking *"What information do you want me to research? Does this paragraph work as a transition?"*

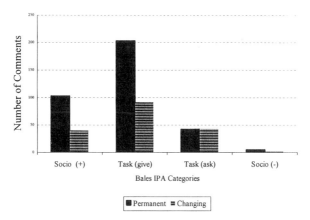

Figure 4. Participants' comments during the interaction: Data for the end of the semester

The mid-semester and end-of-the semester comments were very similar. Figure 4 shows the end-of-the-semester results. From this figure it is quite clear that there is much greater participation in the permanent groups than there is in the changing groups, both in the socio-emotional and task area. Although the participation in both socio-emotional and task areas is greater in the permanent group, the ratio of socio-emotional to task comments appears about the same for both groups. In both cases there seemed to be activity in both areas, but with greater numbers of comments in the task (talking about writing) area.

One of the questions that this research set out to address was whether writing groups would remain effective if they stayed together for an entire semester, they would experience "burn out," grow stale and be non productive, or they would continue to develop trust and cohesion. Thus, it is significant that the Bales Interaction Process Analyses of the permanent groups' discussions at the end of the semester were very similar to the ones at mid-semester. The permanent groups kept the same high level of activity, the same flow of conversation. Although there was no significant increase in the number of negative socio-emotional comments, there was no decrease either, indicating the groups had not become bored, passive, and disinterested in either collaborative writing or one another.

3.2 Qualitative Analysis: Reflecting on the Writing Process

3.2.1 Student Evaluations

Each student *journal* was charted according to the following categories: name, total number of entries, journal entries worth quoting, positive/negative, general/specific, length, socio-emotional comments, and task-oriented comments about the writing process. I followed the same procedure as above for their *evaluative essays*. I also noted how they used the *peer assessment form*.

3.2.2   Categorization of Observations

To categorize my observations, I used Tuckman's (1965) terminology, i.e., *orientation* (forming), *conflict* (storming), *cohesion* (norming), *performance* (performing), and *dissolution* (adjourning); these terms have been used to reflect sequential stages of group development (see also Tuckman, & Jensen, 1977). In the context of this discussion, however, these categories are not used in a similar manner, but rather in reference to a system for classifying group behaviour. This system was used for comparing the differences in behaviour between the permanent groups and the changing groups.

I visited each group condition once during weeks 3 and 5, for several concurrent class periods during weeks 7 and 8, and for the whole last week of the semester. Initially, I sensed the tension associated with being thrust into an unfamiliar classroom situation, an unfamiliar writing task, with an unfamiliar group of people. Slowly, however, I began to notice a few differences arising between the two conditions. The permanent groups seemed to be moving toward cohesion, engaged in writing together, while the changing groups vacillated between orientation and conflict. They approached their task as "divide and conquer." Overall, though, these initial observations seem to suggest that most students had adjusted somewhat, felt more at ease than at first, and overall, had enjoyed participating in their groups.

During weeks 7-8, a few more differences appeared between the changing group and the permanent group classes. Whereas the changing groups' behaviour did not seem to have altered much from earlier observations, the permanent groups continued toward cohesion. Both permanent and changing groups responded similarly to individuals who had not done their part; they attempted to "write them off" or to exclude them. However, they did deal with conflict differently. The permanent groups were more vocal in expressing their displeasure with the individual causing the problem. For example, when one member of a permanent group who had been acting as a "social loafer," remarked *"I don't know how to write a thesis statement,"* the group leader openly voiced her hostility with *"Maybe that's why you're taking English for the fourth time."* This student ended up withdrawing from the course. Changing groups kept their feelings guarded; there was more an underlying tension among members, an "unspoken" hostility than any open expression of conflict. Despite obvious polarization, the changing groups still managed to write collaboratively and perform their task. The following example illustrates how changing groups kept on task.

Two members began a meeting by each one informing the group of what she planned to do (without considering the others). Margaret opened the group discussion with *"I can do the introduction."* Gwynne immediately followed with *"I want to write the conclusion."* She then began telling the other two group members to write the body of the paper; *"...really just a paragraph each."* The group then began discussing the project: what values should appear in what part of the paper, who would write what. Throughout the group discussion concerning what information they were going to include in their paper, I heard many *"right's,"* often offered as Tracy or Ron's attempt to participate in the group discussion, and their responses are the only example of positive socio-emotional response; the conversation was almost totally oriented toward exploring their writing task. This lack of socio-emotional involvement, their task-orientation focus is clearly seen in the group's reaction to one of its members casually mentioning a personal problem. When they were trying to arrange a time to meet the next evening at the library, Gwynne unabashedly announced, *"I have an AA meeting then."* The only reply came from Ron who startlingly said, *"You're in AA?" "Yeah,"* she said matter-of-factly, and without any pause she returned the conversation to writing concerns. Nobody else said anything; no one encouraged her to reveal any more. Finally, in a tone more business-like than sympathetic, Margaret and Ron responded, *"We'll wait for you."* Gwynne shrugged. Despite the lack of personal exchange, this changing group cohered enough to write collaboratively and accomplish their task.

The last week in the semester the students worked on one final project: to define the main idea and important sub-ideas of the course, comparing and contrasting how their readings contributed. The changing groups were now working in their fourth group. As expected, major differences in group cohesion arose at this point. An easy flow of communication was occurring in the permanent groups, showing a balance between task-oriented and socio-emotional responses. On the other hand, the changing groups spent much of their group class time working silently, individually. The permanent groups exuded a much greater feeling of group solidarity, of the task having become the group's responsibility rather than the weakly-connected product of several individuals (see Appendix B for researcher observations). The major difference between what happened in the permanent groups and what did not happen in the changing groups can best be illustrated by one of the last conversations of a permanent group.

Revising the final group essay, Scott sought one last clarification from his group:

> "So what did we learn? Do we understand each other better?"
> Debbie answered Scott: "We want to learn from each other; we learned to be more patient with each other."
> Jeff: "Yeah, we can put that in there, too."
> Debbie continued: "We learned to let others voice their opinion; we learned the responsibility of being somewhere at a certain time and having the paper ready and how you worked under the stress of being with another person....When you work with a group of people, you get mad at yourself and everybody else, too" she said laughing.

The process had been incorporated in the product; this permanent group had recognized that the value of this class was actually the process they had been involved in. They had become dialogic communicators: they understood that the group process in which they had been involved was an essential part of the knowledge they had produced.

4   DISCUSSION

4.1 Collaborative versus Traditional Learning

A first-level analysis of the quality of the products students wrote at the end of the semester would suggest that all students, those who had participated in permanent groups, in changing groups, and those who had written independently, improved their writing significantly. However, a closer look at the results demonstrates that collaborative learning was superior to the traditional, teacher-centred classroom: students improved their writing, they exchanged ideas in a more active way, they came to class more frequently, and they withdrew from class less than when they worked individually. Succinctly, the results of this study seem to corroborate theses developed by the social constructionist framework and the educational philosophy of Dewey, and Freire, among others. The results corroborate research findings that have attested to the positive effects of peer response groups in composition coopera-tive learning. As demonstrated, knowledge is socially constructed, gained through social interaction; the role of the teacher is important for facilitating the creation of a social context for critical thinking to occur. Despite differences between permanent and changing groups, writing collaboratively offers students more benefits than writ-ing individually in a composition class.

The quantitative results showed that students who worked in collaborative writ-ing groups learned to write as well as those who wrote individually all semester. Students in all three conditions began statistically equivalent in writing ability, and students in all conditions significantly improved their writing as individuals. Thus, collaborative writing groups performed equal to the individual writers. Whether they were in changing groups or permanent groups, students learned how to perform their assigned tasks and achieved their goals together – they learned how to write collabo-ratively.

Additional support for the use of collaborative writing groups was found in the significantly high retention and attendance rates for the group classes compared to the individual writer classes. Students working in both group conditions attended classes with significantly more regularity – the individual writers were absent two to three times more than students working in groups. Equally impressive was the dif-ference in withdrawals from class. Students working in both group conditions with-drew significantly less, one-third less than those students who worked individually. Groups encouraged and motivated students to come to class. Said one student, *"This is the only class I come to, that I am awake for; I have to; I can't let my group down."*

According to Dewey (1938), traditional education has failed students because it did not recognize the community life of the classroom. Working along similar lines, composition theorists stress the importance of establishing an environment within which not only texts may be produced, but also discourse about writing can develop to generate knowledge and help participants develop their strategic thinking about writing. Writing should not be separated from its inherent social nature. In this study, collaborative writing groups established a community life within a language-centred classroom. Students engaged in dialogue continually; they focused on their task to create a piece of writing together. Meaning and knowledge were thus gener-ated through the language of social interactions; group dialogue became central to the learning process. As the teachers reported, their traditionally taught, individual writer classes were silent. The usual pattern of dialogue was teacher-to-student, or student-to-teacher, responding to questions or seeking clarification, with little to no student-to-student interchange. Students played a passive role, waiting for knowl-edge to come from the teacher. In the collaborative classes students did not/could not sit and wait for answers to be given to them. They used language to discover language. One of the teachers noted: *"The students gained power to control their own words and often gave much more effort to the work as they became an absolutely necessary member of the team producing a group product."*

4.2 Permanent versus Changing Groups

While changing groups offered students some benefits that permanent groups did not, permanent groups provided more measurable benefits in almost every category analyzed. The permanent groups talked significantly more about writing, felt they learned more about writing, and improved their writing significantly more than the changing groups. Moreover, permanent groups kept their members – fewer withdrew from permanent groups than any other condition.

Though changing groups did not outscore permanent groups in any measured category, they did provide benefits that the permanent groups did not. For example, they allowed students to move away from particularly dominating personalities that they could not work with. Also, since teachers could observe how all the groups worked, they could sense which individuals would be capable of working together for the next project.

Another benefit changing groups provided students was adaptability. They had no time to develop strong, cohesive bonds, and no time to build trust; they only had time to complete a writing project. Five times during the semester they changed groups; five times they adapted to different working situations and personalities. Yet no one group failed to complete a writing project.

Overall, changing groups performed as well as other groups and improved in their writing as much as the others. Retention rates for these classes were significantly high, along with permanent groups. Students learned to work collaboratively in an ever-changing environment, adapting to meet the needs of the group and the task.

Even though students in all conditions significantly improved their writing (pretest to post-test comparison), a statistically significant difference occurred in the amount of improvement among the groups. The permanent groups improved their individual writing performance significantly more than did the changing groups. They also talked the most. This finding corroborated the idea that discourse generates knowledge.

After tallying the tape-recorded responses of the two groups, the difference in participation between permanent and changing groups was statistically significant. Supporting what the teachers and I had observed, students in permanent groups simply talked significantly more than did students in changing groups. In task-oriented comments, which focused on their writing (the overwhelming majority of response type), and socio-emotional responses, concerned with interpersonal relationships, the permanent groups were significantly more vocal than changing groups and remained so though the end of the semester. After they completed a writing project, they did not move into Tuckman's "adjourning" stage and exhibit signs of increased independence of members, group disintegration, and withdrawal from one another. Rather, they continued to work well together throughout the semester.

What typified the behaviour of the permanent groups was a growth of cohesion. In their initial journal entries, many students in both types of groups became skeptical of group work, hesitant to trust other student to do the work, reluctant to trust them with their grade. As the semester continued, changing groups never seemed to move beyond the polite discourse of information exchanging and task exploring. They spent much of their group time re-establishing a methodology for performing their task with a new set of people. On the other hand, permanent groups had established their methodology for performing their tasks and continued to refine it. The changing groups used group times more simply as individual work time while the taped sessions reveal few periods of silence, more overlapping comments and socio-emotional response happening in the permanent groups. The length of time they spent together taught them how to balance the task-orientation and the socio-emotional response to form cohesive relations and perform the task simultaneously.

Working in permanent groups taught students that they could rely on their group; they could trust their member to do the work; they could and did trust others with their grade. In one of their final essays, not only did permanent group members point out how much they had learned from one another, but some even detailed what specifically they had learned about writing and working together from each of their group members.

Though students in both groups express, *"groups got better the more we worked at it,"* their explanations differed. Many students in changing groups thought the more they did group work, the easier it (the task) became. Permanent group members responded, *"The longer we worked together, the better we worked together."* One group stressed the dominance of task; the other emphasized the importance of relationship. Permanent group members learned that the process they had been involved in was an essential part of the knowledge they gained, not just a way to produce an essay.

4.3 Implications

Given the positive results obtained in the research, one might be tempted to recommend that composition classrooms be changed to collaborative writing classrooms. In group conditions not only did students believe they learn more about writing, they improved their writing. Also, students did not drop – 2 to 3 times more students finished group classes. So teachers grade 2/3 fewer papers, but at no cost to their students. Teachers win and students win. However, certain cautions do exist – collaborative writing may not work equally well for all students or all teachers.

It is difficult to find the most advantageous group mix of students. Further research should be undertaken concerning the effect of students' academic ability on their participation (or lack thereof). Also, disadvantages can occur with a mismatched group or a group with an over-bearing personality who can sometimes shut down the whole group. For success to occur, teachers (like their students) must trust in the process, trust that students can learn from one another, resist interfering too much in the group's interactions. It is the teacher's role to facilitate, to appear disinterestedly interested in what the groups are doing, who, as a member of a community of writers, will offer suggestions and criticisms in the form of "challenging feedback." Although the teacher remains a distinctly active member of this community, s/he must replace teaching the right answers with teaching the right questions. Thus, the implementation of collaborative writing groups in the classroom crucially depends upon teachers' reshaping their own understanding of the factors involved in the collaborative process. Teachers may need to change their attitudes towards students' abilities and to be willing to give them the responsibility for their education. It seems, therefore, that fostering teacher's awareness and developing techniques that would provide teachers with insight on how to implement collaborative writing would be a viable direction to be taken in the future. Indeed, this is a direction worth exploring, since only through this process can we transform classrooms into social contexts of learning.

APPENDICES

APPENDIX A: EXAMPLES OF GROUP-WRITTEN ESSAYS

1   PERMANENT GROUP (TEACHER 1)

Working as a group teaches an individual values, obedience, responsibility, as well as social interaction.

As we worked on each project we learned to delegate work evenly among the group. There were few problems with anyone in the group disobeying their responsibility. In fact, each person was receptive in receiving their command to locate certain items for our papers. Perhaps this was a result of each group person acting out the role of initiator. We learned being the leader all the time has its disadvantages, yet it also has some advantages.

The disadvantages of being the initiator constantly limits your ability to grow with the group. Also when in the initiator role you tend to not listen to others' ideas. Therefore resulting in the others in the group resisting all ideas. However, we learned to express our ideas as an individual by each one of us being the initiator. Thereafter, we evaluated these ideas and decided on which ones would best suit our paper. This helped us not only appreciate each others' ideas, but respect them as well.

When we began to work together as a group we knew little about each other; therefore, being somewhat shy from expressing our true feelings. However, as our group grew, we realized we were constantly influencing each other without our recognizing it. In fact, we discovered many traits about ourselves that we were unaware existed. One important fact is communicating with people can accomplish more if only we provide considerate listening skills. Also if there is a person in the group that becomes resistant to all ideas, do not allow that person to detain the progress of the group.

Many responsibilities were delegated during our papers. In fact, each person spent hours locating items for our research paper. Everyone accepted their responsibility to the group as well as to themselves by locating their items without resistance. Also we each knew if there were a problem locating any material, we could call upon someone in our group for assistance. It was a comfort to have the people in our group interact favourably toward each other. However, it is not to say we never had problems.

There was some resistance in our group but it was quickly smoothed when the others in the group pulled together to complete the assignment. Also, knowing the responsibility of developing a proper paper for class would result in others grades besides ones own, helped each other do a more thorough job. Therefore, we appreciated each other's opinion in what should or should not be allowed in our paper.

Nevertheless, our time together was not always spent on assignments. There were days we spent socializing, yet unknowingly to anyone in our group, we were learning even then. We learned how each person felt about certain issues, therefore, discovering differences of opinion among our group and learning to deal with it in a tactful manner. Due to our group interacting in this manner, we were able to rely upon each other and make sure the assignment was completed.

We all agree that learning social responsibility is extremely important, especially prior to graduation. Therefore, a student should learn social responsibility and social interaction in class so he/she will be prepared for the workforce. An individual cannot be successful without having the knowledge and experience of interacting with others as well as the social responsibility required in today's world.

2   CHANGING GROUP: TEACHER 1

Individuals make up a society. As individuals we must all intermingle and relate with others. It is true that each person is an individual physically, but as part of society you are never individually isolated. We are responsible for our individuality, thus we are responsible for how society functions.

Our values and morals are created, shaped, and passed on through stories and fairytales. We are taught through fairytales that good overcomes evil and that if we are patient and honest good things will come to us. Fairytales use the best values and ethics to create heroes that have these valuable qualities to be examples for society. By passing fairytales and stories form [sic] generation to generation culture is formed. Through the formation of culture our morals and values are instilled in us.

Bartleby was a true individual, completely isolating himself form [sic] society and those around him. We all possess a part of Bartleby's personality, though we do not take extreme isolationism. Bartleby teaches us that we must be content and happy with ourselves in order to be an individual. We are taught by Bartleby that adaptation to our surroundings is a must in order for us to be content and happy.

Milgram shows us the true dependent person. The teachers in Milgram's lab experiments have to be told what to do in order to do it. Just as Bartleby was content with not being told what to do, Milgram's teachers were content with being told what to do. We all possess a dependent quality Milgram's teachers were more concerned with how society viewed them rather than what they were doing to society.

In order to be a truly stable individual in society we must learn to balance our dependency with our individuality. We must take our individuality and link it with society in order for us to be a complete person.

Collaborative work forced us to do our individual work and relate and put it together with others. The purpose was for us to coincide our ideas with the ideas of others.

During group work we were not only expected to work together but we needed to understand and have an open mind toward other people's views. Working together and understanding not necessarily accepting, others views helps us to function in society.

APPENDIX B:
RESEARCHER "END-OF-SEMESTER" OBSERVATIONS OF
GROUP PROCESSES

1   PERMANENT GROUP A – TEACHER 1
(DEBBIE, SCOTT, JEFF, AND JENNIFER)

Debbie never did relinquish control of the group, steadfastly remaining the initiator and coordinator, but she was not the sole evaluator, nor information seeker or giver. Scott's participation increased steadily over the course of the semester; he provided and sought information as well as evaluated group procedures and products. Jennifer's participation increased as well, but not as dramatically as Scott's. She still remained the quiet participator, offering information, seeking information, but minimally. However, she always did her part of the group work, always remained focused on group activities.

Scott also rivalled Debbie in questions directed to the group, e.g., "So, it [the Milgram experiment – how far people will go, i.e., inflict pain on others to obey authority] caught your attention."

Jeff, refusing to acquiesce, said, "I didn't think about it at all. What did you think, Jennifer?"

Before she could respond, Scott interrupted: "You heard what I said. It made you evaluate yourself, take a good look at yourself."

They continued to talk and take notes about what they had learned from each writing assignment. The conversation was punctuated with affirmative, "yeah's," "right's," and "okay's." They concluded they had learned "how to organize our time, our schedules; how to work outside of class together." They referred to the works they read, looking for the values each had taught them. Scott directed them to "Bartleby asking the group "what have we decided about this work?" Debbie remarked how it taught her "how to work with problem people" (with a glance in Jeff's direction).

2   CHANGING GROUP – TEACHER 1 (ALISA, CLIFF, CYNDI, TED)

This representative changing group exemplified a lack of cohesion. They never demonstrated a feeling of group unity; rather they operated as separate individuals who happened to be sitting together, trying (or not trying) to get the task finished.

There was initial joking and laughter at the beginning of the session as they read over what had been written. Alisa was the initiator and coordinator, trying to put together what the others had done. As she read the members' drafts, she would ask for clarification; all group members contributed at various times. Cyndi usually had to be asked specifically what she thought or to clarify a particular point, but then she would contribute. When Alisa had trouble understanding Cliff's ideas, he interpreted her difficulty as a sign of her inability to unravel the complexity of his ideas, not his inability to express himself well. His individual draft was only a few paragraphs long, much shorter than the efforts of the others. Alisa seemed the only one really determined to perform. She read excerpts, writing down those parts of papers, paragraphs, sentences, that worked best. As she read aloud she asked the group for comments and criticisms, changes, additions, deletions, and word choice. They all did contribute to the task, but minimally; Alisa was the energy force pulling bits and pieces from the group. Cliff was more interested in debating with the teacher than he was in working with his group.

APPENDIX C: BALES' INTERACTION PROCESS ANALYSIS:
THE CODING CATEGORIES AND THEIR MAJOR RELATIONS

Socio-emotional area: Positive

A: Positive Reactions
1) *Shows solidarity*, raises other's status, gives help,
2) *Shows tension release*, jokes, laughs, shows satisfaction
3) *Agrees*, shows passive acceptance, understands, concurs, complies
4) *Gives suggestion*, direction, implying autonomy for others

B: Attempted Answers
5) *Gives opinion*, evaluation, analysis, expresses feeling, wish
6) *Gives orientation*, information, repetition, confirmation

Task-area: Neutral

C: Questions
7) *Asks for orientation*, information, repetition, confirmation
8) *Asks for opinion,* evaluation, analysis, expression of feeling
9) *Ask for suggestion*, direction, possible ways of action

Socio-emotional area: Negative

D: Negative Reactions
10) *Disagrees*, shows passive rejection, formality, withholds help
11) *Shows tension*, asks for help, withdraws out of field
12) *Shows antagonism*, deflates other's status, defends or asserts self

REACHING OUT FROM THE WRITING CLASSROOM

Research Writing as a Situated, Public Act

LINDA ADLER-KASSNER, & HEIDI ESTREM

Eastern Michigan University, USA

Abstract. This article analyzes college-level composition by exploring how premises that prevail in current research on context-situated writing inform the design of college-level composition courses. Specifically, the discussion builds on the premise that writing in any context, in school or out, should be seen as a situated, public act that makes sense within a constellation of literacy practices. This chapter illustrates how we have enacted these principles in the design and sequencing of assignments in the first-year research writing course at our own institution, Eastern Michigan University. The design of our first-year research writing course is located within the theoretical premises informing our pedagogy; these challenge the notion that college-level writing courses should focus exclusively on helping students enter an "academic discourse community" and suggest instead that they should help students think strategically and become flexible writers.

Keywords: research writing, multi-genre college composition, alternative discourses, public writing, literacy practices, writing for the community

1   INTRODUCTION

In American colleges and universities, the first-year "research writing" course is a staple. When using the shorthand for describing these courses, instructors will say that they are intended to help students develop writing, reading, and thinking strategies for academic purposes. However, this shorthand description negates a number of complex issues associated with this very description. Currently, the field of composition research would suggest that a different set of questions needs to be raised: Are academic purposes really so distinct from purposes associated with writing in contexts outside of academe? If this is so, how can instructors make courses both engaging and appropriate for students, many of whom are trying to find their ways into this new realm of learning? And what is the relevance of the strategies students develop in these courses once the first year course itself is completed?

Over the last 15 years, research in the field of composition has provided varying responses to these questions. One research strand, situated under the heading "expressivist" approaches to composition, emphasizes student engagement with writing, encouraging student-writers to use this activity as a way of exploring their own "selves" and their personal processes (e.g., Macrorie, 1988; Rohmann, 1965). Researchers who advocate for the "writing in the disciplines" approach (e.g., Behrens, & Rosen 1985; Cooper, 1996; Lester, & Lester, 2002) outline a different set of purposes for composition courses, suggesting that such courses should prepare students to write within *other* major disciplines, which might lead to the concomitant implication that composition as a discipline does not exist save for as a service to the *rest* of the university. A third strand, "social constructivism" (e.g., Berlin, 1996; Weisser, 2002), suggests that writing courses should provide opportunities for students to explore how they, as writers, can create and perpetuate particular relationships with readers, texts, and discourses and learn how to uphold or change power dynamics within and around those relationships. Increasingly, students appropriate valued ways of engaging in public conversations enacted both inside and outside of the academy.

Although it is possible to delineate these different threads in theory, in practice most research writing courses draw to some degree from all of these traditions. Although instructors may identify their theoretical perspectives as "discipline-based," "expressivist," or "social constructivist," most instructors *do* seem to recognize the need for writing to be both personally engaging and socially responsive. In light of this movement toward a mixture of these different theoretical strands, it is worth attending to the ways that these perspectives are balanced. One such integrative attempt is delineated in this chapter which outlines the course we have designed and implemented at Eastern Michigan University. Our aim is to make research writing a meaningful act for students by engaging them, in particular ways, in researching and writing *about* and *in* a variety of local contexts. The discussion develops as follows: First, we present and analyze various scholarly perspectives on first-year writing, considering their theoretical premises and tracing the way by which these have been translated in the form of specific research writing courses. The particular pedagogical practices adopted and implemented at Eastern Michigan University (EMU) are situated within the evolving scholarship of alternative discourses and ethnographically-oriented literacy studies. After illustrating the way we draw from these research traditions, we proceed to delineate the details of the writing program at EMU by focusing on the types of tasks employed, the genres created, their sequencing, and the results obtained.

2   ON THE FIRST YEAR WRITING COURSE: IDENTIFYING ITS PURPOSES

The pedagogies developed for college-level first-year writing courses reflect a shifting conceptualization of the nature of academic writing and the purpose of research writing courses which have evolved within the last 15 years. A significant change in the field was instigated through the publication of David Bartholomae's (1985b) article "Inventing the University" which reshaped many first-year writing programs. In contrast to earlier research focusing on the way cognitive factors affect the writing process, this article suggested that socioculturally shaped parameters (such as students' previous experiences with writing and reading at home) might factor considerably into students' successes in school. Indeed, this suggestion (i.e., that students' struggles with writing could stem from their limited experience with the literacy practices defining the academic culture, parts of which are reflected in expectations for academic writing), has been particularly influential within the sub-field of basic writing (used in reference to "pre-college composition" courses for students who are designated as not prepared for first-year writing) (cf., Harrington, & Adler-Kassner, 1998). As Bartholomae put it,

> Every time a student sits down to write for us, he has to invent the university for the occasion .... The student has to appropriate (or be appropriated by) a specialized discourse, and he has to do this as though he were easily and comfortably one with his audience...; he has to invent the university by assembling and mimicking its language while finding some compromise between idiosyncrasy, a personal history, on the one hand, and the requirements of convention, the history of a discipline, on the other (Bartholomae, 1985b: 134-135).

Bartholomae's article resonated powerfully within the broader field of composition studies because the argument he delineated in it reflected a purpose for composition and rhetoric courses that, according to historians of the field like Sharon Crowley, has long served as the modus operandi for these classes. As noted, "the introductory composition course has always been justified... in instrumental terms: this is the site wherein those who are new to the academy learn to write its prose" (Crowley, 1995: 227).

Gradually, as the goals of composition courses have been reconceptualized, the purposes implied in the article "Inventing the University" have come under close scrutiny as well. Some researchers have directly challenged the article's key tenets and pedagogies that emerged from it (e.g., Adler-Kassner, & Harrington, 2002; Hindman, 1993; Schroeder 2001). Alternative conceptions – such as that of the "contact zone" (Pratt, 1990) – have been introduced, leading many researchers (including Bartholomae [cf. "The Tidy House"]) to re-imagine composition courses less as sites where students learn to "invent the university," and more as places where they would grapple with conflicting ideas and, likely, challenge their own ideas and values and, perhaps, the ideas and values represented in university curricula (Bartholomae, 1993: 14-15, 19).

Other recently published work has not only challenged the existence of the "academic discourse community" assumed in works like "Inventing the University" but has also raised concerns about the concomitant principle that writing in composition classes should prepare students exclusively for writing in academic contexts. As Royster (2002: 24) argues, the notion of "the academic discourse community" can be invoked to elide both the powerful ideologies reflected in ideas of "goodness" (that is, "good language" or "good ideas") within particular disciplines, and to erase the astounding diversity that exists among language use within contexts and communities, including "the academy." It is because of the *artificial* constraints imposed both by the presumed existence of an "academic discourse community," and by the constraints of disciplinary convention, that Bizzell (1999, 2000, 2002) notes the increasing prevalence of "mixed form" genres in academic writing. These forms, which blend conventional and non-conventional voices, are becoming more prevalent precisely because they make possible a certain way students may engage with academic work; this cannot be attained through pedagogical practices that reinforce highly constrictive, conventionalized ideas about language in academic settings. And lest compositionists become concerned that such mixed forms are unwelcome in other disciplines, co-authors Christopher Thaiss, & Terry Myers Zawacki (2002) draw on evidence from interviews with faculty from five disciplines other than composition/English to note that these faculty do not want students to "imitate disciplinary discourses"; instead, they wanted students to "summarize and analyze, write clear and logical arguments, situate themselves within the conversations of the field, and engage critically with these conversations" (Thaiss, & Zawacki, 2002: 89). To develop these strategies, the faculty whom Thaiss, & Zawacki interviewed required that students produce a variety of genres, from letters to the editor to opinion-editorial pieces. In short, echoing Royster, and Bizzell, Thaiss, & Zawacki's research supports the idea that academic discourse is not a homogeneous entity; "boundaries around disciplinary discourses are more permeable than we indicate to students.... How a writer writes within the discipline seems a compromise between the conventions of discourse and the idiosyncrasies of the writer" (Thaiss, & Zawacki, 2002: 92).

In addition to questioning the idea of the "academic discourse community" as a principle for capturing a specific context that shapes writing, the basic goal which some writing courses set out to attain – to help students develop writing strategies for audiences *only* inside of the academy – has also been under heavy criticism. Instead, it is suggested that writing in any context should *always* be seen as a public act, even a political activity, that is relevant for the writer and for audiences beyond the writer (and the instructor/class where the writing is being produced). Weisser (2002) notes that this conception of composition is most visible in courses reflecting Freirian pedagogies; these are courses that invoke "the public sphere" (through writing of "public" genres, like letters to the editors), and service-learning courses (where students engage in work for not-for-profit organizations/causes, and explicitly reflect on that work, as a part of their work of the composition class). In both of these course structures, students consider the expectations of a number of contexts and audiences, such as their classmates, the instructor, the audiences outside of the classroom who read and use their work, the individuals or organizations who serve as the subject of the work (e.g., in a grant application). They also reflect on how the strategies they are developing through this writing are applicable in contexts with which they are familiar, inside and outside of school.

3   THE CONTEXT OF TEACHING AND LEARNING AT EMU

Before we discuss the particular approach we have taken in first-year research writing course at Eastern Michigan University (EMU), it is important to provide some context about the institution. A comprehensive, mid-sized university of approximately 26,000 students, EMU has a strong reputation as a "teaching school" – both a place where faculty care about teaching, and a campus that has long been devoted to educating future teachers. This reputation, in part, attracts students from around southeastern Michigan and northwestern Ohio. Other factors associated with EMU also make it popular: it is one of Michigan's least expensive universities and it is close to both the Detroit (Michigan) and Toledo (Ohio) metropolitan areas. The mix of students that comprise EMU's student body is quite diverse. Some outward signs of this diversity are immediately apparent for instance, 16 percent of all students are non-white (12% African American, 2.1% Latino, 1.3% Asian, and 1.0% Native American) and 58 percent of the student population is female. There are less visible signs of diversity, as well. Students come with a range of experience with critical thinking, reading, and writing; students also bring a variety of life experiences to EMU. Some of the statistics related to this less obvious diversity are alarming. 35 percent of entering first-year students do not continue to attend EMU from one fall to the next, and EMU's six-year graduation rate is only 33 percent (http://www.emich.edu/aboutemu/fastfacts/EMU statistics). Thus, in designing a research writing course for EMU's first-year students, we needed to consider how best to accommodate and engage the broad range of students' interests and experiences.

4   WRITING AND RESEARCHING THE PUBLIC EXPERIENCE AT EMU

The first-year research writing course offered at EMU is almost never called by its official title, "Composition II: Researching and Writing the Public Experience"; instead, it is referred to by its course designator, "English 121," which we will also use here. This course is taken by the vast majority of the first-year students at EMU; typically, we offer 65-70 sections a semester and each section enrols 25 students. English 121 reflects the reconceptualizations of research writing outlined above. Working from the understanding that writing can and should be a locally responsive act, our first-year writing pedagogies and practices lead to a greater understanding for all of us – students, teachers, and administrators alike – of the public nature of written discourse.

Echoing the work of Bizzell (1999) and Royster (2002), our pedagogy in English 121 is founded on the idea that composition courses cannot, and should not, prepare students to reproduce some uniform "discourse" that prevails in the academy. Instead, the outcomes for the course outline the conception of writing reflected in it:

> students will develop habits of mind that are important for writers: assessing audience expectations; reading critically; engaging with others' ideas in analytic and research-based writing; developing control over surface features of writing; and discovering, cultivating, and being reflective about their writing processes. This development takes place recursively – that is, students master these strategies by practicing with them repeatedly through their work in [this course] and others at EMU.
> (http://www.emich.edu/public/english/fycomp/outcomes/index.htm)

This statement reflects our belief that perhaps the most important strategy we can help writers to develop is *flexibility*. As Royster puts it, "…when we position literacy instruction as helping students to understand and to participate flexibly in multiple discourses, and especially multiple academic discourses, then part of the pedagogical mandate is a question of identifying, negotiating, and reconfiguring certain communicative gaps" (Royster, 2002: 28). Implicit in this notion of flexibility is the importance of engaging students in careful examinations of contextually-embedded writing: analysis is directed to both situations and audiences for writing, as well as to writing within and across various situations and audiences.

To investigate these questions in English 121, we have designed a curriculum that asks students to *begin* with specific contexts, and move from them into specific acts of engagement, reflection, and presentation. Recognizing that students need to become more aware of genre conventions as well as attend to how those genres are shaped in specific acts of communication between a writer and multiple audiences, we draw upon ethnographic literacy studies and alternative discourse theory (in part, the work of Bizzell, Royster, and Thaiss, & Zawacki cited earlier) to inform the research writing strategies we wish to develop in the classroom. Briefly, students conduct an ethnographically-oriented study, writing about it in several ways, produce a multigenre essay, and then collaborate on projects for the Celebration of Student Writing, described below. In this section, we outline these research projects and the strategies for research writing that underlie English 121.

4.1 Grounding Research Writing in Specific, Local Contexts

For many students in English 121, the notions "good writing" and "good literacy" point to valid terms, instantiating a part of what Street calls "autonomous... separate, reified set of 'neutral' competencies [separate] from social context" (Street, 1995: 114). From conversations conducted with students over years of writing classes, as well as from interviews with students placed in pre-first-year composition courses conducted as part of a larger study (cf., Adler-Kassner, & Harrington, 2002), we found that many students believe that the rules they have learned about writing ("Never use *I* in research writing; the thesis is always the last sentence of the first paragraph," and so on) represent the absolute truth. Yet, they have never had the opportunity to connect writing acts to particular contexts or to revisit these rules as guidelines which represent specific ways of thinking.

In contrast to approaches viewing of literacy practices as universal constructs disassociated from specific contextual parameters, the research writing pedagogy in English 121 is grounded in the notion of contextually-bound and context-shaped literacy practices. In essence, we are adapting and extending Barton, & Hamilton's notion of "literacy practices," which has been developed and used in reference to "the general cultural ways of utilizing written language which people draw upon in their lives.... literacy practices are more usefully understood as existing in the relations between people, within groups and communities, rather than as a set of properties residing in individuals" (Barton, & Hamilton, 2000: 7-8).

This notion has been extended in two specific ways. The first step taken is asking students to root their investigations in specific sites – generally, physical (as opposed to virtual) spaces – that are interesting to them. For the first 4-6 weeks of the semester (depending on the section of 121), students spend 1-2 hours a week conducting field research in this site. This ethnographically-oriented research work in 121 draws heavily on Chiseri-Strater, & Sunstein's (2002) research writing rhetoric, *Field Working* (2nd ed.) (For a discussion on the rationale for conducting ethnographic work with composition students, see Bishop [1999] and Zebroski [1994]).

For this segment of the course, students choose communities or cultures where they conduct fieldwork by becoming participant-observers, conducting interviews, and collecting written and spoken documents. They listen to what stories are told and valued by community members, what rituals and traditions are observed by these community members. The definition of "ritual" and "tradition" depends on the site, of course – it can range from watching white and black students sit only with other white or black students at a campus restaurant, to lighting ritual candles at a religious observance. Here, students are clearly required to ground the outcomes of their research in specific sites; the practices of those sites are the subjects of their work.

Throughout their observation work, instructors and students work together, in writing and discussion, to make visible both the process of doing ethnographically-oriented work and to generate initial research questions based on their observations. While these research questions are not always directly bound up with "literacy practices" as Barton, & Hamilton (2000) define them – that is, they are not always concerned with *written* language – they are nevertheless grounded in the social and cultural practices that suffuse and help to shape definitions of literacy practices in specific sites. Campus dorms, religious sites (mosques, temples, churches), restaurants, coffee shops, and libraries are just a few examples of the places students have chosen; through their observations, they have investigated topics as diverse as the role of smoking for female college students to the culture of a reform Jewish congregation in a Detroit suburb.

4.2 Thinking Strategically: From Context-specific to Cross-contextual Writing

While our approach reflects the position that "good writing" is necessarily context-appropriate writing and that the writing strategies students draw on are responses to specific, local contexts, we also recognize that there may exist certain tasks and text types that are valued both within the academy as well in many contexts outside of it. These include producing summaries, developing a clear position, engaging in dialogue with others interested in the issues focused upon in the writing, and so on. The cross-contextual nature of these elements is echoed, for instance, in Thaiss, & Zawacki's (2002) study of writing expectations among faculty in five disciplines (other than English) at their university; while these faculty asked students to employ what might be considered "alternative discourse" practices (that is, their assignments asked students to create genres not typically produced in "academic" writing), they did so because they believed these practices would help students to achieve key strategies that they thought would be useful for students' academic work. Their research echoes Jolliffe's (1994: 188) assertion that while composition courses cannot "transcend" all disciplines and purposes, they can provide an orientation to ways of engaging with knowledge.

English 121, similarly, engages students in work with strategies that are often invoked in a number of situations: considering audience expectations; making conscious choices (about everything from content, to evidence, to stylistic and grammatical conventions); expressing cogent, insightful analysis; supporting that analysis with evidence from a variety of sources; critically assessing and engaging in dialogue with sources in meaningful ways; and employing conventions (of language, punctuation, and citation) "appropriately" (as "appropriateness" is defined by particular disciplines, situations, and contexts).

However, consistent with the position that literacy strategies should always be analyzed as situated in specific contexts, the meaning and the site-specific nature of these strategies is made clear and co-constructed through repeated conversations between the students and the instructor as well as through analyses of the reflective texts produced by the students. Students are immediately engaged in this process of analysis of and negotiation among contexts while they conduct their site-specific research projects. As they work to describe these sites, students in many sections of 121 are asked to consider how they might (re)present images to several audiences: their fellow students, their instructor, the community they studied (some instructors ask students to give a copy of their draft to the community members for a "member check") and, looking ahead to the end of the semester, the larger campus community attending a large, end of the semester event called the Celebration of Student Writing (which we describe more fully below). Students also must extend beyond their own immediate research interests (developed from their site observations) to conduct library research, locating articles (with the instructor's assistance) in academic journals and books that enable them to situate their interests in broader conversations. Because of the immediacy of these multiple, overlapping audiences, students encounter tough ethical and rhetorical situations that they must write their ways through: How can writers draw from their research in a way that is "fair"? What are the pitfalls of researching a site/subject to which they are close? How can they meaningfully draw on scholarly sources to inform their research? How do they negotiate their own perceptions, the data they have collected, and the perceptions of the people they have researched?

Providing examples of student projects might be important for illustrating the kind of learning achieved. For example, one student chose as her community to study the "CTG"s, or Campus Tour Guides – students who train to give tours on campus for prospective students and their parents. As she did so, she began to record how these workers were taught to "market" various aspects of the campus (academic support services, for example) while not mentioning other particulars (drinking in the dorms, for example). As she worked through her study, she then formulated a final project that showed these various "faces" of campus life. Another student chose to focus on his dorm suite as a community. Through research into social status and work behaviours, he realized that the most popular of his roommates maintained his social status by actively portraying himself as a "slacker" – that this persona, in fact, seemed to be valued not only by this student's suitemates but also by friends, as well. In his final study, he portrayed the various personas that could be adopted in college and followed them through to what he saw as their "logical" conclusions – success, failure, mediocrity – and mapped his *own* plan that would enable other students to achieve success in college. While studies like these described here might seem apparent to a seasoned observer of campuses, these findings were new and surprising for these students. Through their work in their communities and with their researched essay models, they came to see themselves not as observers of removed phenomena, but as authors with some degree of agency to take action regarding issues of interest to them.

As students interpret and reflect on "their" sites, they develop "habits of mind" particular to both the specific projects they are all engaged in and that will continue to serve them as they engage in researched writing projects beyond English 121: audience analysis, critical reading of sources, balancing evidence and argument.

4.3 Identifying Audience Expectations

Even among different disciplines within the academy, audience expectations vary considerably – what might be acceptable form and style in a literature class, for instance, would be considered completely inappropriate in a physics lab report. In 121, students must also take into account the expectations of audiences outside of their classrooms and, often, outside of the university, as well. Thus, students are faced with the task of making careful, conscious decisions about the audience(s) for their writing, assessing what their audience(s) expect, and deciding on the choices they need to make so that they meet (or do not meet) those expectations. In English 121, students engage most actively in this work in the multi-genre essay (Romano, 2000), typically assigned as a cumulative, capstone project for the course. For this essay, students must identify a specific, real audience whom they believe will benefit from what they have learned about their research question. Then, they work towards creating anywhere between 4-6 specific genres – ranging from a "hard news" story to a monologue to a talk-show script – that they believe will most effectively communicate various perspectives about or aspects of what they have learned to the audience they identified. To create these genres, students conduct close analyses of their conventions so that they can accurately reproduce them in their own work; they must also synthesize their relevant findings – from academic journal articles and books, from interviews, and from their observations – into these genres. After creating the genres, students also write a comprehensive reflection on their work that summarizes how they have worked on what we are here calling issues of "localness" – local practices in their sites, expectations of their audiences, and conventions of the genres. The following excerpts from student-written multi-genre essays – the first a tabloid-style newspaper article, the second in the style of a more mainstream publication like *Newsweek* – illustrate how the students-authors of these articles, Jessica M. and Meghan H., have borrowed conventions from the genres they have chosen to present their research for particular audiences. (Note that these authors also created *all* elements of these genres, including the "authors" name and journal name.)

N.Y. Senator's daughter yanked out of prestigious academy

Shock waves bolted through the entertainment scene on Monday when *Entertainment Tonight* revealed that renowned pop star Pat Healy and her sophisticated hubby, Sen. Bill Healy, yanked their daughter Meghan from New York's prestigious Archmere Academy.

Sources say that the famous couple was enraged that Meg, their little genius, wasn't receiving any attention for her hard work at school.

Astonished by the two hours of homework little kindergartner Meg was bringing home every night, the busy and loving parents went straight to their daughter's teacher to give her a piece of their minds.

The little tike's teacher, Dr. Linda Adler, former professor of English at Eastern Michigan University, told the *Gazette* that she saw "no need" for Mr. and Mrs. Healy's frustrations, and remarked that "they should become accustomed to long hours of work. I mean come on, they're sending their daughter to Archmere, a school which prides itself on providing its students with a top-notch education."

Cindy Young, fellow pop star and best friend to singing beauty Pat, revealed that the final straw that broke the Healy duo's backs was the day Meg came home crying because her teacher, a so-called professional, would not tell her she liked the picture of her family she had colored.

Sources close to the family say that prior to Meg's heart-wrenching outburst, the usually school-loving little girl had stopped wanting to do her homework at all and started dragging her feet on the walk up the front steps to Archmere every morning.

Approaching his daughter's teacher a second time on the matter, the New York Senator was told that it is not the school's philosophy to praise students for everything they do. According to Archmere administrators, leading research demonstrates that in order for students to become more diligent in their studies, they need to be involved in activities that are naturally intriguing and not induced by praise.

Adler told reporters that the Senator left their meeting in a ranting fury after she may have implied to him that his daughter Meghan "might not feel so neglected and hate going to school if her parents were around her more during the hours she spends outside of Archmere."

"Bill is Mr. Family. He is not going to let anyone imply that he and his wife do not give their child enough attention," affirms Connecticut Senator Jacob Blumner on the issue.

After much controversy and uproar, the star-studded Archmere PTA made their way into the fracas. Of these parents, the sultry Pamela Lee and the gorgeous Tom Cruise started an all-out screaming match with the Academy's Head Master upon learning that he strictly insists the Academy's teachers develop a style of teaching that includes little, if any, praise or rewards for its students' achievements. In a shameful attempt to smooth things over with the Hollywood elites, the school published an interview with Alfie Kohn, a top researcher in the field of teacher praise.

Singing sensations daughter is smiling again, but only after leaving her prestigious private academy for the NYC public schools

This dull interview highlighted Kohn's opinion that "while students would certainly like to have the goody itself — the pizza or money or gold star — none of us enjoys having the very things we desire used as levers to control our behavior...If you're doing something boring, your interest level may already be at rock bottom...that doesn't give us license to treat kids like pets when the task is uninteresting."

Using this "respect the student and they will respect you back" view, Archmere stands strong in the belief that if students are engaged in tasks they find interesting and complete those tasks without the need for bribery or a "good work," they will achieve more in their futures.

The pop star's agent says that Mr. and Mrs. Healy fully agree with Kohn when he says that a child's "desire to learn, commitment to good values, and so on," are very important. However, they find it extremely difficult to believe that telling a kindergartner that she did a good job coloring and reciting her ABC's will inhibit the appearance of these values in her.

Angered and disappointed in the prestigious school, the singing sensation and the handsome politician pulled their five year old out of the academy and placed her in the 75th street public school near their Park Avenue townhouse.

Hillary Clinton, a New York Senator and friend of the Healy family, weighed in on the issue. "Bill has been a strong advocate for the New York Public School system. He feels that it is the best place for his daughter to receive a nourishing education when she is away from his and Pat's caring supervision," she said. "Institutions like Archmere are not educationally well-rounded for young children."

A teacher at the 75th street School assures us that "Meghan is a wonderful addition to our community. All her classmates love her and although the work is at times very easy for her, she is having fun simply being a kindergartener."

- - *Ellen Finnegan*

Children's Choices in the Classroom

More and more teachers are calling for children to have choices in their education. But is it really such a good idea?

BY MARIA GARCIA

Rachel Wolfgrahm has been having a lot of trouble in school lately. Her teacher has been trying to help her understand the assignments that are given out but Meghan still struggles in school. Meghan's father, Senator Victor Wolfgrahm, has been keep trying to help his daughter on a national level. Senator Wolfgrahm recently introduced a bill into Congress which encouraging more creative education in public schools. A very new idea to many people.

But this idea of imaginative education in schools is not new. Carolyn Berge has been doing something most teachers never even consider-- allowing her students to choose their

own spelling words. While most people would assume that kids would choose the easiest words they could find, that isn't the case in Berge's room. "There are still some kids that are learning words like 'cat' and "hat," Berge explained, "but I have other students who have a hard time trying to find words that they don't know how to spell."

Carolyn Berge is one of the teachers who want to see children given more opportunities to make choices in their learning. When talking about why she believes children need to be given more choices, Berge said "I don't see myself as someone who rules over these students' learning process, but as a choreographer or guide, someone who helps them through the process and is

able to watch them grow along the way."

Berge also includes increasing self esteem as one of the big advantages to giving students choices in their learning processes. "When a child sees that they learned something all on their own, it gives them a confidence in their abilities to learn. They know they can learn anything they want. It's important to me that they know that."

While some teachers do not share Berge's enthusiasm for giving kids more freedom in their studies, others are beginning to. Mary Latige had never even thought about letting her students choose how they wanted to do their book reports until a friend urged her to. "I thought it sounded crazy at first," said Latige. "I thought the kids needed more order than that because it was what they have always had." But when Latige did take her friend's advice and tried the "choosy" book reports, she was surprised with what she found. "Every child did something different and put a lot more work into it than they probably would have. I had some students who I couldn't get to do their work turn in extraordinary pieces of art with their reports."

Steven Wolk, author of "The Benefits of Exploratory Time" explained why giving children choices in their education is not looked upon as favorably as some would hope. Wolk talks about exploratory time as a time in which students are given the choice on what and how they want to study for roughly an hour each day in school. "In today's schools, kids are judged primarily on one-time things like tests and reports," he says, "most teachers do not see how these 'exploratory times' could help their kids on things like the standard assessment tests or the math test they have at the end of the week. In

the long run, however, exploratory time could boost students' test scores because we are helping students care about their learning-- and caring changes a person's attitude about learning." Wolk also extolled benefits of exploratory time, "It nurtures a love for learning, encourages meaningful learning through intrinsic motivation, creates true communities of learners, develops self esteem and celebrates uniqueness, uses real-world sources, brings more content into the classroom, teaches skills, and nurtures childrens' gifts of creativity and imagination."

However, Wolk also said that the child's exploratory time could not be a success if the teacher does not show the students how life is one big lesson people learn all their lives. This time would not simply be a 'free-time' for the kids as many teachers think it would be, but a journey the kids need to do alone,

with some guidance from the teacher.

"Creativity is a self-led process," says Wilma McNess, a featured author in L. V. Kosinski's *Readings on Creativity and Imagination in Literature and Language.* McNess has been a strong supporter of giving children more choices from the beginning.

Sunshine and Happy Things

artwork by
Amber · age 8

"Giving children their own choices allows them to deal with their own successes and failures. It also changes the driving force for their work from the teacher or the due date to themselves."

Ruth Shagoury Hubbard and Karen Ernst have also been trying to get teachers to see the importance of including children in the decision making processes in their education. In their recent book, *New Entries: Learning by Writing and*

Drawing, they talk about letting students create their own works of art to help them express their feelings and interests and later turn those into words.

"We came in contact with a lot of students who had a hard time finding something to write about," Hubbard said in a recent interview. "But when you let them create their own stuff, they can come up with all kinds of ideas on what they want to write about, sometimes they just write about the art itself."

The children in these creative classrooms seem to agree with teachers that imagination is important. Said one little girl from Berge's class, "If you really want to have a good life you need imagination because if you don't pretend you'll be grumpy all the time."

However, with all good ideas, there are always drawbacks. "Some of the parents are not always thrilled with my methods," confessed Berge. "I've had parents come to me complaining

NEW WAYS: Mary Latige's classroom tries to encourage creativity.

that they don't think my teaching is helping their student as much as traditional methods would. But when I see an individual student struggling, I usually make some special concessions for the student. I've never had parents say they didn't like any of it."

Parents also seem to be more comfortable when their children are being taught the way they were taught when they were children. "There will always be someone who isn't happy with the way kids are being taught no matter what you do," Latige commented. "Sometimes you just have to be happy knowing that you can't please everyone. Most of the kids I have seen have done a lot better

in school because of these methods, and they're the ones I'm the most concerned about."

While these creative educational methods are currently being taught primarily in "open" schools, many of the ideas are slowly creeping into other public and private classrooms. "I'm hoping that someday every child will have an atmosphere in their classroom where their imagination is nurtured and developed." Latige expressed. "I hope that every child will get the best possible education, no matter what school they go to or what teacher the have."

The multi-genre essay is where students bring together and enact the multiple foci of 121. These foci are rooted in questions that are engaging to students, questions that are themselves grounded in sites of particular interest to their creators. Students also identify audiences for their projects that are relevant to them as writers, and who are (ideally) interested in learning about what students have learned. Then, to create the genres that comprise much of the essay, students engage in extensive audience analysis – what genres would best "speak" to their chosen group? Once students have chosen genres that they feel will be most effective for their work, they analyze the conventions of these genres (e.g., what does an obituary look/sound like?) in order to creatively employ them within the multi-genre essay. Within each genre, they also synthesize evidence from a variety of sources, which requires close reading and careful analysis. Then, they consciously reflect on each choice that they made and discuss the reasons they made it in the reflective essay. Thus, these essays accomplish the goals for the course: the research for them is situated within particular contexts chosen by students, and the essays created by students are intended for a particular audience. Again, the overarching process is complex and each phase of their research process helps them connect to the next writing situation they encounter within the course. To make decisions about how best to reach that audience, students must carefully consider the expectations and culture(s) of their audience; they, then, analyze the conventions of the genres they feel will be most effective *for* that audience and employ those in their writing to achieve the desired effect. The result is a written product (which also may include visual or auditory elements) that reflects students' attention to the literacy practices within the community they have studied and the audience whom they have chosen.

We cannot say that, of the approximately 800 multi-genre essays written during a typical term, *every* one is a vibrant document that demonstrates students' engagement with not only their subjects, but also with their audiences. However, we have by now compiled enough evidence – anecdotal evidence from our own classrooms and those of other instructors, as well as data from surveys administered to students near the end of their 121 courses – to have a sense that this approach does make research writing relevant for students inside and outside of the classroom. As part of a pilot study administered during the fall 2002 semester (n=128), for instance, the changes in students' confidence with key strategies linked to understanding (and, apparently, experiencing) researched writing as a meaningful act through which one engaged in dialogue while simultaneously developing writing, reading, researching, and critical thinking skills were significant at the point .01-.00001 level. These included using a variety of research strategies, using evidence and ideas from other sources in writing, using writing to discover and develop ideas, identifying the patterns shaping – i.e., the "rules" surrounding – the form and language in any piece of writing, understanding and using conventions of written English expected in writing at the university, knowing where to find resources if unsure of conventions, and using academic citation systems.

4.4 "Going Public" in Particular Contexts

While the multi-genre essay asks students to write for an audience outside of the classroom, this activity does not guarantee that students will circulate their work to the chosen audience. Yet, to understand writing as a public act, reaching audiences outside of the classroom is crucial. As Weisser notes, courses emphasizing public writing as an act, like English 121, need to "consist[..] of more than expressing your opinion on a current topic; [they] entail [..] being able to make your voice heard on an issue that directly confronts or influences you" (Weisser, 2002: 94). According to Weisser, "engaging students in public writing in "meaningful ways" means providing students with opportunities to learn how contexts (for speaking) and audiences affect what can be said, how it can be said, who hears what is said, and how that hearing affects actions (Weisser, 2002: 94-99). To provide this kind of opportunity in 121, we created the Celebration of Student Writing.

The Celebration, as it is known, takes place near the end of every semester. It is held in a large space – a ballroom and several adjoining rooms – for 1-1/2 hours on an appointed day. For this event, students attending English 121 create, display, and discuss with the hundreds of Celebration attendees products that represent the research work they have done throughout the semester. In two years, the Celebration has grown from 550 (student) participants to over 800. Participating students also comprise a large part of the audience for the event; they are joined by faculty, administrators, staff, and teachers and students from surrounding colleges and high schools, as well as prospective students and parents. As classes work on Celebration projects, they focus on the questions that underscore our approach to 121: Who is the audience for this event? What are their expectations for the event? What would you like the audience to know about, and take away from, their encounter with your work? What will be the most effective way for you to communicate with them about that? These questions can be particularly powerful when students consider the typical, persistent perception of first-year students (and, often, those beyond the first year, as well) that they "cannot write," that they have little interest in engaging with meaningful questions, that their capacities for sustained attention are ever-dwindling. For some students – and certainly, for us as organizers of the event – the Celebration is an occasion to address and, possibly, change the minds of at least some who hold these perceptions.

It is difficult to capture in writing the visceral sensation that is the Celebration. Spectators mill around the large, open space now crowded with displays and people talking with students about their work. In one corner is a video of students interviewing others on campus about their perceptions of race relations at EMU; in the middle of the room stands a 12-foot cardboard tower covered by representations of men and women from popular magazines read by college students. Directly in front of the entrance doors is a 4 ft. x 3 ft. pegboard display of fishing lures, artifacts representing the author's ethnography of a fishing boat; next to it a display features newspapers and other artifacts from another author's ethnographic work in a Nation of Islam temple. Directly beyond are several "magazines" on aspects of EMU campus life, their articles written by students and based on their research work on student life: dorm rituals, music preferences, nutritional practices, leisure activities, study habits, and so on. Circulating through the room are two "living presentations," students who have covered themselves with conflicting gender representations (one representation on their fronts, another on their backs). The room is loud, boisterous, bright, active, crowded. Spectators mill around the large, open space, talking to students about the research work they have done and the projects they have created.

Students' work for the Celebration and comments collected in Celebration assessments do tell us that productive, reflective, challenging learning experiences are happening within the context of this activity. To some extent, the Celebration embodies a moment when first-year students collectively have a powerful voice that is, even if only for a moment, heard clearly by those who attend the event. In surveys administered after the event, for instance, many students commented on how their ideas about themselves as writers – that is, as individual contributors with voices to be heard – changed after the Celebration. For example, comments demonstrate how the authors' self-images as writers changed after this public exposure. Typical are remarks like, *"showing off my writing ability to the public has helped build my confidence."* Other comments focused on students' discoveries with regard to the abilities of themselves and other writers in 121 courses. They reveal an understanding of how their peers – those with whom they share this campus community – write themselves into this public space. For example, many students echo the comment that *"writers [at EMU] are taken more seriously than I thought."* Additionally, students focused on what they learned by conceiving of writing *as* a public act designed to affect a particular audience. One student's comment that *"I ... had to be more careful in case I accidentally offended someone. I wrote for an audience and by being an audience myself, I knew we had to pick and choose our choice of words"* echoed many others' sentiments. While only a few selected from hundreds of survey responses, these comments are not exceptional; most students reported similar reactions to the Celebration. Simply adding a public forum for their work – one in which each student's work is both individual *and* collaborative – the event itself evokes the image of a carnival-like mosaic, with each project and display adding to the texture of the overall piece.

4.5 First-year Writing as a Site for Conversation

On any university campus, faculty and students alike embrace commonsense notions of what writing is for. Just as the research writing that students engage with in 121 can lead them to challenge preconceived ideas they might have had about what research and writing in college are about, part of our work has been to challenge preconceived notions about *student* writing that are present on campus. The Celebration makes certain that, for at least several hours each semester, instructors, students, administrators, and visitors are focused specifically on students' real work of writing. As at many schools, 121 (or its equivalent) is the one course that nearly all students on campus take, but while the importance of writing and writing instruction are almost universally acknowledged across campus, the actual work of 121 is not. The Celebration provides one important venue for important local conversations about student work on campus; our students themselves provide another. As they begin to see themselves as having a voice on campus, and as their understanding of writing as a complex, locally situated act grows, they then take this perspective with them into their other courses. In asking students to investigate communities closely, they begin to see how practices are shaped within contexts. Our first-year writing courses then must encourage them to make the link between what they are observing and how they might then act on the world so that they begin seeing themselves as *participants* in their education, not just *observers*.

5   CONCLUSION

As the coordinators of this approach to 121, we also embrace the reflective and re-flexive mindset we ask students to engage with as we study, reflect on, and write about the text of the first-year writing program. Just as we encourage students to engage in projects that are both individually relevant and also attendant to the larger social contexts within which they work, we try to do the same with the writing instructors with whom we work closely. And just as students observe aspects of their communities that trouble them, we see aspects of our approach that both encourage and unsettle us. As both administrators and classroom teachers, our commitment to reflective, locally situated practice leads us to acknowledge very real tensions present in both our program and our classrooms – tensions that are productive for us to consider, again and again, as we seek to work with instructors and students to continue creating research writing experiences that are relevant and contextualized.

On an administrative level, we recognize that one very real tension of enacting and encouraging a relevant curriculum for students – one that pushes students to find personal relevance and a public voice – is that first-year writing instructors often cannot engage in a similar kind of relevant pedagogical curriculum for themselves. The majority of our first-year writing courses are taught by part- and full-time lecturers, fewer by teaching assistants, and only a handful each semester by full-time faculty. Because of the very real hierarchies in place, how to both provide models and enact change even while acknowledging how threatening pedagogical change can be for instructors is an ethical dilemma that we often reflect upon.

As classroom teachers, we struggle to balance academic requirements with the engaged, reflective classroom practices we value. We want students to leave their first-year writing courses knowing that writing *is* relevant on many levels. We are aware, though, that for many students, their goal for 121 is to be able to check off that particular requirement among the many they must complete for their degree. While this focus on requirements, credits, and "doing what the teacher asks" can be frustrating, we have found it more productive to acknowledge what Durst (1999) calls students' "pragmatic instrumentalism" by giving them ways to research topics, communities, and questions that *do* relate directly to their goals, and from this research work to develop the flexible strategies alluded to by Royster above. Undoubtedly there will always be a few students who leave English 121 with little sense of writing as anything more than a product that they must produce for their instructor. The reasons for these students' experiences will be as diverse as students themselves. Some may leave the class steadfastly maintaining their belief in autonomous literacy, a notion that is surely scrutinized during the fourteen weeks of English 121. Others may find that they were not as engaged as they thought they would be in the site they chose for research and their lack of engagement may mean that they "just couldn't get into the research." Others may dislike the dialogic nature of the course, requiring as it does close contact between instructor and students. A student of our colleague Clarinda Flannery, who pioneered the multi-genre essay in our department, said that she didn't like creating this capstone project for the course because she "couldn't do it in one sitting; I had to really think about it piece by piece. There was no way I could do it at the last minute" (evaluation). Such comments remind us that, while not all of the students in English 121 are just out of high school, many are; as Haswell so aptly put it, "We are not teachers of writing. We are teachers of this eighteen-year old, writing" (Haswell, 1991: 1). Still, as instructors and as program administrators we work to use the space of a required course, with required assignments, products, practices, and expectations, as one that challenges the very notions students often have of what school-based work is.

REFERENCES

Abadiano, H. (1995). Cohesion strategies and genre in expository prose: An analysis of the writing of children of ethnolinguistic cultural groups. *Pragmatics, 5*(3), 299-324.

Ackerman, J.M. (1989). *Reading and writing in the academy.* Unpublished doctoral dissertation. Carnegie Mellon University, Pittsburgh, PA.

Ackerman, J.M. (1991). Reading, writing and knowing: The role of disciplinary knowledge in comprehension and composing. *Research in the Teaching of English, 25*(2), 133-178.

Adler-Kassner, L., & Harrington, S.M. (2002). *Basic writing as a political act: Public conversations about writing and literacies.* Cresskill, NJ: Hampton.

Alamargot, D., & Chanquoy, L. (Eds.) (2001a). *Through the models of writing.* Dordrecht: Kluwer Academic Press.

Alamargot, D., & Chanquoy, L. (2001b). Planning process. In G. Rijlaarsdam (Series Ed.), & D. Alamargot, & L. Chanquoy (Vol. Eds.), *Through the models of writing* (pp. 33-64). Dordrecht: Kluwer Academic Press.

Albuquerque, E.B.C. de, & Spinillo, A.G. (1997). O conhecimento de crianças sobre diferentes tipos de textos. Psicologia: *Teoria e Pesquisa, 13*(3), 329-338.

Albuquerque, E.B.C. de, & Spinillo, A.G. (1998). Consciência textual em crianças: Critérios adotados na identificação de partes de textos. *Revista Galego Portuguesa de Psicoloxia e Educación, 3*(2), 145-158.

Allal, L. (2000). Metacognitive regulation of writing in the classroom. In A. Camps, & M. Milian (Eds.), *Metalinguistic activity in learning to write* (pp. 145-166). Amsterdam: Amsterdam University Press.

Allal, L. (2001). Situated cognition and learning: From conceptual frameworks to classroom investigations. *Revue suisse des sciences de l'éducation, 23*, 407-422.

Allal, L. (2004). Integrated writing instruction and the development of revision skills. In G. Rijlaarsdam (Series Ed.) & L. Allal, L. Chanquoy, & P. Largy (Vol. Eds.), *Revision: Cognitive and instructional processes* (pp. 139-155). Dordrecht: Kluwer Academic Press.

Allal, L., & Mottier Lopez, L. (2002, July). *Revision as a process of self- and peer regulation in learning to write.* Paper presented at the Writing 2002 Conference, Stafford, England.

Anderson, D.D. (2002). Casting and recasting gender: Children constituting social identities through literacy practices. *Research in the Teaching of English, 36*, 391-427.

Angelova, M., & Riazantseva, A. (1999). "If you don't tell me, how can I know?": A case study of four international students learning to write the U.S. way. *Written Communication, 16*, 491-525.

Anson, C.M. (2000). Response and the social construction of error. *Assessing Writing, 7*, 5-21.

Applebee, A.N. (1981). *Writing in the secondary school: English and content areas.* Urbana, IL: National Council of Teachers of English.

Ashwell, T. (2000). Patterns of teacher response to student writing in a multiple-draft composition classroom: Is content feedback followed by form feedback the best? *Journal of Second Language Writing, 9*(3), 227-257.

Au, K.H. (1993). *Literacy instruction in multicultural settings.* Fort Worth, TX: Harcourt Brace Jovanovich.

Baker, M. (2002). Forms of cooperation in dyadic problem solving. *Revue d'Intelligence Artificielle, 16* (4-5), 587-620.

Bakhtin, M. (1981). *The dialogic imagination* (C. Emerson, & M. Holquist, trans.). Austin: University of Texas Press.

Bakhtin, M.M. (1986). *Speech genres and other late essays.* (V.W. McGee, trans.; C. Emerson & M. Holquist, Eds.). Austin: University of Austin Press.

Bales, R.F. (1950). *Interaction process analysis.* Cambridge, MA: Addison-Wesley.

Bales, R.F. (1965). The equilibrium problem in small groups. In A.P. Hare, E.F. Borgatta, & R.F. Bales (Eds.), *Small groups: Studies in social interaction* (pp. 424-456). New York: Knopf.

Ball, A. (1992). Cultural preference and the expository writing of African-American adolescents. *Written Communication, 9*(4), 501-532

Barnes, D. (1976). *From communication to curriculum.* London: Penguin.

Barré-de Miniac, C., Cros, F., & J. Ruiz, J. (1993). *Les collégiens et l'écriture: Des attentes familiales aux exigences scolaires.* Paris: INRP-ESF.

Bartholomae, D. (1985a). Inventing the university. In G. Blalock (Ed.), *The Bedford handbook for writers* (pp. 14-26). Boston: St. Martin's Press.

Bartholomae, D. (1985b). Inventing the university. In M. Rose (Ed.), *When a writer can't write: Studies in writer's block and other composing-process problems* (pp. 134-165). New York: Guilford.

Bartholomae, D. (1985c). Inventing the university: An alternative to basic skills. *Journal of Basic Writing, 2*, 85-109.

Bartholomae, D. (1993). The tidy house: Basic writing in the American curriculum. *Journal of Basic Writing, 12*(1), 4-21.

Bartlett, F.C. (1932). *Remembering*. Cambridge: Cambridge University Press.

Barton, D. (1994). The social impact of literacy. In L. Verhoeven (Ed.), *Functional literacy* (pp. 185-198). Amsterdam: John Benjamins.

Barton, D., & Hamilton, M. (1998). *Local literacies: Reading and writing in one community*. London: Routledge.

Barton, D., & Hamilton, M. (2000). Literacy practices. In D. Barton, & M. Hamilton (Eds.), *Situated literacies: Reading and writing in context*. London: Routledge.

Barton, E.L. (1995). Contrastive and non-contrastive connectives: Metadiscourse functions in argumentation. *Written Communication, 12*(2), 219-239.

Basso, K. (1974). The ethnography of writing. In R. Bauman, & J. Sherzer (Eds.), *Explorations in the ethnography of speaking* (pp. 425-432). Cambridge: Cambridge University Press.

Bauman, R., & Briggs, C. (1990). Poetics and performance as critical perspectives on language and social life. *Annual Review of Anthropology, 19*, 59-88.

Bauman, Z. (1995). *Postmodern etik*. [Postmodern ethics.] Gothenburg: Daidalos.

Bautier, E. (1995). *Pratiques sociales, pratiques discursives*. Paris: L'Harmattan.

Bautier, E. (1996). Rapport aux savoirs et au lycée des 'nouveaux lycéens'. *Le français aujourd'hui, 115*, 23-30.

Bautier, E., & Bucheton, D. (1997). *Conduites d'écriture*. Paris: CNDP.

Bautier, E., & Rochex, J.Y. (1997). Apprendre: des malentendus qui font la différence. In J.P. Terrail (Ed.), *La scolarisation de la France: Critique de l'état des lieux* (pp. 105-122). Paris: La Dispute.

Bawarshi, A. (2000). The genre function. *College English, 62*, 335-360.

Bazerman, C. (1988). *Shaping written knowledge: The genre and activity of the experimental article in science*. Madison, WI: Wisconsin University Press.

Bazerman, C. (1994a). *Constructing experience*. Carbondale: Southern Illinois University Press.

Bazerman, C. (1994b). Systems of genre and the enactment of social intentions. In A. Freedman, & P. Medway (Eds.), *Rethinking genre* (pp. 79-101). Madison: University of Wisconsin Press.

Bazerman, C., & Paradis, J. (Eds.) (1991). *Textual dynamics of the professions*. Madison, WI: University of Wisconsin Press.

Bazerman, C., & P. Prior (Eds.) (2004). *What writing does and how it does it: An introduction to analyzing texts and textual practices*. Mahwah, NJ: Lawrence Erlbaum Associates.

Beard, J.D., Rymer, J., & Williams, D.L. (1989). An assessment system for collaborative writing groups: Theory and empirical evaluation. *Journal of Business and Technical Communication, 3*, 29-51.

Beaufort, A. (1997). Operationalizing the concept of discourse community: A case study of one institutional site of composing. *Research in the Teaching of English, 37*, 486-529.

Beaufort, A. (1999). *Writing in the real world: Making the transition from school to work*. New York: Teachers College Press.

Beaufort, A. (2000). Learning the trade: A social apprenticeship model for gaining writing expertise. *Written Communication, 17*, 185-223.

Beaven, M.H. (1977). Individualized goal setting, self-evaluation, and peer evaluation. In C.R. Cooper, & L. Odell (Eds.), *Evaluating writing: Describing, measuring, judging* (pp. 135-156). Urbana, IL: National Council Teachers of English.

Begoray, D.L. (1994). *Collaborative writing in a high-technology company*. Unpublished doctoral dissertation. University of British Columbia.

Behrens, L., & Rosen, L. (1985). *Writing and reading across the curriculum*. New York: Longman.

Belanger, K., & Greer, J. (1992). Beyond the group project: A blueprint for a collaborative writing course. *Journal of Business and Technical Communication, 6*, 99-115.

Belcher, D., & Hirvela, A. (Eds.) (2001a). *Linking literacies: L2 reading-writing connections*. Ann Arbor: The University of Michigan Press.

Belcher, D., & Hirvela, A. (Eds.) (2001b). Voice in L2 writing. Special issue. *Journal of Second Language Writing, 10*(1-2).

Bereiter, C., & Scardamalia, M. (1983). Does learning to write have to be so difficult? In A. Freedman, I. Pringle, & J. Yalden (Eds.), *Learning to write: First language/second language* (pp. 20-33). London: Longman.

Bereiter, C., & Scardamalia, M. (1987). *The psychology of written composition.* Hillsdale, NJ: Lawrence Erlbaum Associates.

Berkenkotter, C., & Huckin, T.N. (1988). Conventions, conversations, and the writer: Case study of a student in a rhetoric PhD program. *Research in the Teaching of English, 22,* 9-44.

Berkenkotter, C., & Huckin, T.N. (1993). Rethinking genre from a sociocognitive perspective. *Written Communication, 10*(4), 475-509.

Berkenkotter, C., & Huckin, T.N. (1995). *Genre knowledge in disciplinary communication.* Hillsdale, NJ: Lawrence Erlbaum Associates.

Berkenkotter, C., Huckin, T.N., & Ackerman, J. (1991). Social context and socially constructed texts: The initiation of a graduate student into a writing research community. In C. Bazerman, & J. Paradis (Eds.), *Textual dynamics of the professions* (pp. 191-215). Madison, WI: University of Wisconsin Press.

Berlin, J. (1996). *Rhetorics, poetics, and cultures: Refiguring English studies.* Urbana, IL: National Council of Teachers of English.

Berliner, D. (1979). *Tempus educare.* In P.L. Peterson, & H.J.Walberg (Eds.), Research on teaching. Berkeley: McCutchan

Berman, R.A., & Slobin, D.I. (Eds.) (1994). *Relating events in narrative: A cross-linguistic developmental study.* Hillsdale, NJ: Lawrence Erlbaum Associates.

Bernstein, B. (1958). Some sociological determinants of perception: An enquiry into sub-cultural differences. *British Journal of Sociology, 9,* 159-174.

Besnier, N. (1995). *Reading, emotion, and authority: Reading and writing on a Polynesian atoll.* Cambridge: Cambridge University Press.

Bétrix Köhler, D. (1995). *Orthographe en question(s).* Lausanne: Centre Vaudois de Recherche Pédagogiques.

Bhatia, V. K. (1993). *Analysing genre: Language users in professional settings.* London: Longman.

Bhatia, V.K. (2000). Genres in conflict. In A. Trosborg (Ed.), *Analysing professional genres* (pp. 147-161). Amsterdam: John Benjamins.

Biber, D. (1995). *Dimensions of register variation: A cross-linguistic comparison.* Cambridge: Cambridge University Press.

Birenbaum, M. (1995). *Who is afraid of a research project?* Tel-Aviv: University Enterprises Publishers, Ltd. (in Hebrew).

Bishop, W. (1999). *Ethnographic research writing: Writing it up, writing it down, and reading it.* Portsmouth, NH: Boynton-Cook/Heinemann.

Bizzell, P. (1982). Cognition, convention and certainty: What we need to know about writing. *PRE/TEXT, 3,* 213-243.

Bizzell, P. (1990). Beyond anti-foundationalism to rhetorical authority: Problems defining cultural literacy. *College English, 52,* 661-675.

Bizzell, P. (1992). *Academic discourse and critical consciousness.* Pittsburgh: University of Pittsburgh Press.

Bizzell, P. (1999). Hybrid academic discourses: What, why, how. *Composition Studies, 27*(2), 9-21.

Bizzell, P. (2000). Basic writing and the issue of correctness, or what to do with "mixed" forms of academic discourse. *Journal of Basic Writing, 19*(1), 4-12.

Bizzell, P. (2002). The intellectual work of "mixed" forms of academic discourses. In C. Scheroder, H. Fox, & P. Bizzell (Eds), *Alt dis: Alternative discourses and the academy* (pp. 1-10). Portsmouth: Boynton/Cook-Heinemann.

Bliss, J., Askew, M., & McCrae, S. (1996). Effective teaching and learning: Scaffolding revisited. *Oxford Review of Education, 22,* 37-61.

Bloom, D. (1989). *Classrooms and literacy.* Norwood, NJ: Ablex.

Bloom, D., & Bailey, F.M. (1992). Studying language and literacy through events, particularity, and intertextuality. In R. Beach, J.L. Green, M.L. Kamil, & T. Shanahan (Eds.), *Multidisciplinary perspectives on literacy research* (pp. 181-210). Urbana, IL: National Council of Teachers of English.

Bloom, D., & Egan-Robertson, A. (1993). The social construction of intertextuality in classroom reading and writing events. *Reading Research Quarterly, 28,* 305-333.

Boissevain, J., & Mitchell, J.C. (Ed.) (1973). *Network analysis: Studies in human interaction.* The Hague: Mouton.

Boissinot, A. (1992). *Les textes argumentatifs.* Toulouse: Bertrand- Lacoste.

Bordum, A. (2001). *Diskursetik og den positive selvreference - Jürgen Habernas' kommunikative etik.* [Discursive ethics and the positive self reference - Jürgen Habermas' communicatice ethics]. Fredriksberg (Denmark): Samfundslitteratur.

Bosley, D. S. (1989). A national study of the uses of collaborative writing in business communication courses among members of the ABC. *Dissertation Abstracts,* 50-09A, 2759.

Bosher, S. (1998). The composing processes of three Southeast Asian writers at the post-secondary level: An exploratory study. *Journal of Second Language Writing, 7,* 205-241.

Bourdieu, P. (1989). *Outline of a theory of practice.* Cambridge: Cambridge University Press.

Bouton, C., & Garth, R. (1983). *Learning in groups.* San Francisco: Jossey-Bass.

Bouton, K., & Tutty, G. (1975). The effects of peer-evaluated compositions on writing improvement. *The English Record, 26,* 64-67.

Bracewell, R.J., Frederiksen, C.H., & Frederiksen, J.E. (1982). Cognitive processes in composing and comprehending. *Educational Psychologist, 17,* 146-174.

Bremer, K., Robers, C., Vasseur, M-T., Simonot, M., & Broeder, P. (1996). *Achieving understanding: Discourse in intercultural encounters.* London: Longman.

Brewer, C. (1985). The story schema: Universal and culture-specific properties. In D.R. Olson, N. Torrance, & A. Hildyard (Eds.), *Literacy, language and learning: The nature and consequences of reading and writing* (pp. 167-194). Cambridge: Cambridge University Press.

Brice-Heath. S. (1983). *Ways with words.* New York: Cambridge University Press.

Britton, J., Burgess, T., Martin, N., McLeod, A., & Rosen, H. (1975) *The development of writing abilities (11-18).* London: Macmillan.

Brown, J.S., Collins, A., & Duguid, P. (1989). Situated cognition and the culture of learning. *Educational Researcher, 18*(1), 32-42.

Brown, A., & Palincsar, A. (1989). Guided, cooperative learning and individual knowledge acquisition. In L. Resnick (Ed.), *Knowing, learning, and instruction* (pp. 393-451). Hillsdale, NJ: Erlbaum,.

Brown, A.L., & Campione, J. C. (1990). Communities of learning and thinking, or a context by any other name. *Human Development, 21,* 108-126.

Brown, G., & Yule, G. (1983*). Discourse analysis.* Cambridge: Cambridge University Press.

Bruffee, K. (1978). The Brooklyn Plan: Attaining intellectual growth through peer-group tutoring. *Liberal Education, 64,* 447-68.

Bruffee, K. (1983). *Writing and reading as collaborative or social acts.* In J.N. Hays, J.R. Ramsay, & R.D. Foulke (Eds.), *The writer's mind* (pp. 159-170). Urbana, IL: National Council of Teachers of English.

Bruffee, K.A. (1984). Collaborative learning and the "conversation of mankind." *College English, 46,* 635-652.

Bucha, E.R. (1994). An ethnographic study of collaborative writing in the workplace. *Dissertation Abstracts,* 55-12A, 3825.

Bühler, K. (1934/1965). *Sprachtheorie.* Stuttgart: Fischer,

Cain, K., & Oakhill, J. (1996). The nature of the relationships between comprehension skill and the ability to tell a story. *British Journal of Developmental Psychology, 14,* 187-201.

Cairney, T., & Ashton, J. (2002). Three families, multiple discourses: Parental roles, constructions of literacy and diversity of pedagogic practice. *Linguistics and Education, 13*(3), 303-345.

Campos, T.N., Del Prette, Z.A.P., & Del Prette, A. (2000). (Sobre)vivendo nas ruas: habilidades sociais e valores de crianças e adolescentes. *Psicologia: Reflexão e Crítica, 13*(3), 517-528.

Canale, M. (1983). From communicative competence to communicative language pedagogy. In J. Richards, & R. Schmidt (Eds.), *Language and communication* (pp. 2-27). London: Longman,

Carlo, G., & Koller, S.H. (1998). Desenvolvimento moral pró-social em crianças e adolescentes: Conceitos metodologias e pesquisas no Brasil. *Psicologia: Teoria e Pesquisa, 14*(2), 161-172

Candlin, C., & Hyland, K. (Eds.) (1999). *Writing: Texts, processes, and practices.* London: Longman.

Carraher, T.N. (1984). Face-saving and literacy in Brazil. *Sociological Abstracts, 32,* 40-41.

Carraher, T.N. (1986). Alfabetização e pobreza: Três faces da realidade. In S. Kramer (Ed.), *Alfabetização: Dilemas da prática* (pp.47-98). Rio de Janeiro: Dois Pontos Editora.

Carraher, T.N. (1987). Illiteracy in a literate society: Understanding reading failure in Brazil. In D. Wagner (Ed.), *The future of literacy in a changing world* (pp. 95-110). Oxford: Pergamon Press.

Carrell, P.L., & Eisterhold, J.C. (1988). Schema theory and ESL reading pedagogy. In P. Carrell, J. Devine, & D. Eskey (Eds.), *Interactive approaches to second language reading* (pp. 73-92). Cambridge: Cambridge University Press.

Casanave, C. (1995). Local interactions: Constructing contexts for composing in a graduate sociology program. In D. Belcher, & G. Braine (Eds.), *Academic writing in a second language* (pp. 83-112). Norwood, NJ: Ablex.

Casey, M. (1993). *The meaning of collaborative writing in a college composition course.* Unpublished doctoral dissertation. University of California, Riverside.

Cazden, C.B. (1986). Classroom discourse. In M.C. Wittrock (Ed.), *Handbook of research on teaching* (pp. 432-463). New York: Macmillan.

Cazden, C.B. (1988). *Classroom discourse: The language of teaching and learning.* Portsmouth, NH: Heinemann.

Chafe, W. (1982). Integration, and involvement in speaking, writing and oral literature. In D. Tannen (Ed.), *Spoken and written language: Exploring orality and literacy* (pp. 35-54). Norwood, NJ: Ablex.

Charalambopoulos, A., & Chatzisavidis, S. (1998). *Didaskalia tis liturgikis xrisis tis glossas.* [Teaching of the functional use of language]. Thessaloniki: Kodikas.

Charney, D. (1996). Empiricism is not a four-letter word. *CCC, 47*(4), 567-593.

Chenoweth, C., & Hayes, J.R. (2001). Fluency in writing: Generating text in L1 and L2. *Written Communication, 18,* 80-98.

Chiseri-Strater, E., & Sunstein, B. (2002). *Field working.* Boston: Bedford/St. Martin's.

Christie, F., & Martin, J.R. (Eds.) (1997). *Genre and institutions: Social processes in the workplace and school.* London: Cassell.

Clyne, M. (1987). Cultural differences in the organization of academic texts. *Journal of Pragmatics, 11,* 211-247.

Cobb, P., Gravemeijer, K., Yackel, E., McClain, K. & Whitenack, J. (1997). Mathematizing and symbolizing: The emergence of chains of signification in one first-grade classroom. In D. Kirshner, & J.A. Whitson (Eds.), *Situated cognition, social, semiotic, and psychological perspectives* (pp. 151-233). Mahwah, NJ: Lawrence Erlbaum Associates.

Cobb, P., Stephan, M., McClain, K., & Gravemeijer, K. (2001). Participating in classroom mathematical practices. *Journal of the Learning Sciences, 10,* 113-164.

Collins, J.L. (1984). The development of writing abilities during the school years. In A.D. Pellegrini, & T.D. Yawkey (Eds.), *Oral and written language in social contexts* (pp. 201- 211). Norwood, NJ: Ablex.

Collins, J.L. (1998). *Strategies for struggling writers.* New York: The Guilford Press.

Connor, U. (1995). Examining syntactic variation across three English-speaking nationalities through a multi-feature/multidimensional approach. In D.L. Rubin (Ed.), *Composing social identity in written language* (pp. 75-87). Hillsdale, NJ: Lawrence Erlbaum Associates.

Connor, U. (1996). *Contrastive rhetoric: Cross-cultural aspects of second-language writing.* Cambridge: Cambridge University Press.

Connor, U., & Asanavage, K. (1994). Peer response groups in ESL writing: How much impact on revision? *Journal of Second Language Writing, 3*(3), 257-276.

Connor, U.M., & Kramer, M.G. (1995). Writing from sources: Case studies of graduate students in business management. In A. Belcher, & G. Braine (Eds.), *Academic writing in a second language: Essays on research and pedagogy* (pp. 155-181). Norwood, NJ: Ablex.

Connor, U., & Lauer, J. (1988). Cross-cultural variation in persuasive student writing. In A.C. Purves (Ed.), *Writing across languages and cultures: Issues in contrastive rhetoric* (pp. 138-59). Newbury Park: Sage.

Conrad, S.M., & Goldstein, L.M. (1999). ESL student revision after teacher-written comments: Texts, contexts, and individuals. *Journal of Second Language Writing, 8*(2), 147-179.

Cook Gumperz, J. (1986) *The social construction of literacy.* Cambridge: Cambridge University Press.

Cooper, A. (1996). *Thinking and writing by design: A cross-disciplinary reader.* New York: Longman.

Cooper, C. (1977). Holistic evaluation of writing. In C. Cooper, & L. Odell (Eds.), *Describing, measuring, and judging* (pp. 3-31). Urbana, IL: National Council of Teachers of English.

Cooper, M., & Holzman, M. (Eds.) (1989). *Writing as social action.* Portsmouth, NH: Heinemann.

Cope, B., & Kalantzis, M. (1993). *The powers of literacy: A genre approach to teaching writing*. London: The Falmer Press.

Coupland, N. (2002). Language, situation and the relational self: Theorizing dialect-style in sociolinguistics. In P. Eckert, & J.R. Rickford (Eds.), *Style and sociolinguistic variation* (pp. 185-210). Cambridge: Cambridge University Press.

Cox, B.E., Shanahan, T., & Sulzby, E. (1990). Good and poor elementary readers' use of cohesion in writing. *Reading Research Quarterly, 25*, 47-65.

Crabbe, D. (2003). The quality of language learning opportunities. *TESOL Quarterly, 37*(1), 9-34.

Craidy, C.M. (1998). *Meninos de rua e analfabetismo*. Porto Alegre: Artmed.

Cross, G.A. (2000). Collective form: An exploration of large-group writing. *Journal of Business Communication, 37*, 77-100.

Crowhurst, M. (1987). Cohesion in argument and narration at three grade levels. *Research in Teaching of English, 21*, 185-201.

Crowhurst, M. (1991). Interrelationships between reading and writing persuasive discourse. *Research in the Teaching of English, 25*(3), 314-338.

Crowley, S. (1995). Composition's ethic of service, the universal requirement, and the discourse of student need. *Journal of Advanced Composition, 15*(2), 227-39.

Culler, J. (1982). *On deconstruction: Theory and criticism after structuralism*. Ithaca: Cornell University Press.

Curtin, E.H. (1988). *The research paper in high school writing programs: Examining connections between goals of instruction and requirements of college writing*. Unpublished doctoral dissertation. Carnegie Mellon University, Pittsburgh, PA.

Cushman, E. (1996). The rhetorician as an agent of social change. *College Composition and Communication, 47*, 7-28.

Czerniewska, P. (1992). *Learning about writing*. Oxford: Blackwell.

Daiute, C., & Dalton, B. (1988). "Let's brighten it up a bit": Collaboration and cognition in writing. In B. A. Rafoth, & D.L. Rubin (Eds.), *The social construction of written communication* (pp. 249-269). Norwood, NJ: Ablex.

DeBaryshe, B. (1995). Maternal belief systems: Linchpin in the home reading process. *Journal of Applied Developmental Psychology, 16*, 1-20.

De Fina, A. (1997). An analysis of Spanish *bien* as a marker of classroom management in teachers'-student interaction. *Journal of Pragmatics, 28*, 337-54.

Deem, R., & Brehony, K. (2000). Doctoral students' access to research cultures – are some more unequal than others? *Studies in Higher Education, 25*, 149-165.

Degenne, A., & Forse, M. (1999). *Introducing social networks*. London: Sage.

Department for Education and Employment (1998). *The National Literacy Strategy. A Framework for Teaching*. London: DfEE.

Department for Education and Employment/Qualifications and Curriculum Authority (1999). *The National Curriculum for England: English*. London: HMSO.

Derewianka, B. (1996). *Exploring the writing of genres*. Shepreth: UKRA.

Deutsch, M. (1949a). An experimental study of the effects of cooperation and competition upon group process. *Human Relations, 2*, 199-231.

Deutsch, M. (1949b). A theory of cooperation and competition. *Human Relations, 2*, 129-152.

Deutsch, M. (1968). Field theory. In G. Lindzey, & E. Aronson (Eds.), *Handbook of social psychology*. Reading, Mass: Addison Wesley.

Dewey, J. (1897). My pedagogic creed. *The School Journal, 54*, 77-80.

Dewey, J. (1938). *Experience and education*. New York: The Macmillan Company.

Dewey, J. (1952). Introduction. In E.R. Clapp (Ed.), *The use of resources in education* (pp. vii-xi). New York: Harper.

Diamondslon, J.V. (1997). Contested relations and authoritative texts. *Written Communication, 14*(2), 189-220.

Dias, P. (2000). Writing classrooms as activity systems. In P. Dias, & A. Parré (Eds.), *Transitions: Writing in academic and workplace settings* (pp. 11-29). Cresskill, NJ: Hampton Press.

Dias, P., & Parré, A. (Eds.) (2000). *Transitions: Writing in academic and workplace settings*. Cresskill, NJ: Hampton Press.

Dickinson, D.K. (Ed.) (1994). *Bridges to literacy: Children, families, and schools*. Oxford, UK: Blackwell.

DiPardo, A., & Freedman, S. W. (1988). Peer response groups in the writing classroom: Theoretic foundations and new direction. *Review of Educational Research, 58*(2), 119-149.

Doise, W., & Mugny, G. (1984). *The social development of the intellect.* Oxford: Pergamon Press.

Donahue, C. (2002a). The Lycée to university progression in French students' development as writers. In D. Russell, & D. Foster (Eds.), *Writing and learning in cross-national perspective* (pp. 134-191). Urbana, IL: National Council of Teachers of English.

Donahue, C. (2002b). Quelles stratégies pour mieux aider l'étudiant-écrivain à gérer la polyphonie énonciative invitée par un travail avec d'autres textes? *Enjeux, 54,* 67-81.

Donahue, C. (2002c). Les effets de construction du Sujet textuel produits par l'écrit. *Spirale,* 29, 75-108.

Donato, R. (1994). Collective scaffolding in second language learning. In J. Lantoff, & G. Appel (Eds.), *Vygotskian approaches to second language learning research* (pp. 33-56). Norwood, NJ: Ablex.

Dorr-Bremme, D.W. (1990). Contextualization cues in the classroom. *Language in Society, 19,* 379-402.

Dowswell, P. (1994). *Tales of Real Escape.* London: Usborne.

Drew, P., & Heritage, J. (1992). Analyzing talk at work: An introduction. In P. Drew, & J. Heritage (Eds.), *Talk at work: Interaction in institutional settings* (pp. 1-65). Cambridge: Cambridge University Press.

Duranti, A. (1997). *Linguistic anthropology.* Cambridge: Cambridge University Press.

Duranti, A., & Goodwin, C. (Eds.) (1992). *Rethinking context: Language as an interactive phenomenon.* Cambridge: Cambridge University Press.

Durst, R. (1999). *Collision Course: Conflict, negotiation, and learning in college composition.* Urbana, IL: National Council of Teachers of English.

Duszack, A. (1997). *Culture and styles of academic discourse.* Berlin: Mouton de Gruyter.

Dyson, A.H. (1993). *Social worlds of children learning to write in an urban primary school.* New York: Teachers College, Columbia University.

Dyson, A.H. (1999). Coach Bombay's kids learn to write: Children's appropriation of media material for school literacy. *Research in the Teaching of English, 33,* 367-402.

Eckert, P. (2000). *Linguistic variation as social practice.* Oxford: Blackwell.

Eco, U. (1989). *Lector in fabula: Le rôle du lecteur ou la coopération interprétative dans les textes narratifs.* Paris: Librairie Générale Française.

Ede, L.S., & Lunsford, A. (1990). *Singular texts/plural authors: Perspectives on collaborative writing.* Carbondale, IL: Southern Illinois University Press.

Edwards, D., & Mercer, N. (1987). *Common knowledge: The development of understanding in the classroom.* New York: Falmer Press.

Edwards, A.D., & Westgate, D.P.G. (1994). *Investigating classroom talk* (2nd ed). London: Falmer.

Elbow, P. (1973). *Writing without teachers.* Oxford: Oxford University Pres.

Englert, C.S. (1972). Writing instruction from a sociocultural perspective: The holistic, dialogic, and social enterprise of writing. *Journal of Learning Disabilities, 25,* 153-172.

Englert, C.S., Raphael, T.E., & Anderson, L.M. (1992). Socially mediated instruction: Improving students' knowledge and talk about writing. *The Elementary School Journal, 92,* 411-444.

Englert, C.S., Berry, R., & Dunsmore, K. (2001). A case study of the apprenticeship processes: Another perspective on the apprentice and the scaffolding metaphor. *Journal of Learning Disabilities, 34,* 152-171.

Erickson, F. (1984). School literacy, reasoning, and civility: An anthropologist's perspective. *Review of Educational Research, 54,* 525-46.

Erickson, F., & Schultz, J. (1981). When is a context? Some issues and methods in the analysis of social competence. In J. Green, & C. Wallat (Eds.), *Ethnography and language in educational settings* (vol. 5) (pp. 147-160). Norwood, NJ: Ablex.

Esperet, E., & Piolat, A. (1991). Production: Planning and control. In G. Denhiere, & J.P. Rossi (Eds.), *Text and text processing.* (pp. 317-x.). Elsevier: North Holland.

Evans, L., & Tsatsaroni, A. (1994). Language and "subjectivity" in the mathematics classroom. In S. Lerman (Ed.), *Cultural perspectives on the mathematics classroom* (pp. 169-190). Dordrecht: Kluwer.

Evensen, L.S. (2003). *Femistil framelskes.* http://www.dagbladet.no/kunnskap/2003/04/02/365494.html

Fairclough, N. (1989). *Language and power.* London: Longman.

Fairclough, N. (1995). *Critical discourse analysis: The critical study of discourse.* London: Longman.

Faigley, L. (1985). Nonacademic writing: The social perspective. In L. Odell, & D. Goswami (Eds.), *Writing in non academic settings* (pp. 232-248). New York: Guild.

Faigley, L. (1986). Competing theories of process: A critique and a proposal. *College English, 48,* 527-542.

Faigley, L., & Hansen, K. (1985). Learning to write in the social context. *College Composition and Communication, 36,* 140-149.

Faigley, L., & Miller, T. P. (1982). What we learn from writing on the job. *College English, 44,* 557-569.

Faigley, L., & Witte, S. (1981). Analyzing revision. *College Composition and Communication, 32,* 401-414.

Farrell, L. (1996). A case study of discursive practices and assessment processes in multi-ethnic context. *Journal of Pragmatics, 26,* 267-289.

Ferreira, R.M.F. (1979). *Meninos de rua: Expectativas e valores de menores marginalizados em São Paulo.* São Paulo: CEDEC.

Ferreiro, E., & Teberosky, A. (1982). *Literacy before schooling.* Exeter, NH: Heinemann.

Ferris, D. (1995a). Student reactions to teacher response in multiple-draft composition classrooms. *TESOL Quarterly, 29,* 33-53.

Ferris, D. (1995b). Teaching students to self-edit. *TESOL Journal, 4*(4), 18-22.

Ferris, D.R. (1995c). Student reactions to teacher response in multiple-draft composition classrooms. *TESOL Quarterly, 29,* 33-53.

Ferris, D. R. (1997). The influence of teacher commentary on student revision. *TESOL Quarterly, 31,* 315-339.

Ferris, D.R., & Hedgcock, J. (Eds.) (1998). *Teaching ESL composition.* Mahwah, NJ: Lawrence Erlbaum Associates.

Finlayson, R., & Slabbert, S. (1997). "I'll meet you halfway with language": Code-switching within a South African urban context. In M. Putz (Ed.), *Language choices: Conditions, constraints, and consequences* (pp. 381-422). Amsterdam: John Benjamins.

Fitzgerald, J., Spiegel, D.L., & Cunningham, J.W. (1991). The relationships between parental literacy level and perceptions of emergent literacy. *Journal of Reading Behaviour, 23,* 191-213.

Floriani, A. (1993). Negotiating what counts: Roles and relationships, texts and contexts, content and meaning. *Linguistics and Education, 5,* 241-273.

Flower, L., & Hayes, J. (1981a). A cognitive process theory of writing. *College Composition and Communication, 32,* 365-387.

Flower, L., & Hayes, J. (1981b). Plans that guide the composing process. In C. Frederiksen, & J. Dominic (Eds.), *Writing: The nature, development, and teaching of written communication* (vol. 2) (pp. 39-58). Hillsdale, NJ: Lawrence Erlbaum Associates.

Flower, L., Stein, V., Ackerman, J., McCormick, K., Peck, W., & Kanz, M. (1990). *Cognitive and social processes in reading to write.* New York: Oxford University Press.

Folman, S. (1997). Cycles of academic literacy: From source text to target text. Even Yehuda, Israel: *Reches Educational Enterprises* (in Hebrew).

Folman, S. (2000a). *Constructing meaning from text:Cognitive-communicatice considerations in coherence production and discourse analysis.* Tel Aviv: Diyonon, Tel Aviv University (in Hebrew).

Folman, S. (2000b, April). *The discoursal construction of expertise in genres of academic writing from sources.* Paper presented at the AAAL, Salt Lake City, U.S.A.

Folman, S. (sumitted). Local markedness versus internatinalism: Can they be wedded? *L1-Educational Studies in Language and Literature.*

Folman, S., & Connor, U. (1997). Intercultural rhetorical differences in construction a high school research paper. Meggamot: *Journal for research in behavioral sciences, 38*(2), 247-280 (in Hebrew).

Forman, E.A., Minick, N., & Stone, C.A. (Eds.) (1993). *Contexts for learning: Sociocultural dynamics in children's development.* New York: Oxford University Press.

Foster, D., & Russell, D.R. (Eds.) (2002). *Writing and learning in cross-national perspective: Transitions from secondary to higher education.* Mahwah, NJ: Lawrence Erlbaum Associates.

Foucault, M. (1972). *The archaeology of knowledge and the discourse on language* (trans AM. Sheriman). London: Tavistock.

François, F. (1998). *Le discours et ses entours.* Paris: L'Harmattan.

François, F. (2000). Quelques remarques sur interpréter un texte, un texte scolaire, une dissertation de philosophie. *CALAP, 19,* 55-73.

François, F. (2002). Personal communication.

Freadman, A. (1994). Anyone for Tennis? In A. Freedman, & P. Medway, (Eds.), *Genre and the new rhetoric* (pp. 43-66). London: Taylor & Francis.

Freedman, S.W., & Sperling, M. (1985). Written language acquisition: The role of response and the writing conference. In S.W. Freedman (Ed.), *The acquisition of written language* (pp. 106-130). Norwood, NJ: Ablex.

Freire, P. (1971). *Pedagogy of the oppressed* (M. Bergman Ramos, trans.). New York: Herder and Herder.

Fuchs, L.S., Fuchs, D., Bentz, J., Phillips, N.B., & Hamlett, C.L. (1994). The nature of student interactions during peer tutoring with and without prior training and experience. *American Educational Research Journal, 31*, 75-103.

Garton, A., & Pratt, C. (1998). *Learning to be literate: The development of spoken and written language.* Oxford: Blackwell Publishers.

Gauvain, M. (2001). Cultural tools, social interaction and the development of thinking. *Human Development, 44*, 126-143.

Gebhardt, R. (1980). Teamwork and feedback: Broadening the base of collaborative writing. *College Composition and Communication, 31*, 69-74.

Gee, J.P. (1990). *Social linguistics and literacies: Ideology in discourses.* New York: Falmer Press.

Gee, J.P. (1996). *Social linguistics and literacies: Ideology in discourses.* 2nd edition. New York: Falmer Press.

Gee, J.P. (2001). Reading as situated language: A sociocognitive perspective. *Journal of Adolescent and Adult Literacy, 44*, 714-725.

Genette, G. (2002). *Figures* V. Paris: Seuil.

George, D. (1984). Working in peer groups in the composition classroom. *College Composition and Communication, 35*, 320-326.

Gergits, J.M., & Schramer, J.J. (1994). The collaborative classroom as a site of difference. *Journal of Advanced Composition, 14*, 187-202.

Gibbons, P. (2003). Mediating language learning: Teacher interactions with ESL students in a content-based classroom. *TESOL Quarterly, 37*(2), 247- 273.

Giles, H., & Smith, P. (1979). Accommodation theory: Optimal levels of convergence. In H. Giles, & R. St. Clair (Eds.), *Language and social psychology* (pp. 45-65). Oxford: Blackwell,

Gilly, M., Fraisse, J., & Roux, J.-P. (1988). Résolution de problèmes en dyades et progrès cognitifs chez des enfants de 11 à 13 ans: Dynamiques interactives et mécanismes socio-cognitifs. In A.-N. Perret-Clermont, & M. Nicolet (Eds.), *Interagir et connaitre* (pp. 73-92). Cousset, Switzerland: Delval.

Giora, R. (1985). *Informational structuring of the linear ordering of texts.* Unpublished doctoral dissertation. Tel-Aviv University, Israel (in Hebrew).

Goffman, E. (1981). *Forms of talk.* Philadelphia, PA: University of Pennsylvania Press.

Goldenberg, C., & Patthey-Chavez, G. (1995). Discourse processes in instructional conversations: Interactions between teacher and transition readers. *Discourse Processes, 19*, 57-73.

Golder, C., & Coirier, P. (1994). Argumentative text writing: Developmental trends. *Discourse Processes, 18*, 187-210.

Goldstein, J.R., & Malone, E. (1985). Using journals to strengthen collaborative writing. *The Bulletin of the Association for Business Communication, 48-49*, 24-28.

Gombert, J.E. (1992). *Metalinguistic development.* Harvester: Wheatsheaf.

Goodburn, A., & Ina, B. (1994). Collaboration, critical pedagogy, and struggles over difference. *Journal of Advanced Composition, 14*, 131-147.

Grabe, W. (1987). Contrastive rhetoric and text-type research. In U. Connor, & R.B. Kaplan (Eds.), *Writing across languages: Analysis of L2 text* (pp. 115-135). Reading, MA: Addison – Wesley.

Grabe, W., & Kaplan, R.B. (Ed.) (1996). *Theory and practice of writing.* London: Longman.

Graves, D.H. (1983). *Writing: Teachers and children at work.* Portsmouth, NH: Heinemann.

Graves, P.R., & Noll, C.L. (1999). Collaborating using conferencing software. *Delta Pi Epsilon Journal, 41*, 1-13.

Green, J.L, & Meyer, L.A. (1991). The embeddedness of reading in classroom life: Reading as a situated process. In C. Baker, & A. Luke (Eds.), *Towards a critical sociology of reading pedagogy* (pp. 141-160), Philadelphia: John Benjamins.

Green, J.L., & Wallat, C. (Eds.) (1991). *Ethnography and language in educational settings.* Norwood, NJ: Ablex.

Greene, S. (1993). The role of task in the development of academic thinking through reading and writing in a college history course. *Research in the Teaching of English, 27*(1), 46-75.

Greene, S. (1995). Making sense of my own ideas: The problems of authorship in a beginning writing classroom. *Written Communication, 12*(2), 186-218.

Gregory, E. (2001). Sisters and brothers as language and literacy teachers: Synergy between siblings playing and working together. *Journal of Early Childhood Literacy, 1*(3), 301-322.

Gregory, E., Williams, A., Baker, D., & Street, B. (2004). Introducing literacy to four year olds: Creating classroom cultures in three schools. *Journal of Early Childhood Literacy, 4*(1), 85-107.

Guidelines for Research Paper Writing. (1991). Ministry of Education and Culture. Jerusalem, Israel.

Gumperz, J.J. (1982a). *Discourse strategies.* Cambridge: Cambridge University Press.

Gumperz, J.J. (1982b). *Discourse and social identity.* Cambridge: Cambridge University Press.

Gumperz, J.J., & Hernandez, E. (1971). Communication aspects of bilingual communication. In W.H. Whitely (Ed.), *Language use and social change: Problems of multilingualism with special reference to Eastern Africa* (pp. 111-125). London: Oxford University Press.

Gunnarsson, B-L. (1997). The writing process from a sociolinguistic viewpoint. *Written Communication, 14,* 139-188.

Gunnarsson, B-L., Linell, P., & Nordberg, B. (Eds.) (1997). *Professional discourse.* London: Addison Wesley Longman.

Gutierrez, K. (1994). How talk, context, and script shape contexts for learning: A cross-case comparison of journal sharing. *Linguistics and Education, 5,* 335-365.

Gutierrez, K.D., & Stone, L.D. (2000) Synchronic and diachronic dimensions of social practice: An emerging methodology for cultural-historical perspectives on literacy learning. In C.D. Lee, & P. Smagorinsky (Eds.), *Vygotskian perspectives on literacy research* (pp. 150-164). Cambridge: Cambridge University Press.

Habermas, J. (1984). *The theory of communicative action.* (Vol. 1). Boston: Beacon.

Habermas, J. (1998/1988). *Postmetaphysical thinking: Philosophical essays. London: Polity Press.* (Paperback published in English 1995, reprinted 1998).

Hall, J.K., & Verplaetse, L.S. (2000). *Second and foreign language learning through classroom interaction.* Mahwah, NJ: Lawrence Erlbaum Associates.

Halliday, MAK (1967). *Intonation and grammar in British English.* The Hague: Mouton.

Halliday, MAK (1978). *Language as social semiotic.* London: Arnold.

Halliday, MAK (1985). *An introduction to functional grammar.* London and New York: Arnold.

Halliday, MAK (1994). *An Introduction to functional grammar. 2nd* edition. London: Arnold.

Halliday, MAK, & Hasan, R. (1976). *Cohesion in English.* London: Longman.

Hammond, J., & Derewianka, B. (2001) An introduction to genre. In D. Nunan, & R. Carter (Eds.), *The ELT handbook* (pp. 32-57). Cambridge: Cambridge University Press.

Harré, R., & van Langenhove, L. (1991). Varieties of positioning. *Journal for the Theory of Social Behaviour, 21*(4), 393-407.

Harré, R., & van Langenhove, L. (Eds.) (1997). *Positioning theory: Moral contexts of intentional action.* London: Blackwell.

Harrington, S., & Adler-Kassner, L. (1998). The dilemma that still counts: Basic writing at a political crossroads. *Journal of Basic Writing, 17,* 3-24.

Harris, J. (1997). *A teaching subject: Composition since 1966.* New Jersey: Prentice-Hall.

Haswell, R. (1991). *Gaining ground in college writing: Tales of development and interpretation.* Dallas: Southern Methodist University Press.

Hayes, J.R., & Flower, L.S. (1980). Identifying the organisation of writing processes. In L.W. Gregg, & E.R. Steinberg (Eds.), *Cognitive processes in writing* (pp. 3-30). Hillsdale, NJ: Lawrence Erlbaum Associates.

Hayes, J.R. (1996). A new model of cognition and affect in writing. In M. Levy, & S. Ransdell (Eds.), *The science of writing* (pp. 1-27). Hillsdale, NJ: Erlbaum.

He, A.W. (1998). *Reconstructing institutions: Language use in academic counselling encounters.* Stamford: Ablex.

Heath, S.B. (1982). What no bedtime story means: Narrative skills at home and school. *Language and Society, 2,* 49-76.

Heath, S.B. (1983). *Ways with words: Language, life, and work in communities and classrooms.* Cambridge: Cambridge University Press.

Hedge, T. (1988) *Writing.* Oxford: Oxford University Press.

Helmreich, R.L. (1982). *Pilot selection and training.* Paper presented at the annual meeting of the American Psychological Association, Washington, D.C.

Helmreich, R.L., Beane, W., Lucker, G.W., & Spence, J.T. (1978). Achievement motivation and scientific attainment. *Personality and Social Psychology Bulletin, 4,* 222-226.

Helmreich, R.L., Sawin, L.L., & Carsrud, A.L. (1986). The honeymoon effect in job performance: Temporal increases in the predictive power of achievement motivation. *Journal of Applied Psychology, 71,* 185-188.

Helmreich, R.L., Spence, J.T., Beane, W.E., Lucker, W., & Matthews, K.A. (1980). Making it in academic psychology: Demographic and personality correlates of attainment. *Journal of Personality and Social Psychology, 39,* 896-908.

Herndl, C.G., & Nahrwold, C.A. (2000). Research as social practice: A case study of research on technical and professional communication. *Written Communication, 17,* 258-296.

Herzberg, B. (1994). Community service and critical teaching. *College Composition and Communication, 45,* 307-319.

Hicks, D. (1990). Narrative skills and genre knowledge: Ways of telling in the primary school grades. *Applied Psycholinguistics, 11*(1), 83-104.

Hicks, D. (Ed.) (1996). *Discourse, learning, and schooling.* Cambridge: Cambridge University Press.

Hicks, D. (1997). Working *through* discourse genres in school. *Research in the Teaching of English, 31*(4), 459-485.

Hindman, J. (1993). Reinventing the university: Finding a place for basic writers. *Journal of Basic Writing, 12,* 55-76.

Hinds, J. (1987). Reader versus writer responsibility: A new typology. In U. Connor, & R.B. Kaplan (Eds.), *Writing across languages: Analysis of L2 text* (pp. 141-152). Reading, MA: Addison-Wesley.

Hipple, T. (1972). The grader's helpers-colleagues, peers, scorecards. *English Journal, 61,* 690-693.

Hirvela, A., & Belcher, D. (2001). Coming back to voice: The multiple voices and identities of mature multilingual writers. *Journal of Second Language Writing, 10,* 83-106.

Hogan, K., & Pressley, M. (1997). *Scaffolding student learning: Instructional approaches and issues.* Cambridge, MA: Brookline Books.

Hogg, M.A., & Terry, D.J. (2000). Social identity and self-categorization processes in organizational context. *The Academy of Management Review, 1,* 121-140.

Hornsey, M.J., & Hogg, M.A. (2000). Intergroup similarity and subgroup relations: Some implications for assimilation. *Personality and Social Psychology Bulletin, 26,* 948-958.

http://www.emich.edu/aboutemu/fastfacts/ EMU statistics

http://www.emich/edu/public/english/fycomp/outcomes/index.htm

Hulbert, C.M. (1989). Toward collectivist composition: Transforming social relations through classroom practices. *Writing Instructor, 8,* 166-176.

Hull, G., & Schultz, K. (Eds.) (2002). *Schools out!: Bringing out-of-school literacies with classroom practice.* New York: Teachers College Press.

Hunt, K. (1965). *Grammatical structures written at three grade levels.* Urbana, IL: National Council of Teachers of English.

Hunt, K. (1983). Sentence combining and the teaching of writing. In M. Martlew (Ed.), *The Psychology of written language: A developmental approach* (pp. 99-125). New York: Wiley.

Hyland, K. (2000). *Disciplinary discourses: Social interactions in academic writing.* Edinburgh: Pearson Education.

Hyland, K. (2002). *Teaching and researching writing.* London: Longman.

Hyland, K., & Hamp-Lyons, L. (2002). EAP: Issues and directions. *Journal of English for Academic Purposes, 1,* 1-12.

Hymes, D.H. (1974). *Foundations in sociolinguistics: An ethnographic approach.* Philadelphia: University of Pennsylvania Press.

Hyon, S. (1996). Genre in three traditions: implications for ESL. *TESOL Quarterly, 30*(4), 693-722.

Inghilleri, A. (1989). Learning to mean as a symbolic and social process: The story of ESL writers. *Discourse Processes, 12,* 391-411.

Itakura, H. (2001). *Conversational dominance and gender: A study of Japanese in first and second language contexts.* Amsterdam/Philadelphia: John Benjamins.

Ivanič, R. (1998). *Writing and identity: The discoursal representation of identity in academic writing.* Amsterdam: John Benjamins.

Ivanič, R., & Camps, D. (2001). I am how I sound: Voice as self-representation in L2 writing. *Journal of Second Language Writing, 10,* 3-33.

Jacoby, S., & Ochs, E. (1995). Co-construction: An introduction. *Research on Language and Social Interaction, 28*(3), 171-183.

James, D. (1981). Peer teaching in the writing classroom. *English Journal, 70,* 48-50.

Janssen, D., van Waes, L., & van den Bergh, H. (1996). Effects of thinking aloud on writing processes. In C.M. Levy, & S. Ransdell (Eds.), *Theories of writing and frameworks for writing research* (pp. 233-250). Mahwah, NJ: Lawrence Erlbaum Associates.

Jauss, H.R. (1978). *Pour une esthétique de la réception.* Paris: Gallimard.

Johns, A. (Ed.) (2002). *Genre in the classroom: Multiple perspectives.* Mahwah, NJ: Lawrence Erlbaum Associates.

Johnson, D.W., & Johnson, R.T. (1989). *Leading the cooperative school.* Edina, MN: Interaction.

Johnson, D.W., & Johnson, R.T. (1991). *Learning together and alone* (3rd ed.). Englewood Cliffs, NJ: Prentice Hall.

Johnson, D.W., & Johnson, R.T. (1994). *Learning together and alone: Cooperative, competitive and individualistic learning* (4th ed.). Boston: Allyn & Bacon.

Johnson, N.S., & Mandler, J.M. (1980). A tale of two structures: Underlying and surface forms in stories. *Poetics, 9,* 51-86.

Johnson-Laird, P.N. (1980). Mental models in cognitive science. *Cognitive Science, 4,* 71-115.

Jolliffe, D. (1994). The myth of transcendence and the problem of the "ethics" essay in college writing instruction. In P. Sullivan, & D. Qualley (Eds.), *Pedagogy in the age of politics: Writing and reading (in) the academy* (pp. 183-194). Urbana, IL: National Council of Teachers of English.

Kamberelis, G. (1999). Genre development and learning: Children writing stories, science reports, and poems. *Research in the Teaching of English, 33*(4), 403-460.

Kamberelis, G., & Bovino, T.D. (1999). Cultural artifacts as scaffolds for genre development. *Reading Research Quarterly, 34*(2), 138-170.

Kamberelis, G., & de la Luna, L. (2004). Children's writing: How textual forms, contextual forces, and textual politics co-emerge. In C. Bazerman, & P. Prior (Eds.), *What writing does and how it does it: An introduction to analyzing texts and textual practices* (pp. 239-277). Mahwah, NJ: Lawrence Erlbaum Associates.

Kanz, M. (1989a). *Written rhetorical synthesis: Processes and products synthesis* (Reading–to-write Report No. 1). Center for the Study of Writing at the University of California, Berkeley and at the University of Carnegie – Mellon, Pittsburgh.

Kanz, M. (1989b). *Primises of coherence: Weak content and strong organization: An analysis of the students' texts* (Reading – to-Write Report No.3). Center for the Study of Writing at the University of California, Berkeley and at the University of Carnegie – Mellon, Pittsburgh.

Kaplan, R.B. (1966). Cultural thought patterns in inter-cultural education. *Language Learning, 16,* 1-21.

Kaplan, R.B. (1987). Cultural thought patterns revisited. In U. Connor, & R.B. Kaplan (Ed.), *Writing across languages: Analysis of L2 text* (pp. 9-21). Massachusetts: Addison-Wesley.

Kennedy, M.L. (1985). The composing processes of college students writing from sources. *Written Communication, 2,* 234-456.

Kent, T. (1999). *Post-process theory: Beyond the writing-process paradigm.* Carbonale and Edwardsville: Southern Illinois University Press.

Kern, R. (2000). *Literacy and language teaching.* Oxford: Oxford University Press.

Kintsch, W., & van Dijk, T.A. (1978). Towards a model of text comprehension and production. *Psychological Review, 85*(3), 394-363.

Kirsch, G., & Roen, D.H. (Eds.) (1990). *A sense of audience in written communication.* London: Sage.

Knobel, M. (1999). *Everyday literacies: Students, discourse, and social practice.* New York: Peter Lang.

Knudson, R.E. (1992). The development of written argumentation: An analysis and comparison of argumentative writing at four grade levels. *Child Study Journal, 22*(3), 167-184.

Koku, E., Nazer, N., & Wellman, B. (2000). Netting Scholars: Online and offline. *American Behavioral Scientist, 43.*

Kong, A., & Pearson, P.D. (2003). The road to participation: The construction of a literacy practice in a leanrign community of linguistically diverse learners. *Research in the Teaching of English, 38*(1), 85-124.

Korolija, N. (1998). Recycling cotext: The impact of prior conversation on the emergence of episodes in a multiparty radio talk shown. *Discourse Processes, 25*(1), 99-125.

Korolija, N., & Linell, P. (1996). Episodes: Coding and analyzing coherence in multiparty conversation. *Linguistics, 34,* 799-831.

Kostouli, T. (2000). On writing conferences: The structuring of meaning negotiation in Greek classrooms. In I. Austad, & E.T. Lessand (Eds.), *Literacy: Challenges for the new millenium* (pp. 73-88). Stavenger, Norway: Center for Reading Research.

Kostouli, T. (2002). Teaching Greek as L1: Curriculum and textbooks in Greek elementary education. *L1-Educational Studies in Language and Literature, 2*, 5-23.

Kress, G. (1994). *Learning to Write*. London: Routledge.

Kress, G. (1997). *Before Writing: Rethinking the paths to literacy*. London: Routledge.

Kress, G., & van Leeuwen, T. (1996). *Reading images: The grammar of visual design*. London: Routledge.

Kroll, B. (Ed.) (1990). *Second language writing*. Cambridge: Cambridge University Press.

Kroll, B. (Ed.) (2003). *Exploring the dynamics of second language writing*. Cambridge: Cambridge University Press.

Kumpulainen, K., & Mutanen, M. (1999). The situated dynamics of peer group interaction: An introduction to an analytic framework. *Learning and Instruction, 9*, 449-473.

Labov, W. (1978). *Le parler ordinaire*. Paris: PUF.

Labov, W., & Waletzky, J. (1968). Narrative analysis: Oral versions of personal experience. In J. Helm (Ed.), *Essays on the verbal and visual art* (pp. 12-44). Seattle: University of Washington Press.

Lage, N. (1987). *Estrutura da notícia*. São Paulo: Editora Ática.

Lacasa, P., Reina, A., & Alburqueque, M. (2002). Adults and children share literacy practices: The case of homework. *Linguistics and Education, 13*(1), 39-64.

Langer, J.A. (1985). Children's sense of genre: A study of performance on parallel reading and writing tasks. *Written Communication, 2*, 157-187.

Langer, J.A. (1986). *Children reading and writing: Structures and strategies*. Norwood, NJ: Ablex.

Langer, J.A., & Nicholich, M. (1981). Prior Knowledge and its effect on reading comprehension. *Journal of Reading Behaviour, 13*(4), 375-378.

Langleben, M. (1981). Latent coherence, contextual meanings, and the interpretation of a text. *Text 1*(3), 287-296.

Lantoff, J.P. (Ed.) (2000). *Sociocultural theory and second language learning*. Oxford: Oxford Univerity Press.

Lantoff, J.P., & Appel, G. (1994). Theoretical framework: An introduction to Vygotskian approaches to second language research. In J.P. Lantoff, & G. Appel (Eds.), *Vygotskian approaches to second language research* (pp. 1-32). Norwood, NJ: Ablex.

Largy, P., Chanquoy, L., & Dédéyan, A. (2004). Orthographic revision: The case of subject-verb agreement in French.. In G. Rijlaarsdam (Series Ed.), & L. Allal, L. Chanquoy, & P. Largy (Vol. Eds.), *Revision: Cognitive and instructional processes* (pp. 39-62). Dordrecht: Kluwer Academic Press.

Lave, J., & Wenger, E. (1991). *Situated learning. Legitimate peripheral participation*. New York: Cambridge University Press.

Lee, C.D., & Smagorinsky, P. (Eds.) (2000). *Vygotskian perspectives on literacy research*. Cambridge: Cambridge University Press.

Lemke, J. (1989). Social semiotics: A new model for literacy education. In D. Bloome (Ed.), *Classrooms and literacy* (pp. 289-309). Norwood, NJ: Ablex.

Lemke, J. (1990). *Talking science: Language, learning, and values*. Norwood, NJ: Ablex.

Lemon, H. (1988). *Collaborative strategies for teaching composition: Theory and practice*. Paper presented at the Conference on College Composition and Communication. St. Louis.

Leont'ev, A.N. (1981). The problem of activity in psychology. In J.W. Wertsch (Ed.), *The concept of activity in Soviet psychology* (pp. 37-71). Armonk, NY: M.E. Sharpe.

Lester, J., & Lester, J. (2002). *The essential guide to research across the disciplines*. New York: Longman.

Levinson, J. (Ed.) (1998). *Aesthetics and ethics: Essays at the intersection*. Cambridge: Cambridge University Press.

Lewis, C. (2001). *Literacy practices as social acts: Power, status and cultural norms in the classroom*. Mahwah, NJ: Lawrence Erlbaum Associates.

Linell, P. (1998). *Approaching dialogue: Talk, interaction and contexts in dialogical perspectives*. Amsterdam/Philadelphia: Benjamins.

Linell, P., & Luckman, T. (1991). Asymmetries in dialogue: Some conceptual preliminaries. In I. Markova, & K. Foppa (Eds.), *Asymmetries in dialogue* (pp. 1-20). Hemel Hempsted: Harvester & Whitsheaf.

Liu, J., & Hansen, J.G. (2002). *Peer response in second language writing classrooms.* Ann Arbor: University of Michigan Press.

Loban, W. (1976). *Language development: Kindergarten through grade twelve.* Urbana, IL: National Council of Teachers of English.

Lu, M. (1987). From silence to words: Writing as struggle. *College English, 49,* 437-448.

Luke, A. (1988). *Literacy, textbooks and ideology.* Lewes: Falmer.

Luke, A., & Freebody, P. (1997). Shaping the social practices of reading. In S. Muspratt, A. Luke, & P. Freebody (Eds.), *Constructing critical literacies: Teaching and learning textual practice* (pp. 185-225). Cresskill, NJ: Hampton Press.

Mabrito, M. (1992). Computer-mediated communication and high-apprehensive writers: Rethinking the collaborative process. *The Bulletin,* December, 26-30.

MacArthur, C.A., Schwartz, S.S., & Graham, S. (1991). Effects of a reciprocal peer revision strategy in special education classrooms. *Learning Disabilities Research and Practice, 6,* 201-210.

MacArthur, C.A., Harris, K.R., & Graham, St. (1994). Improving students' planning processes through cognitive strategy instruction. In E.C. Butterfield (Ed.), *Advances in cognition and educational practice* (vol. 2) (pp. 173-198). Greenwich: JAI.

Macrorie, K. (1970). *Telling writing.* Rochelle Park, NJ: Hayden.

Macrorie, K. (1980). *Searching writing.* Upper Montclair, NJ: Boynton/Cook.

Macrorie, K. (1984). *Writing to be read.* Upper Montclair, NJ: Boynton/Cook.

Macrorie, K. (1988). *The I-search paper.* Portsmouth, NH: Boynton/Cook-Heinemann.

Manchon, R.M., de Larios, J.R., & Murphy, L. (2000). An approximation to the study of backtracking in L2 writing. *Language and Instruction, 10,* 13-35.

Mandler, J.M., & Johnson, N.S. (1977). Remembrance of things parsed: Story structure and recall. *Cognitive Psychology, 9,* 111-151.

Many, J.E., Fyfe, R., Lewis, G., & Mitchell, E. (1996). Topical landscape: Exploring students' self-directed reading – writing research processing. *Reading Research Quarterly, 31*(1), 12-35.

Markova, I., & Foppa, K. (Eds.) (1990). *Dynamics in dialogue.* Hemel Hempsted: Harvester & Whitsheaf.

Markova, I., & Foppa, K. (Eds.) (1991). *Asymmetries in dialogue.* Hemel Hempsted: Harvester & Whitsheaf.

Marshall, H.H. (Ed.) (1992). *Redefining student learning: Roots of educational change.* Norwood, NJ: Ablex.

Martin, J.R. (1985*). Factual writing: Exploring and challenging social reality.* Oxford: Oxford University Press.

Martin, J.R (1997). Analyzing genre: Functional parameters. In F. Christie, & J. R. Martin (Eds.), *Genre and institutions. Social processes in the workplace and school* (pp. 3-39). London & Washington: Cassell.

Martin, J.R., & Rothery, J. (Eds.) (1986). *Working Papers in Linguistics 4*: Writing Project Report 1986. Linguistics Department: University of Sydney.

Martins, R.A. (2002). Uma tipologia de crianças e adolescentes em situação de rua baseada na Análise de Aglomerados (Cluster Analysis). *Psicologia: Reflexão e Crítica, 15*(2), 251-260.

Mayes, P. (2003). *Language, social structure, and culture: A genre analysis of cooking classes in Japan and American.* Amsterdam: John Benjamins.

Maynard, O. (1989). *Japanese conversation: Self-contextualization through structure and interactional management.* Norwood, NJ: Ablex.

McAllister, C. (1985). The effects of word processing on the quality of writing: Fact or illusion? *Computers and Composition, 2,* 36-41.

McCormic K.K. (1990). *The cultural imperatives underlying cognitive acts* (Technical Report No. 28). Pittsburgh, PA: Center for the Study of Writing, Carnegie Mellon University.

McGee, L.M. (1982). Awareness of text structure: Effects on children's recall of expository text. *Reading Research Quarterly, 17*(4), 581-590.

McGinley, W. (1992) The role of teaching and writing while composing from sources. *Reading Research Quarterly, 27*(3), 226-248.

Melzi, G. (2000). Cultural variations in the construction of personal narratives: Central American and European American mothers' elicitation styles. *Discourse Processes, 30*(2), 153-177.

Mercer, N. (1995) *The guided construction of knowledge.* Multilingual Matters: Clevedon.

Mercer, N. (1996). The quality of talk in children's collaborative activity in the classroom. *Learning and Instruction*, 6, 359-377.

Meyer B., & Rice, E. (1977). The structure of text. In M. Barr, M.L. Kamil, & P. Mosenthal (Eds.), *Handbook of reading research* (vol. I) (pp. 319-352). New York: Longman.

Meyer, B. (1975). *The organization of prose and its effects on memory.* Amsterdam: North Holland.

Meyer, B., Brandt, D.M., & Bluth, B.J. (1980). Use of top-level structure in text: Key from reading comprehension of ninth-grade students. *Reading Research Quarterly*, 16, 72-103.

Michaels, S. (1981). "Sharing time:" Children's narrative styles and differential access to literacy. *Language in Society*, 10, 423-442.

Michaels, S. (1987). Text and context: A new approach to the study of classroom writing. *Discourse Processes*, 10, 321-346.

Miller, C. (1984). Genre as social action. *Quarterly Journal of Speech*, 70 (1), 151-167.

Milroy, J. (1992). *Linguistic variation and change: On the historical sociolinguistics of English.* Oxford: Blackwell.

Milroy, L. (1987). *Language and social networks.* (2ed.). Oxford UK: Basil Blackwell.

Milroy, L., & Milroy, J.M. (1992). Social network and social class: Toward an integrated sociolinguistics. *Language in Society*, 21, 1-26.

Milroy, L., & Wei, L. (1995). A social network approach to code-switching: The example of a bilingual community in Britain. In L. Milroy, & P. Muysken (Eds.), *One speaker, two languages: Cross-disciplinary perspectives on code-switching* (pp. 136-157). Cambridge: Cambridge University Press.

Mische, A., & White, H. (1998). Between conversation and situation: Public switching dynamics across network domains. *Social Research*, 65, 695-724.

Moffett, J. (1968). *Teaching the universe of discourse.* Boston: Houghton Mifflin.

Moje, E.B., & O'Brien, D.C. (Eds.) (2001). *Constructions of literacy: Studies of teaching and learning in and out of secondary schools.* Mahwah, NJ: Lawrence Erlabaum Associates.

Moll, L.C. (Ed.) (1990). *Vygotsky and education: Instructional implications and applications of sosiohistorical psychology.* Cambridge: Cambridge University Press.

Montes-Alcala, C. (2001). Written code-switching: Powerful bilingual images. In R. Jacobson (Ed.), *Code switching Worldwide II. Trends in Linguistics: Studies and monographs* (pp. 193-219). Germany: de Gruyter.

Morgan, M. (1994). Women as emergent leaders in student collaborative writing groups. *Journal of Advanced Composition*, 14, 203-219.

Morgan, M., Allen, N., Moore, T., Atkinson, D., & Snow, C. (1987). Collaborative writing in the classroom. *Bulletin for the Association for Business Communication*, 50, 20-26.

Morgan, M., Allen, N. & Atkinson, D. (1989). Evaluating collaborative assignments. In R. Louth, & A. M. Scott (Eds.), *Collaborative technical writing: Theory and practice.* Hammond, LA: Association of Teachers of Technical Writing.

Morgan, W. (1997). *Critical literacy in the classroom.* Routledge: London

Mottier Lopez, L. (2001). Temps d'interaction collective dans la classe de mathématiques: Un temps privilégié de participation aux pratiques sociales de la communauté classe. *Canevas de thèse en sciences de l'éducation*, Université de Genève.

Murray, D. (1968). *A writer teaches writing: A practical method of teaching composition.* Boston: Houghton Mifflin.

Myers, G. (1990). *Writing biology: Texts in the social construction of scientific knowledge.* Madison: University of Wisconsin Press.

Myers, M. (1980). *A procedure for writing assessment and holistic scoring.* Urbana, IL: National Council of Teachers of English.

Myhill, D.A. (1999). Writing matters. *English in Education*, 33 (3), 70-81

Nash, J.G., Schumacher, G.M., & Carlson, B.W. (1993). Writing from sources: A structure mapping model. *Journal of Educational Psychology*, 85(1), 159-170.

Nelson J. (1990a). This was an easy assignment: examining how students interpret academic writing tasks. *Research in the Teaching of English*, 24, 362-396.

Nelson, J. (1990b). *Constructing a research paper: A study of students goals and approaches* (Technical Report No. 43). Center for the study of writing, University of California and Pittsburgh, PA: Carnegie Mellon University.

Nelson, J., & Hayes, J. (1988). *How the writing context shapes college students strategies for writing from sources*. (Technical Rep. No. 16). Berkeley, Ca: Center for the Study of Writing. University of California and Pittsburgh, PA: Carnegie Mellon University.

Neuman, S.B., & Celano, D. (2001). Access to print in low-income and middle-income communities: An ecological study of four neighbourhoods. *Reading Research Quarterly, 30*(1), 8-26.

New London Group (1996). A pedagogy of multiliteracies: Designing social futures. *Harvard Educational Review, 57*, 421-444.

Newman, D., Griffin, P., & Cole, M. (1989). *The construction zone: Working for cognitive change in school*. Cambridge: Cambridge University Press.

Nida, E.A. (1992). Sociolinguistic implications of academic writing. *Language in Society, 21*, 477-485.

Nida, E.A.., & Wonderly, W.L. (1971). Communication roles of languages in multilingual societies. In W.H. Whiteley (Ed.), *Language use and social change: Problems in multilingualism with special reference to Eastern Africa* (pp. 57-74). London: Oxford University Press.

Ninio, A., & Snow, C. (1996). *Pragmatic development*. Boulder, CO: Westview.

Northern Examination and Assessment Board (2002). GCSE 2001 Report on the Examination: English. London: AQA, Norwood, NJ: Ablex.

Nutbrown, C. (1994). *Threads of thinking*. London: Paul Chapman

Nystrand, M. (1982). *What writers know: The language, process and structure of written discourse*. New York: Academic Press.

Nystrand, M., Gamoran, A., Kachur, R., & Prendergast, K. (1997). *Opening dialogue: Understanding the dynamics of language and learning in the English classroom*. New York/London: Teachers College Press.

Nystrand, M., Greene, S., & Wiemelt, J. (1993). Where did composition studies come from? An intellectual history. *Written Communication, 10*, 267-333.

O'Brien, D.G., Moje, E.B., & Stewart, R.A. (2001). Exploring the context of secondary literacy: Literacy in people's everyday school lives. In E.B. Moje, & D.C. O'Brien. (Eds.), *Constructions of literacy: Studies of teaching and learning in and out of secondary schools* (pp. 27-48). Mahwah, NJ: Lawrence Erlbaum Associates.

O'Donnell, A.M. (1999). Structuring dyadic interaction through scripted cooperation. In A.M. O'Donnell, & A. King (Eds.), *Cognitive perspectives on peer learning* (pp. 179-196). Mahwah, NJ: Lawrence Erlbaum Associates.

Ochs, E. (1988). *Culture and language development*. Cambridge: Cambridge University Press.

Ongstad, S. (1996). Literacies and Mother Tongue Education. The challenge of task ideologies in a semiotic-didactic perspective. In F. Christie, & J. Foley (Eds.), *Some contemporary themes in literacy research* (pp. 266-296). New York and Berlin: Waxmann.

Ongstad, S. (1997). *Sjanger, posisjonering og oppgaveideologier. Et teoretisk-empirisk bidrag til et tverrfaglig, semiotisk og didaktisk sjangerbegrep* [Genre, positioning, and task ideologies. A theoretical-empirical contribution to an interdisciplinary, semiotic and didactic genre concept]. Unpublished doctoral dissertation. NTNU, Trondheim.

Ongstad, S. (1999a). Self-positioning(s) and students' task reflexivity – a semiotic macro concept exemplified. *Journal of Structural Learning & Intelligent Systems, 14*(2), 125-152.

Ongstad, S. (1999b). Vad är positioneringsanalys? "Självpositionering' i en (post)modern skola som exempel [What is positioning analysis? 'Self positioning' in a (post)modern school as example]. In C. A. Olofsson, & L. Östman (Eds.), *Textanalys. En introduktion til syftesrelaterade analyser* [Text analysis. An introduction to purpose related analyses]. Lund: Studentlitteratur.

Ongstad, S. (2001, September). *Positioning aesthetics: Epistemology and ethics in didaktik of subjects*. Paper at ECER, Lille, France, 5 - 8 September.

Ongstad, S. (2002a). Positioning early research on writing in Norway. *Written Communication, 19*(3), 345-381.

Ongstad, S. (2002b). Genres - from static, closed, extrinsic, verbal dyads to dynamic, open, intrinsic, semiotic triads. In R. Coe, L. Lingard, & T. Teslenko (Eds.), *The Rhetoric and ideology of genre: Strategies for stability and change* (pp. 297-320). Cresskill, NJ: Hampton Press.

Ongstad, S. (2004). *Språk, kommunikasjon og didaktikk*. [Language, communication and didaktik]. Bergen: Fagbokforlaget and Landslaget for norskundervisning.

Ongstad, S. (forthcoming a). Bakhtin's triadic epistemology and ideologies of dialogism. In F. Bostad, C. Brandist, L.S. Evensen, & S. Faber (Eds.), *Bakhtinian perspectives on language and culture: Meaning in language, art and new media*. London: Palgrave Macmillan.

Ongstad, S. (forthcoming b). *Facing the blindness of language focusing: 'Habermasian' and 'Halliday-ian' framing of validation*. In C. Ilie (Ed.), Proceedings from ASLA's conference in Örebro 2003. Örebro University.

Paltridge, B. (1997). *Genre, frames and writing in research settings*. Amsterdam: Johns Benjamins.

Pappas, C.C., & Zecker, L.B. (Eds.) (2001). *Transforming literacy curriculum genres: Working with teacher researchers in urban classrooms*. Mahwah, NJ: Lawrence Erlbaum Associates.

Pasch, H. (1997). The choice of linguae francae in triglossic environments in Africa. In M. Putz (Ed.), *Language choices: Conditions, constraints, and consequences* (pp. 45-54). Amsterdam: John Benjamins.

Paulus, T.M. (1999). The effect of peer and teacher feedback on student writing. *Journal of Second Writing, 8*(3), 265-89.

Peckham, I. (1978). Peer evaluation. *English Journal, 67*, 61-63.

Peirce, C.S. (1940/65). *Collected Papers*. Cambridge, Mass.: Belknep Press.

Perera, K. (1984). *Children's writing and reading: Analysing classroom language*. Oxford and New York: Blackwell.

Pérez, B., McCarty, T.L., Watahomigie, L.J., Dien, T.t., Chang, J-M., Smith, H.L., de Silva, A.D. (1998). *Sociocultural contexts of language and literacy*. Mahwah, NJ: Lawrence Erlbaum Associates.

Perreault, H., & Moses, D. (1992). A comparison of face-to-face and group ware meeting approaches on a collaborative writing project. *Delta Pi Epsilon Journal, 34*, 151-166.

Perret-Clermont, A-N. (1979). *La construction de l'intelligence dans l'interaction sociale*. Bern: Lang.

Person, N.K., & Graesser, A. G. (1999). Evolution of discourse during cross-age tutoring. In A.M. O'Donnell, & A. King (Ed.), *Cognitive perspectives on peer learning* (pp. 69-86). Mahwah, NJ: Erlbaum.

Peterson, S. (2003). Peer response and students' revisions of their narrative writing. *L1- Educational Studies in Language and Literature, 3*(3), 239-272.

Postmes, T., Spears, R., & Lea, M. (2000). The formation of group norms in computer-mediated communication. *Human Communication Research, 26*, 341-371.

Pratt, C., & Grieve, R. (1984). The development of metalinguistic awareness: An introduction. In W.E. Tunmer, C. Pratt, & M.L. Herriman (Eds.), *Metalinguistic awareness in children: Theory, research and implications* (pp. 2-11). New York: Springer-Verlag.

Pratt, M.L. (1986a). Ideology and speech-act theory. *Poetics Today, 7*, 59-72.

Pratt, M.L. (1986b). Fieldwork in common places. In J. Clifford (Ed.), *Writing culture* (pp. 27-50). Berkeley: University of California Press..

Pratt, M.L. (1990). The arts of the contact zone. In D. Bartholomae, & A. Petrosky (Eds.), *Ways of reading* (pp. 527-543). Boston: Bedford Books.

Prince, G. (1973). *A grammar for stories*. The Hague: Mouton.

Prior, P. (1991). Contextualizing writing and response in a graduate seminar. *Written Communication, 8*, 267-310.

Prior, P. (1995a). Tracing authoritative and internally persuasive discourses: A case study of response, revision and disciplinary enculturation. *Research in the Teaching of English, 29*, 288-325.

Prior, P. (1995b). Redefining the task: An ethnographic examination of writing and response in graduate seminars. In D. Belcher, & G. Braine (Eds.), *Academic writing in a second language: Essays on research and pedagogy* (pp. 47-82). Norwood, NJ: Ablex.

Prior, P. (1998). *Writing Disciplinarity: A sociohistoric account of literate activity in the academy*. Mahwah, New Jersey: Lawrence Erlbaum Associates.

Publication Manual of the American Psychological Association (1995), Fourth Edition. Washington, DC: American Psychological association.

Purcell-Gates, V. (1996). Stories, coupons, and TV Guide: Relationships between home literacy experiences and emergent literacy knowledge. *Reading Research Quarterly, 31*(4), 406-428.

Purcell-Gates, V., & Dahl, K. (1991). Low-SES children's success and failure at early literacy learning in skill-based classrooms. *Journal of Reading Behavior, 23*, 1-34.

Purcell Gates, V., Degener, S.C., Jacobson, E., & Soler, M. (2002). Impact of authentic adult literacy instruction on adult literacy practices. *Reading Research Quarterly, 37*, 70-92.

Purves, A.C. (Ed.) (1988). *Writing across languages and cultures*. Newbury Park: Sage.

Putz, J. (1970). When the teacher stops teaching--an experiment with freshman English. *College English, 32*, 50-57.

Qualifications and Curriculum Authority (1999). *Improving Writing at Key Stages 3 and 4*. London: QCA.

Qualifications and Curriculum Authority (2002) *Standards at Key Stage 2: English, Maths and Science*. London: QCA.

Rafoth, B.A. (1988). Discourse community: Where writers, readers, and texts come together. In B.A. Rafoth, & D.L. Rubin (Eds.), *The social construction of written communication* (pp. 131-146). Norwood, NJ: Ablex.

Ramanathan, V. (2002). *The politics of TESOL education: Writing, knowledge, critical pedagogy*. New York and London: RoutledgeFalmer.

Ramanathan, V., & Atkinson, D. (2000). Ethnographic approaches and methods in L2 writing research: A critical guide and review. *Applied Linguistics, 20*(1), 44-70.

Ramanathan, V., & Kaplan, R.B. (2000). Genres, authors, discourse communties: Theory and application for (L1 and) L2 writing instructors. *Journal of Second Language Writing, 9*(2), 171-191.

Randolph, G.F. (1997). *"Fused horizons": Collaboration and co-authored texts. A case study of a freshman writing group*. Dissertation Abstracts, 58-02A, 404.

Raphael, T.E. (Ed.) (1984). *The contexts of school-based literacy*. New York: Random House.

Raphael, T.E., & Boyd, F.B. (1991). *Synthesizing information from multiple sources: A descriptive study of elementary students' perceptions and performance of discourse synthesis*. East Lansing, MI: The Center for the Learning and Teaching of Elementary Subjects: Institute for Research on Teaching, Michigan State University.

Raudenbush, S.W., Rowan, B., Cheong, Y.F. (1993). Higher order instructional goals in secondary schools: Class, teacher, and school influences. *American Educational Research Journal, 30*(3), 523-553.

Reddy, M. (1979). The conduit metaphor. In A. Ortony (Ed.), *Metaphor and thought* (pp. 284-324). Cambridge: Cambridge University Press.

Rego, L.L.B. (1985). Descobrindo a língua escrita antes de aprender a ler: Algumas implicações pedagógicas. *Revista Brasileira de Estudos Pedagógicos*, 66(152), 5-27.

Rego, L.L.B. (1986). A escrita de histórias por crianças: As implicações pedagógicas do uso de um registro lingüístico. *Revista de Documentação de Estudos em Linguística Teórica e Aplicada*, 2(2), 165-180.

Rego, L.L.B. (1995). *Literatura infantil: Uma nova perspectiva da alfabetização na pré-escola*. São Paulo: FTD.

Rego, L.L.B. (1996). Um estudo exploratório dos critérios utilizados pelas crianças para definir histórias. In M.G.B.B. Dias, & A.G. Spinillo (Eds.), *Tópicos em psicologia cognitiva* (pp. 120-140). Recife: Editora Universitária da UFPE.

Reid, I. (Ed.) (1987). *The place of genre in learning*. Deakin, Australia: Deakin University Press.

Resnick, L.B. (1990). Literacy in school and out. *Daedalus, 119*, 169-185.

Resnick, L.B., Pontecorvo, C. & Säljo, R. (1997) (Eds.). *Discourse, tools, and reasoning: Essays on situated cognition*. Berlin: Springer.

Ricoeur, P. (1981). *Hermeneutics and the human sciences*. Cambridge: Cambridge University Press.

Rijlaarsdam, G., Couzijn, M., & Van den Bergh, H. (2004). The study of revision as a writing process and as a learning-to-write process: Two prospective research agendas. In G. Rijlaarsdam (Series Ed.), & L. Allal, L. Chanquoy, & P. Largy (Vol. Eds.), *Revision: Cognitive and instructional processes* (pp. 189-207). Dordrecht: Kluwer Academic Press.

Ringelmann, M. (1913). Research on animate sources of power: The work of man. *Annales de l'Institut National Agronomique*, 2e serie, XII, 1-40.

Rogoff, B. (1990). *Apprenticeship in thinking: Cognitive development in social context*. New York: Oxford University Press.

Rohmann, G. (1965). Pre-writing: The stage of discovery in the writing process. *College Composition and Communication, 46*, 106-112.

Romano, T. (2000). *Blending genre, altering style*. Portsmouth, NH: Boynton/Cook-Heinemann.

Rommetveit, R. (1974). *On message structure*. London/New York: Wiley.

Rommetveit, R. (1992). Outlines of a dialogically based social-cognitive approach to human cognition and communication. In A.H. Wold (Ed.), *The dialogical alternative: Towards a theory of language and mind* (pp. 19-44). Oslo: Scandinavian University Press.

Rose, M. (1989). *Lives on the boundaries*. New York: Simon and Schuster.

Rouiller, Y. (2004). Collaborative revision and metacognitive refection in a situation of narrative text production. In G. Rijlaarsdam (Series Ed.), & L. Allal, L. Chanquoy, & P. Largy (Eds.), *Revision: Cognitive and instructional processes* (pp. 171-187). Dordrecht: Kluwer Academic Press.

Royster, J. (2002). Academic discourses or small boats on a big sea. In C. Schroeder, H. Fox, & P. Bizzell (Eds), *Alt dis: Alternative discourses and the academy* (pp. 23-30). Portsmouth: Boynton/Cook-Heinemann.

Ruben, B.D., & Budd, R.W. (1975). *Human communication handbook.* Rochelle Park, NJ: Hayden.

Russell, D.R. (1995). Activity theory and its implications for writing instruction. In J. Petraglia (Ed.), *Reconceiving writing, rethinking writing instruction* (pp. 51-78). Mahwah, NJ: Lawrence Erlbaum Associates.

Russell, D.R. (2002). The kind-ness of genre: An activity theory analysis of high school teachers' perception of genre in portfolio assessment across the curriculum. In R. Coe, L. Lingard, & T. Teslenko (Eds.), *The rhetoric and ideology of genre: Strategies for stability and change* (pp. 225-242). Cresskill, NJ: Hampton Press.

Salomon, G., & Perkins, D.N. (1998). Individual and social aspects of learning. *Review of Research in Education, 23*, 1-24.

Salomon, G., Perkins, D.N., & Globerson, T. (1991). Partners in cognition: Extending human intelligence with intelligent technologies. *Educational Researcher, 20*, 2-9.

Santa Barbara Classroom Discourse Group (1992). Constructing literacy in classrooms: Literate action as social accomplishment. In H. Marshall (Ed.), *Redefining student learning: Roots of educational change* (pp. 119-150). Norwood, NJ: Ablex.

Santa Barbara Classroom Discourse Group (1995). Constructing an integrated inquiry-oriented approach in classrooms: A cross case analysis of social, literate and academic practices. *Journal of Classroom Interaction, 30*(2), 1-15.

Sarig, G. (1991a). *Learning – promoting strategies in composing a discourse synthesis.* Paper presented at the College Composition and Communication Convention, Boston, MA.

Sarig, G. (1991b). Children's intuitive discourse synthesis skills. *Hachinuch Husvivo, 1992). 11, 101-131* (in Hebrew).

Sarig, G., & Folman, S. (1993). *Testing academic literacy: An integrative approach.* Hachinuch Husvivo, *15*, 125-145 (in Hebrew).

Saunders, W.M. (1989). Collaborative writing tasks and peer interaction. *International Journal of Educational Research,, 13*, 101-112.

Schegloff, E. (1984). On some question and ambiguities in conversation. In J. Atkinson, & J. Heritage (Eds.), *Structures of social action: Studies in conversation analysis* (pp. 28-52). Cambridge: Cambridge University Press.

Schieffelin, E.A., & Ochs, E. (Eds.) (1986). *Language socialization across cultures.* Cambridge: Cambridge University Press.

Schiffrin, D. (1987). *Discourse markers.* Cambridge: Cambridge University Press.

Schiffrin, D. (1994). *Approaches to discourse.* Oxford: Blackwell.

Schilb, J. (1990). The ideology of "epistomological ecumenicalism": A response to Carol Berkenkotter. *Journal of Advanced Composition*, 153-155.

Schroder, C. (2001). *Reinventing the university: Literacies and legitimacy in the postmodern academy.* Logan: Utah State University Press.

Schwegler, R., & Shamoon, L. (1982). The aims and process of the research paper. *College English, 44*, 817-824.

Scollon, R., & Scollon, S.B.K. (1981). The literate two-year-old: The fictionalization of self. In R. Scollon, & S.B.K. Scollon (Eds.), *Narrative, literacy, and face in interethnic communication* (pp. 57-98). Norwood, NJ: Ablex

Scribner, S., & Cole, M. (1981). *The psychology of literacy.* Cambridge, MA.: Harvard University Press.

Sénéchal, M., LeFreve, J-A., Thomas, E.M., & Daley, K.E. (1998). Differential effects of home literacy experiences on the development of oral and written language. *Reading Research Quarterly, 33*(1), 96-116.

Shapiro, R.L., & Hudson, J.A. (1997). Coherence and cohesion in children's stories. In J. Costermans, & M. Fayol (Eds.), *Processing interclausal relationships: Studies in the production and comprehension of text* (pp. 23-48). Mahwah, NJ: Lawrence Erlbaum Associates.

Sharples, M. (1999). *How we write: Writing as creative design.* London: Routledge.

Shaughnessy, M. (1977). *Errors and expectations.* New York: Oxford University Press.

Shine, S., & Roser, N.L. (1999). The role of genre in preschoolers' response to picture books. *Research in the Teaching of English, 34,* 197- 251.

Sinclair, J., & Coulthard, R. (1975). *Towards an analysis of discourse: The English used by teachers and pupils.* London: Oxford University Press.

Slavin, R.E. (1983). When does cooperative learning increase student achievement? *Psychological Bulletin, 94,* 429-45.

Smagorinsky, P. (Ed.) (1994). *Speaking about writing. Reflections of research methodology.* London and Thousand Oaks, CA: Sage.

Smidt, S. (2001). "All stories that have happy endings have a bad character": A young child's response to televisual texts. *English in Education, 35*(2), 25-33.

Sommers, N. (1982). Responding to student writing. *College Composition and Communication, 33,* 148-156.

Sommers, N. (2002). Personal interview.

Sormunen, C., & Ray, C.M. (1996). Teaching collaborative writing with group support systems software – an experiment. *Delta Pi Epsilon Journal, 38,* 125-138.

Spear, K. (1988). *Sharing writing.* Portsmouth, NH: Boynton/Cook.

Sperling, M. (1994). Discourse analysis of teacher-student writing conferences: Finding the message in the medium. In P. Smagorinsky (Ed.), *Speaking about writing: Reflections on research methodology* (pp. 205-224). Thousand Oaks: Sage

Spinillo, A.G., & Oliveira, P. (1999). *The use of connectives by children when producing narrative and argumentative texts.* (p. 126). Proceedings of the IXth European Conference on Developmental Psychology. Island of Spetses, Greece.

Spinillo, A.G., & Pinto, G. (1994). Children's narratives under different conditions: A comparative study. *British Journal of Developmental Psychology, 12,* 177-193.

Spinillo, A.G. (2001). A produção de histórias por crianças: A textualidade em foco. In J. Correa, A.G. Spinillo, & S. Leitão (Eds.), *Desenvolvimento da linguagem: Escrita e textualidade* (pp. 73-116). Rio de Janeiro: Nau Editora.

Spinillo, A.G., Albuquerque, E.G.C. de, & Lins e Silva, M.E. (1996). "Para que serve ler e escrever?" O depoimento de alunos e professores. *Revista Brasileira de Estudos Pedagógicos, 77*(184), 477-496.

Spivey, N.N. (1984). *Discourse Synthesis: Constructing texts in reading and writing.* Newark, DE: International Reading Association.

Spivey, N.N. (1988). *Comprehending and composing: The synthesis of comparative text.* Unpublished manuscript. Carnegie – Mellon University.

Spivey, N.N. (1990). Transforming texts: Constructive processes in writing. *Written Communication, 7,* 256-287.

Spivey, N.N. (1997). *The constructivist metaphor.* New York: Academic Press.

Spivey, N.N., & King, J.R. (1989). Readers as writers composing from sources. *Reading Research Quarterly, 24,* 7-26.

Stahl, S., Hynd, C.A., Britton, B.K., Mcnish, M.M., & Bosquet, D. (1996). What happens when students read multiple source documents in history? *Reading Research Quarterly, 31*(4), 430-457.

Starobinski, J. (1970). *La relation critique.* Paris: Gallimard.

Stedman, L.C. (1996). An assessment of literacy trends, past and present. *Research in the Teaching of English, 30*(3), 283-302.

Stein, N.L. (1982). What's in a story: Interpreting the interpretations of story grammar. *Discourse Processes, 5,* 319-335.

Stein, N.L. (1988). The development of children's storytelling skill. In M. Franklin, & S. Barten (Eds.), *Child language: A book of readings* (pp.282-297). Oxford: Oxford University Press.

Stein, V. (1989). *Elaborations: Using what you know.* (Reading-to-write Report No. 6, Technical Report No. 25). Berkeley, CA: Center for the Study of Writing, University of California and Pittsburgh, PA: Carnegie – Mellon University.

Stets, J.E., & Burke, P.J. (2000). Identity theory and social identity theory. *Social Psychology Quarterly, 63,* 224-237.

Stotsky, S. (1991). On developing independent critical thinking. *Written Communication, 8,* 193-212.

Street, B. (1995). *Social literacies: Critical approaches to literacy in development, ethnography, and education.* New York: Longman.

Swales, J. (1990). *Genre analysis: English in academic and research settings.* Cambridge: Cambridge University Press.

Tan Bee, Tin (2000). Multi-dimensionality of idea framing in group work in academic settings. *Language and Education, 14*(4), 223-249.

Tan Bee, Tin (2003). Creativity, diversity and originality of ideas in divergent group discussion tasks: The role of repetition and addition in discovering 'new significant', or 'original' ideas and knowledge. *Language and Education, 17*(4), 241-265.

Tannen, D. (Ed.) (1982). *Spoken and written language: Exploring orality and literacy.* Norwood, NJ: Ablex.

Tannen, D. (1993). What's in a frame? Surface evidence for underlying expectations. In D. Tannen (Ed.), *Framing in discourse* (pp. 14-56). Oxford: Oxford University Press.

Taylor, D., & Dorsey-Gaines, C. (1988). *Growing up literate: Learning from inner city families.* Portsmouth, NH: Heinemann.

Teale, W.H. (1986). Home background and young children's literacy development. In W.H. Teale, & E. Sulzby (Eds.), *Emergent literacy* (pp.173-206). Norwood, NJ: Ablex.

Teale, W.H., & Sulzby, E. (1989). Emergent literacy: New perspectives. In D. Strickland, & L.M. Morrow (Eds.), *Emerging literacy: Young children learn to read and write* (pp. 1-15). Newark, DE.: International Reading Association.

Teberosky, A. (1990). Reescribiendo noticias: Una aproximacion a los textos de niños y adultos. *Anuário de Psicologia, 47*, 43-63.

Teberosky, A. (1992). Reescribiendo textos: produccion de adultas poco escolarizadas. *Infancia y Aprendizage, 58*, 107-124.

Tebo-Messina, M. (1993). Collaborative learning: how well does it work? *Writing on the Edge, 4*, 63-79.

Thaiss, C., & Zawacki T.M. (2001). Questioning alternative discourses: Reports from across the disciplines. In C. Schroeder, H. Fox, & P. Bizzell (Eds), *Alt dis: Alternative discourses and the academy* (pp. 80-96). Portsmouth: Boynton/Cook-Heinemann.

Tharp, R., & Gallimore, R. (1988). *Rousing minds to life: Teaching, learning, and schooling in social context.* Cambridge: Cambridge University Press.

Thatcher, B.L. (2000). L2 professional writing in a US and South American context. *Journal of Second Language Writing, 9*(1), 41-69.

Tracy, K. (1998). Analyzing context: Framing the discussion. *Research on Language and Social Interaction, 31*(1), 1-28.

Trimbur, J. (1985). Collaborative learning and teaching writing. In B.W. McClelland, & T.R. Donovan (Eds.), *Perspective on research and scholarship in composition* (pp. 87-109). New York: Modern Language Association.

Triplett, N. (1898). The dynamogenic factors in pace making and competition. *American Journal of Psychology, 9*, 507-533.

Trosborg, A. (Ed.) (2000). *Analyzing professional genres.* Amsterdam: John Benjamins.

Tuckman, B. (1965). Developmental sequences in small groups. *Psychological Bulletin, 63*, 384-399.

Tuckman, B.W., & Jensen, M.A.C. (1977). Stages of small group development revisited. *Group and Organizational Studies, 2*, 419-427.

U.S. Department of Education, National Center for Educational Statistics (1991). The Condition of Education, 1991, vol. I. Elementary and Secondary Education. Washington, DC: Author.

Valsinger, J. (1988). Epilogue: Ontogeny of co-construction of culture within socially organized environment settings. In J. Valsinger (Ed.), *Child development within culturally structured environments* (vol. 2) (pp. 283-298). Norwood, NJ: Ablex.

van de Kopple, W. (1985). Some exploratory discourse on metadiscourse. *College Composition and Communication, 36*, 82-93.

van Dijk, T.A. (1972). *Some aspects of text grammars.* The Hague: Mouton.

van Dijk, T.A. (1977). *Text and context: Explorations in the semantics and pragmatics of discourse.* London: Longman.

van Dijk, T.A. (1980). *Macrostructures: An interdisciplinary study of global structures in discourse, interaction, and cognition.* Hillsdale, NJ: Lawrence Erlbaum Associates.

van Dijk, T.A. (1981). *Studies in the pragmatics of discourse,* The Netherlands: Mouton.

van Dijk, T.A. (1992). *La ciencia del texto: Un enfoque interdisciplinario.* Barcelona: Ediciones Paidós.

van Dijk, T.A. (1995). *Estructuras y funciones del discurso.* México: Siglo Veintiuno Editores.

van Dijk, T.A. (1997). The study of discourse. In T.A. van Dijk (Ed.), *Discourse as structure and process* (pp. 1-34). London: Sage Publications.

Vasconcellos, M. (1993). *Le système éducatif.* Paris: Editions La Découverte.

Veel, R. (1997). Learning how to mean – scientifically speaking: Apprenticeship into scientific discourse in the secondary school. In F. Christie, & J.R. Martin (Eds.), *Genre and institutions. Social processes in the workplace and school* (pp. 161-195). London & Washington: Cassell.

Voigt, J. (1994). Negotiation of mathematical meaning and learning mathematics. *Educational Studies in Mathematics, 26*, 275-298.

Vygotsky, L.S. (1962). *Thought and language*. Cambridge, MA: MIT Press.

Vygotsky, L.S. (1978). *Mind in society* (M. Cole, V. John-Steiner, S. Scribner, & E. Souberman, Eds.). Cambridge, MA: Harvard University Press.

Vygotsky, L.S. (1987). *Thought and language* (Kozulin, A., Ed.). Cambridge: Cambridge University Press.

Wagner, E. (1975). How to avoid grading compositions. *English Journal, 64*, 2-8.

Walker, C.P., & Elias, D. (1987). Writing conference talk: Factors associated with high- and low-rated writing conferences. *Research in the English of Teaching, 21*(3), 266-215.

Wall, S.V., & Hull, G.A. (1989). The semantics of error: What do teachers' know? In C.M. Anson (Ed.), *Writing and response: Theory, practice, and research* (pp. 261-269). Urbana, IL: National Council of Teachers of English.

Wang, L. (2003). Switching to first language among writers with differing second-language proficiency. *Journal of Second Language Writing, 12*, 347-375.

Webb, N. (1989). Peer interaction and learning in small groups. *International Journal of Educational Research, 13*, 21-39.

Weisser, C. (2002). *Moving beyond academic discourse: Composition studies and the public sphere.* Carbondale: Southern Illinois University Press.

Wellman, B. (1997). An electronic group is virtually a social network. In S. Kiesler (Ed.), *Culture of the internet* (pp. 179-205). Hillsdale, NJ: Lawrence Erlbaum Associates.

Wells, G. (1985). Preschool literacy-related activities and success in school. In D.R. Olson, N. Torrance, & A. Hildyard (Eds.), *Literacy, language and learning: The nature and consequences of reading and writing* (pp. 229-255). Cambridge: Cambridge University Press.

Wells, G. (1986). *The meaning makers: Children learning language and using language to learn.* London: Hodder and Stoughton.

Wells, G. (1999). *Dialogic inquiry: Towards a sociocultural practice and theory of education.* New York: Cambridge University Press.

Wells, G., & Chang-Wells, G. (1992). *Constructing knowledge together: Classrooms as centers of inquiry and literacy.* Portsmouth, NH: Heinemann.

Wenger, E. (1998). *Communities of practice: Learning, meaning, and identity.* Cambridge: Cambridge University Press.

Wertsch, J. (1985). *Vygotsky and the social formation of mind.* Cambridge: Cambridge University Press.

Wertsch, J. (1991). *Voices of the mind.* Cambridge, Mass.: Harvard University Press.

Wertsch, J. (1998). *Mind as action.* New York/Oxford: Oxford University Press.

White, E.M. (1986). *Teaching and assessing writing.* San Francisco: Jossey-Bass Publishers.

Winograd, P. (1984). Strategic difficulties in summarizing texts. *Reading Research Quarterly, 19*(4): 404-25.

Winter, J.K., & Neal, J.C. (1995). Group writing: student perceptions of the dynamics and efficiency of groups. *Business Communication Quarterly, 58*, 21-24.

Witte, S.P. (1983). Topical structure and writing quality: Some possible text-based explanations of readers' judgments of student writing. *Visible Language, XVII* (2), 177-205.

Witte, S.P. (1985). Revising, composing theory, and research design. In S.W. Freedman (Ed), *The acquisition of written language: Response and revision* (pp. 250-284). Norwood, NJ: Ablex.

Wolfe, J. (2002). Marginal pedagogy: How annotated texts affect a writing from sources task. *Written Communication 19*(2), 297-333.

Wolff, D. (2000). Second language writing: A few remarks on psycholinguistic and instructional issues. *Learning and Instruction, 10*, 107-112.

Wood, D., Bruner, J. & Ross, G. (1976). The role of tutoring in problem solving. *Journal of Child Psychology and Psychiatry, 17*, 89-100.

Woodall, B.R. (2002). Language-switching: Using the first language while writing in a second language. *Journal of Second Language Writing, 11*, 7-28.

Wray, D., & Lewis, M. (1997). *Extending Literacy.* London: Routledge

Wyatt-Smith, C., & Murphy, J. (2001). What English counts as Writing Assessment? *English in Education, 35*(1), 12-31.

Yackel, E., & Cobb, P. (1996). Sociomathematical norms, argumentation, and autonomy in mathematics. *Journal for Research in Mathematics Education, 27*, 458-477.

Yates, J., & Orlikowski, W.J. (1992). Genres of organizational communication: A structurational approach to studying communication and media. *Academy of Management Review, 17*(2), 299-326.

Yates, J., & Orlikowski, W.J. (2002). Genre systems: Chronos and kairos in communicative interaction. In R. Coe, L. Lingard, & T. Teslenko (Eds.), *The rhetoric and ideology of genre: Strategies for stability and change* (pp. 103-121). Cresskill, NJ: Hampton Press.

Young, K.M., & Leinhardt, G. (1998). Writing from primary documents: A way of knowing in history. *Written Communication, 15*(1), 25-68.

Young, R., & He, A.W. (Eds.) (1998). *Talking and testing: Discourse approaches to the assessment of oral proficiency*. Amsterdam: Benajamins.

Zamel, V. (1985). Responding to student writing. *TESOL Quarterly, 19*, 79-102.

Zamel, V. (1987). Recent research on writing pedagogy. *TESOL Quarterly, 21*, 697-715.

Zammuner, V.L. (1995). Individual and cooperative computer-writing and revising: Who gets the best results? *Learning and Instruction, 5*, 101-124.

Zebroski, J. (1994). *Thinking through theory: Vygotskian perspectives on the teaching of writing*. Portsmouth, NH, Boynton/Cook-Heinemann.

Zecker, L.B. (1996). Early development in written language: Children's emergent knowledge of genre-specific characteristics. *Reading and Writing, 8*, 5-25.

Zimmerman, R. (2000). L2 writing: Sub-processes, a model of formulating and empirical findings. *Learning and Instruction, 10*, 73-99.

AUTHOR INDEX

Abadiano H., 14
Ackerman J., 170
Ackerman J.M., 166
Adler-Kassner L., 16, 22, 26, 231, 234
Alamargot D., 73, 188, 193
Allal L., 16, 22, 23, 25, 70, 72, 73, 76, 80, 90, 96
Anderson D.D., 5
Anderson L.M., 70
Angelova M., 190
Anson C.M., 21
Appel G., 19, 96
Applebee A.N., 14, 177
Asanavage K., 20
Ashton J., 7
Ashwell T., 20, 21
Askew M., 69
Atkinson D., 9
Au K.H., 96, 149

Bailey F.M., 21
Baker D., 81
Baker M., 81
Bakhtin M.M., 1, 3, 4, 49, 53, 54, 55, 58, 66, 137, 138, 141, 142
Bales R. F., 213, 216, 217, 227
Ball A., 123
Barnes D., 69
Bartholomae D., 138, 140, 145, 146, 151, 230, 231
Bartlett F.C., 119
Barton D., 2, 3, 6, 7, 94, 138, 234, 235
Barton E.L., 138, 172
Basso K., 11, 94
Bauman R., 12
Bauman Z., 56
Bautier E., 138, 139, 145, 157
Bawarshi A., 187
Bazerman C., 2, 3, 4, 6, 17, 187
Beard J.D., 211
Beaufort A., 2, 16, 187, 188
Beaven M.H., 208, 209

Begoray D.L., 208, 209
Behrens L., 230
Belanger K., 209, 210
Belcher D., 3, 101, 190, 191
Bentz J., 69
Bereiter C., 17, 89, 166, 196
Berkenkotter C., 2, 6, 17, 138
Berlin J., 230
Berman R.A., 35
Bernstein B., 138
Berry R., 70
Besnier N., 5
Bétrix Köhler D., 90
Bhatia V. K., 17
Biber D., 15, 25
Birenbaum M., 172
Bishop W., 234
Bizzell P., 138, 140, 145, 172, 231, 232, 233, 234
Bliss J., 69
Bloom D., 2, 16, 21, 95, 142
Boissevain J., 187
Boissinot A., 140
Bordum A., 56
Bosher S., 193
Bosley D. S., 208, 209, 210
Bourdieu P., 58
Bouton C., 208, 209
Bouton K., 208, 209
Bovino T.D., 31
Boyd F.B., 177
Bracewell R.J., 166
Brehony K., 203
Bremer K., 15
Brewer C., 34
Brice-Heath. S., 138
Brown A.L., 70
Brown G., 5, 102, 119
Bruffee K.A., 208, 209
Bucha E.R., 208, 209
Bucheton D., 157
Budd R.W., 211, 212

Bühler K., 49, 53, 56, 58, 66
Burke P.J., 188

Cain K., 31
Cairney T., 7
Campione J. C., 70
Campos T.N., 33
Camps D., 190
Canale M., 12
Candlin C., 5, 18
Carlo G., 33
Carlson B.W., 171
Carraher T.N., 28, 29, 30, 43, 48
Carrell P.L., 11, 119
Casanave C., 15, 187
Casey M., 208
Cazden C. B., 69, 94
Celano D., 28, 30
Chafe W., 4
Chang-Wells G., 21
Chanquoy L., 73, 90, 188, 193
Charalambopoulos A., 100
Charney D., 138
Chatzisavidis S., 100
Chenoweth C., 186
Cheong Y.F., 177
Chiseri-Strater E., 234
Christie F., 2, 17
Clyne M., 18
Cobb P., 71, 72
Coirier P., 14
Cole M., 18, 28, 69
Collins J.L., 14, 17, 70
Connor U.M., 15, 16, 20, 22, 23, 24, 128,
    138, 140, 142, 193
Conrad S.M., 21
Cook-Gumperz J., 122
Cooper A., 230
Cooper C., 215
Cooper M., 3
Cope B., 2, 17, 121
Coulthard R., 94
Coupland N., 189
Couzijn M., 89
Cox B.E., 14
Crabbe D., 21, 94
Craidy C.M., 33
Cross G.A., 87, 169, 208, 209, 235
Crowhurst M., 14
Crowley S., 231
Culler J., 139, 145

Cunningham J.W., 28
Curtin E.H., 165, 166, 176
Czerniewska P., 119, 135

Dahl K., 28
Daiute C., 70, 72, 89
Daley K.E., 28
Dalton B., 70, 72, 89
De Fina A., 102
de la Luna L., 20
DeBaryshe B., 28
Dédéyan A., 90
Deem R., 203
Degenne A., 188
Del Prette A., 33
Del Prette Z.A.P., 33
Derewianka B., 118, 119, 120
Deutsch M., 209
Dewey J., 220
Dias P., 2, 18, 19
Dickinson D.K., 2
DiPardo A., 207, 208
Doise W., 72
Donahue C., 16, 22, 23, 24, 143, 146
Donato R., 96
Dorr-Bremme D.W., 102
Drew P., 6, 10
Dunsmore K., 70
Duranti A., 5, 6, 9, 10, 54
Durst R., 245
Duszack A., 14
Dyson A.H., 20

Eckert P., 187
Eco U., 145
Ede L.S., 208, 209
Edwards A.D., 94, 119
Edwards D., 94
Egan-Robertson A., 95
Eisterhold J.C., 11, 119
Elbow P., 208, 209
Elias D., 21, 96
EMU statistics, 233
Englert C.S., 7, 70, 72
Erickson F., 54, 102
Evans L., 58

Faigley L., 2, 18, 53, 96, 208, 209
Fairclough N., 18, 140
Farrell L., 14

Ferreira R.M.F., 33
Ferreiro E., 28
Ferris D., 20, 21, 95
Ferris D.R., 20, 21, 95
Finlayson R., 190
Fitzgerald J., 28
Floriani A., 21
Flower L.S., 73, 119, 166, 177, 193
Folman S., 16, 22, 23, 24, 142, 166, 172, 180
Foppa K., 98
Forman E.A., 18
Forse M., 188
Foucault M., 83, 118, 142
Fraisse J., 72
François F., 137, 141, 142, 145, 146, 157
Freadman A., 54, 55
Frederiksen C.H., 166
Frederiksen J.E., 166
Freebody P., 16, 101
Freedman S. W., 21, 96, 207, 208
Freire P., 220
Fuchs D., 69
Fuchs L.S., 69

Gallimore R., 19
Garth R., 208, 209
Garton A., 31
Gauvain M., 188, 193
Gebhardt R., 209
Gee J.P., 3, 5, 11, 21, 104, 110, 113, 130, 186, 187
Genette G., 145
George D., 36, 211
Gergits J.M., 209
Gibbons P., 97
Giles H., 190
Gilly M., 72, 81
Giora R., 171
Globerson T., 69
Goffman E., 10, 145
Goldenberg C., 2
Golder C., 14
Goldstein J.R., 212
Goldstein L.M., 21
Gombert J.E., 31
Goodburn A., 209
Goodwin C., 5, 6, 9, 54
Grabe W., 13, 14
Graesser A. G., 69
Graham S., 70

Gravemeijer K., 71
Graves D.H., 70, 209, 210
Graves P.R., 70, 209, 210
Greene S., 165, 166, 170, 171, 172
Greer J., 209, 210
Gregory E., 15, 97, 98
Grieve R., 31
Griffin P., 69
Guidelines for Research Paper Writing., 168, 177
Gumperz J.J., 6, 10, 12, 13, 102
Gutierrez K., 2, 4, 94
Gutierrez K.D., 2

Habermas J., 49, 53, 56, 57, 58, 66
Hall J.K., 97
Halliday M.A.K., 9, 13, 49, 53, 54, 58, 66, 144, 145
Hamilton M., 2, 3, 6, 7, 94, 234, 235
Hamlett C.L., 69
Hammond J., 118
Hamp-Lyons L., 15
Hansen J.G., 208, 209
Hansen K., 18
Harré R., 58
Harrington S., 231
Harrington S.M., 231, 234
Harris J., 143, 145
Hasan R., 9, 13
Haswell R., 246
Hayes J.R., 73, 119, 166, 177, 178, 180, 186, 188, 193
He A.W., 10, 11, 12
Heath S.B., 2, 5, 19, 28, 96
Hedgcock J., 20, 21, 95
Hedge T., 119
Helmreich R.L., 209
Heritage J., 6, 10
Hernandez E., 190
Herndl C.G., 187
Hicks D., 2, 19, 31
Hindman J., 231
Hipple T., 209
Hirvela A., 3, 101, 190, 191
Hogan K., 98
Hogg M.A., 188
Holzman M., 3
Hornsey M.J., 188
Huckin T.N., 2, 6, 17, 138
Hudson J.A., 35
Hulbert C.M., 209

Hull G., 2
Hunt K., 13
Hyland K., 2, 5, 15, 17, 18, 96
Hymes D.H., 9, 10, 15, 20
Hyon S., 17

Ina B., 209
Inghilleri A., 96
Itakura H., 104
Ivanič R., 3, 138, 140, 141, 142, 143,
   145, 157, 187, 190

Jacobson E., 9
Jacoby S., 11
James D., 209
Janssen D., 193
Jauss H.R., 145
Jensen M.A.C., 218
Johns A., 17, 95
Johnson D.W., 34, 69, 209, 211, 212
Johnson N.S., 34
Johnson R.T., 34, 69, 209, 211, 212
Johnson-Laird P.N., 119
Jolliffe D., 235

Kalantzis M., 2, 17, 121
Kamberelis G., 20, 31, 34
Kanz M., 166
Kaplan R.B., 13, 14
Kennedy M.L., 166
Kent T., 15, 17
Kern R., 2
King J.R., 142, 166, 176
Kirsch G., 14
Knobel M., 2, 7
Knudson R.E., 14
Koku E., 188
Koller S.H., 33
Kong A., 4
Korolija N., 107
Kostouli T., 16, 22, 23, 25, 70, 100
Kramer M.G., 193
Kress G., 118, 119, 120, 126, 130, 131,
   135
Kroll B., 3
Kumpulainen K., 81

Labov W., 11, 138
Lacasa P., 15
Lage N., 36

Langer J.A., 14, 31, 135
Lantoff J.P., 19, 96, 97
Largy P., 90
Lave J., 3, 15, 18, 19, 70
Lee C.D., 2, 7, 94
Leinhardt G., 166, 177
Lemke J., 3, 18
Lemon H., 209
Lester J., 230
Levinson J., 56
Lewis C., 12
Lewis M., 119
Linell P., 8, 9, 98, 104, 107
Lins e Silva M.E., 29
Liu J., 208, 209
Loban W., 13
Lu M., 171
Luckman T., 98
Luke A., 16, 101, 119

Mabrito M., 210
MacArthur C.A., 70
Macrorie K., 209, 230
Malone E., 212
Manchon R.M., 186
Mandler J.M., 34
Many J.E., 33, 36, 123, 125, 130, 131,
   142, 216, 222, 224
Markova I., 98
Marshall H.H., 94
Martin J.R., 2, 17, 18, 53, 54, 58, 118,
   119, 127
Martins R.A., 33
Mayes P., 5, 11
Maynard S., 102
McAllister C., 16, 22, 23, 26, 215
McClain K., 71
McCormick K., 178
McCrae S., 69
McGinley W., 165, 166, 178
Melzi G., 19
Mercer N., 21, 69, 94, 119
Meyer B., 11, 171
Meyer L.A., 7, 21
Michaels S., 18, 19, 100
Miller C., 17
Miller T. P., 2, 208, 209
Milroy J., 189
Milroy J.M., 189
Milroy L., 187, 189
Minick N., 18

Mische A., 203
Mitchell J.C., 187
Moffett J., 208, 209
Moje E.B., 5, 19
Moll L.C., 7, 94
Montes-Alcala C., 185
Morgan M., 209, 212
Morgan W., 119, 120, 121, 127, 135
Moses D., 210
Mottier Lopez L., 74, 76, 96
Mugny G., 72
Murphy L., 118, 122
Murray D., 209
Mutanen M., 81
Myers G., 2
Myers M., 215
Myhill D.A., 16, 22, 23, 24, 124

Nahrwold C.A., 187
Nash J.G., 171
Neal J.C., 209, 210
Nelson J., 165, 166, 169, 177, 178, 180
Neuman S.B., 28, 30
New London Group, 6
Newman D., 69, 71, 91
Nicholich M., 135
Nida E.A., 189
Ninio A., 97
Noll C.L., 209, 210
Nordberg B., 8
North S., 31, 138
Nutbrown C., 119
Nystrand M., 3, 21, 53

Oakhill J., 31
Ochs E., 3, 4, 11, 97, 100
Oliveira P., 31
Ongstad S., 16, 22, 23, 25, 50, 51, 53, 55,
    58, 61, 62, 64, 65, 66
Orlikowski W.J., 17

Paltridge B., 17, 139, 142, 144, 145, 147
Pappas C.C., 7
Paradis J., 2
Parré A., 2, 19
Pasch H., 189
Patthoy Chavez G., 2
Paulus T.M., 21, 95
Pearson P.D., 4, 172
Peckham I., 209

Perera K., 14
Pérez B., 96
Perkins D.N., 69, 71
Perreault H., 210
Person N.K., 69
Peterson S., 96
Phillips N.B., 69
Pinto G., 34, 35
Piolat A., 188, 194
Pontecorvo C., 71
Pratt C., 22, 23, 31
Pratt M.L., 137, 141, 142, 143, 158, 231
Pressley M., 98
Prince G., 34
Prior P., 2, 4, 6, 9, 75, 117, 119, 122, 127
Purcell-Gates V., 28, 29, 43, 188
Purves A.C., 169
Putz J., 209

Rafoth B.A., 70
Ramanathan V., 9, 13, 15
Randolph G.F., 208, 209
Raphael T., 7
Raphael T.E., 70, 177
Raudenbush S.W., 177
Ray C.M., 209, 210
Reddy M., 18
Rego L.L.B., 28, 32, 34
Reid I., 58
Resnick L.B., 70, 71
Riazantseva A., 190
Rice E., 171
Ricoeur P., 58, 66
Rijlaarsdam G., 26, 89, 90
Ringelmann M., 209
Rochex J.Y., 145, 157
Roen D.H., 14
Rogoff B., 4, 18, 19, 95
Rohmann G., 230
Romano T., 237
Rommetveit R., 11
Rose M., 138
Rosen L., 230
Roser N.L., 47
Rothery J., 119
Rouiller Y., 72, 73, 89
Rowan B., 177
Royster J., 231, 232, 233, 234, 245
Ruben B.D., 211, 212
Russell D.R., 16, 94

Säljo R., 71
Salomon G., 69, 71
Santa Barbara Classroom Discourse
    Group, 7, 21, 94, 95
Sarig G., 166, 177
Saunders W. M., 70
Scardamalia M., 17, 89, 166, 196
Schegloff E., 99, 107
Schieffelin E.A., 3
Schiffrin D., 6, 10
Schilb J., 138
Schramer J.J., 209
Schultz J., 54, 102
Schultz K., 2
Schumacher G.M., 171
Schwartz S.S., 70
Schwegler R., 177
Scollon R., 3, 28
Scollon S.B.K., 3, 28
Scribner S., 28
Sénéchal M., 28, 29
Shamoon L., 177
Shanahan T., 14
Shapiro R.L., 35
Sharples M., 131
Shaughnessy M., 138
Shine S., 47
Sinclair J., 94
Slabbert S., 190
Slavin R.E., 209
Slobin D.I., 35
Smagorinsky P., 2, 94
Smidt S., 123
Smith P., 190
Snow C., 44, 97
Sommers N., 160
Sormunen C., 209, 210
Spear K., 209, 211, 212
Sperling M., 21, 96
Spiegel D.L., 28
Spinillo A.G., 22, 23, 29, 31, 32, 34, 35,
    36, 37
Spivey N.N., 166, 170, 171, 176, 177
Stahl S., 176
Starobinski J., 145, 157
Stedman L.C., 177
Stein N.L., 34, 166
Stein V., 34, 166
Stephan M., 71
Stets J.E., 188

Stewart R.A., 5
Stone C.A., 18
Stone L.D., 2
Stotsky S., 181
Street B., 27, 39, 41, 42, 43, 44, 45, 47,
    234
Sulzby E., 14, 28
Sunstein B., 234
Swales J., 2, 15, 17, 119, 120, 138, 143,
    186, 187

Tannen D., 4, 5, 119
Taylor D., 2
Teale W.H., 28, 43
Teberosky A., 28, 36
Tebo-Messina M., 209
Terry D.J., 188
Thaiss C., 232, 234, 235
Tharp R., 19
Thatcher B.L., 14
Thomas E.M., 28
Tracy K., 14, 218
Trimbur J., 209
Triplett N., 209
Trosborg A., 17
Tsatsaroni A., 58
Tuckman B., 218, 221
Tuckman B.W., 218
Tutty G., 208, 209

Valsinger J., 71
van de Kopple W., 172
van Dijk T.A., 34, 171
van Langenhove L., 58
van Leeuwen T., 130, 131
Vasconcellos M., 140
Veel R., 18
Verplaetse L.S., 97
Voigt J., 71
Vygotsky L.S., 3, 66, 94, 100, 208

Wagner E., 209
Waletzky J., 11
Walker C.P., 21, 96
Wallat C., 21
Wang L., 186
Webb N., 89
Wei L., 187
Weisser C., 230, 232, 243
Wellman B., 186

Wells G., 21, 28, 127
Wenger E., 3, 15, 18, 19, 70
Wertsch J., 18
Westgate D.P.G., 94, 119
White E.M., 44, 203, 215
White H., 44, 203, 215
Whitenack J., 71
Wiemelt J., 53
Winter J.K., 209, 210
Witte S.P., 14, 73, 96
Wolfe J., 166
Wolff D., 186
Wonderly W.L., 189
Wood D., 98
Woodall B.R., 198
Wray D., 119

Wyatt-Smith C., 118, 122

Yackel E., 71
Yates J., 17
Young K.M., 166, 177
Young R., 11, 12
Yule G., 5, 102, 119

Zamel V., 20, 21
Zammuner V.L., 70
Zawacki T.M., 232, 234, 235
Zebroski J., 234
Zecker L.B., 7, 31
Zimmerman R., 185

SUBJECT INDEX

activity types, 1, 4, 6, 94
approximative systems, 165

co-construction, 1, 7, 11, 12, 16, 18, 22,
    71, 72, 77, 81, 84, 85, 87, 88, 91, 94,
    97, 98, 105, 115
coherence, 60, 66, 146, 179, 183, 194
cohesion, 13, 18, 60, 207, 210, 211, 217,
    218, 219, 222, 226
collaborative learning, 93, 97, 207, 208,
    210, 220
college composition
    multi-genre, 229
community
    discourse, 15, 26, 70, 121, 122, 141,
        143, 145, 172, 180, 185, 186, 187,
        188, 191, 199, 200, 203, 211, 229,
        231, 232
composition
    college, 207, 208, 209, 210, 231
composition
    multi-genre college, 229
connectives, 14, 31, 117, 121, 128, 129,
    130, 132, 146
context
    cultural, 8, 27, 32, 138, 141, 165, 166,
        169
contextualization, 1, 10, 12, 13, 19, 78,
    93, 101, 102
convention, 120, 137, 140, 141, 143, 146,
    151, 153, 157, 231

dialogism, 1, 53, 66, 142
discourse
    analysis, 4, 138, 141, 146, 160
    argumentative, 24, 137, 140
    secondary school, 137
    synthesis, 165, 166, 176, 177
discourses
    alternative, 229, 230

genre
    expectations, 49, 59, 60, 61, 143
    learning, 93, 108
genres
    text, 2, 23, 27, 30, 31, 33, 34, 39, 41,
        46, 47, 121

interaction
    peer, iii, 2, 22, 23, 25, 69, 70, 71, 72,
        80, 81, 90, 91, 100
    whole-class, 69, 70, 71, 73, 74, 76, 77,
        78, 88
intercultural
    rhetorical differences, 165
intertextuality, 3, 93, 95, 101, 106, 108,
    139, 140, 141, 142, 145, 151

knowledge
    of the world, 119
    prior knowledge, 11, 24, 106, 117,
        118, 119, 120, 122, 123, 124, 127,
        130, 131, 134, 135, 166, 170

letters, 23, 27, 28, 29, 31, 32, 34, 35, 36,
    37, 39, 40, 41, 42, 43, 44, 45, 46, 54,
    90, 125, 166, 232
literacy
    events, 1, 4, 6, 9, 11, 13, 15, 18, 19,
        29, 93, 94, 101, 107
    home, 27, 28, 29, 43, 127
    practices, 3, 4, 6, 15, 16, 22, 26, 70,
        95, 229, 231, 234, 235, 242
    school, 22, 27, 47, 117, 120, 135
    street, 27, 47, 48
    visual, 117
literacy, 1, 3, 4, 5, 6, 7, 9, 11, 12, 13, 15,
    16, 17, 18, 19, 21, 22, 23, 24, 25, 26,
    27, 28, 29, 30, 34, 45, 46, 47, 70, 93,
    94, 95, 96, 97, 98, 99, 100, 101, 102,
    107, 108, 110, 117, 118, 119, 120, 121,
    122, 126, 127, 130, 131, 140, 144, 158,

165, 166, 178, 180, 229, 230, 231, 233, 234, 235, 236, 242, 246
literate arts, 137, 141, 142, 143, 159

meaning
    semiotic, 49, 60, 64, 117
mediation
    social, 69, 70, 71, 72, 73, 74, 88, 91

negotiation, 21, 23, 24, 72, 91, 94, 96, 98, 99, 103, 104, 135, 137, 140, 141, 142, 143, 151, 157, 159, 160, 236
newspaper articles, 23, 27, 29, 32, 34, 36, 37, 39, 40, 41, 42, 43, 45, 46, 47, 182
norm-based products, 165

planning processes, 185, 186, 194, 203

Reading events, 107, 108
repetition, 51, 97, 102, 114, 154, 227
research
    paper, 25, 165, 166, 167, 168, 169, 170, 172, 174, 175, 177, 178, 179, 180, 181, 184, 188, 203, 211, 212, 224
    paper evaluation, 165
    sociocognitive, 1
revision, iii, 25, 69, 70, 71, 72, 73, 74, 75, 76, 77, 78, 79, 80, 81, 82, 83, 84, 85, 86, 87, 88, 89, 90, 91, 100, 115, 140, 193

scaffolding, 19, 31, 69, 70, 93, 96, 97, 98, 99, 103, 104, 111, 112
schemata, 5, 8, 11, 19, 23, 24, 96, 117, 119, 120, 123, 124, 127, 135, 170, 182, 194, 208
self-positioning, 49, 51, 58, 65
shared texts, 207
social mediation, 69, 70, 71, 72, 73, 74, 88, 91

social writing network, 26, 185, 188, 190, 191, 193, 199, 203, 204
stories, 23, 27, 29, 31, 32, 34, 35, 37, 38, 39, 40, 41, 42, 43, 44, 46, 51, 103, 110, 123, 131, 156, 224, 235
style, 10, 14, 34, 35, 36, 37, 51, 52, 137, 147, 150, 153, 157, 167, 172, 175, 176, 179, 184, 216, 237
synthesizing styles, 165, 166, 175, 177

taxonomy, 165, 170, 172, 174, 178
text
    genres, 2, 23, 27, 30, 31, 33, 34, 39, 41, 46, 47, 121
    layout, 24, 117, 130, 131
    types, 23, 31, 32, 118, 120, 121, 127, 135, 235
textual
    knowledge, 23, 27, 32, 46, 47
    movement, 137, 141, 143, 145, 151

writing
    as sociocultural practice, 1, 2
    assessment, 165
    collaborative, 207, 208, 209, 210, 211, 212, 217, 220, 222, 223
    conferences, 5, 13, 20, 21, 25, 70, 93, 95, 96, 98, 100, 101, 102, 103, 105, 106, 112, 114
    for the community, 229
    groups, 207, 208, 209, 217
    public, 229, 243
    research, 194, 229, 230, 232, 233, 234, 242, 244, 245
    school writing, 2, 3, 4, 24, 49, 51, 63, 66, 117, 121, 122, 123, 127, 131, 135, 137, 138, 141, 152, 165, 177
    second language, 105
    situated, 1, 4, 6, 7, 16, 229
    task, 9, 49, 70, 100, 122, 124, 132, 135, 165, 192, 194, 207, 210, 216, 218, 219

LIST OF CONTRIBUTORS

Alexia Forget, Assistant, Faculty of Psychology and Educational Sciences, University of Geneva, Switzerland. E-mail: Alexia.Forget@pse.unige.ch.

Alina G. Spinillo, Associate Professor, Department of Psychology, Federal University of Pernambuco, Recife, Brazil. E-mail: spin@ufpe.br.

Carole McAllister, Professor of English, Department of English, Southeastern Louisiana University, USA. E-mail: cmcallister@selu.edu.

Chris Pratt, Full Professor, School of Psychological Science, La Trobe University, Melbourne, Australia. E-mail: c.pratt@latrobe.edu.au

Christiane K. Donahue, Assistant Professor of English, University of Maine- Farmington, USA & Associated member of the THEODILE Research Group, University of Lille. E-mail: tdonahue@maine.edu.

Debra Myhill, Senior Lecturer in Education, School of Education and Lifelong Learning, University of Exeter, Exeter, UK. E-mail: D.A.Myhill@exeter.ac.uk.

Heidi Estrem, Assistant Professor, Assistant Director of First-Year Writing Program, Eastern Michigan University, USA. E-mail: hestrem@emich.edu.

Katia Lehraus, Assistant, Faculty of Psychology and Educational Sciences, University of Geneva. E-mail: Katia.Lehraus@pse.unige.ch.

Linda Adler-Kassner, Associate Professor of English, Director of First-Year Writing Program, Eastern Michigan University, USA. E-mail: Linda.Adler-Kassner@emich.edu.

Linda Allal, Professor, Faculty of Psychology and Educational Sciences, University of Geneva. E-mail: Linda.Allal@pse.unige.ch.

Lucie Mottier, Assistant, Faculty of Psychology and Educational Sciences, University of Geneva. E-mail: Lucie.Mottier@pse.unige.ch.

Orna Ferenz, EFL Unit, Bar Ilan University, Israel. E-mail: ferenzo@mail.biu.ac.il.

Shoshana Folman, Senior Lecturer, General Studies, The Academic College of Tel-Aviv, Yaffo, Tel-Aviv, Israel. E-mail: folman@mta.ac.il.

Sigmund Ongstad, Professor, Faculty of Education, Oslo University College, Norway. E-mail: Sigmund.Ongstad@lu.hio.no.

Triantafillia Kostouli, Assistant Professor in Applied Linguistics and Language in Education, Department of Education, Aristotle University of Thessaloniki, Thessaloniki, Greece. E-mail: kostouli@eled.auth.gr.

Illa Connor, Professor, English Department, Indiana University, Indianapolis, USA. E-mail: uconnor@iupul.edu.

Studies in Writing

7. P. Tynjälä et al. (eds.): *Writing as a Learning Tool.* 2001
    ISBN HB 0-7923-6877-0; PB 0-7923-6914-9
8. L. Tolchinsky (ed.): *Developmental Aspects in Learning to Write.* 2001
    ISBN HB 0-7923-6979-3; PB 0-7923-7063-5
9. D. Alamargot and L. Chanquoy: *Through the Models of Writing.* 2001
    ISBN HB 0-7923-6980-7; PB 0-7923-7159-3
10. T. Olive and C.M. Levy (eds.): *Contemporary Tools and Techniques for Studying Writing.* 2001   ISBN HB 1-4020-0035-9; PB 1-4020-0106-1
11. S. Ransdell and M-L. Barbier (eds.): *New Direction for Research in L2 Writing.* 2002   ISBN HB 1-4020-0538-5; PB 1-4020-0539-3
12. L. Björk, G. Bräuer, L. Rienecker and P. Stray Jörgensen (eds.): *Teaching Academic Writing in European Higher Education. 2003*
    ISBN HB 1-4020-1208-X; PB 1-4020-1209-8
13. L. Allal, L. Chanquoy and P. Largy (eds.): *Revision: Cognitive and Instructional Processes.* 2004   ISBN HB 1-4020-7729-7
14. G. Rijlaarsdam, H. van den Bergh, M. Couzijn (eds.) *Effective Learning and Teaching of Writing: A Handbook of Writing in Education.* 2004
    ISBN HB 1-4020-2724-9; PB 1-4020-2725-7
15. T. Kostouli (ed.): *Writing in Context(s): Textual Practices and Learning Processes in Sociocultural Settings.* 2005.   ISBN HB 0-378-24237-6; PB 0-378-24238-4

For Volumes 1-6 please contact Amsterdam University Press, at www.aup.nl